The
Heritage
of American Catholicism

A TWENTY-EIGHT-VOLUME SERIES DOCUMENTING THE HISTORY
OF AMERICA'S LARGEST RELIGIOUS DENOMINATION

EDITED BY

Timothy Walch

ASSOCIATE EDITOR
U.S. Catholic Historian

A Garland Series

Inner Wealth and Outer Splendor

NEW ENGLAND TRANSCENDENTALISTS VIEW
THE ROMAN CATHOLIC CHURCH

HELENA SANFILIPPO, R. S. M.

Garland Publishing, Inc.
New York & London
1988

LIBRARY OF CONGRESS CATALOGING-IN-PUBLICATION DATA
Sanfilippo, Helena.
  Inner wealth and outer splendor.
  (The Heritage of American Catholicism)
  Originally presented as the author's thesis (Ph. D.--University of Notre Dame, 1972).
  Bibliography: p.
  1. Catholic Church. 2. Transcendentalism (New England) 3. Transcendentalists (New England)
I. Title. II. Series.
BX1397.S28 1988   282   88-9787
ISBN 0-8240-4100-3 (alk. paper)

DESIGN BY MARY BETH BRENNAN

PRINTED ON ACID-FREE, 250-YEAR-LIFE PAPER
MANUFACTURED IN THE UNITED STATES OF AMERICA

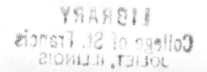

PREFACE

The New England variety of the transcendental philosophy is exciting no little comment today among students of religious and intellectual history. For the most part, examination of the large body of writings of the transcendentalists consists as yet in surveys and compilations. The present study undertakes to scrutinize in greater depth one aspect of the opinions which the published transcendentalist writings disclose--their views on the Catholic Church. It does not draw theological comparisons, nor does it discuss transcendentalist opinion in areas common to all Christian Churches. Rather, it focuses upon matters specifically referred to by the transcendentalist writers as "Catholic" or "Romanist." A few short studies have already been done in this regard on single relevant issues, but transcendentalist opinion concerning the complete system of Catholic belief and practice has never been subjected to a thorough analysis. To offer such an analysis is the purpose of this study.

My thanks are due to the library staffs of the Universities of Notre Dame, California at Berkeley, and California at Los Angeles, and in a special way to the staff of the Library of Congress. Additional thanks are due to numerous friends and mentors, most particularly Professors Philip Gleason and Ernest Sandeen, both of the University of Notre Dame, for their invaluable assistance and encouragement.

i

TABLE OF CONTENTS

LIST OF ABBREVIATIONS

BoQR   Boston Quarterly Review

BrQR   Brownson's Quarterly Review

CE   Christian Examiner

JN   Journals and Miscellaneous Notebooks of Ralph Waldo Emerson

MQR   Massachusetts Quarterly Review

MJAUA Monthly Journal of the American Unitarian Association

NAR   North American Review

QJAUA Quarterly Journal of the American Unitarian Association

SA   Spirit of the Age

UR   Unitarian Review

WM   Western Messenger

CHAPTER I

NEW ENGLAND TRANSCENDENTALISM

THE MEANING OF TRANSCENDENTALISM IN NEW ENGLAND

In mid-nineteenth century New England there appeared a small group of individuals whose influence was destined to spread out of all proportion to their numbers. Their significance arose from the nature and scope of what they tried to do, briefly, to provide for Americans a new set of ideals and values that would transform their lives.

The American dream did not always lie in the rags-to-riches saga. During what has been called a "God-ridden" epoch,[1] some men were inspired by a loftier vision. Among these was a group that aspired to a realm of living that transcended the play of the senses, where they might find peace and happiness through communion with Nature and with Nature's God. They were unorganized and scattered in a variety of callings. Yet their shared hopes and their impatience of routine and tradition drew them together into a recognizable group. Their contemporaries called them dreamers, or sometimes "transcendentalists." This was a term of derision, but it caught on; historically they are known as the New England transcendentalists.

Who were they? What did they believe? What were their hopes and dreams? These questions cannot be answered simply, since the transcendentalists were united more by a state of mind than by a systematic creed or philosophy.[2] What they produced is perhaps best described as a ferment--a ferment that was intellectual, social, and aesthetic, but above all religious. Further, depending on how we approach these opinions, there may be room for more or fewer names of persons to be included in their ranks.[3] Yet this welter of sentiments does admit of analysis and generalization, and its principal adherents can be fairly well identified.

Until recently the majority of the transcendentalists excited little commentary, although the extent of their own literary output is staggering. But the general quality of their thought and writing is high, and in their religious dedication they stand, in the American tradition, second only to the great figures of seventeenth century New England Puritanism. An examination of their writings leads the historian to a set of productions by scholars and artists; preachers and reformers; socialists and individualists; journalists, historians, poets, and musicians. In short, these men and women were drawn from the intellectual elite in a variety of fields.

Can such a motley group display anything in common? In this case they can. For though means may have differed, both their goals and their basic framework were the same, since the fundamental tenet of transcendentalism was held by them all. Concisely stated, it was the belief that man has a faculty which provides him with knowledge transcending that offered by the senses.[4] Contrary to the then popular philosophy of Lockean sensationalism, the transcendentalists held that man can acquire truth from a source other than experience. The faculty by which he does this they variously called Intuition, Reason, or Instinct. Its function was to put each individual into direct contact with a higher world than the palpable one, a world of divine realities.[5]

Most of the transcendentalists were Unitarian ministers. For the majority, the nature of this higher realm was nothing less than the absolute reality, a personal God. For others, their faith in even the most fundamental concepts of the Judaic-Christian creed had dwindled to a mere selectivism. According to these, the nature of the other world might best be comprehended in the term coined by one of their number, Ralph Waldo Emerson. Emerson used the term Over-Soul to name the impersonal but divine force that permeated--or better, was permeated by-- all mankind. Hence man's dignity approached the divine, nay, perhaps was divine.[6] In either case, all the transcendentalists believed the object of their life to be union with this divinity, however conceived.

Practically speaking, this assumption that supernatural attributes reside in the natural constitution of man amounted to an assertion of the inalienable worth of the individual. All was goodness within, and the deep-rooted Calvinistic notion of inherent evil in man was ignored or denied. Further, if the "unerring witness in the soul," as George Ripley termed it,[7] was the source of truth, then the individual man was his own interpreter of the universe and of his part in it. The rights of the individual had been asserted in the eighteenth century, but this group added the right to be different, to forsake authority and obey oneself, or rather God as heard in oneself. This "still voice within"[8] constituted "the rock to build on in the human soul," and disclosed all external organizations to be foundations built of sand.[9]

What, then, of institutions, especially the church? The answer was simple—they were not needed. Emerson, the most extreme iconoclast of the transcendentalists, rejected entirely all outward ecclesiastical authority. And he went so far as to charge the historical church with having sinned inexcusably against the human race by setting up a material machine to perform spiritual functions. The creation of this apparatus, he charged, amounted to a denial of the direct affinity of the soul with the divine.[10] Other transcendentalists did not share Emerson's extreme view. They accepted churches, traditions, and sacred books, but only insofar as these offered a revelation which did not conflict with the inner lumination of the soul. As James Marsh put it, the knowledge that comes from "living from a great depth...no man can draw for another"; each must draw it for himself.[11] Religion, therefore, was to be a personal matter for each man, not to be dictated from without. Educational systems could draw forth and cultivate the divinity in man, but, in the conception of the pioneer educator of the group, Amos Bronson Alcott, these systems should never deteriorate to an external imposition of knowledge upon passive minds.[12] As for the world of creeds and rituals, it was often idolatrous. Since the divine element was within man, the temple of God was the soul, and it was there primarily that man ought to worship.

Historian Vernon L. Parrington views this subjective religion as an insufferable egoism on the part of the transcendentalists.[13] In some cases it undoubtedly was. But the discriminating observation of an early commentator should not go unnoticed:

> ...they were innovators, and this circumstance naturally attracted a good deal of their attention to themselves. But transcendentalism was too considerable a fact to be disposed of by reducing it to egotism or sentimentalism. Applied to Emerson, the most prominent figure among the transcendentalists, such a description, everyone will feel, would be preposterous....
> Intuition, with him, means something very different from infallible knowledge; it means, to use his own words, the openness of the human mind to new influx of light and power from the divine Mind.[14]

Such an interpretation makes intelligible Cyrus Bartol's startling affirmation: "Sometimes Isaiah is not worth a farthing, I have such inward wealth;...."[15] The most systematic thinker of the group, Orestes Brownson, also commented correctly on the nature of transcendentalist individualism. During the peak of his transcendental period he wrote:

> We must not confound this interior light with mere feeling, impression, or affection of the sensibility. By inspiration we must understand light, not sentiment....It may be termed, as we have sometimes termed it, the spontaneous activity of the Reason; but only when Reason is taken absolutely, as God's Reason, and not man's.

And lest anyone would be confused as to how Reason could be distinguished from impulse, he concluded: "...it [is] the same at all times, in all places, and with all individuals;...."[16]

Practically speaking, not all transcendentalists agreed wtih Brownson. If there was anything absolute for them, it was the absoluteness of freedom; in actual practice, the "truth" as grasped from the light within often differed widely from one to another. This extreme individualism makes the transcendentalists elusive and difficult to categorize. Yet this very individualism, as Santayana notes, constitutes the secret of the remarkable tenacity with which the transcendental "philosophy" has held onto the minds of both Americans and British. For it is a method, he observes, "which enables a man to renovate all his beliefs, scientific and religious, from the inside, giving them a new status...so that he does not seem to himself to reject anything, and yet is bound to nothing, except to his creative self."[17]

Yet it must still be insisted that the thrust of the transcendentalists' intuitionism was religious. Far from being a worship of self, their focus on themselves had as its purpose an ever deepening communion of the self with God. Although the entire movement had literary, philosophical, and social dimensions, it was primarily a religious phenomenon. As a matter of fact, only a superficial study of the major literary productions could lead to any other conclusion. While it is true that the transcendentalists started with nature, they inevitably led through it to God, since as Emerson made clear, they were convinced of the union-- though not the identity--of the three elements of God, nature, and man.[18] In transcendentalist Theodore Parker's expression, the intuiting of God by the soul was nothing more nor less than the supreme height of an "Absolute Religion."[19] So definitely predicated was transcendentalism on the reality and naturalness of the spiritual element in man, that its believers saw God everywhere. They saw him in the yearning impulse of every heart, in its feeling for the Infinite, in the moralizing voice of every conscience, in the beauty of all creation. All of this, as Perry Miller has commented, was as obvious to them as the certitude of mathematical demonstration.[20]

This species of religion was criticized by some as "sheer naturalism."[21] Certain writings of Parker or Thoreau, for example, might justify such a conclusion. On the other hand, there are critics who call it "sheer mysticism."[22] The latter judgment is more nearly correct. Any effort to reestablish contact with the root source of all things, where that root is regarded as a God, is mysticism. In that case, the majority of the transcendentalists were mystics, for they added to the naturalism of the eighteenth century a religious dimension which the Aufklärung never thought of.

They were mystics then. But how far they were Christian mystics is another question. Those who like Emerson and Thoreau nearly worshipped nature, or who like Parker regarded the "natural" elements in Christianity as the only permanent ones, were furthest from being Christian in the traditional sense of the word. The middle-of-the-roaders who preferred to remain within the mainstream of traditional Christianity were for the most part Unitarians. As such they were inclined to minimize the vital role played by Jesus Christ as Savior-God, the role in which orthodox Christianity had known him. But they regarded him as the greatest mystic of them all, for his nobility, in their eyes, lay in his perfect openness to the divine Spirit within him. And this spirit was in direct "correspondence" with the divine spirit in men.[23]

Still others may be called "Christian transcendentalists," insofar as they used the tenets of transcendentalism in the interests of the Christian faith in its basic formulations.[24] Yet Brownson's ironic judgemnt of their Christianity-- after he had left their ranks and become a Catholic--has merit. It places such a Christianity within the broader context of their total religion, with its natural- istic bias:

> Christianity is accepted [by the transcendentalists]; o yes, and as
> divine; for it is one of the forms with which the human race has sought
> to clothe its religious sentiment, or in which it has sought to realize
> its conceptions of the Greatest and Best. By the same title they accept
> the Fetichism of the African negroes, the Polytheism of the Greeks and
> Romans, Brahminism, Buddhism, Mahometanism, and all other religions which
> have been or are. They are all divine, because they are all human--the
> product of the human race.[25]

The Sacred Oracle, then, dwelt within, and it must be obeyed, for it announced the inmost promptings of the divine will. This leads us to another rather elusive characteristic of the transcendentalists. Not only did they search for all that was true; they also sought whatever was beautiful and good as additional manifes- tations of the divinity and its perfections. This helps further to explain their preoccupation with Nature, and by extension, their close observation of all that was beautiful in man and in the arts. Their interest in external beauty may appear inconsistent in those who sought knowledge beyond the evidence of the senses, but it is important to keep in mind that here we have no coherent or systematic philosophy. On the contrary, inconsistencies abound. In the investigation of these inconsistencies we might well recall the wry comment of their sage: "A foolish consistency if the hobgoblin of little minds."[26]

What Paul Kaufman calls "a renascence of wonder"[27] pervaded the consciousness of these men and women in the face of truth as beauty. Their aesthetic interests did not consist solely in an appreciation of the artistic qualities of a given masterpiece; in fact sometimes it did not even reach such an appreciation. Rather, contemplation of both creative and aesthetic experiences was the same as communion with Nature—both constituted an absorption in the divine.[28] From their viewpoint the creative and the aesthetic were one, since, at least in the mind of Emerson and some of his closest followers, art was the projection of intuition, and it was that which gave Nature, man, and all history their meaning. The process of this might be reduced to a formula as follows: The pinnacle of all truth, beauty and goodness exists in the Absolute Being, the universal soul, or God. This Being is the divinity perceived by the Reason, intuition, or spirit of man. Finally, that which is perceived is projected onto the outside world in the form of art. Conversely, contemplation of the outside world, whether of nature or of art, brings a closer recognition of what already exists in the soul. The universal quality of truth as it thus exists in all these facets of the world constitutes the law of "correspondence," or the symbolic nature of the universe.[29]

But the transcendentalists did not stop at abstractions. At least most of them did not. Their sense of the transcendent perfection of the universe did not blind them to the realities of the misdeeds and misfortunes of society. Putting together their joy in life and their total confidence in their "divine" nature, they maintained an indomitable hope for the future of the race, a steady optimism that looked forward to the ultimate moral and social perfection of individuals and of society. The did accept the dictum then current in philosophical circles that this was the best possible world. But this in no way seemed a contradiction to their goal of making it perfect. Frederic Henry Hedge, one of the scholars among them, gingerly made the distinction: "If this world is not the best possible world, then the God of Theism is not that world's creator: the best possible, not as a present finality, but as means and method of the perfect good."[30]

This sanguine view of the world bore fruit in two areas of operation where some of the transcendentalists made their most important mark. In the first place they developed a philosophy of history which descried a neat pattern of perfectibility and progress in the evolution of historical man, especially historical religious man. Secondly, they applied the progressive patterns gleaned from the past to their prognosis of an ever more perfect future. To hasten this process of perfection, they made much of the moral implications of Christianity, as these were perceived true by the perception of the intuition. They exhorted men to holiness so that life might be nothing less than a divine life lived here and now, a life modeled on "Christ's spirit, Christ's virtue,...the Sermon on the Mount...." This likeness to Christ some of the transcendentalists held up as "the one thing needful." All other things, whether churches, laws, events or influences, were "utterly worthless" when separated from it.[31] Others were more careful to separate the identities of religion and morality, but all agreed that the inward and outward reformation of character was essential for true religion and ultimate happiness.

The perfecting of the world did not end, however, with oneself; society too had to be reformed. Justice had to be done by man to man; human rights and especially liberties had to be extended on as wide a plane as possible—to all men, in fact. Besides preaching private morality, therefore, many of the transcendentalists turned their speculations into action in the areas of temperance, education, abolitionism, economic equality, peace, and social justice. It was easy for them

to take their place among the vanguard during this age of reform, since they were

enemies of conformism and complacency,and their optimistic, religious spirit made

them confident of success.

The most distinctive attempt to reform society tried by the transcendental-

ists was the establishment of utopian communities. Two of these that were actually

implemented were Fruitlands, founded by Amos Bronson Alcott and Charles Lane, and

the more famous Brook Farm, initiated by George Ripley. An early participant in

the latter experiment gives witness to the religious and reformist motivation

that prompted Ripley in the undertaking:

> The new departure was not a going away from religious thought, but it
> joined the intellect and heart....It ignored faith alone. It did not
> believe that faith stood above works. It pointed always towards action.
> It summed up the lesson and meaning of all good doctrines, that man
> should lead a better life here,....[32]

The fact that both these experiments were organizational failures does not detract

from their value as a symptom of the social character of the transcendentalist

movement.

Less well-known activities for the betterment of the life of men were the

efforts of Theodore Parker, Isaac Hecker, and especially Orestes Brownson on behalf

of the laboring man, and Brownson's attempts to bring about a kind of Christian

socialism; Parker's work--and to a lesser extent that of almost every other tran-

scendentalist--in the anti-slavery movement; Alcott and Elizabeth Peabody's reform

methods in education; Thoreau's non-conformist attitude toward particular laws of

the state; and Margaret Fuller's abortive efforts for women's rights in America

and for Italy's liberation from Church domination. The most ambitious project of

them all was also the most unrealistic: the program of William Henry Channing for

the transformation of the United States into an organized Christian Commonwealth.[33]

Few of the millenialist hopes of the transcendentalists were realized. But

this does not make them fanciful idealists. In many respects they were precursors of the Social Gospel movement that was to gain headway in numerous Protestant and Unitarian circles later in the century.

Such were some of the more recognizable traits common to most of the transcendentalists. Within this framework they played a distinctive role in giving some shape to the fluid religious and social climate of their day.

THE DEVELOPMENT OF NEW ENGLAND TRANSCENDENTALISM

Transcendentalism in New England did not spring full blown from barren or hostile soil. In one sense the movement was certainly an original one, but in another, it can be seen to have roots both in America and abroad. An examination of some of these may help to clarify the transcendentalist position within its proper context.

The transcendentalists drew light from their own souls and from the contemplation of nature and the arts. But they drew light from other external sources as well. Most significant of these was their reading. The library and reading lists of several of them reveal a wide selection from the classic writers of antiquity, Christian Fathers and Doctors oriental mystics, and men of scholarship or piety from every age, as well as the sacred books of every major religion. Some of the transcendentalists, of course, were more scholarly than others, but those at the head of the movement were among the best educated men and women of their day.

While it is possible to trace the influence of many of these sources on our group, the most obvious thing about the transcendentalists is that they were primarily men of nineteenth century New England. If we adopt R.W.B. Lewis's approach to the analysis of a given moment of history, we will see that the transcendentalists entered upon what resembles "a protracted and broadly ranging conversation" with their environment.[34] The result of this dialog constituted what Isaac Hecker described as "a spontaneous growth of the New England mind."[35] Later studies of the transcendentalists have confirmed Hecker's point.[36] One of the most sig-

nificant facts brought to light by these studies is that the transcendentalists

were "Puritans to the core."[37] They were Puritans in their character: sincere,

unselfish in adherence to an ideal, morally heroic. They were Puritans also in

their emphasis on the practical. But they were Puritans above all in the reli-

gious tendency of their spirit.

Perhaps even more vivid than the likenesses to Puritanism are those to be

found between the transcendentalists and other religious sects that flourished

--or were persectued--in early New England: antinomians, anabaptists, Quakers,

"New Lights." Going back further still, we can detect other sources of transcen-

dental thought in the Protestant emphasis on individual freedom. The transcen-

dentalists' many comments on their evolution out of Protestantism provide indis-

putable testimony of their own understanding of this development of their beliefs.[38]

Brownson even went so far as to say that in the Protestant principle of private

judgment lay the foundation for the "fundamental proposition of transcendentalism"

--namely, "that each and every man is in himself the exact measure of truth and

goodness."[39] They were heirs, too, of the "benevolent naturalism" of the Enlighten-

ment--though adding a religious dimension--and of the liberal, progressive, and

rational elements found in Unitarianism. Particularly relevant here was the Uni-

tarian stress on individual responsibility, which cleared the way for a rejection

of the Calvinistic doctrine of human depravity and for the consequent affirmation

of the dignity of man.

In this historical context, a comment of Brownson's is enlightening. Alluding

as a Catholic to the transcendendalists' religious aspirations, he remarked:

> ...we [Americans] have a strong religious nature,...and have a persuasion
> that there must be a true religion of some sort, though we know not
> precisely what or where it is. We are best represented by those who have
> outgrown all the forms of dogmatic Protestantism, and are looking, like
> Emerson and Parker, for something beyond the reformation....[40]

Brownson's point was that although Americans had inherited "a strong religious nature" from the past, they had developed an aversion for the forms through which it had expressed itself. Indeed, it was as "insurgents"[41] against their traditional religious heritage that the transcendentalists at length crystallized their aspirations into a more or less distinct movement. The major form of religion which they rejected was Calvinism. For Calvinism prevented the religious man's escape from total depravity to a joyous recognition that he was a being permeated by the divine. Rejection of Calvinism, however, was not enough. The prevailing rational religion of the educated New Englander also had to be repudiated. It had grown authoritarian and cold, "corpse-cold," according to Emerson. Like the outworn forms of orthodox religion, it had lost its urgency and had to be replaced. Yet an adequate replacement for once meaningful forms is not easy to find. The transcendentalists therefore adopted the simplistic formula of a return to basic Christianity--clear away the accretions of the centuries and adopt the law of the gospel, the simple and pure law which Parker was wont to sum up in an oft-repeated phrase, "love to God and love to man."

Besides the indigenous roots which can easily be traced in the historical soil of New England, other influences shaped this new sytle of religion. These influences are much more difficult to determine, but several historians have attempted to highlight them. Two studies are particularly useful in identifying the German writers of the idealist and romantic schools who were read by individial transcendentalists, and in discerning similarities in the thought of the two groups. These studies reveal that Emerson confined himself almost exclusively to the more mystical German writers, but the other transcendentalists read much more widely.[42] Most of them, however, did not read the German in the original. The doctrines of German idealism came to them from Kant through the French writers Madame DeStael, Benjamin Constant, and Victor Cousin, and from there to England through Coleridge, Carlyle, and Wordsworth.[43] Only the more scholarly took directly to the German writers,[44] especially if they had studied in Germany.

Because of this wide familiarity with the German school, some historians imply that American transcendentalism sprang from the German sod.[45] Most, however, disagree.[46] It is true that the transcendentalists later adopted much of the vocabulary of German idealism—for example, Kant's use of "Reason"—but the New England variety had its own beginnings long before. Further, the Americans never carried through Kant's philosophy systematically. Rather, in accepting the Kantian notion of Reason they arbitrarily applied it to suit their own purposes.

Another question on influences concerns the New Englanders' connection with the European romantic movement. In a sense they were part of that larger phenomenon, but only insofar as they adopted its positive doctrines in confirmation of their own. They did not accept the romantics' return to medievalism; for, unlike the romantics, they were preoccupied more with the future than with the past—or better, with the past only inasmuch as it concerned the future. Secondly, they rejected the "moral anarchy" of romanticism.[47] Lastly, and perhaps above all, they resisted certain elements in the romantic appeal of the Catholic Church.

To summarize, the German school did exert a good deal of influence on New England transcendentalism, especially as mediated by the French and English writers. But as Hecker wrote later: "Its real authors were Channing, Alcott, and Emerson, who were neither affected at their start nor afterward—or if at all but slightly—by foreign extraneous influences."[48] The Americans, as Alexander Kern and others have shown, were obviously affected by their reading of German books. Yet, as Kern concludes, they "were not pale reflections of a European movement, but an indigenous group who met American problems in a distinctive way."[49]

Over and above literary influences on the movement are the historical circumstances of its rise, those events which provided the particular time, place and manner of its flowering. The general outlines of this development can be more briefly sketched than subtle cultural and intellectual roots. Its earliest stages were situated in the 1820's, with James Marsh's introduction of Coleridge into the University of Vermont, "the first asylum for transcendental idealism in America."[50] The studies of Edward Everett, Frederic Henry Hedge, and George Bancroft in the German universities and their subsequent influence in America also belong to this early period. But the more tangible and significant developments occured as a result of a polarization of thought which took place within the ranks of New England Unitarianism.

Imperceptible beginnings of dissent early in the 1830's led to a recognizable split among Unitarian clergymen by 1838. Perhaps the common aim of the Boston radicals in the denomination during that decade was, as Brownson later maintained, "to distinguish between the transient and the permanent in religion."[51] Or perhaps it was an "inevitable...TRANSCENDENTAL-REFORMATORY movement" that arose, as is claimed by another transcendentalist, James Freeman Clarke.[52] More specifically, the radical or progressive wing of Unitarianism emerged through a series of events, the principal of which were: first, a challenging of the reliability of man's senses in providing the supernatural knowledge of revelation; second, and by an extension of the first, a rejection of the miracles of the New Testament as sources of revelation; third, a succession of tirades against traditional Christianity by transcendentalism's foremost pulpit preacher, Theodore Parker; and, lastly, the most famous of the early statements of transcendentalism, Emerson's "Divinity School Address" of 1838. By means of these particulars, the "latest form of infidelity" took shape.[53]

In addition to open dissent, there was a gradual clustering of the like-minded liberals into small groups. As early as September of 1836 a handful of them began to meet informally about once a week for conversation on philosophy and literature. Later they met irregularly about once a month at the home of one or another member of the liberal wing. The meetings continued for the next fourteen years, achieving notoriety as the "Transcendental Club" of unorthodox Unitarians. These years of early and intense enthusiasm were the springtime years of the "newness," as the movement was sometimes called. The individuals who adopted the transcendental mode of thought during this period--the first generation tran- scendentalists, if you will--we shall next classify, one by one, as the "New England Transcendentalists."[54]

NOTES

[1]Harold C. Gardiner, ed. American Classics Reconsidered: A Christian Appraisal (New York, 1958), p. vii.

[2]"We called ourselves," said one of them," the club of the likeminded; I suppose because no two of us thought alike" (James Freeman Clarke, as cited in Henry David Gray, Emerson: A Statement of New England Transcendentalism As Expressed in the Philosophy of Its Chief Exponent [New York,1958], p. 12).

[3]William Hutchison sums up the difficulty neatly: "Almost any concise definition of the methods and aims of this group will either be theoretically broad enough to include all philosophical idealists from Plato through Bradley or else so narrowly technical as to exclude persons who were consciously and actively a part of what is called American Transcendentalism" (William R. Hutchison, The Transcendentalist Ministers: Church Reform in the New England Renaissance [New Haven, 1959], p. 22).

[4]Of the transcendentalists themselves, James Freeman Clarke put it most succinctly: "I am a transcendentalist. I do not believe that man's senses tell him all he knows" (Clarke, Essentials and Non-Essentials in Religion. Six Lectures Delivered in the Music Hall, Boston [Boston, 1877], p. 19, hereafter cited as: Clarke, Essentials).

[5]For a few of the many references to this faculty in the writings of the transcendentalists, see for example, George Ripley, Letter to the Church in Purchase Street, October 1, 1840, as cited in Perry Miller, The Transcendentalists: An Anthology (Cambridge, Massachusetts, 1950), p. 255; James Marsh, ed., in Aids to Reflection, in the Formation of a Manly Character, on the Several Grounds of Prudence, Morality, and Religion: Illustrated by Select Passages from Our Elder Divines, Especially from Archbishop Leighton by Samuel Taylor Coleridge. Preliminary Essay and Additional Notes by James Marsh (Burlington, Vermont, 1829), p. 317; Ralph Waldo Emerson, "The Transcendentalist," in Emerson, The Complete Works of Ralph Waldo Emerson (New York, 1926 [c. 1903]), I, 340, hereafter cited as: Emerson, Works; Frederic Henry Hedge, "Natural Religion," CE, LII (January, 1852), 122; Christopher Pearse Cranch, "Gnosis," The Dial, I (July, 1840), 98.

[6]"Once they had decided that men were capable of ascertaining divine truth by an examination of their own minds, the transcendentalists saw that this capacity must be of the same nature as divinity itself" (George Hochfield, ed., Selected Writings of the American Transcendentalists [New York, 1966], p. xvii, hereafter cited as: Hochfield, Selected Writings). Yet, contrary to a popular assumption, the transcendentalists were,for the greatest part, not pantheistic. Some of Alcott's statements might lead to such a conclusion, but his letters, especially in his later life, definitely reveal his belief in a personal God (The Letters of A. Bronson Alcott, ed. Richard L. Herrnstadt [Ames, Iowa, 1969], especially his letter to Miss Cleaver, July 6, 1879, p. 770, hereafter cited as: Alcott, Letters).

Only by stretching the term can we call Emerson pantheistic, and certainly not the others (see in particular a discussion of the distinction between God and man in Emerson, Review of A Letter to Rev. William E. Channing by O.A. Brownson [Boston, 1842], The Dial, III [October, 1842], 276-277).

[7]George Ripley, Letter to the Church in Purchase Street, October 1, 1840, as cited in Miller, The Transcendentalists, p. 255.

[8]Emerson, JN (Cambridge, Massachusetts, 1960-   ), 1833, IV, 109.

[9]Cyrus Augustus Bartol, "The Tidings," in The West Church, Boston: Commemorative Services on the Fiftieth Anniversary of Its Present Ministry and the One Hundred and Fiftieth of Its Foundation, on Tuesday, March 1, 1887. With Three Sermons by Its Pastor (Boston, 1887), p. 93.

[10]Emerson, Works, I, 117-151. See A. Robert Caponigri, "Brownson and Emerson: Nature and History," New England Quarterly, XVIII (September, 1945) 370-371.

[11]Marsh, Preface to Aids to Reflection by Coleridge.

[12]Alcott, Journal, September 21, 1828, in The Journals of Bronson Alcott, selected and ed. Odell Shepard (Boston, 1938), p. 12, hereafter cited as: Alcott, Journals.

[13]Vernon Louis Parrington, The Romantic Revolution in America, 1800-1860, vol. II of Main Currents in American Thought: An Interpretation of American Literature from the Beginnings to 1920 (New York, 1927), p. 382, hereafter cited as: Parrington, Romantic Revolution.

[14]James Elliot Cabot, A Memoir of Ralph Waldo Emerson (New York, 1887), I, 251, hereafter cited as: Cabot, Memoir of Emerson.

[15]Bartol, The Rising Faith (Boston, 1873), p. 51.

[16]Brownson, "Transient and Permanent in Christianity," BoQR, IV (October, 1841), 460, hereafter cited as: Brownson, "Transient and Permanent."

[17]George Santayana, The Genteel Tradition, ed. Douglas L. Wilson (Cambridge, Massachusetts, 1967), p. 85.

[18]Emerson, Works, I, 1-77.

[19]Parker, The Transient and Permanent in Christianity, ed. George Willis Cooke (Boston, 1908), especially pp. 1-39, hereafter cited as: Parker, Transient and Permanent.

[20]Perry Miller, The American Transcendentalists: Their Prose and Poetry (Garden City, New York, 1957), p. 49.

[21]Brownson, "Transcendentalism," BrQR, 1845, 1846, in The Works of Orestes Brownson, ed. Henry F. Brownson (Detroit, 1882-1887), VI, 2, hereafter cited as: Brownson, Works. The article was written after Brownson became a Catholic.

[22]Parrington, Romantic Revolution, p. 384.

[23]William Henry Channing, William Henry Furness, James Freeman Clarke, and James Marsh most clearly reflect this understanding of the "divinity" of Christ. Put another way, "The divine message of the Gospel corresponds to the divine instincts of the soul" (George Ripley, as cited in Hochfield, ed., Selected Writings, [no source given], p. xv).

[24]Ronald Vale Wells, Three Christian Transcendentalists: James Marsh, Caleb Sprague Henry, Frederic Henry Hedge (New York, 1943), p. 48 and passim.

[25]Brownson, "Parkerism, or Infidelity," BrQR, II (April, 1845), 234, hereafter cited as: Brownson, "Parkerism."

[26]Emerson, Works, II, 57.

[27]Paul Kaufman, "The Romantic Movement," in The Reinterpretation of American Literature, ed. Norman Foerster (New York, 1928), p. 120.

[28]See Vivian Constance Hopkins, Spires of Form: A Study of Emerson's Aesthetic Theory (Cambridge, Massachusetts, 1951), p. 198.

[29]The law of correspondence was adopted by Emerson from Swedenborg. Transcendentalist poet and caricaturist Christopher Pearse Cranch clarified in verse the two corollaries of this proposition. In "Correspondences" (The Dial, I [January, 1841], 381), he rhapsodized on Nature as universal types speaking to the senses and spirit of man; in "The Pines and the Sea" (1877, as cited in Miller, American Transcendentalists, pp. 269-270), he depicted the complementary principle, that what is perceived in Nature is what has been projected from the self as a symbol of the mind. Each of these, of course, verifies the other, according to the theory.

[30]Frederic Henry Hedge, Ways of the Spirit, and Other Essays (Boston, 1878), p. 250.

[31]William Ellery Channing, The Works of William Ellery Channing (Boston, 1841-1843), VI, 187, hereafter cited as : Channing, Works.

[32]John Thomas Codman, Brook Farm: Historic and Personal Memoirs (Boston, 1894), p. 5.

[33]See especially his periodical, Spirit of the Age, which ran less than one year, 1849-1850.

[34]R.W.B. Lewis, The American Adam (Chicago, 1955), p. 2.

[35]Isaac Hecker, "The Transcendental Movement in New England," Catholic World, XXIII (July, 1876), 530, hereafter cited as: Hecker, "Transcendental Movement."

[36]George Willis Cooke, An Historical and Biographical Introduction to Accompany The Dial (New York, 1961 [c. 1902], I, 10, hereafter cited as: Cooke, Historical Introduction to The Dial; Hochfield, Selected Writings, p. xx; Cabot, Memoir of Emerson, I, 253-254; Caponigri, "Brownson and Emerson," p. 369; Perry Miller, "Jonathan Edwards to Emerson," New England Quarterly, XIII (December, 1940), 589-617; Bartholow V. Crawford, Henry David Thoreau: Representative Selections, with Introduction, Bibliography and Notes (New York, 1934), p. xxix; Harold Clarke Goddard, Studies in New England Transcendentalism (New York, 1908), Chapter II; Franklin Benjamin Sanborn, Henry D. Thoreau (Boston, 1886), p. 126.

[37]Goddard, Studies in New England Transcendentalism, p. 188.

[38]The subject of religious development will be treated in Chapter V.

[39]Brownson, "Protestantism Ends in Transcendentalism," BrQR, July, 1846, in Brownson, Works, VI, 127.

[40]Brownson, "Questions of the Soul," BrQR, April, 1855, in Brownson, Works, XIV, 541.

[41]The term is Miller's, The Transcendentalists, p. 9.

[42]Stanley Morton Vogel, German Literary Influence on the American Transcendentalists (New Haven, 1955), passim; Henry A. Pochmann, German Culture in America: Philosophical and Literary Influences, 1600-1900, with the assistance of Arthur R. Schutz and Others (Madison, Wisconsin, 1957), provides a detailed listing of all possible German influences on each of the transcendentalists.

[43]See Howard Mumford Jones, "The Influence of European Ideas in Nineteenth Century America," American Literature, VII (November, 1935), 260-261; Van Wyck Brooks, The Flowering of New England, 1815-1865, rev. ed. (New York, 1940), p. 193; William Henry Channing, in Memoirs of Margaret Fuller, ed. Ralph Waldo Emerson, W.H. Channing, James Freeman Clarke, 2 vols. (Boston, 1851), II, 12-13; Cooke, Historical Introduction to The Dial, I, 42; Alexander Kern, "The Rise of Transcendentalism, 1815-1860," in Transitions in American Literary History, ed. Harry Hayden Clarke (Durham, N.C., 1953), pp. 273-275.

[44]Notably Hedge, Parker, Bancroft, Brownson, Marsh, and Charles Timothy Brooks.

[45]For example, Octavius Brooks Frothingham, Transcendentalism in New England: A History (New York, 1876), Chapter I; Wells, Three Christian Transcendentalists, pp. 147-148.

[46]John Edward Dirks, The Critical Theology of Theodore Parker (New York, 1948), p. 17; Henry Steele Commager, Theodore Parker, 2nd ed. (Boston, 1947), p. 153; Rene Wellek, "The Minor Transcendentalists and German Philosophy," New England Quarterly, XV (December, 1942), 679; Wellek, "Emerson and German Philosophy," New England Quarterly, XVI (March, 1943), 62; Vogel, German Literary Influence on the American Transcendentalists, p. xiv; Cabot, Memoir of Emerson, I, 248; Perry Miller, "New England's Transcendentalism: Native or Imported," in Literary Views: Critical and Historical Essays, ed. Charles Carroll Camden (Chicago, 1964), pp. 115-129.

[47]Jones, "Influence of European Ideas in Nineteenth Century America," p. 262; Paul Elmer More, "Thoreau's Journal," in Shelburne Essays, Fifth Series (New York, 1908), p. 115.

[48]Hecker, "Transcendental Movement," p. 530.

[49]Kern, "Rise of Transcendentalism," pp. 273-275, 309.

The transcendentalism peculiar to New England was also affected by varying doses of oriental mysticism, Platonism, and neo-platonism. This is particularly true of Emerson and Thoreau. See especially Stuart G. Brown, "Emerson's Platonism,"

New England Quarterly, XVIII (September, 1945), 325-345; Hopkins, Spires of Form; Kenneth Walter Cameron, in Emerson, Indian Superstition, ed. with a Dissertation on Emerson's Orientalism at Harvard, by Cameron (Hanover, New Hampshire, 1954); Frederic Ives Carpenter, Emerson and Asia (Cambridge, Massachusetts, 1930).

[50]Pochmann, German Culture in America, p. 132.

[51]Brownson, "Emerson's Prose Works," Catholic World, May, 1870, in Brownson, Works, III, 211.

[52]Clarke, "Polemics and Irenics: An Address on Theology, Before the Ministerial Conference, at Bedford Street Chapel, Wednesday, May 31, 1854," CE, LVII (September, 1854), 181.

[53]The term "latest form of infidelity" comes from a rebuttal to Ripley made by the "pope of Unitarianism," Andrews Norton, in his "Discourse on the Latest Form of Infidelity," 1839, in Hochfield, ed., Selected Writings, pp. 203-209.

Miller (The Transcendentalists, p. 173) claims that the Unitarian organ, The Christian Examiner, was closed to transcendentalists after January, 1837, once Emerson's "Nature" was published. But an examination of the periodical in the ensuing years reveals that it was anything but closed. Over 100 articles from the pens of transcendentalists appear from that date until 1869. As a matter of fact, the man whose name was used in a term that was synonymous for the Transcendental Club--the "Hedge Club"--was its editor from 1857 to 1861.

[54]After the 1850's transcendentalism lost its momentum. It is difficult to understand why, and few have attempted to do so. Miller believes that it died out as a movement probably because it had won its point (Miller, The Transcendentalists, p. 13). Wells speculates that as the movement progressed it became secular in interest and content, and as the attempt of the Christians within it to give it an ecclesiastical embodiment failed, it had neither a religious basis nor a religious organization to stand on (Wells, Three Christian Transcendentalists, p. 151). Stow Persons attributes the decline of transcendentalism to much the same cause, which he calls a "new naturalism" which rode in on the wave of scientific evolutionary thought after 1859. The primacy of intuitionism gave place once again to the primacy of a Lockean or empirical sensationalism, and the much-vaunted inner voice of Reason was drowned out (Persons, Free Religion, An American Faith [New Haven, 1947], p. 108). More simply, Hochfield maintains that it could live only as long as it could believe in its vision of the future (Hochfield, Selected Writings, p. xxviii). In the end, the real world was too much for it.

CHAPTER II

THE NEW ENGLAND TRANSCENDENTALISTS

The number of transcendentalists whom we can classify as belonging to the
first generation is twenty-eight. We cannot give anything resembling an adequate
biographical account of each of these. Neither can we present a full exposition
of elements which constitute the unique position of each within the "loose federation we call transcendentalism."[1] Rather, we shall introduce them in clusters
according to either the varying contributions they made to the movement, or the
particular avenue through which they approached it.

THE PRECURSOR

We begin with the forerunner William Ellery Channing (1780-1842), without
whom transcendentalism in New England could not have taken the direction it did.
Channing cannot be called a full-fledged transcendentalist. Yet more than any
other single individual in the United States he gave Unitarianism its liberal
thrust away from Calvinism. His departure from orthodox Christianity was so unique,
and his incipient transcendentalism so pronounced, that he may be regarded as the
first of the transcendentalists. His fellows of the transcendental persuasion
often pointed to him as the first inspiration of their movement, and even his
opponents referred to him on occasion as a transcendentalist.[2]

Channing attended only the first meeting of the Transcendental Club, but he
usually gave his blessing to its undertakings. He was too much of a Unitarian
Christian, however, to accept fully the transcendental doctrine of complete reliance on unaided individual reason.[3] Yet his style of Christianity closely resem-
bled that of the more authentically Christian transcendentalists in that he saw
in every man the potentiality of becoming like God, as Christ was. Thus it was
he who planted the vital seed that flowered in transcendentalism, although he
lived too soon to be placed at its center. His repeated insistence upon "inward

20

sanctity, pure love, disinterested attachment to God and man, obedience of heart and life, sincere excellence character," and his reminder that "all things else ...[are] utterly worthless when separated from this" are definitely within the stream of transcendentalism.[4]

Channing himself was a mild-mannered person who hated controversy and loved peace; a Unitarian minister who early made tolerance of other faiths his business. He was a remarkably popular religious leader, by both the appeal of his personality and the strength of his preaching.[5] These factors add to his significance as the central figure in what has been called "the first act" of the transcendental drama.[6]

THE INDIVIDUALISTS

The name of Ralph Waldo Emerson (1803-1882) springs to mind more than any other whenever the term transcendentalist occurs. This is in part due to the genial personality which made Emerson a popular lecturer even in as remote places as England and California. More important was the literary genius that made him the favorite American essayist of the nineteenth century. Finally and most significantly, Emerson gave the fullest, the most memorable, the most radical expression to the transcendental spirit.[7]

For Emerson, the individual was all, the individual was near-divine; no one need go beyond the borders of his own soul for happiness. He preached this; he practiced it; he sincerely believed this doctrine to be the one thing necessary for universal happiness. He saw therefore no need to go out to others, to join reform groups or cooperative ventures--all perfection comes from within. It was a personally agreeable doctrine, for as his private journals reveal, Emerson was never comfortable in the company of any but his closest friends. As he himself admitted, "I like man, but not men."[8]

Emerson's desire to be alone and to commune with nature has often caused him to be regarded as a mystic. But his was less a genuinely religious mysticism than a kind of poetic musing that often took a religious turn and became a sort of arm-chair philosophizing about life.[9] His interpretation of Christianity was likewise more humanistic and moralistic than profoundly religious. In an essay significantly entitled "Natural Religion Universal and Sympathetic," he wrote: "I am glad to believe society contains a class of humble souls...who do not wonder that there was a Christ, but that there were not a thousand; who have conceived an infinite hope for mankind; who believe that the history of Jesus is the history of every man, written large."[10] In Emerson, then, the individual stands supreme.

The transcendentalist who most consistently adopted the individualist posture by his very life was Henry David Thoreau (1817-1862). In his emphasis upon the primary significance of nature, upon the concept of correspondences, and upon individual nonconformity, Thoreau is strictly within the transcendental fold. On the other hand, if the movement derived its sole definition from his position within it, it would scarcely be called a religious one. Though he called himself "a mystic, a transcendentalist, and a natural philosopher to boot,"[11] these three perhaps are best seen in ascending order. Probably his early biographer and close friend, William Ellery Channing the Younger, characterized him most accurately as a "poet-naturalist."[12] This is not to say that Thoreau was a gifted poet, but that he approached his study of nature in a poetic spirit.

While Thoreau's themes were largely drawn from nature, and his observations flowed from a total acceptance of nature's every aspect, his individualism took form in a rather egoistical resentment against men and society. Any attempt to disprove this by pointing up his contacts with men and the shortness of his two-year retreat to Walden is doomed to failure upon a close perusal of both his published works and his private journal. His friend Emerson was the first to recognize this basic streak of social hostility in Thoreau, writing of him in 1853:

> Henry is military. He seemed stubborn and implacable; always manly and wise, but rarely sweet. One would say that, as Webster could never speak without an antagonist, so Henry does not feel himself except in opposition. He wants a fallacy to expose, a blunder to pillory, requires a little

sense of victory, a roll of the drums, to call his powers into full exercise.[13]

Hence Thoreau has become the patron saint of individualist non-conformists and an idol of all who protest seriously against submission to convention and super- ficiality.

All this is in addition to Thoreau's holding a place of honor in American letters. But it puts him in a somewhat isolated position--literally and figura- tively--in the transcendental movement. It makes him even less a religious figure than Emerson and causes the image of New England transcendentalism to take on a more earthy tone than the other transcendentalists alone would have lent it. If he was indeed deeply religious, he never showed it, obeying always his self- imposed demand that religion be "that which is never spoken."[14] In any case, both he and Emerson were forever done with the Christianity of their day--whatever form it took, from orthodox Calvinism to Christian transcendentalism. This they made clear in the highly selective approach to it that they reveal in all their writ- ings. Where it was deemed by their inner voice to be useful to their peculiar versions of transcendentalism, they accepted it; where it was not, they could no longer incorporate it into their approach to the sacred.

THE MINISTER-SCHOLARS

The largest group of transcendentalists consists of those who maintained some connection with the clerical profession, primarily within the liberal wing of the Unitarian fold. As were all the transcendentalists, they were intellectuals, but intellectuals with a definitely scholarly orientation. They were not only well- read, but remarkably profuse in their own verbal output, whether through the pul- pit or the press, and ordinarily through both.

The most outspoken as well as the most radical of this group was Theodore Parker (1810-1870). Parker was a Congregational Unitarian minister in Boston whose prime of life coincided with the most flourishing period of transcendentalism.

A prodigious reader and a vigorous and outspoken preacher, Parker adopted every current cause as his own and attempted to apply to it the Christian principles as he saw them. At first he interpreted them in an orthodox manner, and excoriated all deviations from the simple primitive gospel. But as time went on he discarded as arbitrary and contrary to Reason more and more of what was contained "between the lids of the Bible."[15] He defended this approach by arguing that only certain elements of Christianity--the "natural" ones--were permanent, and the rest transient.

The fact, however, that Parker watered the Christian message down to "almost nothing,"[16] did not make him any less ardent in its defense. With all his transcendental fervor he hammered mercilessly at the God and the message that the nineteenth century churches offered to men. Not only was the Christianity of his day contrary to the original gospel; it was contrary to the real God and the inspirations of that God which men could find entirely within their own souls.[17] It was here, in man's soul, not in creed or book, that truth lay. Parker had reached the point where he had so cleared away the transient in Christianity that, as Isaac Hecker put it years later, he was two-thirds infidel.[18] Even his own transcendentalist fellows could not always abide his ruthless pruning. In a eulogy Cyrus Bartol praised Parker's sincerity but found his religion entirely wanting. Parker "could do nothing with enduring institutions and operative principles in the life of mankind, but analyze and reduce them to ashes in the crucible of a speculative brain." After hearing Parker's "Transient and Permanent" sermon, John Weiss, a later transcendentalist and Parker's biographer, asked plaintively "Where is the permanent?" In Samuel Osgood's milder phrase, Parker was the "last word of Puritan individualism."[19] So sure of himself was Parker that he predicted that the religion he preached, "not known in the Old Testament or the New,"[20] would last a thousand years.[21] Hardhitting, tactless Parker was indeed, as one of Channing's biographers suitably phrased it, "the enfant terrible" of transcendentalism.[22]

More typical of the genial and broadly tolerant aspects of transcendentalism were the other prolific writers of the ministerial group: James Freeman Clarke, Frederic Henry Hedge, Orestes A. Brownson, George Bancroft, and Samuel Osgood.

The first of these, James Freeman Clarke (1810-1888), is best known for his pioneer work in comparative religion, Ten Great Religions.[23] Clarke immensely enjoyed examining various religions to discover and adopt whatever was true in each. So broadly tolerant was he, that Brownson later charged him with being "as open to the reception of error as to the reception of truth."[24]

Clarke possessed a firm belief in Christianity of the liberal Unitarian type.[25] His expression of this version of emancipated Christianity was more definitely transcendental than Channing's. He claimed belief in Christ as one who possessed the fulness of divinity just as all men can possess it. Thus he reduced Christianity to a natural transcendental religion that was similar to Parker's, but more palatable to traditional believers. "Religion," he wrote, "wherever you find it, as far as it goes, is always one and the same thing. It is always reverance, faith, obedience, gratitude, hope, love."[26] He held to many of the orthodox Christian beliefs as well, albeit with his own rendering of each. He did a great deal of writing and was one of the leading shapers of nineteenth century Unitarianism,[27] but he did not confine himself to exhortation. In 1840 he established the Church of the Disciples among his own congregation in Boston. This was the only transcendental Church to outlive its founder.[28]

Frederic Henry Hedge (1805-1890) was another Unitarian whose preaching and pen were tireless. Unlike Clarke, Hedge made not only religion but German literature and philosophy his areas of specialization. He had studied in Germany for four years as a young man, and was undoubtedly one of the principal channels through which European influences reached New England. He honestly admitted that transcendentalism, especially under Emerson and Alcott, flourished without any need of European ingredients, but his erudition in German transcendentalism was clearly significant.

More Christian than Clarke, Hedge endeavored to keep within the fold of "ecclesiastical" Christianity, and eventually did revert to a more traditionally orthodox position. In an 1867 article, in fact, he virtually repudiated transcendentalism--a system which he foresaw could not survive.[29] A staunch Unitarian, Hedge contributed to the Unitarian Review, the Unitarian Monthly, and the Christian Examiner, the last of which he also edited for four years. His contributions to these and other publications caused his contemporaries to rank him as "the ablest theologian the Unitarians have produced."[30] In addition to working in theology, he was minister to three Unitarian congregations over a period of about forty years, and served three terms as president of the American Unitarian Association. Through all these channels he strove to liberalize the Unitarian body without damaging its essential spirit. His own phrase, "enlightened conservatism" succinctly describes his position.[31]

In the early days Hedge was in the vanguard of the transcendental movement. Indeed, the Transcendental Club was in the beginning called the Hedge Club owing to the fact that it often met at his home in Bangor, Maine. With Emerson and Ripley, he was one of the original founders of the club. At that time he feared the associationist tendencies of some of his fellow transcendentalists,[32] but in later years he espoused the more social aspects of Christianity himself. In the springtime years of transcendentalism he had shared the belief that man's progress is to be brought about only by individual inspiration and reformation. But two decades of reflection eventually convinced him that social effort, particularly through the organized church, was mankind's only hope.[33]

The most philosophical and systematic thinker of all the transcendentalists was Orestes Augustus Brownson (1803-1876).[34] Brownson began his association with what was to become the transcendentalist group in about 1834. Transcendentalism was just beginning then to take shape, and Brownson's voluminous writings contributed to its formulation.[35] But he was only a temporary member of the group. His transcendental period, approximately from 1836 through 1842, coincides with the period of his most zealous efforts for religious and social reform. For years, Brownson searched relentlessly for answers to questions troubling him about the nature and purpose of life. His "iron pen"[36] moved tirelessly and at great length in an effort to work out with minute precision an understanding of the means and goals of human perfection.[37] The result was a spiritual pilgrimage which took him successively through Presbyterianism (1822), Universalism (1824), scepticism (1830), Unitarianism (1832), and transcendentalism (1836). Finally, his inexorable logic led him to a permanent station inside the Catholic Church (1844).[38]

Brownson was an avid student of philosophy. From his reading of the German transcendentalists and the French eclectics he developed some of the convictions that remained with him the rest of his life. In each new period of his religious evolution, he repudiated elements from the prior stage with a show of certitude that led to charges of inconsistency and irresponsibility.[39] But his overall pattern was set within a consistent frame of reference and pursued with a single aim--to seek out the truth. Many years later Isaac Hecker wrote in his defense: "Without seeing clearly this passionate love of truth in him, it is, I think, hardly possible to understand him."[40]

Alluding to Brownson's Catholic period, Arthur Schlesinger, Jr., accuses him of claiming or disclaiming ever having been a transcendentalist, according as it suited his current purpose.[41] But Brownson was not so arbitrary as that. We must remember that there were many interpretations of transcendentalism. And Brownson made an important distinction in describing what kind of transcendentalist he was:

> So far as transcendentalism is understood to be the recognition in man
> of the capacity of knowing truth intuitively, or of attaining to a scien-
> tific knowledge of an order of existence transcending the reach of the
> sense, and of which we can have no sensible experiences, we are transcen-
> dentalists. But when it is understood to mean, that feeling is to be
> placed above reason, dreaming above reflection, and instinctive intima-
> tion above scientific exposition, in a word, when it means the substitu-
> tion of a lawless fancy for an enlightened understanding...we must disown
> it, and deny that we are transcendentalists.[42]

During his transcendental period Brownson sought to cooperate with others of a like mind. But his domineering manner put off many in the Transcendental Club[43] and at Brook Farm. Nor would the group consent to use his Boston Quarterly Review as their mouthpiece; instead, they created their own, The Dial. Others, however, overlooking his formidable exterior, genuinely appreciated his gifts. A Brook Farmer's comment on his visits to the farm is typical of the mingled reactions that awaited him when he visited there: "Mr. Brownson is expected to be here next Sunday, in which I don't rejoice, but many are glad;...."[44]

To his search for truth, Brownson added an insatiable urge for reforming the social order. His efforts in behalf of the working classes, and his transcendental Society for Union and Progress were tangible fruits of his abstract speculations. They demonstrate well the fusion of the theoretical and the practical in this most dynamic of the transcendentalists.

A more lasting product of Brownson's energetic mind and his zeal for religious and social reform was his Boston Quarterly Review (1838-1842). The total project amounted to five weighty tomes, the first three of which constituted almost a single-handed performance. Just before becoming a Catholic Brownson founded a new journal with a more accurate title, Brownson's Quarterly Review. Except for a seven-year hiatus from 1865 to 1872, this "intellectual athlete"[45] continued to edit the review and to write most of its articles himself for the next thirty-two years. Through its pages every major topic of the day received sometimes controversial but always perceptive treatment.

George Bancroft (1800-1891) was another transcendental scholar, but of an entirely different stamp. Like Hedge, Bancroft had studied in Germany. And like the former, he was thoroughly acquainted with the German writers of the transcendental persuasion and helped spread their teachings to America.

After practicing his Unitarian ministry for only one year, Bancroft turned to the study of the past. The history he then began to write became enormously popular, owing to its subjective interpretation of the place of the United States in the history of nations. Throughout a period of forty years, beginning in 1834, Bancroft wrote what Americans wanted to hear--that their country was at the pinnacle of God's providential plan for the perfection of the human race. With the possible exception of Emerson, Bancroft was the most well-known of all the transcendental writers.

Bancroft's first expression of a transcendental theory of history came in 1835, when the movement was just getting under way. In his "Office of the People,"[46] he stated the general principles that were to guide his multi-volume and oft-revised History of the United States. Although the period during which the transcendental strain was highest in him extended only through 1852,[47] its influence continued to color his entire sense of history. It caused him to perceive in all the variegated events of the past an inevitable surge toward the perfection of the race, particularly as it blossomed in American democratic institutions. As Brownson correctly observed: "Properly speaking, he does not write history, nor even commentaries on history; he uses history for the purpose of setting forth, illustrating, confirming, and disseminating his speculative theories on God, man, and society."[48]

Of the other minister-scholars, the one whose writings we will most often have occasion to cite is Unitarian Samuel Osgood (1812-1880). Until he became an Eposcopalian minister in 1869, Osgood produced a number of books, articles, and essays on a variety of subjects. He was a transcendentalist of the milder type, one who could look upon a Theodore Parker as only "our great iconoclast."[49] Of a temperament similar to Clarke, whose close friend he was, Osgood demonstrated the more amiable qualities of the transcendental mind. His genuine acceptance of differences between religious groups accorded more with the transcendentalists' doctrine of tolerance than did that of any other member of the group. Moreover, he appears to have been the least provincial of the lot. That he lived much of his life in New York helps to explain both these differences.

Another moderate transcendental minister-scholar was Congregationalist turned Episcopalian, Caleb Sprague Henry (1804-1884). Like Hedge and Osgood, Henry was a professor, holding a chair of "mental and moral philosophy" at New York University during the peak of the transcendental period. The topics of Henry's writings covered a broad spectrum: slavery, education, morality, peace, history, psychology, social welfare. In the area of religious belief, he opted for what several of the transcendentalists called a "Broad Church" and a "practical Christianity"--it would be broad in its acceptance of every shade and variety of opinion, and practical in its orientation toward the betterment of society.[50]

Several other minister-scholars were lesser lights in the movement, but were just as dedicated to liberal religion. Convers Francis (1795-1863) was a Unitarian clergyman keenly interested in German philosophy and theology. When the Hedge Club met in Watertown, it was at his home. Here, and in his few writings, this quiet professor seemed to have been able to offer praise and blame with equal ease on a variety of topics in the field of theology. Though like the others in being an advocate of an individualistic and personal religion, he could not share the extreme views of such a one as Parker, although the two were close friends.

Poet and scholar Charles Timothy Brooks (1815-1883) was a Unitarian minister and like Hedge an avid student of German literature. But where Hedge's primary attention, at least till the latter part of his life, was given to the philosophical and theological features of the German authors, Brooks' chief interest was a literary one.[51] An early biographer, Charles W. Wendte, describes Brooks as a transcendentalist by nature, though never an obtrusive one.[52] On the other hand we have the unequivocal praise extended to him by the German scholar who is perhaps most familiar with Brooks' achievements. Camillo von Klenze writes: "We do no violence to the facts by asserting that no American ever entertained greater regard for the temper and genius of the German people, and that no American of his day--not even Hedge or Bayard Taylor--equalled his intimacy with German prose and verse."[53] It is by combining the judgments of these two critics that we can best see the place of Brooks in the stream of New England transcendentalism.

Unitarian William Henry Furness (1802-1896) was a lifetime friend of Emerson, though he spent most of his fruitful years in Philadelphia. His most important writings dealt with the life and teachings of Christ. In them he combined an inspirational point of view with the latest methods of Biblical criticism and the latest form of Unitarian liberalism.

The German immigrant Charles Follen (Karl Theodore Christian Follen, 1796-1840 lost his life in a shipwreck while transcendentalism in New England was reaching its peak. He did not contribute to the mainstream of transcendental thought, since he was not closely connected with the Concord group. However, his writings on theology and religious history, his marked intuitionism, his eclectic method, and his emphasis on heart over head bolstered the transcendental influence.[54]

James Marsh (1794-1842) was another who died too soon to participate in the full flowering of transcendentalism, but he definitely affected its incipient stages. A student of classical philosophy, Marsh was President of the University of Vermont from 1826 to 1833 and a professor there for another decade. From this vantage point he exercised a decisive influence at the head of the Vermont tran-scendentalists. His earliest and most significant contribution to transcendental-ism was his Preface to Coleridge's Aids to Reflection,[55] in which he argued for the importance of individual inspiration. The preface was widely read and became a seminal document in the development of American transcendentalism, since Marsh was well versed in transcendentalism of the German variety. He and his disciples built the entire University of Vermont curriculum upon a conservative version of the philosophy, which looked to human progress through religious, not social reform.[96] Marsh was thus not too sympathetic with the more liberal and sometimes superficial elements of Boston transcendentalism.[57]

THE REFORMERS

The reformist urge of several of the minister-scholars, especially Brownson, had a fuller expression in the writings and activities of another group of their colleagues. Most were associationists to the core. But they displayed their individuality in the unique ways in which each developed his utopian dreams.

Numbered here was William Ellery Channing's nephew, William Henry Channing (1810-1884). Channing was one of the least realistic of the transcendentalists. He spun elaborate plans on paper but never bore fruit in any permanent association. Still less did the idealistic "positive Christian Commonwealth" that he envisioned for the nation or the world ever become a reality, even on a small scale.

Although overshadowed by his uncle, William Henry was equally gifted. Yet he could never quite appraise his hopes in terms of concrete feasibility, and he thus comes across as a dreamer. But this was less unrealism than uncertainty. He had, as Van Wyck Brooks has expressed it, as many doubts as talents.[58] His vagueness is appraent particularly in his dabbling in various religious groups in search of the most viable alternative. After a preliminary investigation of Roman Catholicism, he decided it did not give enough room for the individual. In this regard, it seemed to him that transcendentalism had all that Catholicism did not. His associationist impulse therefore took him to Brook Farm for a trial there. Unsatisfied with this endeavor, he established a socialistic "Religious Union of Associationists" (1847-1850). Only after making these attempts did he create his elaborate but stillborn scheme for a universal socialistic Christianity. Despite his impracticality, however, those who knew Channing attest to the radiance of his presence and the unexcelled power of his preaching.[59] In this way at least, he did exert a good deal of influence over his fellows.

A better known if not better understood advocate of transcendental communisn was Amos Bronson Alcott (1799-1888). Alcott was the dreamiest and most opaque thinker of them all and was even more unrealistic than Channing. Yet he was the

most original and earliest of the indigenous transcendentalists. Probably little
that crystallized later in the brighter and more intelligible language of an
Emerson or a Parker had not already had some part in his own thought. His biographer
and editor of his journal, Odell Shepard, classes him as the only complete representative of American transcendentalism.[60]

Alcott was perhaps a greater iconoclast than Parker, for Parker retained till
the end a solid strain of piety. Alcott, however, had little of the devotedness
to God that is usually regarded as the essence of piety--at least not until his
later years. His contemplation of the divine took more the form of admiration of
the divine within the human, sometimes verging on pantheism. Moreover, Alcott
rarely prayed, in the usual sense of the word, and both Channing and George Ripley
regarded him as a near-atheist. Hecker, too, had little regard for Alcott's
piety, dismissing him as "an innocent charlatan." But Emerson and Thoreau viewed
him far differently. Emerson wrote with warm admiration: "Our Alcott (what a
fruit of Connecticut!) has only just missed being a seraph." And Thoreau characterized effectively:

> I have devoted most of my day to Mr. Alcott. He is broad and genial,
> but indefinite; some would say feeble; forever feeling about vainly in
> his speech and touching nothing....The feelers of his thought diverge,
> --such is the breadth of their grasp,--not converge; and in his society
> almost alone I can express at my leisure...my vaguest but most cherished
> fancy of thought....He has no creed. He is not pledged to any institution.
> The sanest man I ever knew;....[61]

Alcott's conception of the divinity within his own soul caused him to be
regarded as an insufferable egotist. "Whom could he pray to?" wondered Hecker.
"Was not Bronson Alcott the greatest of all?" And Brownson, sarcastic perhaps
because of his own uncertain position in 1843, wrote: "A. Bronson Alcott,...who
himself boasts of being to the nineteenth century what Jesus was to the first."[62]

Despite his vagueness, Alcott's idealism led to more concrete action than did
that of most of the others. He established the "heretical" Temple School (1834-
1839) for children, in which he combined an autocratic regime with the most radical

freedom of inquiry for his young pupils. Further, he spread his doctrine by various concrete means—his numerous lecture tours as far as the midwest, his Journal of Speculative Philosophy, and his Concord School of Philosophy. He is probably best known, however, for the utopian community he established at Fruitlands in 1844. The eleven-member vegetarian community nearly died of starvation after seven months, but it did not dull the idealism of its founder.

Alcott's partner in the Temple School was one of the two women transcendentalists of note, Elizabeth Palmer Peabody (1804-1894). In cooperation with Alcott, her goal was to stimulate the child's intuitive knowledge through Alcott's inquiry method of education. She also established significant contacts with the other transcendentalists. Her bookstore, which she opened in Boston in 1840, became a center for discussions by the Boston intelligentsia, in particular the Hedge Club and Margaret Fuller's Conversation Class.

If Alcott can be said to have had any lasting influence, it was through Miss Peabody. After her experiences as a governess and in the Temple School, she concentrated her entire energies on education. Beginning in 1845 she went on to become one of the most significant of the nineteenth century elementary school educators in the country. Most important in this area was her establishment of the first American kindergarten and her pioneer efforts in this field. A historian of the minor transcendental figures gives her this singular tribute: "Perhaps of all members of the 'Hedge Club,' only Miss Peabody achieved a working synthesis of what seem to some critics to be irreconcilable elements in transcendentalism—past and present, society and solitude, moral and aesthetic, education of self and education of others."[63]

Another transcendentalist who tried to join his idealism with a real-life modus operandi was George Ripley (1802-1880). Ripley's communitarian experiment, Brook Farm, ranks with the writings of Emerson and Thoreau as one of the most famous results of New England transcendentalism. Brook Farm was an attempt to

combine manual labor with advanced education for all its residents. It proved
successful for some half dozen years, from 1841 to 1847. But economically it
could not survive. Nor could its combination of mental and physical labor appeal
to many. Yet it remained the idyllic symbol of the transcendental dream at its
height.

Ripley had been a Unitarian minister (1826-1840) before he launched Brook
Farm. His fine mind had led him during that period into two major intellectual
endeavors. The first was his editorship of the fourteen-volume Specimens of
Foreign Standard Literature.[64] The translation and commentary for these German
and French works Ripley did in cooperation with a handful of transcendentalist
friends--Samuel Osgood, Christopher Pearse Cranch, John Sullivan Dwight, and Charles
Timothy Brooks. The second project evolved in the form of a theological controversy which spelled his undoing as an orthodox Unitarian minister and his definitive
establishment in the transcendental camp. The so-called Ripley-Norton controversy
of 1839, a disagreement centering on the reality of New Testament miracles, was the
final event that precipitated the Unitarian split into liberal and conservative
wings.

Ripley endeared himself to all his transcendentalist acquaintances, influen--
cing them as much by his personality as by his intellectual accomplishments. Cranch's
later tribute is representative: "I knew him to be always the same kind, genial,
generous, liberal heart, as in his youth. I have felt his loss deeply....He never
changed as other friends have changed...." Brownson, a very different sort of person from Cranch, also spoke highly of Ripley: "In the formation of my mind, in
systematizing my ideas, and in general development and culture, I owe more to him
than to any other man among Protestants....I loved him as I have loved no other
man."[65]

After Ripley's transcendental pilgrimage, he moved to New York and took up
other pursuits, mainly in journalism. It is doubtful, however, that he broke off

all association with Boston transcendentalism as one authority has asserted.[66]
Association in a specifically defined manner he perhaps did sever, but in his
writings of the period we can still discern a reflection of the same general perspective of his earlier years.

The last transcendentalist whom we shall classify as reformer has far fewer
tangible reform achievements to her credit. Yet as an intellectual, Margaret
Fuller (1810-1850) ranks among the finest of the century. And as a transcendentalist she undoubtedly earned the title Brownson bestowed upon her--its high
priestess.[67]

Miss Fuller was tending toward transcendentalism as early as 1830, but her
major contribution to the movement came at a later date, in her campaign to popu-
larize it. Her "conversations" in Elizabeth Peabody's bookstore during the years
1839-1844 had this purpose, as did her journalistic efforts as editor of The Dial
and as a columnist for the New York Tribune during the ensuing six years. As a
Tribune correspondent from revolutionary Italy (1847-1850), she voiced her aspirations for the emancipation of the mind of man from bondage to corporate authority.
And in a particular way she was also spokesman for the freedom and equality of
woman. Her combination of intellectual brilliance, psychic restiveness, and a
passionate longing for reform, marks her as one of the most interesting of the
transcendentalists.

Margaret Fuller's end was tragic. On her return voyage from Italy she met
death, along with her husband and child, in the way she had feared most--by shipwreck. Though her sojourn in Italy had been the occasion for much suffering, it
also brought her the happiness and fulfillment she had been seeking--ironically,
in marriage and motherhood. Her transcendentalist friends mourned her premature
passing with a remarkable devotion.[68] What they perhaps failed to realize was the
change that had come over her during her years in Italy. As she wrote: "Had I
only come [to Rome] ten years earlier! Now my life must be a failure, so much

strength has been wasted on abstractions, which only came because I grew not in the right soil."[69]

OTHER TRANSCENDENTALISTS

Besides these transcendentalists, there were others who came from a variety of callings. John Sullivan Dwight (1819-1893) began his career as a Unitarian minister, but very quickly decided that music was more expressive of the soul of man than preaching, and he eventually disengaged himself from all churches. He was an early member of the Hedge Club and of Brook Farm, a man "full of a German mysticism," as one of his contemporaries described him.[70] Dwight's greatest work consisted in leading later nineteenth century Americans to a genuine appreciation of the European classical and romantic masters of music.[71] Nevertheless, in his earlier years he was a typical transcendentalist. He repudiated the conventional, the institutional, and the external, and tried to express through music what he felt words could not convey--the mystical communion of the soul with God.

Jones Very (1813-1880) also had an artistic temperament, but of a different sort. Very was more genuinely mystical than any of the others. In fact, his single-minded devotion to mysticism caused some of his contemporaries to consider him to be at least at the borderline of mental imbalance. In this regard his transcendentalist associates sometimes came to his defense. Clarke, in an essay extolling Very's "mono-sania," classed him with the most "pure and earnest religionists" of the past. And Emerson, though he could never definitively decide on Very's mental condition, was occasionally moved to write, "he is profoundly sane," and "you will think all insane but he."[72] Very's writings, mainly poetry, are neither vast nor impressive; his chief contribution was in the inspiration he provided for the other transcendentalists.

Unitarian clergyman Cyrus Augustus Bartol (1813-1900) was a deeply pious and gentle human being, warmly venerated and appreciated in his time.[73] The Hedge Club met often at his home in Boston. However, he had little use for the extremes chosen by Emerson and Parker, preferring to remain more closely aligned with traditional Christianity.[74]

Other Unitarian ministers had their own unique though minor roles to play. Sylvester Judd (1815-1853) was a combination clergyman and novel writer who used both professions for the dissemination of transcendental concepts. Christopher Pearse Cranch (1813-1892) was first the poet and then the caricaturist of the move-ment. And lastly, Caleb Stetson (1793[?]-1870) has at least a passing interest owing mainly to a few of his writings that have survived his day.

One of the few men of the movement who were never connected with the ministry was Charles King Newcomb (1820-1894), of Brook Farm. Newcomb is a rather mysteri-ous character who, according to his friend Emerson, did a great deal of reflecting and writing. Early in their acquaintance Newcomb earned from Emerson the encomium: "A purer service to the intellect was never offered than his,--warm, fragrant, religious,...."[75] But Newcomb published little, and in five years Emerson changed his tune: "Charles Newcomb came, and yesterday departed. But I do not ask him again to come. He wastes my time;...the unique, inspired, wasted genius!"[76]

Last and least from the point of view of transcendentalist contributions is Isaac Hecker (1819-1888). But he is far from least from the viewpoint of the transcendentalist interest in Catholicism. During his brief connection with the movement, Hecker displayed the characteristics of both the individualists and the associationists: he sought social and religious reform first by radical changes in society, and then by joining the elite utopias of Fruitlands and Brook Farm. Moreover, his mild and mystical temperament led him on another pilgrimage, a search for inner truth. He therefore undertook a concentrated study of the German tran-scendentalists along with his close friend, Brownson. Unlike the latter, however, it was less a rational conviction than an intuitive vision of truth that led him into the Catholic Church. Through transcendentalism to the Church was for him the most natural way to the perfect life that his transcendentalist colleagues so eagerly sought.

Such was the motley assortment of individuals who comprised the first generation transcendentalist group. Alike in their earnest quest for genuine religious
renewal and in their intellectual and intuitionist approach to it, they nonetheless
each brought his own unique stamp to the movement and to the ultimate solution to,
or disillusionment with, its cause.[77] But in their individuality and the broad-
ness of their platform--what one of their best historians has called their "un-
abashed eclectism"[78]--lay the seeds of their dissolution. Affecting only the
elite of a small geographical area, having no unifying principle or construct,
they succeeded in their reform only to the degree that they encouraged further
individualism and hence further disintegration. Thus is the measure of their
failure the measure of their success. This is the irony of the transcendental
tale.[79]

THE TRANSCENDENTAL PERIODICALS

Before the Unitarian split, the transcendentalists tried to propound their
views in the Unitarian Christian Examiner. But when its editor, Francis Bowen,
commenced an attack upon them in 1837, it became clear that some other organ was
needed as well.

Brownson was the first to act, with his Boston Quarterly Review, begun in
January of 1838--"the most vigorous [journal] of its day."[80] The five hefty volumes of the quarterly constitute a brilliant production by this most profound and
comprehensive transcendentalist.

Only occasionally were the other transcendentalists willing to use Brownson's
journal as a vehicle for their views. Instead, in 1840 the core members of the
group launched their own periodical, The Dial. Ripley, Emerson, Channing, and
Margaret Fuller were the most enthusiastic about the venture. It lasted only four
years, however, because the editorial burdens, which fell to Emerson and Margaret
Fuller, became too taxing. Further, its esoteric columns reached only a small

clientele, and it had no adequate means of support. In later years Hedge commented that its demise was providential, since the movement was "already tending to dissolution"! But, he added, "I prize the four volumes among the choicest treasures of my library."[81]

The Dial has been variously hailed as the greatest contribution of the transcendentalists or dismissed as neither original nor significant. Whatever its position in the realm of American journalism, The Dial does hold first place in the field of American transcendental thought.

The Western Messenger was a periodical that originated in Louisville, Kentucky, even earlier than The Dial. It had started in 1835 as a Unitarian review, but under its transcendentalist editors, Clarke and Osgood, it became the mouthpiece of transplanted Boston transcendentalism.[82] As late as 1840, however, there could be found in its pages severe criticism of "that new and dangerous sect of heretics, known as transcendentalists."[83]

William Henry Channing, who served under Clarke on the staff of the Western Messenger, made two attempts to begin a periodical of his own. The first was The Present, a monthly published in New York in 1843-1844. Channing was neither a good editor nor a capable financial manager, and when the task of editing his uncle's memoirs fell to him, he gave up journalism for a time. In 1849, with Ripley's help, he tried again with The Spirit of the Age. This was an ambitious weekly, but it was even shorter-lived, lasting less than one year. Both these journals expressed in Channing's own way the transcendental philosophy, the second taking on the comprehensive task of crusading for a total reformation of the social order. The prospectus printed in all its issues shows the breadth of its ambition:

> This Weekly Paper seeks as its end the Peaceful Transformation of human
> societies from isolated to associated interests, from competitive to
> co-operative industry, from disunity to unity. Amdist Revolution and
> Reaction it advocates Reorganization. It desires to reconcile conflict-
> ing classes and to harmonize man's various tendencies by an orderly
> arrangement of all relations, in the Family, the Township, the Nation,
> the World. Thus would it aid to introduce the Era of Confederated

Communities, which in spirit, truth and deed shall be the Kingdom of
God and his Righteousness, a Heaven upon Earth.

Theodore Parker too tried his hand at journalism, editing from 1847 to 1830
his own periodical, the Massachusetts Quarterly Review. Hutchison describes the
review succinctly as "a robust journal dealing with all public questions."[84]
Besides a broad range of topics, it displayed an impressive roster of contributors.
Parker initiated the review to afford a channel for outspoken liberals in every
field, and to demonstrate that transcendentalism was not a dreamy idealism. This
undertaking, too, was perhaps overly ambitious.

Finally we have the Harbinger, appearing irregularly from 1845 to 1849.
Edited by Ripley at Brook Farm as a transcendental journal for social and political purposes, the Harbinger became the mouthpiece of the American Union of Associationists when Brook Farm collapsed in 1847.[85]

In addition to these, several other journals were vehicles for transcendental
thought, while not controlled by our group. The transcendentalists certainly
believed in individual inspiration, but they obviously believed in the power of
persuasion as well.

THE TRANSCENDENTALISTS' INTEREST IN THE CATHOLIC CHURCH

As is evident from their many writings,[86] the transcendentalists were interested in a broad range of subjects. Not the least of these, obviously, was reli-
gion--religion in its widest sense, involving the meaning of God, the meaning and
purpose of man, and the relationship between the two. Under this heading they
displayed a keen interest in a number of specific topics. One such is the Catholic
Church.

The transcendentalist concern with Catholicism was more in the academic realm
than in the realm of reality, but there were certain occasions when they did come
into direct contact with the living Church. Most of them, for example, visited
Catholic Europe at least once.[87] We would not expect such an articulate and intellectual group to remain mute before the spectacle that European Catholicism offered

them on these occasions, and certainly our expectation is not disappointed. Numerous observations and critical commentaries on the subject may be found scattered throughout their correspondence, diaries, and journals.[88] Parker, for one, during his 1844 trip to Italy displayed in both letters and journal a genuine desire to learn as much as he could about the Catholic Church. But for the most part his second trip in 1859-1860 found him the bitterest transcendental critic the Catholic Church had.[89] Margaret Fuller, too, as correspondent for the New York Tribune in Rome, demonstrated at first an enthusiastic hope for the liberalization of the Catholic Church under Pope Pius IX. But she very quickly became disillusioned when the Italian liberation movement failed.[90] This did not prevent her, however, from marrying a penniless Catholic aristocrat.

The comments of the other transcendental tourists of Europe are more or less haphazard, but all have left at least some record of their impressions of the Catholic Church there, especially in France and Italy. All of them, too, include comments which show that more than once--and for some, many times--they were drawn inside the European churches for participation in Catholic services.

On this side of the Atlantic, some few attended Catholic Masses and Verpers,[91] though this was quite rare. Even Thoreau ventured inside the Cathedral of Notre Dame in Montreal and the Church of St. Anne in Quebec, but these seem to have been the only instances for him.[92]

Contact with Catholic persons was less common. During Parker's first trip to Europe he made it a point to talk to Catholics about religion. He also made sure that these personages were his intellectual and social peers--a Jesuit priest, a bishop, and a cardinal.[93] Emerson likewise made the acquaintance of some Catholic persons in Europe--mostly monks--but this was only in passing.

At home in Boston and Concord, contacts with Catholics were also few. Boston at the height of the transcendental period was still a predominately Protestant and Unitarian city.[94] And after the surge of Irish immigration began in the late 1840's,

Catholicism seemed to be confined to the ignorant working class. Nonetheless, Emerson and Thoreau do mention a few brief contacts with them.[95] The other transcendentalists who had transient contacts with Catholic clergy and religious are Bartol and Brooks, who both met Catholic nuns while hospitalized; and Alcott, who dined with Catholic priests on one lone occasion. Over and above these meagre instances, Hedge is said to have been the personal friend of a Catholic priest in Brookline, and Furness was purportedly on friendly terms with the Catholic bishop of Philadelphia.[96]

The only Catholic whose memory at least seemed to be known rather widely among the transcendentalists was John Cheverus, Bishop of Boston from 1808 through 1823. A benign and tolerant ecclesiastic, Cheverus was beloved as a humanitarian and respected for his cultivated intellect and manners. Channing admired him greatly, and the two cooperated in such ventures as the advancement of literary associations, and the support of the Mechanics' Association and the Seaman's Aid Society.[97] When in 1823 Cheverus was recalled to France, his departure from Boston was mourned by Catholics and Protestants alike, who joined in bidding him farewell and in petitioning for his return. Twelve years later, on the occasion of Cheverus's death, Channing preached an eloquent sermon and had his church bells tolled in memory of his revered friend.[98]

Finally of course, the transcendentalists had first-hand acquaintance with the few Catholic residents of Brook Farm, and with friends and colleagues who entered the Catholic Church: Brownson, Hecker, the wife of George Ripley, her niece, Sarah Stearns, and other scattered acquaintances.[99]

The transcendentalists' knowledge of Catholicism was not, however, left entirely to chance encounters. Most of them made it their business to gain an understanding of the Church in a more systematic way than random contacts could afford. At Brook Farm, for example, the residents were in varying degrees eager to study both the doctrine and the devotion of the Church. Dwight led the way on

the inspirational level by means of his Mass Clubs at Brook Farm and later in
Boston. Such clubs were primarily choruses specializing in the great Catholic
Masses of Bach, Mozart, and Haydn. As further devotional and intellectual stim-
uli, Brownson, Hecker, Mrs. Ripley, and others brought out such Catholic books as
the Catechism of the Council of Trent, the literature of Dante, the writings of
the Fathers of the Church, and especially the devotional works of Fenelon, Augustine, and aKempis.[100]

At Fruitlands too, the library shelves were heavy with multiple copies of
Catholic devotional or mystical authors: Fenelon, Madame Guyon, Bellarmine,
aKempis, St. Juliana of Norwich, St. Francis DeSales, and St. Bridget.[101] Moreover, several of the transcendentalists individually read and often owned many
of the great Catholic books.[102] And a few of them adopted a self-imposed project
of making a more or less thorough study of the Church in its beliefs, practices,
and history, usually via the Catholic writers themselves.[103]

In the case of Clarke, Hedge, Osgood, and Brownson, interest led to study,
and study to scholarship. The results were that they incorporated certain concepts
of Catholic thinking into their ideas, wrote their own monographs on one or more
aspects of the Church, and in most cases did both. Many of them were quite familiar
either at second hand or very often at first, with the writings of the Fathers[104]
and, to a lesser extent, Doctors of the Church. Further, they made themselves so
knowledgeable about the Church, especially its history, that they felt qualified
to teach courses or deliver lectures on the subject, or at least on the historical
periods of the Church's prime.[105]

As far as contemporary Catholic writers are concerned, Osgood demonstrates
the greatest familiarity with them, while the others show only a spasmodic
interest.[106] As transcendentalists, Brownson and Hecker did read some of the
current Catholic authors, but even as a Catholic, Brownson explained that his
lack of interest in them had been due to the fact that "they were written...in a

dry, feeble, and unattractive style, and abounded with terms and locutions which were...totally unintelligible. Their authors seemed...ignorant of the ideas and wants of the non-Catholic world, engrossed with obsolete questions, and wanting in broad and comprehensive views."[107]

The Catholic Church also figured in the various social conversations initiated by some of our group. An example is Margaret Fuller's Conversation Class, which discussed Roman Catholicism as one of its topics in the 1842-1843 season.[108] And the congregation of Clarke's Church of the Disciples chose as one of its topics of discussion in 1845-1846, "What are the principles and ideas peculiar to Protestantism, as distinguished from those peculiar to the Church of Rome?"[109]

The transcendentalists were, then, indeed interested in the Catholic Church. They did inquire about its nature and functions; they did observe it at first hand when they had the opportunity. What were their conclusions? As with all subjects that came under their scrutiny, they sometimes approached the Church in a tolerant spirit, but always with an individualistic and a selective eye. Their investigations were as broad-based in scope as the Catholic Church itself, and their conclusions as variegated as their own creative minds would allow.

NOTES

[1]Perry Miller, in Consciousness in Concord: The Text of Thoreau's Hitherto
'Lost Journal' (1840-1841). Together with Notes and a Commentary by Perry Miller
(Boston, 1958), Introduction, p. 96, hereafter cited as: Miller, Consciousness in
Concord.
So loose a federation was it that none of the transcendentalists, not even
Emerson, has escaped the judgment from one quarter or another that he was not
really a transcendentalist. For pro and con views on the major transcendentalists,
se:
On Parker: Dirks, Critical Theology of Theodore Parker, pp. 85, 135; Froth-
ingham, Transcendentalism in New England, pp. 125, 149, 302-321; John White Chad-
wick, Theodore Parker: Preacher and Reformer (New York, 1901), Chap. IV; Goddard,
Studies in New England Transcendentalism, pp. 8-9; Herbert Wallace Schneider, A
History of American Philosophy, 2nd ed. (New York, 1963), p. 224; Hilrie Shelton
Smith, "Was Theodore Parker a Transcendentalist?" New England Quarterly, XXIII
(September, 1950), 351-364; George H. Williams, Rethinking the Unitarian Relationship with Protestantism: An Examination of the Thought of Frederic Henry Hedge
(1805-1890) (Boston, 1959), p. 17; Clarence F. Gohdes, The Periodicals of Ameri-
can Transcendentalism (Durham, North Carolina, 1931), p. 248; Henry David Gray,
Emerson: A Statement of New England Transcendentalism, p. 14n; Kern, "The Rise
of Transcendentalism," p. 291.
On Clarke: Cooke, Historical Introduction to The Dial, II, 65-66; Frothing-
ham, New England Transcendentalism, p. 343; John Wesley Thomas, James Freeman
Clarke: Apostle of German Culture in America (Boston, 1959), p. 146n; Hochfield, ed.,
Selected Writings, p. 424; Arthur S. Bolster, James Freeman Clarke, Disciple to
Advancing Truth (Boston, 1954), p. 137.
On Hedge: Orie William Long, Frederic Henry Hedge: A Cosmopolitan Scholar
(Portland, Maine, 1940), p. 21; Wells, Three Christian Transcendentalists, pp. 103-
104, 113; Cooke, Historical Introduction to The Dial, II, 71; Schneider, History
of American Philosophy, p. 240.
On Brownson: Theodore Maynard, Orestes Brownson: Yankee, Radical, Catholic
(New York, 1943), pp. 84, 108, 125; Alvan S. Ryan, "Orestes A. Brownson, 1803-
1876: The Critique of Transcendentalism," in American Classics Reconsidered, ed.
Gardiner, p. 101; Wellek, "The Minor Transcendentalists and German Philosophy,"
p. 669; Matthew A. Fitzsimons, "Brownson's Search for the Kingdom of God: The
Social Thought of an American Radical," Review of Politics, XVI (January, 1954),
passim; C. Carroll Hollis, "Brownson on George Bancroft," South Atlantic Quarterly,
XLIX (January, 1950), 43; Arthur M. Schlesinger, Jr., A Pilgrim's Progress:
Orestes A. Brownson (Boston, 1939), pp. 48, 283; Per Sveino, Orestes A. Brownson's
Road to Catholicism (New York, 1970), Chap. XII.
On Emerson: Most consider him a transcendentalist. Two who do not are New-
ton Dillaway, Prophet of America: Emerson and the Problems of Today (Boston, 1936),
p. 81; Frothingham, Transcendentalism in New England, pp. 226-227. Goddard draws
a useful distinction in Studies in New England Transcendentalism, p.167.
On Thoreau: One historian who has doubts about Thoreau's transcendentalism
is Bartholow V. Crawford, Henry David Thoreau, p. xxviii.
[2]Among the transcendentalists, see for example, Cyrus Augustus Bartol, in
Principles and Portraits (Boston, 1880), p. 351; Elizabeth Peabody, Reminiscences
of Rev. William Ellery Channing (Boston, 1877), p. 364, hereafter cited as: Peabody, Reminiscences of Channing; Isaac Hecker, "The Transcendental Movement," p.
p. 530. James Freeman Clarke established his transcendental Church of the
Disciples in 1841 under Channing's auspices (see Orestes A. Brownson, "The Church

As It Was, Is, and Ought To Be," BrQR, July, 1848, in Brownson, Works, VII, 179, hereafter cited as: Brownson, "The Church As It Was"). Emerson continued to acknowledge his indebtedness to Channing for most of his life (see Arthur W. Brown, William Ellery Channing [New York, 1961], p. 138).

For references of his opponents see David P. Edgell, William Ellery Channing (Boston, 1955), p. 114; Rice, Federal Street Pastor, p. 198; William Henry Channing, in William Ellery Channing, Works, with an Introduction. New and Complete Edition, Rearranged. To Which Is Added The Perfect Life, ed. William Henry Channing (Boston, 1886), p. 928, hereafter cited as: Channing, Works, Complete Edition.

For a review of the literature of Channing's place in transcendentalism, see Conrad Wright, The Liberal Christians: Essays on American Unitarian History (Boston, 1970), pp. 34-38. Channing died in 1842 at the age of sixty-two; the heyday of transcendentalism can roughly be placed between 1836 and 1847.

[3]See for example Channing to Lucy Aiken, July 18, 1840, as cited in Rice, Federal Street Pastor, p. 198; Channing to James Martineau, 1841, in Memoir of William Ellery Channing. With Extracts from His Correspondence and Manuscripts, by William Henry Channing, 3 vols. (Boston, 1848), II, 451, hereafter cited as: Channing, Memoir; Channing to Peabody, June 21, 1841, in Peabody, Reminiscences of Channing, p. 424.

[4]Channing, Works, VI, 223.

[5]Transcendentalist Bartol referred to him as "the prince of our preachers, the Paganini of the pulpit" (Bartol, "Theological Changes," UR, XII [April, 1880], 298).

[6]"To omit Channing in discussing transcendentalism," wrote Goddard (Studies in New England Transcendentalism, p. 28), "would be to omit a large part of the first act of the play."

[7]Especially in such essays as "Nature," 1836; "The American Scholar," 1837; "The Divinity School Address," 1838; "The Method of Nature," 1841; "The Over-Soul," 1841; "Self-Reliance," 1841. See also his "The Transcendentalist," 1842, for the supremely vague expression of transcendentalism.

Emerson was indeed, as Brownson put it, "transcendentalism's "high priest" (Brownson, "Aspirations of Nature," BrQR, October, 1847, in Brownson, Works, XIV, 551).

[8]Emerson, Journal O, 1846, in Emerson, JN, IX, 378. Bartol described Emerson as "an insulated soul...an island rather than a star" (Bartol, "The Nature of Knowledge--Emerson's Way," in Concord Lectures in Philosophy: Comprising Outlines of All the Lectures at the Concord Summer School of Philosophy in 1882, with an Historical Sketch, Collected and Arranged by Raymond L. Bridgman [Cambridge, Mass., 1883], p. 56). This is a trait not often brought out about a man who was so universally loved and admired by the sheer charm of his personality.

[9]Even here we are at a loss as to Emerson's true position. Certainly he was no poet, nor did he have a highly trained or developed aesthetic sense nor philosophical system. About the most that can be said is that he spent long hours reading and reflecting, and that in giving expression to his thoughts he was a master of epigram and a literary genius. It is for his accomplishments in verbal expression that, fairly or unfairly, he is best known to us today.

[10]Emerson, "Natural Religion Universal and Sympathetic," in Freedom and Fellowship in Religion: A Collection of Essays and Addresses, ed. a Committee of the Free Religious Association (Boston, 1875), p. 388.

[11]Thoreau, March 5, 1853, Journal, ed. Bradford Torrey and Francis H. Allen. With a foreward by Walter Harding, 14 vols. in 2 (New York, 1962), V, 4.

[12]William Ellery Channing the Younger, Thoreau the Poet-Naturalist. With Memorial Verses (Boston, 1873).

[13]Emerson, Journal, 1853, in Journals of Ralph Waldo Emerson, with Annotations, ed. Edward Waldo Emerson and Waldo Emerson Forbes, 10 vols. (New York, 1910-1914), VIII, 375, hereafter cited as: Emerson, Journals.

[14]Thoreau, Journal, 1858, XI, 113.

[15]Parker, The World of Matter and the Spirit of Man: Latest Discourses of Religion, ed. George Willis Cooke (Boston, 1907), p. 148, hereafter cited as: Parker, World of Matter and Spirit. See also among many other statements his Discourse of Matters Pertaining to Religion (ed. Thomas Wentworth Higginson [Boston, 1907], p. 257, hereafter cited as Parker, Discourse of Religion), in which he elaborates at length on "what is true in Christianity."

[16]R.W.B. Lewis notes that it is astonishing, "contemplating the vastness of his erudition...how little he finally had to say. A small mouse of a doctrine emerged after all the convulsions of labor by a whole mountain range of information." Lewis's explanation for this is that "on the theological side, his entire intellectual process was reductive. His learning was exploited in the way of refutation and denial. His theology was a singular application of Thoreau's injunction to simplify, simplify, simplify" (Lewis, The American Adam, p. 178).

[17]In all of Parker's writings may be found numerous instances in which he elaborates on the differences between orthodox Christian theology and his own. His own he summarized in one place as "absolute religion--teaching that man is greater than the Bible, ministry, or church, that God is still immanent in mankind, that man saves himself by his own and not another character, that a perfect manly life is the true service, and the only service God requires,..." (Parker, Discourse of Religion, p. 427).

[18]Hecker, "Dr. Brownson in Boston," Catholic World, XLV (July, 1887), p. 472.

[19]Bartol, A Discourse, Preached in the West Church, on Theodore Parker (Boston, 1860), p. 16; Weiss, as cited in Commager, Theodore Parker, p. 76; Samuel Osgood, Our Patriot Scholar: Discourse in Memory of Edward Everett,... (New York, 1865), p. 11. Channing wrote of Parker: "As to our friend Theodore Parker, he deals too much in exaggerations. He makes truth unnecessarily repulsive, and, as I think, sometimes goes beyond the truth (Channing to Elizabeth Peabody, June 21, 1841, in Channing, Memoir, II, 441).

[20]Parker, Autobiography, Poems and Prayers, ed. Rufus Leighton (Boston, 1911 [?]), p. 330, hereafter cited as: Parker, Autobiography.

[21]As cited by Wendte in Parker, Theism, Atheism and the Popular Theology, ed. Charles W. Wendte (Boston, 1907), p. i, hereafter cited as: Parker, Theism.

[22]Edgell, William Ellery Channing, p. 141.

[23]Ten Great Religions: An Essay in Comparative Theology (Boston, 1871).

[24]Brownson, "Steps of Belief," Catholic World, December, 1870, in Brownson, Works, VIII, 289. Clarke had more than once to defend himself against the charge of being a syncretist.

[25]His biographer, Arthur S. Bolster, regards him as a Christian and therefore not a transcendentalist (Bolster, James Freeman Clarke, p. 137).

[26]Clarke, Steps of Belief, or, Rational Christianity Maintained Against Atheism, Free Religion, and Romanism (Boston, 1880), p. 287.

[27]Clarke turned out thirty-two books, nearly 100 pamphlets, and over 1000 articles.

[28]For the principles upon which the Church was founded, see Clarke, The Church of the Disciples in Boston. A Sermon on the Principles and Methods of the Church of the Disciples.... (Boston, 1846), pp. 4-24.

[29]Hedge, "The Destinies of Ecclesiastical Religion," CE, LXXXII (January, 1867), pp. 1-15. See also his "Antisupernaturalism in the Pulpit, An Address Delivered to the Graduating Class of the Divinity School, Cambridge, July 17, 1864," CE, LXXVII (September, 1864), 145-159, where he takes a step in this direction.

Edgell claims that Hedge withdrew from the transcendental movement out of fear of public opinion (Edgell, William Ellery Channing, p. 136). However, a careful examination of Hedge's latter-day writings on the nature of the Church would seem to indicate that he acted more out of conviction.

[30]Cooke, <u>Historical Introduction to The Dial</u>, II, 71. Bartol called him "the Unitarian chief in theology" (Bartol, "Hedge's Reason in Religion," <u>CE</u>, LXXIX [July, 1865], 89).

[31]Hedge, <u>Martin Luther and Other Essays</u> (Boston, 1888), p. 144.

[32]Hedge to Convers Francis, February 14, 1843, in Wells, <u>Three Christian Transcendentalists</u>, pp. 205-206.

[33]See, for example, his "Destinies of Ecclesiastical Religion," pp. 1-15.

[34]Lord Acton classed Brownson as the most penetrating American thinker of his day (as cited by Russell Kirk in Brownson, <u>Selected Essays</u>, ed. Kirk [Chicago, 1955], p. 1). But he is almost forgotten in his own country. Nothing explains this neglect except his conversion to Catholicism. Such at least is the unanimous verdict of Kirk (in <u>ibid</u>., p. 2), Miller (<u>The Transcendentalists</u>, p. 180), Maynard (<u>Orestes Brownson</u>, p. 118), and Seidel Canby (<u>Thoreau</u> [Boston, 1939], p. 58). Per Sveino ascribes it to his contemporaneity (<u>Orestes A. Brownson's Road to Catholicism</u>, p. 16), while Schlesinger adduces other causes (<u>A Pilgrim's Progress</u>, pp. 295-296).

[35]Among Brownson's most significant transcendental contributions are his "Benjamin Constant on Religion," <u>CE</u>, XVII (September, 1834), 63-77; <u>New Views of Christianity, Society and the Church</u>, 1836, in Brownson, <u>Works</u>, IV, 1-56, hereafter cited as: Brownson, <u>New Views</u>; and most of his five-volume <u>Boston Quarterly Review</u>, 1838-1842.

[36]Parker to George E. Ellis, 1838 [?], in Octavius B. Frothingham, <u>Theodore Parker: A Biography</u> (Boston, 1874), p. 106.

[37]The <u>Dictionary of American Biography</u> errs in alluding to the twenty hefty volumes of Brownson's <u>Works</u> as "complete." They are by no means complete, particularly for the period before 1840. What is possibly the best and most original and incisive piece of writing he ever did, "The Laboring Classes" (<u>BoQR</u>, III [July, October, 1840], pp. 358-395, 420-510), is one of the items that does not appear in the collection. This is probably owing less to the social doctrine he propounded --a radical socialized democracy, which if heeded might have been quite significant--as to the fact that the lengthy, two-part article contains a biting attack upon the Christian priesthood. The <u>Works</u> were edited by his son, Henry F. Brownson, a Catholic.

[38]Students of Brownsoniana are not agreed upon the precise date at which Brownson gave up his adherence to transcendentalism. Hutchison, Maynard, and Schlesinger place it at mid-1842 (Hutchison, <u>The Transcendentalist Ministers</u>, p. 165; Maynard, <u>Orestes Brownson</u>, p. 127; Schlesinger, <u>A Pilgrim's Progress</u>, pp. 145-155); and Pochmann sees Brownson only gradually moving away by the <u>end</u> of 1842 (<u>German Culture in America</u>, p. 235). Ryan believes Brownson's transcendentalism began to weaken as early as 1840 ("Orestes A. Brownson, 1803-1876: The Critique of Transcendentalism," p. 104), while Miller considers that date as marking his turning point against the movement (<u>The American Transcendentalists</u>, p. 340), though this would seem to be placing it much too early.

[39]Quipped Clarke, "No man has ever equalled Mr. Brownson in the ability with which he has refuted his own arguments" (Clarke, "Orestes A. Brownson's Argument for the Roman Church," <u>CE</u>, XLVIII [March, 1850], 228).

[40]Hecker, "Dr. Brownson and Bishop Fitzpatrick," <u>Catholic World</u>, LXV (April, 1887), 3.

[41]Schlesinger, <u>A Pilgrim's Progress</u>, p. 46.

[42]Brownson, "Two Articles from the <u>Princeton Review</u>, Concerning the Transcendental Philosophy of the Germans, and of Cousin, and Its Influence on Opinion in This Country," <u>BoQR</u>, III (July, 1840), 322-323.

[43]Hedge seemed to be reflecting wishfully when he recalled that Brownson had only attended one or two meetings of the club (as cited in Lindsay Swift, <u>Brook</u>

Farm: Its Members, Scholars, and Visitors [New York, 1961, c. 1899], p. 7). Actually Brownson was present for many more. Sometimes the club even met at his home (see George Willis Cooke, Ralph Waldo Emerson: His Life, Writings, and Philosophy [Boston, 1881], p. 57).

[44]Marianne Dwight to Anna Q.T. Parsons, September 18, 1844, in Marianne Dwight, Letters from Brook Farm, 1844-1847, ed. Amy L. Reed, with a Note on Anna Q.T. Parsons, by Helen Dwight Orvis (Poughkeepsie, New York, 1928), p. 38.

[45]Hecker, Diary, June 22, 1845, in Walter Elliott, The Life of Father Hecker (New York, 1891), p. 181, hereafter cited as Elliott, Life of Hecker.

[46]Later revised and published as "Progress of Civilization," BoQR, I (October, 1838), 389-407.

[47]See John W. Rathburn, "George Bancroft on Man and History," Transactions of the Wisconsin Academy of Sciences, Arts and Letters, XLIII (1954), 61n; Hollis, "Brownson on George Bancroft," p. 50.

[48]Brownson, "Bancroft's History of the United States," BrQR, October, 1852, in Brownson, Works, XIX, 385.

[49]Samuel Osgood, American Leaves: Familiar Notes of Thought and Life (New York, 1867), p. 378.

[50]Henry, About the Bishop's Declaration on Baptism; with Something About Prayer-Book Revision and Church Progress. A Letter to a Layman (New York, 1872), p. 29; Henry, Politics and the Pulpit: a Tract for the Times (New York, 1860), p. 394.

[51]For a very thorough account of Brooks's writings and numerous translations in this field, see Camillo von Klenze, Charles T. Brooks and the Genteel Tradition (Boston, 1937).

[52]Charles W. Wendte in Brooks, Poems, Original and Translated by Charles T. Brooks, with a Memoir by Charles W. Wendte, ed. W.P. Andrews (Boston, 1885), p. 24, hereafter cited as: Brooks, Poems, Memoir.

[53]Von Klenze, Charles T. Brooks and the Genteel Tradition, p. 76.

[54]See Hutchison, The Transcendentalist Ministers, p. 49; von Klenze, Charles T. Brooks and the Genteel Tradition, p. 18.

[55]Marsh, in Aids to Reflection by Coleridge, pp. vii-liv.

[56]See Lewis S. Feuer, "James Marsh and the Conservative Transcendental Philosophy," New England Quarterly, XXXI (March, 1938), pp. 18, 21, 27, 29; Marjorie H. Nicolson, "James Marsh and the Vermont Transcendentalists," Philosophical Review, XXXIV (January, 1925), 29, 33-34, 36; Pochmann, German Culture in America, p. 132; Wells, Three Christian Transcendentalists, passim.

[57]Marsh to Henry J. Raymond, March 1, 1841, in George B. Cheever, Characteristics of the Christian Philosopher: A Discourse Commemorative of the Virtues and Attainments of Reverend James Marsh, Late President, and Professor of Moral and Intellectual Philosophy in the University of Vermont.... (New York, 1843), Appendix, p. 69.

[58]Van Wyck Brooks, The Life of Emerson (New York, 1932), p. 85.

[59]See for example, Marianne Dwight to Anna Q.T. Parsons, August 11, 1845, in Marianne Dwight, Letters from Brook Farm, p. 112; Brownson, "Channing on the Church," pp. 137-138. See also Van Wyck Brooks, Flowering of New England, pp. 250-251.

[60]Odell Shepard in Alcott, Journals, p. xvii.
As a Catholic Brownson early characterized Alcott as New England transcendentalism's best representative (Brownson, "Transcendentalism," p. 97). And Hecker regarded Alcott, along with Emerson and Channing, as one of the movement's three founders (Hecker, "Transcendental Movement," p. 530).

[61]See Odell Shepard, Pedlar's Progress: The Life of Bronson Alcott (Boston, 1937), p. 37; Hecker, as cited in Elliott, Life of Hecker, p. 76; Emerson, Journals, 1861, IX, 346; Thoreau, Journal, May 9, 1853, V, 130.

[62]Hecker, Diary, March 5, 1888, in Elliott, Life of Hecker, p. 81; Brownson, "The Philosophy of History," Democratic Review, May, June, 1843, in Brownson, Works, IV, 420n.

[63]John B. Wilson, "A Transcendental Minority Report," New England Quarterly, XXIX (June, 1956), 152.

[64](Boston, 1838-1842).

[65]Cranch, Journal, July 28, 1880, in Leonora Cranch Scott, The Life and Letters of Christopher Pearse Cranch (Boston, 1917), p. 311, hereafter cited as: Cranch, Life and Letters; Brownson, The Convert, or Leaves from My Experience, 1857, in Brownson, Works, V, 81. Although Brownson refrained "from motives of delicacy," from naming Ripley here, Schlesinger attests that there can be little doubt that Brownson was referring to Ripley (Schlesinger, A Pilgrim's Progress, p. 52).

[66]Arthur R. Schultz and Henry A. Pochmann, "George Ripley: Unitarian, Transcendentalist, or Infidel?" American Literature, XIV (March, 1942), 17.

[67]Brownson, "Aspirations of Nature," p. 551.

[68]Thoreau brooded on the sands near the scene of the shipwreck; Emerson, Clarke and William Henry Channing cooperated in editing--freely--her memoirs as a kind of testimonial of their admiration for this remarkable woman.

[69]Fuller to Emerson, December 20, 1847, in Memoirs of Margaret Fuller, II, 225.

[70]W.S.B. Mathews, "John S. Dwight, Editor, Critic and Man," Music, XV (March, 1899), 532.

[71]Mainly through Dwight's Journal of Music, which ran from 1852 to 1881, with Dwight as editor.

[72]Clarke, "A Defense of Jones Very's Sanity, by the Reverend James Freeman Clarke, and Poems Published in The Western Messenger But Not Included in Any Edition of Jones Very's Works," WM, VI (March, 1839), 308-314; Emerson to Elizabeth Peabody, October 30, 1838, in Emerson, Letters, II, 171; Emerson to Margaret Fuller, November 9, 1848, in ibid., p. 173.

[73]See Henry Whitney Bellows, "Bartol's Discourses on the Christian Body and Form," CE, LIV (January, 1853), 121; George Willis Cooke, John Sullivan Dwight, Brook-Farmer, Editor, and Critic of Music: A Biography (Boston, 1898), p. 267.

[74]See, for example, Bartol, "Representative Men," CE, XLVIII (March, 1850), 315.

[75]Emerson, Journal W, June 7, 1845, in Emerson, JN, IX, 222.

[76]Emerson, Journals, December 18, 1850, VIII, 154.

[77]A careful tracing of the transcendental spirit within each member of our group reveals that none of them held to this doctrine consistently throughout his life. In most of them who outlived the transcendental epoch it grew lukewarm, decomposed, or at least became somewhat diluted. Even the arch-individualist Emerson found his moments of inner illumination growing dimmer as the years passed, and toward the end of his life he recognized--and attempted to fulfill--the need for at least a minimal adherence to an outward religion. Besides Emerson, there are very obvious signs of the weakening of the transcendental spirit in Hedge, Cranch, Bartol, Osgood, Marsh, Alcott, Ripley, Peabody, Fuller, Bancroft, and of course Brownson and Hecker.

[78]Hutchison, The Transcendentalist Ministers, p. 50.

[79]For further information on the transcendentalists, see the bibliography. The most practical and useful handbook of information about most of them is Hutchison, The Transcendentalist Ministers. For sketches of all but Newcomb, Osgood, and Stetson, see the Dictionary of American Biography.

[80]Miller, The Transcendentalists, p. 180.

[81]Hedge, "Destinies of Ecclesiastical Religion," p. 13.

[82]Clarke was editor from 1836 to 1839; Osgood, associate editor from 1836 to 1837.

[83]"The Duties of the Clergy," WM VII (September, 1840), 226. The article is an anonymous review of Ripley's sermon delivered on the occasion of Dwight's ordination.

[84]Hutchison, The Transcendentalist Ministers, p. 128.

[85]Elizabeth Peabody started a transcendental journal, Aesthetic Papers, in May, 1849, but she was able to get only one number off the press.

[86]The bibliography below lists only those which were useful for this study. It represents approximately one-third of the total transcendentalist output.

[87]Channing, 1822-1823; Bartol, 1855; Fuller, 1847-1850; Dwight, 1861; Brooks, 1865-1866; Peabody, 1867; Ripley, 1865, 1869-1870; Parker, 1843-1844, 1859-1860 (he died in Florence); Hedge, 1818-1822, 1847-1848; Clarke, 1852, 1882; Cranch, 1846-1849, 1856-1863, 1881; William Henry Channing, 1835-1835; Emerson, 1832-1833, 1844, 1847-1848; Bancroft, 1818-1822, 1867-1874 (as U.S. Minister to Prussia). Follen was born in Germany, arriving in the United States for permanent residence in 1824 at the age of twenty-eight.

[88]Particularly those of Emerson, Parker, William Henry Channing, and Cranch. Clarke and Bartol went further and included this subject in the books they produced as a result of their European travels (Clarke, Eleven Weeks in Europe; and What May Be Seen in That Time [Boston, 1852]; Bartol, Pictures of Europe, Framed in Ideas, 2nd ed. [Boston, 1856]).

[89]See John Weiss, Life and Correspondence of Theodore Parker, Minister of the Twenty-Eighth Congregational Society, Boston, 2 vols. (New York, 1864), passim,*

[90]The period of her enthusiasm for the pope lasted from August, 1846, to approximately October, 1847. She grew ambivalent during the period from October, 1847, to April, 1848. Finally, her bitter disappointment in the pope becomes evident for the period April, 1848, through June, 1849 (see Fuller to New York Tribune, in The Writings of Margaret Fuller, ed. Mason Wade [New York, 1941], pp. 409-522, hereafter cited as: Fuller, Writings).

[91]For example, Emerson (in the Catholic Church of St. Augustine, Florida, 1827, and the Baltimore Cathedral, 1843); Dwight and Newcomb (in the Catholic churches of Massachusetts and the Catholic Cathedral of Philadelphia, numerous times). Late in his life Emerson found no objection to taking part in a Catholic wedding (1876; see Ralph Leslie Rusk, The Life of Ralph Waldo Emerson [New York, 1949], p. 499, hereafter cited as: Rusk, Life of Emerson). Alcott ventured into a convent to attend a clothing ceremony of nuns in 1856 (Alcott to Mrs. A. Bronson Alcott, October 25, 1856, in Alcott, Letters, p. 206). Margaret Fuller witnessed a similar ceremony (Fuller to New York Tribune, December 30, 1847, in Fuller, At Home and Abroad: or, Things and Thoughts in America and Europe, ed. Arthur B. Fuller [Boston, 1860], pp. 271-272).

[92]See his Yankee in Canada, in Thoreau, The Writings of Henry David Thoreau, 20 vols. (New York, 1906), vol. V: Excursions and Poems, especially pp. 12-15, hereafter cited as: Thoreau, Excursions.

[93]See Parker, Journal, March 3, 1844, in Weiss, Life of Parker, I, 211-213; Parker to Convers Francis, March 13, 1844, in ibid., pp. 231-232.

[94]As for Concord, Edward Emerson surmises that in 1835 there was probably not a single Catholic there (Edward Emerson, in Emerson, Works, XI, 570n).

[95]Emerson's letter to William Emerson, May 29, 1842, is a sympathetic account of the death of his Irish cook's child (The Letters of Ralph Waldo Emerson, ed. Ralph Leslie Rusk, 6 vols. [New York, 1939], III, 57, hereafter cited as: Emerson, Letters).

[96]Bartol, Rising Faith, p. 318; Brooks, Poems, Memoir, p. 94; Alcott to Mrs. A. Bronson Alcott, October 25, 1856, in Alcott, Letters, p. 206. See also Wells, Three Christian Transcendentalists, p. 135.

[97]Channing was Unitarian pastor on Federal Street in Boston from 1803 to 1842.

*hereafter cited as: Weiss, Life of Parker.

[98]See "Memoir of Bishop Cheverus," Boston Monthly Magazine, I (June, 1825), 12; Hecker, "Transcendental Movement," p. 536; Oliver Johnson, Address, April 7, 1881 [?], in The Channing Centenary in America, Great Britain, and Ireland. A Report of Meetings Held in Honor of the One Hundredth Anniversay of the Birth of William Ellery Channing, ed. Russell Nevins Bellows (Boston, 1881), pp. 179-180, hereafter cited as:Channing Centenary; Peabody, Reminiscences of Channing, pp. 98-99; Louis H. Warner, "Channing and Cheverus: A Study in Early New England Tolerance," The Christian Register, May 4, 1939, pp. 296-299; Annabelle Melville, Jean Lefebvre de Cheverus, 1768-1836 (Milwaukee, 1958), p. 141; Madeleine Hooke Rice, Federal Street Pastor: The Life of William Ellery Channing (New York, 1961), p. 65.

[99]See Emerson to William Emerson, August 11, 1842, in Emerson, Letters, III, 78-79; Emerson to Anna Barker Ward, May 5, 1859, in ibid., V, 142-143; Emerson to Samuel Gray Ward, August 10, 1859 [?], in ibid., 169; Emerson to Lidian Emerson, January 4, 1872, in ibid., VI, 194; Emerson, Journals, 1862, IX,468. See also Georgiana Bruce Kirby, "Reminiscences of Brook Farm," Old and New, V (May, 1872), 523.

[100]Vincent F. Holden, The Early Years of Isaac Thomas Hecker (1819-1844) (Washington, D.C., 1939), pp. 212-213, hereafter cited as: Holden, Early Years of Hecker; Americo D. Lapati, Orestes A. Brownson (New York, 1965), p. 39; Swift, Brook Farm, p. 59, 200; Katherine Burton, "Sophia Dana Ripley," The Missionary, LIII (1939), 42; Georgiana Bruce Kirby, Years of Experience: An Autobiographical Narrative (New York, 1886), p. 135.

[101]See Bronson Alcott's Fruitlands. With Transcendental Wild Oats, by Louisa May Alcott, comp. Clara Endicott Sears (Boston, 1915), pp. 177-179; Howard Mumford Jones, America and French Culture, 1750-1848 (Chapel Hill, North Carolina, 1927), p. 221.

[102]In addition to writings mentioned above, these included the works of Manzoni, Bossuet, DaVinci, Bede, Eusebius and others. For additional books of Catholic piety, see below, Chapter IV.

Of the 12,000 books in Parker's library, many were various editions and languages of one work. He possessed more than 100 editions of the Bible, including Catholic ones most likely; he purchased all the editions of Thomas More (Utopia?) he could find; the works of John Damascene, Vincent of Beauvais, and many other medieval authors; books on demoniacal possession, books on canon law, etc. (see Weiss, Life of Parker, II, 2, 4-7).

Thoreau's great literary interest was in aboriginal America. For the last twelve years of his life he collected material from every source available. Not the least of these was almost the complete set of Jesuit Relations, from 1632 to 1690, which he read omnivorously, and which he trusted above the writings of any other on the subject. He also collected and read any other history of the French in America that he could find, these being particularly the works of Jesuit and Recollet Fathers (see Kenneth Walter Cameron, Companion to Thoreau's Correspondence: With Annotations, New Letters and an Index of Principal Words, Phrases and Topics [Hartford, Connecticut, 1964], pp. 290-292; Lawrence Willson, "Thoreau and Catholicism," Catholic Historical Review, XLII [July, 1956], 160-165; Albert Keiser, The Indian in American Literature [New York, 1933], pp. 211-213).

[103]Particularly Clarke, Brownson, Hecker, Hedge, Emerson, Parker, and Osgood. As Parker wrote, "I have endeavored always to learn their doctrine from their own writers" (Parker, Journal, March 3, 1844, in Weiss, Life of Parker, I, 213).

That prodigious researcher, Kenneth Cameron, has listed all of the reading Emerson did in periodical literature up to the transcendental period. The list contains thirty-nine articles on Catholic subjects (Cameron, Emerson's Workshop: An Analysis of His Reading in Periodicals through 1836 with the Principal Thematic

Key to His Essays, Poems and Lectures. Also Memorabilia of Harvard and Concord, 2 vols. (Hartford, Connecticut, 1964), I, 10-113, passim.

Before Follen's untimely death by shipwreck in 1840, he proposed to establish a journal to be entitled All Sides. Under the heading of Religion was to be included the topic, "Roman Catholicism and Protestantism" (see The Works of Charles Follen, with A Memoir of His Life, 5 vols. [Boston, 1841-1842], I, 634, hereafter cited as: Follen, Works).

104Osgood, for example, used complete sets of the writings and lives of the Fathers, in English and French, for his Studies in Christian Biography (or, Hours with Theologians and Reformers [New York, 1850]), more than half of which concerns Catholic figures. Judging from Parker's citations, we can see that he apparently secured every new edition of the Fathers as soon as it appeared. The other transcendental scholars used them extensively also (see below, Chapters III and V).

105Hedge delivered a course on "Medieval History" at Lowell Institute, Boston, 1853; Brownson, a series of lectures on the Middle Ages, in 1842-1843; Clarke a series of biographical sketches in his church in 1846, among which he included Joan of Arc and Charles Borromeo (Clarke to S.S.C., December 13, 1846, in Clarke, Autobiography, Diary and Correspondence, ed. Edward Everett Hale [New York, 1968, c. 1891], p. 166, hereafter cited as Clarke, Autobiography). Clarke's course in Natural and Revealed Religion given at the Divinity School of Harvard College was divided into three parts, the last of which concerned the relation between Catholic and Protestant Christianity (ibid., pp. 292, 297-298). Emerson delivered a lecture on Thomas More in 1835, and he covered the history of Catholicism as a topic in his sermons (see Kenneth Cameron, "History and Biography in Emerson's Unpublished Sermons," Proceedings of the American Antiquarian Society, LXVI [October, 1956], 113). In 1840 Emerson proposed an institution for instruction--somewhat like what was later created as the Concord School of Philosophy in 1879. Included in the subjects to be taught by Parker would be one on the Catholic Church (Emerson to Fuller, 1840, as cited in John Albee, "A Tribute to Emerson," The Independent, LV [May 21, 1903], 1178). The project did not materialize.

106In Osgood's Mile Stones in Our Life-Journey ([New York, 1854], p. 208, hereafter cited as: Osgood, Mile Stones), he has a Christmas Vesper hymn written by Archbishop John Hughes of New York. More significantly, he has four articles which deal with contemporary Catholic events. His "Education in the West" (CE, XXII [November, 1837], 194-207), is a review of the transactions of three annual meetings of the Western Literary Institute and College of Professional Teachers, Cincinnati, 1834-1836, in which Cincinnati's Catholic Bishop John B. Purcell actively participated. "Debates on the Roman Catholic Religion" (CE, XXIII [September, 1837], 53-64), is Osgood's review of two debates on Catholicism, participated in by Protestant Divines, Bishop Purcell, and Coadjutor Bishop of New York, John Hughes. "Americans and the Men of the Old World" (CE, LIX [July, 1855], 1-77), surveys the church property question then before the New York Senate, as seen through the speeches of Louis Kossuth, Senator E. Brooks, and New York Archbishop John Hughes. "Doctrine of the Holy Spirit" (CE, LXXXI [September, 1866], 217-233), is in part a discussion of The Temporal Mission of the Holy Ghost (New York, 1866) by the Catholic Archibshop of Westminster, Henry Edward Manning.

Clarke also demonstrates familiarity with Manning in his Peter at Antioch; or the Vatican vs. Bismarck and Gladstone. A Sermon Preached by James Freeman Clarke, To the Church of the Disciples,... (Boston, 1875), p. 6. His knowledge of other contemporary Catholic writers is not evident, but he admits that he "sometimes" read polemical Catholic literature (Clarke, "A Sermon on Scolding," MJAUA, III [August, 1862], 343).

Parker has an allusion to the Familiar Letters to John B. Fitzpatrick, the Catholic Bishop of Boston (Boston, 1854), in Parker, The Rights of Man in America, ed. Franklin B. Sanborn (Boston, 1911), p. 355n, hereafter cited as: Parker, Rights of Man.

Brooks has one article in which he discusses ten French Catholic replies to Renan (Brooks, "Renan's Life of Jesus," NAR, XCVIII [January, 1864], 195-233). In Brooks's Simplicity of Christ's Teachings, Set Forth in Sermons (Boston, 1859), pp. 198-200, he discusses Nicholas Cardinal Wiseman.

Others who demonstrate a knowledge of Wiseman are Osgood, in Studies in Christian Biography, p. 2; Hedge, in "Romanism in Its Worship," CE, LVI (March, 1854), 233; and Elizabeth Peabody, in The Identification of the Artisan and the Artist, the Proper Object of American Education. Illustrated by a Lecture of Cardinal Wiseman, on the Relation of the Arts of Design with the Arts of Production. Addressed to American Workingmen and Educators, with an Essay on Froebel's Reform of Primary Education (Boston, 1869), pp. 3-42.

For the transcendentalists' interest in John Henry Newman, see below, pp.

[107]Brownson, The Convert, p. 157.
[108]See Julia Ward Howe, Margaret Fuller (Boston, 1883), p. 114.
[109]Edward Everett Hale, in Clarke, Autobiography, p. 164.

CHAPTER III

TRANSCENDENTAL INDIVIDUALISM AND THE CLAIMS OF THE CATHOLIC CHURCH

There is a good deal of ambiguity in the transcendentalists' evaluation of the Catholic Church. But basically we can see that all their judgments are regulated by a certain dualism. On the one hand there is their insistence upon the individual's inner light as the supreme source of truth. From this it follows that they could not accept the Catholic Church's claim to be a channel of truth at all, let alone the supreme channel. On the other hand, the transcendentalists did see inner light and beauty objectivized in art and nature. They therefore could accept certain religious expressions as found in the Catholic and nowhere else.

But often the authority of the Church--which they rejected--overlapped with the various religious forms which gave it expression. The transcendentalists were therefore perplexed as to the degree of acceptance which they would bring to the total Church. While they became enraptured of the religious beauty which offered itself to their senses, they often censured these very forms as opposed to their own spirit of freedom. At such times it was not the inspiration of the religious expressions that affected them. Rather their irritation sprang from a two-fold objection. Their first objection to this or any "religion of creeds and forms" was its tendency to materialize religion to the point of placing legal purity above moral purity. Their own earnest pursuit of moral perfection made them especially sensitive to the human failings of those who claimed adherence to the only true religion, Catholicism. They were shocked therefore at what they judged the hypocrisy of covering lax living with a mere profession of belief, without any conviction or genuine "experience" of truth through the intuition.[1] Second, and more importantly, they abhorred the replacement of the movements of the inner light with the external forms of authoritative priesthood and "magical" sacraments.

Such legalism seemed to them to sacrifice the religion of the spirit for the sake of the letter of the law, and to deprive its advocates of touch with the divine which came from "natural piety."[2]

At bottom, then, what the transcendentalists objected to was not the art and prayer of the Church--in these they could and did find inspiration. These were rejected only insofar as they embodied a much more objectionable feature of Catholicism, its entire structure of authority and belief. In the creed and organization of the Catholic Church the transcendentalists found little more than spiritual tyranny, a tyranny which sprang primarily from the "immense" and "idolatrous" claims which it made for itself.[3] Occasionally they were forced to acknowledge that the Church's self-assurance in these assumptions had given it an admirable place in the past, and a sometimes enviable position in the present.[4] But for the most part they judged the Church's "pretensions" as unsubstantiated. They were quite familiar with these claims and took pains to discuss and refute them all.

AUTHORITY OF THE CATHOLIC CHURCH

The most basic claim made by the Catholic Church was its belief in itself as the instrument through which God's truth was made known to the world. Such a position was intolerable to the transcendentalist. By what authority, he questioned, could a self-made, visible and tangible organization claim to speak for God, to tell a man what God himself revealed directly and daily in the inner chamber of the soul? The question constituted almost a theme appearing in nearly every comment on the Church's authority made by the transcendentalists. Few subjects provoked even the most unprejudiced among them as did this one. "Whence, indeed," demands the ordinarily gentle Bartol, "comes [the Church's] right to stand between the soul and God?"[5] Even the tolerant Clarke loses his usual placidity whenever discussing the Church's presumptions. Although he is always careful to demonstrate his recognition of the Church's "goodness" and to acknowledge its sincerity, Clarke does not hesitate to label it with a name that even

the vitriolic Parker avoided--antichrist.[6] Nor could the temperate Emerson refrain,
at least in private, from calling Romanism, along with every other popular religion,
"an aggrandized and monstrous individual will," entirely opposed to the divine will
discernible in the goodness of all things. Along with Jupiters, fairies, saints
and devils, the Catholic Church, he mused to himself, was not spiritual therefore,
but "demonological" and fictitious.[7]

Yet with the single exception of his senior essay on the middle ages,[8]
Emerson made no in-depth study of the pro's and con's of the Church's claims. The
more systematic transcendentalists, however, felt an obligation to examine them.
In some, their study had for its purpose to discover how far the claims possessed
validity; in others, it was to provide circumstantial evidence in support of
their own preconceived judgments. For, while in theory the transcendentalists
preferred intuition over evidence, in actuality they frequently turned to the
rational examination of such evidence to confirm what their intuition prompted.

Sources for the transcendental argumentation on the validity of the Catholic
Church were many: the Bible, especially the New Testament; history, or the warrant of tradition; signs of particular virtue in those claiming authority; evidence
of the inspiration of God in individual Catholics or in Church Councils; and
lastly, the unanimous consent of mankind. Parker, Hedge, Clarke, and to a lesser
degree Bartol, were adept at the selective examination of such evidence.

When the transcendentalists used Scripture in this project, they ordinarily
employed the usual Protestant exegesis. The specific texts of the conferring of
the keys and the call of Peter as rock[9] Constitute the primary case in point.[10]
But often they went beyond the common Protestant rendering, as Clarke did in his
exposition of these two texts. From his universalist eminence, Clarke decided
that the Protestant argument did not go far enough here. In his view, the conferral
of the keys was made not to the pope, as Catholics would have it; not to all ministers of the faith, as Protestants would have it; but to all Christians, since the

bestowal of the keys meant nothing more than the bestowal of a living faith.[11] To

the symbolism of Peter and the rock he gave a similar transcendental interpreta-

tion: "This is what the Church of Christ stands upon;...the rock of sincerity and

honesty in the minds of Christian men and women." The Catholic Church had no more

authority than this, an authority held in common with all men.[12]

Besides Scripture, the transcendentalists occasionally referred to the voice

of tradition. In this area, Clarke took exception to the Church's insistence upon

tradition as furthering its claim to supremacy. In his book Orthodoxy: Its Truth

and Errors, he challenged the Church to supply sufficient warrant for a set of

nine of its assumptions, which he took upon himself to refute one by one.[13]

In less measured and scholarly terms Parker too challenged the Church's claims,

denying the arguments from Scripture and tradition, and adding a third to refute:

the Church's claim to authority based on its direct inspiration by God. Direct

inspiration was a part of Parker's transcendental creed, but he could not admit

the right of a church to receive it. The Catholic Church's claims, therefore, were

both "contrary to human reason" and "unscriptural."[14] Later, after he had assumed

the more radical position that there is no supernatural revelation in the Scrip-

tures, he simply dropped the idea of any warrant for spiritual authority, except

the created universe in man and nature.[15]

In these and the comments of others we see the ultimate transcendental posi-

tion. God's inspirations in the soul were sufficient justification for themselves

and did not need to be announced or endorsed by any Church, unless that Church

could claim the entire consent of all humanity.[16] Where the "Church" expressed

the soul, it was acceptable; where it set itself up as a divinely sent institution,

"with God-given authority to dictate and command,"[17] it was not. Since the only

true church was simply the divine element in each individual man,[18] the "papal

church" did not possess the Holy Spirit in its hierarchy, its councils, or its

Scriptures.[19] Wrote Brownson, not long before he did come to accept Catholicism:

"We do not believe the Church...we do not hold it to be a divine institution....
This, I suppose, is the secret of our hostility to ecclesiastical authority."[20]
Even where the divine origin of any institution was acknowledged by the transcendentalists as a distinct possibility of the past, most such institutions were
judged to have lost the divine spark--they were nothing now but empty shells.[21]

If, then, there is no divine authorization for the supremacy of the Catholic
Church or its spokesmen, it follows that there is no basis for the Church's claim
to infallibility. Transcendental attacks on this point, therefore, proceeded
consistently from the above, sometimes with restraint, sometimes with derision;
sometimes after scholarly research and correct understanding; sometimes by means
of sheer polemics.

The transcendentalists' arguments against infallibility were constructed on
the bases of their varying interpretations of the term. Parker early rendered a
precise definition of it in his journal of 1844, after a conversation with a
Roman bishop. But later he came to conceive of the term as the pope's title to
inerrancy in opinions, thoughts, acts, and feelings. As a result, he thought of
the Roman Church as the Catholic's "great idol" precisely because of its infallibility. Bancroft too, second only to Parker in his private abuse of the Church,
was disgusted at the papal assumption. After the Vatican Council's declaration
on papal infallibility in 1870, he seemed to believe his own words that this was
an announcement that the pope was God on earth, "a monstrosity that cannot be
paralleled since the days of the Caesars....The scarlet woman of Babylon is in
a bad way."[22]

The scholarly Clarke could offer no better an understanding of the meaning
of infallibility. In the challenges to the Church which he listed in Orthodoxy,
he asked the Church to prove its infallibility by demonstrating that it had "never
committed any mistake."[23] Four years after the declaration, he presented an
unusually heated discussion of the matter, attempting to warn of its far-reaching

consequences: First, since the Church had authority over faith and morals, and since morals in Clarke's mind were all-inclusive--"everything we do is either right or wrong"--he warned that every action of every American Catholic was now under the direct supervision of a foreign power! Specifically, he singled out Archbishop Henry Edward Manning's insistence on the pope's temporal power, charging that it was a direct attempt of Rome to interfere in the laws and social institutions of this country. Thus he inferred that the declaration of papal infallibility, which he felt the bishops had been "compelled" by the pope to issue, was a clever expedient for the ultimate exercise of a relentless authoritarianism over every facet of life.[24]

Hedge had nothing to say on infallibility at this period, but in the sunny days of transcendentalism he offered an explanation of the term that could not but be palatable to even the most liberal mind. In an 1843 lecture he argued that the infallibility assumed by the Catholic Church

> was only a more emphatic announcement of that authority by which every society provides for the final arbitrament of litigated questions in its own sphere, and which the Catholic Church could claim, with peculiar propriety, on the allowed supposition of a Divine Spirit copresent to every period and phase of its development. The design was not to subject the mind, but to build it up; not to enforce a particular scheme of faith, but to offer guidance and repose....[25]

This diluted version of the Church's notion of infallibility is perhaps best balanced by Furness's simple and direct understanding of the word. Catholics, he wrote, "uphold the Church as the infallible interpreter of Christian Truth."[26]

Given these various understandings of infallibility, a few of the transcendentalists went to work to demolish it. In the process, they employed tools from reason, history, and their own transcendental faith. Arguing from reason, they declared that there was no real rational support for the theory; that its "proofs" were an insult to reason, or at the very least insufficient, since they appealed to the reason without the heart; that changes in the Church's political behavior was a most reasonable sign that its opinions were subject to error.[27] Finally,

Clarke, with less logic than he demanded of the Church, protested that calling the pope infallible did not make him so, and that blunders were just as liable to be made by the pope after the declaration as before it.[28]

History provided further grist for the mill. Clarke, especially, adopted all the favorite Protestant targets of criticism: the crusades against heresy, the St. Bartholomew massacre, the Inquisition, the errors and personal crimes of the Church's ministers and of Catholic monarchs, the Galileo incident. A Church with such a record, they argued, could not possibly offer genuine truth to the world.[29] Even the gentle Channing charged that popery had been "the scourge and curse of Christendom" from this one cause, its "insolent, intolerant pretension to infallibility."[30] "It is blasphemy," cried Hedge late in his life, "when we think of the attribute of Deity vested in a Boniface VIII, an Alexander VI, a John XXIII. Infallible? No! forever no!"[31]

Marshalling further signs from history, some of the transcendentalists thought they observed a definite tendency against the acceptance of the doctrine of infallibility in such figures as Newman, Fenelon, and St. Ambrose.[32] Moreover, they could see no assumption to infallibility on the part of the apostles.[33]

The last word in the argument against infallibility, however, was the transcendental one. Did man need an infallible guide outside himself? Was not the heart guide enough? With painful rhetoric, the better to display the "tangled thicket" of the Catholic position, Clarke argued:

> If an infallible church is necessary, an infallible guide to the infallible church is still more necessary. Nor does the difficulty stop here. We shall also need an infallible witness to the infallible guide. We shall then need an infallible proof of the infallibility of the witness of the infallible guide into the infallible church.[34]

Thus it seemed that the absurdity of the Catholic assumption was in the end its own rebuttal. Once again the only reliable guide to truth seemed to be oneself. "We can have certainty for ourselves," Clarke wrote in another place, "but only for ourselves. Infallibility is inward....There is no outward infallibility to be found anywhere. No church is infallible, no creed is infallible, no book is infallible."[35]

CATHOLIC DOGMATISM

Whether described as a display of blasphemy or as merely a want of reserve, the Catholic claim to infallibility had ramifications that by logical extension the transcendentalists could not or would not accept. For, once the claim to infallibility was made, it was obvious that it would assert itself in the formulation of articles of belief. The writings of the transcendentalists abound with allusions to these "dull superstitions" and "sour opinions" of the Romish Church.[36] Was it not a grave danger to replace Christ and his spirit with man-made creeds?[37] To love God and pursue Christian moral perfection was the whole of the law, and no "creed" further than that was necessary.[38] Besides, creeds were too narrow, too wizened, to cover all the world of ideas which man had received "in his inspired brain from the great God."[39]

Moreover, depending on the need or mood of the moment, the transcendentalists judged the Catholic doctrines false for several often contradictory reasons. At one time the Catholic creed is too rigid; at another too changing. At one time the sources of creeds are a pure desire for union with God; at another they are "immoral, unlovely, and irreligious" teachings based on the mere "said so of somebody who knew no better than we; who took his dreams...for the facts of the universe." At still another, they were produced by a desire to bring the witness of Scripture into line with some favorite system of speculation.[40]

But this was only begging the question. Basically, the transcendentalists were simply being consistent with their fundamental beliefs. If their infallible authority for truth lay within themselves, then the truth itself lay within also. Thus each had his own creed. Thoreau, for example, described his thus: "For my part if I have any creed it is so to live as to preserve and increase the susceptibleness of my nature to noble impulses--first to observe if any light shine on

me, and then faithfully to follow it."[41] That he lived in strictest adherence to
this creed in incontestable. These self-made creeds were what gave the transcendentalists their peculiar élan. Bartol exulted toward the end of his life: "The
movement [transcendentalism] has released us from all dogmatic bonds, and has
disclosed the rock to build on in the human soul, showing that other foundations
are but sand." As he put it elsewhere, "In...variety of opinion, not in dogmatic
stability,...are our life and joy."[42] On the other hand, for the transcendentalist with a reformist orientation, the "authentic creed fo the Church of Christ"
was written not only in the heart of the individual but "in the very heart of this
century,...in two words UNION AND PROGRESS, the mutual solidarity and continuous
progress of the race."[43]

Yet despite their fervent disapproval in principle of all outward authority
in matters of belief, some of the transcendentalists occasionally expressed regret
that their system was so viable. In a journal entry for 1863, Emerson copied a
statement from Varnhagen:

> To have religion, to have a creed, means to give up yourself uncondition-
> ally to an image, to a thought, and who can or must do that, to whom
> that thing succeeds, has incontestably a great hold and consolation....
> Whoever is directed on steady free thinking, whose piety fastens not on
> fixed images, seems in many respects to have a harder lot....And the
> Divinity, who sees the different strivings which belong to it, looks
> surely with greater approbation on those who have the most difficult
> approach to him....[44]

Emerson makes no comment on the passage. He seems to have copied it to reassure
himself, at a time when, as he was growing older, he began to feel the need for a
more secure religious orientation. Bartol too, in his later life at times saw the
need of a set of beliefs to feed the declining enthusiasm of religious groups. In
1886 he issued a call for a definite Unitarian creed. "Must we not admit," he
asked, "that the other sects--Greek, Romish, Catholic, Protestant--are more religious than the Unitarians, in the ritual and documentary sense?...The contents of
special Christian revelation they have done the most to preserve." And while rejecting the concept of "salvation by subscription to a creed," he warned that

"a sect without ideas of its own to urge has no title to be free or to exist."
Hedge likewise betrayed an incipient concern for the future of his own religious
faith when he wrote in 1856 that the early Church had to be dogmatic, for being
so young it was in constant danger of dissolution.[45]

For the most part, however, the transcendentalists continued in their opposition to dogmatizing. Besides opposing it in principle, they lined up an impressive list of ill effects that they believed it had produced. In the first place
they argued that dogmatism had led the Catholic Church to arbitrary scriptural
interpretation and to theological wrangling and hopeless obscurantism.[46] Channing
and Parker deplored the creation of a Christian theology by means of "cold speculation." For them, the pure religion of the heart could never be formed by such
a system.[47] Others pointed with dismay to the bigotry and sectarianism which they
believed Catholic theologizing inevitably produced.[48] For how could the Christian
Church ever be united, if one branch insisted on its sole claim to truth and
denied salvation to any outside its community? This exclusivism[49] exasperated
all the transcendentalists, not only on the basis of their doctrine of the soul
as source of truth. They opposed it further because they were all of a universalist cast: where they concerned themselves with salvation at all, they felt it was
earned by "likeness to Christ," or Christian living, not by "mere assent" to a
creed.[50]

The transcendentalists pointed also to the effects of dogmatism on personal
freedom. Most of them assumed, with certain of their Protestant contemporaries,
that the Catholic Church's imposition of doctrine had the unwholesome effects of
restricting totally the consultation of the Bible,[51] the following of one's own
conscience,[52] and above all the use of reason and free inquiry.[53] A few of them
occasionally glimpsed the fact that these assumptions on the Catholic position
were erroneous. Hedge at one time praised the Church's inspirations and classified the Catholic Church as the one which allowed "the largest liberty of specula-

tion and ...the greatest diversity of view."[54] As for freedom of conscience, Clarke

could on occasion admit that in the last analysis, even the most orthodox Roman

Catholic was obliged to make his own reason the final judge of what the authorita-

tive Church really meant. Everyone who believes, he concluded, whether Catholic

or Protestant, must have "more or less of inward freedom."[55] This was a very

precise rendering of a concept which ordinarily irritated Clarke to an exceptional

degree.

But these voices were whispers in a roar. Most often the transcendentalists

went on to discover other harmful consequences of a Catholic's obedience to the

Church. They felt that the Catholic's submission was a mere outward conformity,

containing little or no inner conviction. It meant servility; it meant hypocrisy.[56]

It might even have meant obedience to a foreign voice ordering the overthrow of

the Constitution and the annexation of the United States to the dominions of

Napoleon![57]

Here again we can find several exceptions to the radical notion of Catholic

obedience which the transcendentalist usually entertained. Paradoxically, it was

his transcendental faith which came to the rescue. For he saw that it could very

well be a genuine faith which led the Catholic to "surrender himself body and

soul" and to "renounce his most sacred rights" at the bidding of conscience. Such

faith was an "implicit trust," which could produce a "sanctified obedience," and

moreover could issue in the "uttermost possible degree of certitude."[58] Thus,

where the transcendentalist could see the inner voice at work, even Catholic

authority could be acceptable.

Another fruit of dogmatism which the transcendentalists often felt was harm-

ful to mankind was the brake it seemed to apply to progress. As will be seen in

Chapter V, they agreed that the Church of the past had been the mother of progress

in western civilization. But they were almost unanimous in appraising the Church's insistence on spiritual submission to "mere men" as a stumbling block for God's designs for the nineteenth century.[59] They believed further that modern advances in science alarmed the Church and made it tighten its authority still more.[60]

Whether this "spiritual violence," as Parker called it,[61] led also to the suppression of civil freedoms and to the antipathy for democracy and republicanism was a point on which the transcendentalists could not agree. And one of them, Bancroft, could not even agree with himself, presenting now one view and now its opposite.[62]

The Catholic Church, then, for its claims to God-given supremacy over the spirit of man, its assumptions of infallibility, and its insistence upon the acceptance of a set of truths as divine, was, more often than not, a spiritual despot. Its absolutist character the transcendentalists saw as a direct outcome of its dogmatism. It had consequently evolved into a kind of Egyptian yoke in Egyptian darkness, a spiritual tyranny.[63] Yet it was, Emerson would add, a tyranny tempered with "a grain of sweetness," a sweetness not always noticed by those transcendentalists who selected from the Church's past the more notorious instances of intolerance.[64] The Catholic Church had become, warned Hedge, "the most powerful spiritual organism" the world had ever known; and it was precisely to her spirit of legalism and arbitrary spiritual power that she owed her position of strength.[65]

THE CATHOLIC CLERGY

Such particular power over souls was a concept odious to the transcendentalists. The men who wielded it, therefore, also came in for their share of criticism. In the first place, the very idea of a special priesthood would naturally give them offense, since the concept of a chosen class or a spiritual elite was totally repugnant to their own system of beliefs. Just as they objected strenuously to any institution, so they rejected outright the idea that any man or class of men was needed to mediate between God and the soul or to establish the unity of men with each other. In their approach to religion, therefore, all men were their own priests, "Every man," wrote Convers Francis, "must feel that it comes to him, and demands of him to be a priest and curate of his own soul."[66] To forget this, as the Catholic Church seemed to do, was equivalent to forgetting the immanence of God in all created things, and especially in the human soul. Naturally they could not object to priests if conceived of as teachers of religion[67]--many of them were such themselves--but it was the peculiar "pretensions" to special authority made by the Catholic clergy and hierarchy that irritated them.[68]

Particularly annoying to the transcendentalists were the honors and worldly recognition that they often saw accorded to Catholic priests and hierarchy. Titles such as Father and Pope came under attack, since they seemed to set a very fallible man at the center of attention and in place of humanity's real axis, God.[69] On this score they were especially sensitive to the honors paid to the pope and to Catholic prelates, particularly the cardinals, and to the display and ceremony that attended them.[70]

More than pomp and show, some of the transcendentalists saw in the hierarchy a sign of the "grand organization" of a Catholic theocracy, monarchy, or aristocracy.[71] They were vividly impressed--whether positively or negatively--by the power and command which the Church's structure had enabled it to exercise through the centuries and up to the present day. Bartol and Clarke got carried away in their metaphors of the Church as a magnificent army, with its officered corps, its cavalry, infantry and artillery, its commissary department, hospitals, ambulances, and telegraph corps. From another point of view Clarke wrote admiringly of the Church's familial organization, with the pope as Father and the other clergy as fathers to smaller families of sons and daughters of God. With less imagination but more realism, Hedge listed ecclesiastical organization, along with ritualism and symbolism, as one of the unique contributions of the Roman Church to what he called the spiritual values of mankind.[72]

If the transcendentalists could rarely acknowledge the right of spiritual authority in a Catholic priest or prelate, they had still less sympathy with the Church's temporal power.[73] It was perhaps for this area that they reserved their most heated attacks on the Catholic clergy. Such twofold power in the hands of men, they argued, could only lead to pride and a lust for glory.[74] The results--priestcraft, clerical fraud, the wiles of the Jesuit--were obvious signs of a stagnant and reactionary clergy, at enmity with humanity, "ignorant of their own ignorance," and inadequate of meet the religious needs of the age.[75]

Still, the transcendentalists had to be true at times to their own belief in the goodness in all men, even Catholics. "It is easy," warned William Henry Channing, "to ascribe to the cunning and love of power of priests the wonderful sovereignty which this spiritual dictator has exerted; but it is proof of surprising superficiality, that these critics do not recognize, that only _sincere_ enthusiasm and truth, however adulterated by errors, can give such a hold upon human will." Clarke could find such sincerity in the "loving and tender spirit" of many of the Catholic clergy; and Convers Francis, in the midst of his diatribe against "popery," could discern "the zeal, fidelity and self-sacrificing kindness with which many of the clergy of that communion, in modern times, have devoted themselves to the temporal and spiritual interests of their flocks." Emerson admitted to having met one good Catholic priest, and Thoreau at least accorded the Catholic priest the title "degenerate saint." Even Parker, in his earlier days, acknowledged that there were a number of Catholic priests and bishops of "sound learning, of true and beautiful philanthropy, of natural piety." Whatever their judgments of the Catholic priest, Osgood advised, it might be well to accept the Catholic hierarchy as descendants of Aaron's line, until the race was perfected, and a "truer civilization" should arise.[76]

CATHOLIC BELIEFS

Although the transcendentalists deplored the imposition of belief by an external authority, this is not to say that they were opposed to any dogmatism at all. Indeed, they were very nearly dogmatic themselves in their insistence upon the truth of specific matters revealed to every individual soul, particularly their own. This becomes more evident when one examines the many theological writings they produced on Christian teachings, both Protestant and Catholic. They spent the greater part of such exercises on doctrines held by all "orthodox" Christians in common, but occasionally they took on a topic which concerned matters of Catholic faith specifically. It is not our purpose to analyze the theological hair-splitting involved in such controversies, but merely to select points of Protestant-Catholic divergence, particularly where these bore most closely upon the transcendental faith.

Practically every Catholic teaching was touched upon by one or other of the transcendentalists, and elaborated on at great length especially by Clarke, Hedge and Parker. Only Clarke, however, undertook to produce systematic studies of Catholic doctrine, and to refute it in an orderly fashion. Parker was undoubtedly sincere in attempting to search out the genuine meaning of Catholic doctrine, but as in all the other fields of human knowledge which he tried to swallow whole, he never allowed himself a chance to assimilate them. In the end, his intolerance of absolute truth got the better of him. Of the other transcendentalists, only Bartol and Bancroft expressed admiration for the unchangeableness of Catholic dogma,[77] while the rest were content to criticize or refute certain ones here or there.

The favorite topics which elicited an expression of transcendental opinion were sin and redemption; the Trinity and Incarnation; the place of the Bible and tradition in revelation; and the doctrinal aspects of baptism and the Eucharist.

In Parker, the method of discussion usually took on the form of polemics, and in his later life, sarcasm and invective. In Hedge,the pattern was more one of scholarly ambivalence; in Brownson, growing acceptance; and in Clarke, a rather thorough mastery of many of the specifics of Catholic dogma. Clarke could speak with equal ease of the Church's teachings regarding Latria and Dulia as types of worship, or of the Catholic understanding of atonement as this differed from the usual Protestant interpretation. He and others, particularly Hedge, could discourse more or less familiarly and accurately on the fine distinctions in the teachings found in Catholic writings, and often used these documents to support their own views.[78]

In some cases the transcendentalists did not attempt to refute the Catholic teaching, but merely to pass it on, as Clarke often did, for example, in his studies on comparative religions.[79] At other times a primary aim was to demonstrate the falsity of the Catholic view or to bring the subject into line with Protestant, Unitarian, or transcendental thought.[80]

As did all good Unitarians, the transcendentalists attacked the Calvinist concepts of sin, depravity, atonement, baptism, heaven and hell with a vengeance. Thus they can also be expected to condemn any Catholic belief which they considered, rightly or wrongly, to be identical or similar in this area. By the same token, where they noticed that the Catholic position differed, they sometimes used it as a counterargument to the Calvinist. Their views on these subjects, therefore, amounted to at least a partial acceptance of the Catholic doctrines concerning salvation and the future life, especially that of purgatory.[81]

In examining the Catholic doctrine of salvation, the transcendentalists were able to accept only what conformed to the moralist stance of their own spirituality--the power of the individual to save himself. Hence they could deny the validity of baptism or the redemptive act of Christ, and contend that faith, hope and love are the only requisites for "salvation," or happiness.[82] For Clarke, heaven and hell were carried about in one's own person by reason of one's moral behavior. And for Hedge, atonement was man's cooperation with the divine creative intelligence, and a "progressive reconciliation of the earthly and heavenly in human life."[83]

On these points the transcendentalists often challenged the Catholic position. But to the Catholic belief in purgatory, they were more amenable. Actually, they were uncertain about the existence of a future life. Hedge dismisses the Protestant notion of heaven as "groundless and preposterous," but views the Catholic idea of purgatory as "a less irrational conception of the future of the soul." Other transcendentalists also wrote rather favorably of purgatory, while not accepting it as a fully established truth: Cranch sees the development of belief in purgatory as "an infiltration of secular common sense and pity," a doctrine established to "leaven the oppressive creed" of sin and punishment. Henry appraises the idea of a modified version of the Catholic purgatory as a very definite possibility, one which "serves to illustrate the awful purity and tender compassion of our God."[84]

It will be recalled that in their first difference with the orthodox Unitarians, the transcendental or liberal wing split on the question of the New Testament miracles. It is noteworthy that some of the major transcendental voices refer in their discussions to the Catholic teachings on the subject. Hedge and Parker both find the Catholic position—belief in miracles both of the New Testament and of later ages—more defensible than the Protestant. And they find the Catholic use of other evidence for Christianity—besides miracles—much more to the point.[85]

As the transcendentalists' beliefs emerged in more specific form, their interest in Christian topics gradually shifted from the subject of miracles to that of the Bible. Here their concept of the individual's direct communion with the spiritual world began to take shape and to modify their approach to the

the Scriptures as the revelation of God. Late in his life, Clarke attacked the

Catholic belief in the "infallibility" and "inspiration" of the Bible, while

early in the transcendental period Brownson warmly approved the Catholic appeal

to the spirit of inspiration or "prophecy" both within and without the Bible. He

contended that the spirit which inspired every prophet from Moses to the Cumaean

Sybil was the same as that which inspires every soul which holds communion with

the spiritual world. This spirit he saw as identical with what Catholic theology

called the Logos, or divine Word.[86]

In another area of Christian theology, the notion of God's self-communication

to man caused Hedge to produce an original though unelaborated theory on the doc-

trine of the Trinity. For the most part the transcendentalists adhered to the

strictly Unitarian repudiation of the doctrine, but Hedge could find in the Cath-

olic view a profounder truth. He judged the Catholic doctrine to be a balanced

combination of the Judaic concept of God, with those of Hellenism, Anselm, Abelard,

and Thomas Aquinas. He saw that the Catholic doctrine of the Trinity, as formu-

lated by the ancient and medieval Fathers, was another expression of an inviolable

transcendental truth, namely, that God forever communicates himself.[87] This point

at least, the transcendentalists could accept.

Carrying the concept a step further, Hedge agreed with the Athanasian dictum

that God the Father communicates himself to God the Son, Christ. Christ, there-

fore, did possess the fulness of divinity. But, added Hedge, to stop there, as

did the Catholics, was to construe the understanding of Christ's nature too nar-

rowly. For God did not dwell by nature in Christ alone; rather, what Christ "by

nature possessed without measure, all men in a measure must also possess."[88]

Brownson put it another way: "When she [the Catholic CHurch] asserted the incar-

nation of the ideal in Jesus, she asserted the truth; when she asserted that it

was and could be incarnated in him only, she erred;...." And he reached the ulti-

mate in transcendental musings on this point by adding: "...but had she properly interpreted the mystery of God made flesh, she would have commanded that the same love and reverence be paid to every man, for every man is, in proportion to the quantity of his being, an incarnation, a visible manifestation of the Divinity."[89]

Perhaps the most apt Catholic doctrine which the transcendentalists could examine with regard to their concepts of divinity in humanity was that of the Eucharist. For the most part, their harsh criticism of the Catholic belief lay in their evaluation of it as too materialistic an interpretation of the words of Christ at the Last Supper. It was an absurdity, a monstrosity, a superstition, a fancy, both idolatrous and irrational, and on the whole the most questionable of all the doctrines put forward by the Catholic Church.[90]

A few of the transcendentalists, however, undertook a more serious look into the implications of the Catholic belief. In their tours of Europe, Bartol and Clarke were strongly impressed by the Catholic concept of the "real presence." Clarke found himself unable to make a definitive statement about the reality or unreality of the doctrine, as others had done. He could only admit that his direct contact with this Roman Catholic belief had been for him a deep religious experience. But others drew out the transcendental implications of the doctrine more specifically. For Bartol, the "real presence" was no monopoly of the Catholic Church, but a privilege common to all Christians. With somewhat the same meaning, Emerson and Furness applied their concepts of symbols and correspondences to the Catholic Eucharist.[91]

A still more spiritual and transcendental view of the Eucharist was that which observed in the Catholic idea of it as "Holy Communion" a profound mode of depicting the solidarity of men with each other and with God.[92] Hedge, in particular, glimpses the relevance of a combination of the transcendental vision with that of the Catholic. He is, as usual, careful first to discredit the Catholic doctrine for the sake of his hearers, to call it "monstrous" and "gross" when taken in its literal sense. But he also points out the power of "the consecrating action of faith" to transmute the material into the spiritual, to discover a spiritual presence and a spiritual nourishment in material things. This he sees as the "true" side of the Catholic doctrine of transubstantiation. Finally, he comes closer than any of the others to an understanding of the potentiality for divine communion inherent in the Catholic belief. He explains his vision of the consecrated bread as a representation of the "looked-for universal transformation of this human world by the communication [through the bread] of a higher and divine life."[93] In this interpretation he gives the Catholic doctrine its most ideally transcendental expression.

Viewed thus in its entirety, a broad consensus becomes apparent in the transcendentalists' appraisal of the institutional Church--the Church in its structures of authority and belief. Perhaps their collective opinion might best be summarized in Channing's comment that it was Catholicism's peculiar error to have exalted the institution above inward sanctity.[94] Inner freedom, total responsiveness to the divine spirit within could not, in their minds, be limited. Above all, it ought never to be so constricted as to force itself into molds set by an external authority, particularly one which they judged was all too often devoid of inner meaning.

It has also become obvious that the transcendentalists acknowledged the Church's remarkable sway over men's minds and consciences, and that they protested this influence. But they admitted in addition that Catholicism had another power, an inner dynamism capable of forming what they liked to call a "spiritual community." This power they could and often did appreciate, perhaps even more than they rejected the other. We shall next examine by what criteria and to what extent they accepted it.

NOTES

[1]Clarke, "Orestes A. Brownson's Argument for the Roman Church," p. 244; Parker, Ten Sermons of Religion (Boston, 1853), p. 152, hereafter cited as: Parker, Ten Sermons; Thomas T. Stone, "Man in the Ages," The Dial, I (January, 1841), 279-280; Furness, as cited by Hedge in "Dr. Furness's Word to Unitarians," CE LXVII (November, 1859), 433; Cranch, "Evolution and the Moral Ideal," UR, XXXVI (August, 1891), 103; Hedge, Reason in Religion (Boston, 1865), pp. 7-8; Emerson, Works, X, 104.
    Where the transcendentalists saw moral virtue in Catholics, they were always quick to commend it (see for example, Convers Francis, Life of Sebastian Rale, Missionary to the Indians, The Library of American Biography, ed. Jared Sparks, XVII (Boston, 1845); Channing, "On the Character and Writings of Fenelon," 1829, Channing, Discourses, Reviews, and Miscellanies (Boston, 1830), pp. 165-215, hereafter cited as: Channing, "On Fenelon"; Bancroft, History of the United States, from the Discovery of the American Continent, 10 vols. (Boston, 1852-1874), passim; Osgood, Studies in Christian Biography, passim; Osgood, "St. Ambrose and the Church of the West," NAR, LXXXI (October, 1855), 414-436, hereafter cited as: Osgood, "St. Ambrose."

[2]Parker, World of Matter and Spirit, p. 65; Parker, Ten Sermons, pp. 92, 328; Osgood, The Coming Church and Its Clergy, 2nd ed. (New York, 1859), p. 6, hereafter cited as: Osgood, The Coming Church; Osgood, Studies in Christian Biography, p. 8; Emerson, JN, 1833, IV, 77; Clarke, Peter at Antioch, p. 4.

[3]Clarke, Vexed Questions in Theology (Boston, 1886), p. 49, hereafter cited as: Clarke, Vexed Questions; Clarke, "Christ and His Antichrists," MJAUA, II (September, 1861), 399; Bancroft to Hamilton Fish, December 8, 1873, in U.S. Congress, House of Representatives, Papers Relating to the Foreign Relations of the United States, 1874-1875, Part I, p. 435, hereafter cited as: U.S. Foreign Papers.

[4]Osgood, God with Men, or Footprints of Providential Leaders (Boston, 1853), p. 253; Parker, World of Matter and Spirit, p. 65; Clarke, Peter at Antioch, p. 4. See also Chapters V and VII below.

[5]Bartol, The Word of the Spirit to the Church (Boston, 1859), pp. 7, 13, hereafter cited as: Bartol, Word of the Spirit.

[6]Clarke, "Christ and His Antichrists," pp. 355-357; Clarke, "A True Theology the Basis of Human Progress," in Christianity and Modern Thought (Boston, 1880), p. 43, hereafter cited as Clarke, "True Theology." Clarke hastened to clarify his position, "to avoid misunderstanding: Let me repeat, not till they come in the name of Christ, saying 'I am he,' do they become antichrist. Whenever, therefore, in the hands of any of its ministers, the Church of Rome forgets or omits this sacrilegious claim, and simply does its work for human souls, it becomes a part of the true body of Jesus Christ on earth;..." (Clarke, Vexed Questions, p. 50).

[7]Emerson, JN, 1829, VII, 167-168. This is perhaps the clearest instance of Emerson's application of his doctrine of Over-Soul to his judgments on the single, visible, organized body of the Church.

[8]Emerson, "Thoughts on the Religion of the Middle Ages," The Christian Disciple, IV (November-December, 1822), 401-408, reprinted in Kenneth W.Cameron, Emerson, Thoreau, and Concord in Early Newspapers: Biographical and Historical Lore for the Scholar and General Reader (Hartford, 1958), pp. 273-276.

[9]Matt. 16:18, 19.

[10]See for example, Osgood, God with Men, pp. 194-198; Parker, Discourse of Religion, pp. 349-350; Bartol, "The Bible," UR, XIX (January, 1833), 42; Clarke, The Hour Which Cometh and Now Is: Sermons Preached in Indiana-Place Chapel, Boston (Boston, 1864), p. 282, hereafter cited as: Clarke, Hour Which Cometh; Clarke, Deacon Herbert's Bible Class (Boston, 1890), pp. 112-113; Clarke, The Christian Doctrine of the Forgiveness of Sin; An Essay (Boston, 1867), pp. 132-135, hereafter cited as: Clarke, Christian Doctrine of Forgiveness; Furness, The Veil Partly Lifted and Jesus Becoming Visible (Boston, 1864), p. 23n, hereafter cited as: Furness, Veil Partly Lifted.

[11]Clarke, Hour Which Cometh, pp. 282-298; Clarke, Christian Doctrine of Forgiveness, pp. 132-134. The passage in Hour Which Cometh is an elaborate discussion of the various spiritual and symbolic meanings of the "keys." In Events and Epochs in Religious History (Being the Substance of a Course of Twelve Lectures Delivered in the Lowell Institute, Boston, in 1880, 3rd ed. [Boston, 1887], pp. 38-39, hereafter cited as: Clarke, Events and Epochs), Clarke makes use of new evidence used in common with Protestants, namely, that in the recently discovered (1854) tombs of the popes in the catacombs of St. Callistus, there was no depiction of Peter's supremacy or his reception of the keys. Later discoveries have provided contrary evidence (see Ludwig Hertling and Englebert Kirschbaum, The Roman Catacombs and Their Martyrs [Milwaukee, 1956], p. 194), but in Clarke's day his research was thorough as far as it could go.

In still more spiritual and characteristic flights of interpretation, Bartol sees the "keys" as simply "the consciousness of God in the human soul" (Bartol, "The Key of the Kingdom," The Monthly Religious Magazine and Independent Journal, XX [July, 1859], 16).

[12]Clarke, Go Up Higher; or Religion in Common Life (Boston, 1877), p. 274.

[13]Clarke, Orthodoxy: Its Truths and Errors, 14th ed. (Boston, 1880 [c. 1866]), pp. 391-396. The nine assumptions he lists as: "(1.) That Jesus founded an outward Church of this kind; (2.) That he made Peter its head; (3.) That he gave Peter power to continue his authority to his successors; (4.) That the bishops of Rome are the successors of Peter; (5.) That this succession has been perfect and uninterrupted; (6.) That the Roman Catholic Church is infallible, and has never committed any mistake; (7.) That it is Catholic, and includes all true Christians; (8.) That it is at one with itself, having never known divisions; (9.) That it is the only holy Church,..." (ibid., p. 395). Clarke later takes up the same matter in greater detail in Steps of Belief, pp. 197-216.

Clarke's cited sources on this subject are few. He is familiar with Guericke and Bellarmine, but he makes no allusions to the Fathers and Doctors of the Church who treated the subject rather fully. Moreover, although well-read in comparative religions, he missed two of the books which were fast becoming standard texts in Catholic seminaries throughout the country: Francis Patrick Kenrick, A Vindication of the Catholic Church, in a Series of Letters Addressed to the Right Reverend John Henry Hopkins, Protestant Episcopal Bishop of Vermont (Baltimore, 1855); and Kenrick, The Primacy of the Apostolic See Vindicated, 3rd ed. (New York, 1848).

The redoubtable Brownson, now a Catholic, took upon himself the task of debating Clarke's argumentation. He published a prompt and spirited point-by-point refutation of Clarke's defense (Brownson, "Steps of Belief," 378-399). In addition to the usual Catholic exegesis, Brownson challenged Clarke to look to his own transcendental ideal. If, he argued, "God teaches and commands in the human soul... God must be in all souls alike, and teach all alike....Then all religions, however they contradict one another, are true and good. Why, then, declaim against the Catholic religion,...?" (ibid., p. 395).

[14]Parker, Discourse of Religion, pp. 370-373.

[15]Parker, Transient and Permanent, p. 300.

[16]Bartol, Reason and Rome in Education. A Sermon... (Boston, 1879), p. 16; Bartol, Character: The Man and the Physician. A Sermon... (Boston, 1878), p. 23.

[17]Hedge, "The Churches and the Church," CE, XLI (September, 1846), 200.

[18]W.H. Channing, The Christian Church and Social Reform, 1848, as cited in Brownson, "Channing on the Church and Social Reform," BrQR, April, 1849, in Brownson, Works, X, 154.

[19]Osgood, "Doctrine of the Holy Spirit," p. 217.

[20]Brownson, "Origin and Ground of Government," Democratic Review, 1843, in Brownson, Works, XV, 349.

Almost alone among the transcendentalists, however, Brownson did not give up his early recognition of the possibility of a spiritual church as holding supreme authority (Brownson, New Views [1836], pp. 12-13). His "Parker's Discourse" (BoQR, V [October, 1842], 385-512) is a virtual refutation of Parker's assertion of the soul's superiority over the "church." At this time Brownson still conceived of the "church" as a purely "spiritual" organism, though possessing, in some intangible way, the right to interpret Scripture and command the body of Christ (ibid., pp. 489-510).

[21]Thoreau, Journal, 1851, II, 403-404; Emerson, Works, X, 227; Bartol, Pictures of Europe, pp. 238-239; Brownson, New Views, p. 5; Brownson, "The Church Question," BrQR, January, 1844, in Brownson, Works, IV, 472; Cranch, The Bird and the Bell, with Other Poems (Boston, 1875), p. 16.

[22]Parker, Journal, March 3, 1844, as cited in Weiss, Life of Parker, I, 212; Parker, World of Matter and Spirit, pp. 62-63; Parker, Discourse of Religion, in a chapter entitled, "The Catholic Party," p. 371; Parker, Theism, p. 171; Bancroft to J.C. Bancroft Davis, September 4, 1870, in M.A. DeWolfe Howe, The Life and Letters of George Bancroft, 2 vols. (New York, 1908), II, 240, hereafter cited as: Howe, Life of Bancroft.

George Ripley was in Rome at the time of the Vatican Council, writing articles on it for the New York Tribune, with what his biographer calls "detached scepticism." But he was "appalled" at the drive to define the dogma of papal infallibility, and he left the city gladly in a matter of months (see Charles Crowe, George Ripley: Transcendentalist and Utopian Socialist [Athens, Georgia, 1967], p. 257).

[23]Clarke, Orthodoxy, p. 395.

[24]Clarke, Peter at Antioch, entire sermon; Clarke, Steps of Belief, pp. 202-204. Bancroft also believed that the acceptance of the infallibility of "a foreign and alien sovereign" by American Catholics clearly brought with it subordination within no defined bounds (Bancroft to Hamilton Fish, May 26, 1873, in U.S. Foreign Papers, 1873-1874, Part I, p. 290).

[25]Hedge, Martin Luther and Other Essays, p. 137.

[26]Furness, Discourses (Philadelphia, 1855), p. 193.

[27]Parker, World of Matter and Spirit, p. 63; Hedge, "Luther and His Work," Atlantic Monthly, LII (December, 1883), 817; Clarke, Common-Sense in Religion: A Series of Essays (Boston, 1873), p. 344, hereafter cited as: Clarke, Common-Sense; Clarke, "Orestes A. Brownson's Argument fo the Roman Church," p. 236.

[28]Clarke, Common-Sense, p. 344.

[29]Clarke, "Orestes A. Brownson's Argument for the Roman Church," p. 236; Clarke, Orthodoxy, p. 345; Clarke, Peter at Antioch, p. 3; Clarke, Steps of Belief, p. 209.

[30]Channing, Sermon, October, 1834, in Channing, Memoir, III, 248.

[31]Hedge, "Luther and His Work," [1883], p. 817.

[32]Clarke, "On a Recent Definition of Christianity," in Clarke and Francis Ellingwood Aboot, The Battle of Syracuse: Two Essays. The Index Tracts, No. 15 (Boston, 1875), p. 9; Channing, "On Fenelon," p. 174; Osgood, "St. Ambrose," p. 425.

[33]Clarke, "Orestes A. Brownson's Argument for the Roman Church," p. 243.

[34]Clarke, Steps of Belief, p. 213. Clarke used the same line of reasoning in "Orestes Brownson's Argument for the Roman Church," pp. 240-241. In private, Channing did likewise (Channing to Joseph Blanco White, September 10, 1847, in Channing, Memoir, II, 375).

[35]Clarke, Common-Sense, p. 104.

The transcendentalists were even more opposed to the implicit claims of Protestants regarding the infallibility of Creed or Book (Examples of their allusions to Protestant infallibility abound. For instances where they compare it unfavorably with Catholic infallibility see Clarke, Letter in The Radical, I [May, 1866], 344; Clarke, "Inspiration of the New Testament," MJAUA, VIII [May, 1867], 163; Clarke,

Common-Sense, p. 91; Clarke, Vexed Questions, pp. 142-143; Channing, Memoir, I, 417; Hedge, Reason in Religion, p. 201; Hedge, "The Churches and the Church," p. 201; Parker, Discourse of Religion, p. 396). Some of them declared that if they had to choose between only two alternatives, the Protestant or the Catholic type of infallibility, they would have chosen the latter, as the most venerable, ancient, and esteemed of them all (Channing, "Letter on Catholicism to the Editor of the Western Messenger, 1836" in Channing, Works, II, 269, hereafter cited as: Channing, "Letter on Catholicism"; Channing, as cited in Ernest Renan, "Channing and the Unitarian Movement in the United States, A.D. 1780-1842," in Leaders of Christian and Anti-Christian Thought. Studies in Religious History and Criticism. First Series [London, 1895], p. 12; Hedge, "The Cause of Reason the Cause of Faith," CE, LXX [March, 1861], 210).

[36]Dwight, "Music," Aesthetic Papers, May, 1849, p. 32; Parker, Lessons from the World of Matter and the World of Man, ed. Rufus Leighton (Boston, n.d.), p. 226, hereafter cited as: Parker, Lessons from Matter and Man; Emerson, JN, 1822, II, 30; Bartol, "Discourse on Dr. Mayhew," in The West Church and Its Ministers (Boston, 1856), p. 122; Bartol, Word of the Spirit, p. 11; Bancroft to Osgood, February 21, 1868, in Howe, Life of Bancroft, II, 203; Channing, "Dangers of Liberality," The Christian Disciple, III (May, 1815), 134; Fuller, Diary, January 5, 1849, in Leona Rostenberg, "Margaret Fuller's Roman Diary," Journal of Modern History, XII (June, 1940), 212; Cranch, The Bird and the Bell, p. 90. The reference to doctrine as mere opinion is also a common usage (see for example Clarke, Orthodoxy, p. 23; Clarke, Vexed Questions, p. 108; Hedge, "Life and Character of St. Augustine," Putnam's Monthly Magazine, V [March, 1856], 229, hereafter cited as: Hedge, "Life of St. Augustine").

[37]Marsh, "Evils of Creeds," Christian Palladium, Extra No. 2, 1841, p. 1; Furness, The Story of the Resurrection Told Once More; With Remarks Upon the Character of Christ and the Historical Claims of the Four Gospels (Philadelphia, 1885), p. 147, hereafter cited as: Furness, Story of the Resurrection; Bartol, Christ the Way. A Sermon... (Lancaster, Mass., 1847), p. 4.

[38]Hedge, "Life of St. Augustine," p. 229; Channing, "Letter on Catholicism," p. 271; Ripley, Letters on the Latest Form of Infidelity, Including a View of the Opinions of Spinoza, Schleiermacher, and DeWette (Boston, 1840), First Letter, p. 6; Judd, Margaret: A Tale of the Real and the Ideal, 2 vols. (Boston, 1851), II, 16-17; W.H. Channing, Sermon, as cited in Marianne Dwight, Letters from Brook Farm, p. 125; Parker to Convers Francis, February 14, 1840, as cited in Dirks, Critical Theology of Theodore Parker, p. 106; Parker, Transient and Permanent, p. 28; Parker, The American Scholar, ed. George Willis Cooke (Boston, 1907), p. 447; Parker, World of Matter and Spirit, p. 369; Marsh, "Evils of Creeds," p. 8; Clarke, Every-Day Religion, 4th ed. (Boston, 1886), p. 73.

[39]Parker, Lessons from Matter and Man, p. 226.

[40]See for example, Channing, Works, V, 408; Marsh, "Evil of Creeds," p. 3; Francis, Popery and Its Kindred Principles Unfriendly to the Improvement of Man (Cambridge, Mass., 1833), p. 13, hereafter cited as: Francis, Popery; Parker, Discourse of Religion, p. 388; Parker, World of Matter and Spirit, p. 241; Parker, Transient and Permanent, pp. 349, 353; Ripley, Discourses on the Philosophy of Religion: Addressed to Doubters Who Wish To Believe (Boston, 1836), p. 57.

[41]Thoreau to Isaiah T. Williams, September 8, 1841, in Miller, Consciousness in Concord, p. 60.

[42]Bartol, "The Tidings," p. 93; Bartol, "Martin Luther," UR, XX (December, 1883), 515.

[43]Brownson, "Parker's Discourse," p. 508. As was the case with infallibility, the transcendentalist scholars inveighed against Protestant dogmatism far more often than against Catholic.

[44]Varnhagen, Writings, I, 45, in Emerson, Journals, 1863, IX, 495. Note the Calvinistic slant in the conclusion, a rather rare instance in the later Emerson.

[45]Bartol, "The Unitarian Idea and Situation," UR, XXVI (September, 1886), 197, 206; Hedge, "Life of St. Augustine," pp. 229-230.

[46]Parker, World of Matter and Spirit, p. 369; Parker, Discourse of Religion, pp. 301, 354, 401; Clarke, Vexed Questions, p. 153; Clarke, "The Bible," in Unitarian Affirmations: Seven Discourses Given in Washington, D.C., by Unitarian Ministers (Boston, 1879), p. 37; Clarke, "Orestes A. Brownson's Argument for the Roman Church," p. 235; Newcomb, Journal, September 13, 1866, in The Journals of Charles King Newcomb, ed. Judith Kennedy Johnson (Providence, R.I., 1946), p. 257, hereafter cited as: Newcomb, Journals; Emerson, "Natural Religion Universal and Sympathetic," p. 384; Channing, Works, VI, 212; Bartol, Reason and Rome in Education, p. 12.

[47]Channing, "Dangers of Liberality," p. 134; Channing, "Letter on Catholicism," pp. 271-272; Parker, World of Matter and Spirit, p. 369. Parker classes the Catholic Church along with popular theology in the category of Arabian Nights entertainments (ibid., p. 321).

It will be noticed that Hedge's name does not appear in these citations nor in those of n. 49 above. He could not identify Catholic theology with a sterile intellectualism because he judged the preponderance of devotional feelings over dogma to be one of the peculiar merits of the Catholic Church (Hedge, "Ecclesiastical Christendom," CE, LI [July, 1851], 123-124).

[48]Parker, Transient and Permanent, p. 27, Newcomb, Journals, 1866, p. 257; Channing, "On Fenelon," p. 180; Channing, Works, III, 155, 209; Marsh, "Evils of Creeds," pp. 6-8; Hedge, "The Churches and the Church," pp. 194-196.

[49]The transcendentalists interpreted in various ways the Church's understanding of itself as the "exclusive" vehicle for salvation. Clarke, for example, saw it as an arrogant claim to a monopoly on virtue and as the presumption of complete security within the Church's walls (Clarke, Steps of Belief, pp. 199, 261-262, 277). Other transcendentalists also subscribed to definitions of the term which neither they nor Catholics could accept (see for example, Peabody, "The Dorian Measure, with a Modern Application," Aesthetic Papers, May, 1849, p. 102; Channing, Works, VI, 227; Parker, Theism, p. 147; Parker, World of Matter and Spirit, p. 127). On Parker's first trip to Rome he imbibed a correct understanding of the doctrine, which he recorded accurately in letter and journal (Parker to Convers Francis, March 18, 1844, in Weiss, Life of Parker, I, 232; Parker, Journal, March 3, 1844, in ibid., pp. 212-213). Only Clarke attempted to refute the doctrine, using, however, the common Protestant argumentation (Clarke, Steps of Belief, pp. 210-211; Clarke, Vexed Questions, pp. 32-33).

[50]Bartol, Reason and Rome in Education, p. 11; Judd, Margaret, II, 16-17; Parker, Discourse of Religion, pp. 370, 385, 392; Parker, World of Matter and Spirit, pp. 58-62; Channing, Works, VI, 186-187; Osgood, "Doctrine of the Holy Spirit," pp. 217-218, 225, 231; Osgood, "The Schleiermacher Centennial and Its Lesson," CE, LXXXVI (March, 1869), 180; Brownson, New Views, p. 11; Furness, The Exclusive Principle Considered: Two Sermons on Christian Union and the Truth of the Gospels (Boston, 1845), p. 9; Emerson, as cited in Cabot, Memoir of Emerson, I, 318; Ripley, "Religion in France," CE, X (July, 1831), 286; Clarke, Anti-Slavery Days: A Sketch of the Struggle Which Ended in the Abolition of Slavery in the United States (New York, 1883), p. 122; Clarke, Orthodoxy, p. 279.

Channing regarded Protestant exclusivism as worse than Catholic (Channing, Remarks on Creeds, Intolerance, and Exclusion [Boston, 1837], p. 20).

[51]Bartol, Church and Congregation: A Plea for Their Unity (Boston, 1858), pp. 32, 95; Clarke, Orthodoxy, p. 56; Jones Very, Sermon 14, as cited in Paschal Reeves, "Jones Very As Preacher: The Extant Sermons," Emerson Society Quarterly, LVII (1969), 21; Emerson, JN, 1822, II, 17.

[52]Newcomb, Journals, 1866, p. 257; Francis, Popery, p. 12; Brownson, Charles Elwood, or, The Infidel Converted, 1840, in Brownson, Works, IV, 250; Clarke, Peter at Antioch, p. 6; Channing, Sermon, in Channing, Memoir, III, 248; Hedge, Ways of the Spirit, p. 83; Parker, Discourse of Religion, pp. 345, 374; Parker, Rights of Man, p. 354.

[53]Thoreau, The Writings of Henry David Thoreau, vol. II: Walden; or, Life in the Woods, p. 226; ibid., vol. V: Excursions, p. 46; Judd, Philo: An Evangeliad (Boston, 1849), p. 108; Francis, Popery, pp. 7-10; Henry, in General History of Civilization in Europe, from the Fall of the Roman Empire to the French Revolution by Francois Pierre Guizot, 3rd American, from the 2nd English Edition, with Occasional Notes by Caleb Sprague Henry (New York, 1842), p. 120, hereafter cited as: General History by Guizot; Emerson, JN, 1822, II, 17; Emerson, Journals, 1870, X, 337; Bancroft to Osgood, December 25, 1871, in Howe, Life of Bancroft, II, 263; Channing, Works, III, 102; Channing, Works, Complete Edition, p. 998; Channing, The Worship of the Father: A Service of Gratitude and Joy (Boston, 1838), p. 39; Osgood, Studies in Christian Biography, p. 130; Bartol, Word of the Spirit, p. 46; Bartol, Reason and Rome in Education, pp. 11, 15; Brownson, "Laboring Classes," pp. 386, 435; Brownson, New Views, p. 13; Brownson, Literary Notice of Life of Cardinal Cheverus, Archbishop of Bordeaux, Formerly Bishop of Boston, Massachusetts by J. Huen-Dubourg, trans. E. Stewart (Boston, 1849), BoQR, II (July, 1839), 388; Parker, Sins and Safeguards of Society, ed. Samuel B. Steward (Boston, 1909), p. 121, hereafter cited as: Parker, Sins and Safeguards; Parker, Transient and Permanent, p. 299; Parker, "Hennell on the Origin of Christianity," The Dial, IV (October, 1843), 137; Parker, St. Bernard and Other Papers, ed. Charles W. Wendte (Boston, 1911), p. 150; Parker to Convers Francis, March 18, 1844, in Weiss, Life of Parker, I, 232; Parker to P.D. Moore, n.d., in ibid., p. 404; Clarke, "Polemics and Irenics," p. 168; Clarke, "Orestes A. Brownson's Argument for the Roman Church," p. 247; Clarke, The Ideas of the Apostle Paul Translated into Their Modern Equivalents (Boston, 1884), p. 390, hereafter cited as: Clarke, Ideas of Paul; Clarke, "Sermon on Scolding," pp. 341-343; Clarke, Common-Sense, p. 255; Clarke, Go Up Higher, pp. 246-247; Clarke, "True Theology," pp. 44-45; Clarke, Steps of Belief, pp. 276-277; Cranch, The Bird and the Bell, pp. 1-22, 90-93, 257; W.H. Channing, "Ernest the Seeker," The Dial, I (October, 1840), 241-242. See also Octavius Brooks Frothingham, Memoir of William Henry Channing (New York, 1886), p. 438.

[54]Hedge, Ways of the Spirit, pp. 74-77.

On his way to the Catholic Church, Brownson also developed a more correct understanding of the place of intellectual freedom in its theology (see a summary of his lectures on the middle ages, delivered in 1842-1843, in Henry F. Brownson, Orestes A. Brownson's Early Life: From 1803 to 1844 [Detroit, 1898], especially pp. 383-384; see also Brownson, Literary Notice of Life of Cardinal Cheverus by Huen-Dubourg, p. 388).

[55]Clarke, Letter in The Radical, I (December, 1865), 149-151.

[56]Follen, Works, II, 252; Bancroft to Professor Nippoli, March 5, 1869, as cited in David Levin, History As Romantic Art: Bancroft, Prescott, Motley, and Parkman (New York, 1959), p. 125; Bartol, Reason and Rome in Education, passim; Brooks, Simplicity of Christ's Teachings, pp. 78-79; Ripley, Philosophical Miscellanies, Translated from the French of Cousin, Theodore Jouffroy, and Benjamin Constant, with Introductory and Critical Notes by George Ripley, 2 vols. (Boston, 1838), II, 302-303, hereafter cited as: Ripley, Philosophical Miscellanies; Thoreau, Excursions, p.64; Hedge, "The Cause of Reason the Cause of Faith," pp. 208-213; Clarke, "Christ and His Antichrists," p. 357; Clarke, Steps of Belief, pp. 214-216; Clarke, Hour Which Cometh, pp. 291-292; Clarke, "Orestes A. Brownson's Argument for the Roman Church," pp. 233, 240-242; Clarke, Peter at Antioch, passim; J.K. Ingalls, "Creed," SA, I (July 7, 1849), 11-12; Parker, West Roxbury Sermons, 1837-1848 (Boston, 1902), p. 228; Parker, Rights of Man, p. 356; Parker, World of

Matter and Spirit, p. 370; Parker, Ten Sermons, p. 358; Francis, Popery, p. 10; Channing, Letter on Creeds, &c. (London, 1839), p. 6; Channing to Joseph Blanco White, February 27, 1841, in Channing Memoir, II, 378; Brownson, "Laboring Classes," p. 435; Judd, The Church: In a Series of Discourses (Boston, 1854), p. 53.

[57]Clarke, Steps of Belief, p. 266. This is Clarke's charge that the Catholic Brownson had published a statement indicating exactly that degree of servitude to the pope. Brownson's incisive reply proved the quotation had been falsified. It also provided Brownson with an opportunity to refute Clarke's entire theory of the "steps to belief," that is, to transcendentalism (Brownson, "Steps of Belief," pp. 378-399).

In Peter at Antioch Clarke warned that Catholic obedience to the pope could undermine the most cherished American institutions, in the same way that obedience to the Fugitive Slave Law had done (passim).

[58]W.H. Channing, "The Church of God with Us," SA, I (December 1, 1849), 344; Furness, The Authority of Jesus. A Discourse... (Philadelphia, 1867), p. 13; Osgood, Studies in Christian Biography, pp. 191-192; Brownson, "Parker's Discourse," pp. 507-508; Parker, Ten Sermons, p.150; Hedge, "Ecclesiastical Christendom," p. 123.

[59]Francis, Popery, pp. 7-8; Newcomb, Journals, 1866, p. 257; Clarke, Ideas of Paul, p. 391; Parker to Rev. Mr. Senkler, January 22, 1860, in Weiss, Life of Parker, I, 372-375; Parker, St. Bernard and Other Papers, p. 148; Parker, Theism, pp. 32-35; Parker, Rights of Man, p. 354; Parker, Autobiography, p. 22; Parker, World of Matter and Spirit, p. 130; Parker, The Great Battle Between Slavery and Freedom ...Considered in Two Speeches Delivered Before the American Antislavery Society, at New York, May 7, 1856 (Boston, 1856), pp. 48-49; Hedge, Martin Luther and Other Essays, p. 174; Hedge, "Luther and His Work," p. 817; Hedge, "The Churches and the Church," p. 202.

William Henry Channing lamented this charge. In "Ernest the Seeker" (The Dial, I [July, 1840], 54), he pointed to the Catholic colleges where the best scientific, philosophic, historical, and literary knowledge of all times was offered, and to the "mile-long libraries, stored with the choicest literature of all ages, and thrown liberally open for the world of scholars to consult;...."

[60]Clarke, Peter at Antioch, pp. 5-10 and passim; Clarke, Steps of Belief, pp. 203-204; Parker, Theism, p. 14; Brownson, The Convert, p. 158.

Clarke, Bancroft and Parker saw in papal centralization a highly systematized Jesuit plot (see, among others, Clarke, Steps of Belief, pp. 202-204; Clarke, Peter at Antioch, p. 10; Parker, Theism, p. 35; Bancroft to J.C. Bancroft Davis, September 4, 1870, in Howe, Life of Bancroft, II, 240; Bancroft to Osgood, December 25, 1871, in ibid., II, 263).

[61]Parker, Journal, February, 1844, in Weiss, Life of Parker, I, 207.

[62]For opinions favoring the view that Catholicism was inimical to civil freedom, see for example, Parker, American Scholar, pp. 278-280; Clarke, "Literary Notices," WM, II(August, 1836), 71; Bancroft to C.C. Perkins, June 12, 1869, in Howe, Life of Bancroft, II, 228; Brownson, New Views, p. 13.

For argumentation and evidence that Catholic dogmatism promotes freedom, see Bancroft, History of the United States, 3rd ed. (Boston, 1858), VII, 159; Ripley, in Philosophical Miscellanies, p. 235; W.H. Channing, as cited in Hecker, Questions of the Soul, 4th ed. (New York, 1855), pp. 220-221.

[63]Hedge, Ways of the Spirit, p. 83; Parker, Autobiography, pp. 381-382; Parker, West Roxbury Sermons, p. 188; Henry, in General History by Guizot, p. 120; Very, Sermon 14, 1860, as cited in Reeves, "Jones Very As Preacher," p. 21; Clarke, Steps of Belief, p. 202; Clarke, Orthodoxy, p. 334; Clarke, Peter at Antioch, p. 5; Parker, Discourse of Religion, pp. 385-388; Parker, Autobiography, p. 314; Channing, "On Fenelon," p. 179; Hedge, Sermons (Boston, 1891), p. 169; Brownson, Charles Elwood, p. 250; Bancroft to Osgood, February 21, 1868, in Howe, Life of Bancroft, II, 203-204; Bancroft, History of the United States, VII, 159.

[64]Emerson, Works, I, 394; Channing to Joseph Blanco White, February 27, 1841, in Channing, Memoir, II, 377-378; Channing, "Dangers of Liberality," p. 134; Ripley, Letters on the Latest Form of Infidelity, First Letter, pp. 5-6; Parker, Discourse of Religion, pp. 286-287; Parker, Ten Sermons, p. 162; Clarke, Common-Sense, pp. 255-256; Clarke, Go Up Higher, p. 247; Clarke, Steps of Belief, pp. 262-266.

[65]Hedge, Ways of the Spirit, pp. 299-306; see also his Reason in Religion, p. 342, and his Presidential Remarks, Thirty-Fifth Annual Meeting of the American Unitarian Association, May 29, 1860, MJAUA, I (July, 1860), 303.

[66]Francis, Popery, p. 16. See also Clarke, Vexed Questions, p. 44; Brownson, "Laboring Classes," p. 384.

[67]See especially Brownson, "Laboring Classes," pp. 387, 439-441. Brownson sees the duties of the Catholic priest as still spiritual and therefore still relevant, in contradistinction to those of the Protestant minister, which he judges to have become merely functional (ibid., pp. 443-446).

[68]Parker, Autobiography, pp. 86-87; Parker, Rights of Man, p. 355; Hedge, "Ecclesiastical Christendom," p. 127; Francis, Popery, p. 16; Clarke, Steps of Belief, pp. 243-244; Clarke, Common-Sense, pp. 266-267; Channing, Works, VI, 207; Emerson to Anna Barker Ward, May 5, 1859, in Emerson, Letters, V, 143n; Osgood, The Coming Church, pp. 7-8; Bartol, "Key of the Kingdom," pp. 2, 16; Brownson, "Laboring Classes," especially pp. 385-386.

Occasionally they adopted the Protestant argument from Scripture, by means of which they insisted that Christ did not intend to institute a special priesthood (Bartol, Church and Congregation, pp. 90-91; Brownson, "Laboring Classes," p. 384).

[69]W.H. Channing, as cited in Marianne Dwight to Anna Q.T. Parsons, October 19, 1845, in Marianne Dwight, Letters from Brook Farm, p. 125; Clarke, Vexed Questions, p. 44; Clarke, "Christ and His Antichrists," p. 355; Osgood, God with Men, p. 196; Parker, Theism, p. 171; Fuller to New York Tribune, January 10, 1848, in Fuller, At Home and Abroad, p. 276.

[70]W.H. Channing, "Church and State," SA, I (September 8, 1849), 152-153; Emerson, JN, 1833, IV, 152-153; ibid., 1835, V, 69; ibid., 1829, VI, 90; Fuller to New York Tribune, January 10, 1848, in Fuller, At Home and Abroad, p. 278; Cranch, The Bird and the Bell, p. 90.

Parker delighted in heaping scorn upon the cardinals (Parker to [?], April 19, 1856, as cited in Frothingham, Theodore Parker, p. 302; Parker to [?], 1858, as cited in ibid., p. 496; Parker, Sins and Safeguards, p. 228; Parker to Convers Francis, March 18, 1844, in Weiss, Life of Parker, I, 230; Parker to Miss Hunt, October 31, 1857, in ibid., p. 311; Parker to John Manley, November 5, 1859, in ibid., II, 378). In these and other passages Parker so often wrote capriciously of hoping for a red hat and robes for himself, that one wonders if he coveted them.

[71]Clarke, Peter at Antioch, p. 4; Parker, Sins and Safeguards, p. 92; Parker, American Scholar, p. 419; Peabody, "A Glimpse of Christ's Idea of Society," The Dial, II (October, 1841), 217; Hedge, "Romanism in Its Worship," pp. 231-232; Judd, The Church, p. 86; W.H. Channing, "Church and State," p. 153.

[72]Bartol, Word of the Spirit, p. 51; Clarke, Peter at Antioch, pp. 4-5; Clarke, Ten Great Religions, p. 26; Hedge, Sermons, pp. 166-169.

[73]Clarke, Peter at Antioch, passim; Parker to Rev. Mr. Senkler, January 22, 1860, in Weiss, Life of Parker, I, 375; Osgood, "St. Ambrose," p. 425; Ripley, Book Review of Materialism in Religion: or Religious Forms and Theological Formulas by Philip Harwood (London, n.d.), The Dial, I (October, 1840), 269; Bancroft, Poems (Cambridge, Mass., 1823), p. 73.

[74]Parker, Rights of Man, pp. 355-356; Parker, Sins and Safeguards, p. 93; Parker, Social Classes in a Republic, ed. Samuel A. Eliot (Boston, nd.), p. 31, hereafter cited as: Parker, Social Classes; Parker to Mrs. Ednah Cheney, December 31, 1859, in Weiss, Life of Parker, II, 405; Channing, Works, III, 259; Clarke,

Events and Epochs, p. 33; Clarke, Peter at Antioch, p. 5; Emerson, JN, 1835, V, 69; Francis, Popery, pp. 15-16; Fuller, Diary, January 1, 1849, in Rostenberg, "Margaret Fuller's Roman Diary," p. 211; Osgood, Book Review of Symbolism: or, Exposition of the Doctrinal Differences Between Catholics and Protestants, As Evidenced in Their Symbolical Writings by John Adam Moehler (New York, 1844), CE, XXXVII (July, 1844),   121; W.H. Channing, "Thanksgivings and New-Year Wishes," The Present, I (January 15, 1844), 225; Brooks, "The Revelation of St. John," CE, XLIV (May, 1848), 391-392; Brownson, Charles Elwood, p. 250; Brownson, "Laboring Classes," p. 385; Brownson, "Truth Not Dangerous," BoQR, III (April, 1840), 172.

[75]Emerson, Works, VIII, 14; Emerson, JN, 1822, I, 309; ibid., 1827, III, 116; Emerson, "Thoughts on the Middle Ages," p. 404; Parker, Theism, pp. 35, 177; Parker, Sins and Safeguards, pp. 93-94; Parker, The Nebraska Question: Some Thoughts on the New Assault Upon Freedom in America, and the General State of the Country in Relation Thereunto, Set Forth in a Discourse... (Boston, 1854), p. 70; Parker, Rights of Man, pp. 356-357; Parker to Convers Francis, March 18, 1844, in Weiss, Life of Parker, I, 232; Parker to Mrs. Apthorp, September 21, 1857, in ibid., p. 309; Parker to John Manley, September 3, 1859, in ibid., II, 350; Parker, Journal, 1859, in ibid., p. 386; Parker to Ripley, 1860, in ibid., p. 432; Newcomb, Journals, 1865, 1868, pp. 203, 272; Judd, Philo, p. 233; Fuller to New York Tribune, December 17, 1847, and January 10, 1848, in Fuller, At Home and Abroad, pp. 260, 278-279; Fuller to New York Tribune, April 19, 1848, in Fuller, Writings, p. 466; Clarke, Peter at Antioch, p. 5; Clarke, Steps of Belief, p. 202; Clarke, Hour Which Cometh, p. 5; Bancroft to Osgood, December 25, 1871, in Howe, Life of Bancroft, II, 263; Thoreau, as cited by William Ellery Channing the Younger, in Franklin B. Sanborn, The Life of Henry David Thoreau: Including Many Essays Hitherto Unpublished and Some Accounts of His Family and Friends (Boston, 1917), p. 341, hereafter cited as: Sanborn, Life of Thoreau; Channing, "On Fenelon," p. 176; Brownson, The Convert (referring to his transcendental period), p. 158; Hedge, "Destinies of Ecclesiastical Religion," p. 8; Ripley, "Religion in France," pp. 278-279; Francis, Popery, p. 16.

[76]W.H. Channing, "Call of the Present, No. 3--Oneness of God and Man," The Present, I (December 15, 1843), 150-151; Clarke, Peter at Antioch, p. 5; Francis, Popery, p. 16; Emerson, JN, 1843, VIII, 340; Thoreau, Journal, December, 1839, I, 101n; Parker, Theism, p. 35; Parker to Convers Francis, March 18, 1844, in ibid., pp. 232-233; Osgood, God with Men, pp. 50-56.

[77]Bartol, "Theological Changes," p. 294; Bancroft, History of the United States, VII, 159.

[78]Clarke, Orthodoxy, passim; Clarke, The Christian Doctrine of Prayer: An Essay (Boston, 1854), pp. 170-175; Clarke, Christian Doctrine of Forgiveness, pp. 107-108; Ripley to Andrews Norton, 1840, in Letters on Infidelity, Second Letter, pp. 75-77; Hedge, Reason in Religion, pp. 310, 406-412; Hedge, "Christianity in Conflict with Hellenism," UR, XXI (January, 1884), 14-15; Hedge, "Shedd's History of Christian Doctrine," NAR, LXXXII (April, 1864), passim; Hedge, "The Doctrine of Endless Punishment," CE, LXVII (July, 1859), passim; Alcott, "Philosophemes," Journal of Speculative Philosophy, IX (April, July, 1875), 196-197, 258-259.
    The reason for citing the Fathers of the Church in support of their own opinions was given by Brownson. "The early Christian Fathers," he wrote in 1841, "were transcendentalists" (Brownson, "Emerson's Essays," BoQR, IV [July, 1841], 300).

[79]Clarke, Ten Great Religions, passim. On the sacraments in general: Clarke, Common-Sense, p. 116. On future life: Henry, Endless Future of the Human Race: A Letter to a Friend (New York, 1879), pp. 64-72. On various subjects: Clarke, Orthodoxy, passim.

[80]On tradition as a source of revelation: Judd, The Church, p. 231. On the doctrinal aspects of devotion to Mary: Hedge, "Antisupernaturalism in the Pulpit,"

p. 145; Parker, Transient and Permanent, p. 354. On indulgences: Emerson, JN, 1822 [?], I, 188; Parker to Convers Francis, January 28, March 18, 1844, in Weiss, Life of Parker, I, 227-228, 233. On the Trinity: Hedge, Ways of the Spirit, pp. 346-351; Judd, The Church, p. 231; Parker, Discourse of Religion, p. 373; Ripley, The Doctrines of the Trinity and the Transubstantiation Compared (Boston, 1833), pp. 4-12, hereafter cited as: Ripley, Doctrines of Trinity and Transubstantiation; Emerson, Works, XI, 479; and many more. Clarke touches upon all these, especially throught Steps of Belief and Orthodoxy.

[81]On free will: Parker, Theism, pp. 288-289; (Osgood describes with approval a correct understanding of the Catholic position on free will: Osgood, Book Review of Symbolism by Moehler, p. 120). On baptism: Clarke, "Little Children. A Discourse ...," MJAUA, III (December, 1862), 531, 536; Clarke, Deacon Herbert's Bible Class, pp. 119-120, 126-127; Clarke, Orthodoxy, pp. 357, 412; Clarke, Steps of Belief, pp. 221-239; "The Disease of the Age and the Cure," The Present, I (December 15, 1843), 173-180; Judd, The Birthright Church: A Discourse (Augusta, Maine, 1853), pp. 15-18; Judd, The Church, pp. 124, 131. On sin and depravity: Osgood, Studies in Christian Biography, p. 33; Osgood, Mile Stones, p. 299; W.H. Channing, "Edwards and the Revivalists," CE, XLIII (November, 1847), 384, 389. On hell: Parker, Theism, pp. 161-170, 261-263, 266; Parker, World of Matter and Spirit, pp. 133-134. On atonement: Clarke, Christian Doctrine of Forgiveness, pp. 107-108; Bartol, Discourses on the Christian Spirit and Life, 2nd ed. (Boston, 1850), p. 189, hereafter cited as: Bartol, Discourses on Christian Spirit; Hedge, Ways of the Spirit, pp. 100-101, 238-239; Parker, Discourse of Religion, pp. 375-376.

[82]Parker and Clarke insist on this again and again.

[83]Clarke, Common-Sense, p. 155 and passim; Hedge, Ways of the Spirit, pp. 100-101; Hedge, Sermons, pp. 339-340.

[84]Hedge, "Thoughts on the Origin and Destination of the Soul," UR, II (September, 1874), 105; Clarke, Orthodoxy, p. 372; Cranch, "Symbolic Conceptions of the Deity," UR, IX (March, 1878), 250; Henry, Endless Future of the Human Race, pp. 34-36; 68-70. Emerson vacillates from one position to the other (Emerson, JN, 1837, V, 380; Emerson, Works, VIII, 328-329; 346-347).

[85]Parker, Discourse of Religion, pp. 249-251, 328-329; Hedge, "The Mythical Element in the New Testament," in Christianity and Modern Thought (Boston, 1880), 166-167; Ripley to Andrews Norton, 1839, in Ripley, Letters on the Latest Form of Infidelity, First Letter, pp. 51-52; Brownson, "Transient and Permanent in Christianity," pp. 448-449.

[86]Clarke, Vexed Questions, pp. 147-153; Clarke, "The Bible," p. 37; Brownson, "Transient and Permanent in Christianity," p. 449.

[87]Hedge, Reason in Religion, p. 310; Hedge, "Christianity in Conflict with Hellenism," p. 15. Alcott too, in his rather opaque way, commented favorably on the self-communication of God as depicted by the Athanasian creed (Alcott, Orphic Saying No. 12, as cited in Franklin B. Sanborn and William T. Harris, A. Bronson Alcott: His Life and Philosophy, 2 vols. [Boston, 1893], II, 559).

[88]Hedge, Ways of the Spirit, pp. 346-351.

[89]Brownson, "Church of the Future," BoQR,, January, 1842, in Brownson, Works, IV, 63-64.

[90]Newcomb, Journals, April 24, 1867, p. 264; Hedge, "Romanism in Its Worship," pp. 240-242; Hedge, Sermons, p. 228; Clarke, Orthodoxy, p. 56; Furness, The Power of Spirit Manifested in Jesus of Nazareth (Philadelphia, 1877), pp. 34-40, hereafter cited as: Furness, Power of Spirit; Bartol, Church and Congregation, pp. 51, 135; Bartol, Word of the Spirit, p. 11; Bartol, Discourses on the Christian Body and Form (Boston, 1852), p. 96, hereafter cited as: Bartol, Discourses on the Christian Body; Osgood, "Debates on the Roman Catholic Religion," p. 64; Osgood, "The Poet of Puseyism," CE, XXXV (September, 1843), 46; Parker, Discourse of Religion, p. 29.

[91]Clarke, Eleven Weeks in Europe, p. 182; Bartol, Church and Congregation, p. 141; Furness, in The Character of Jesus Portrayed, a Biblical Essay by Daniel Schenkel, 3rd German ed., trans. and ed. William Henry Furness, 2 vols. (Boston, 1866), I, 248; ibid., II, 245-246; Emerson, Works, XI, 9, 12. Brooks has an elaborate defense of the wholly symbolic interpretation of the Eucharist, although he is not particularly concerned with correspondences (Brooks, Simplicity of Christ's Teachings, pp. 198-213).

[92]Brownson, "Leroux on Humanity," BoQR, July, 1842, in Brownson, Works, IV, 123-124; Hedge, Reason in Religion, p. 312; Bartol, "Our Fellowship," in The West Church, Boston, p. 102; Bartol, Church and Congregation, p. 20. Clarke also insisted upon the importance of the Lord's Supper as a sign of humanity's unity, but from a thoroughly Protestant point of view (Clarke, Vexed Questions, pp. 221-228).

[93]Hedge, Ways of the Spirit, pp. 354-355.

[94]Channing, Works, VI, 208.

CHAPTER IV

RELIGIOUS EXPRESSION

MYSTICISM AND ASCETICISM

The transcendentalists approached the praying Church with a good deal more cordiality than they exhibited for the teaching and governing Church. This would naturally be the case, since prayer, or communion with the divine in one form or another, was the core element in their belief.[1]

It will be recalled that for the transcendentalist, the highest form of human existence consisted in communion with the life of God present in the soul. So identified is this concept with traditional Christian mysticism as practiced in the Catholic Church, that the transcendentalists found little difficulty in adopting most of the concepts of prayer as prescribed by the Catholic mystics. In these figures of the past they discovered every aspect of prayer and the inner life that the transcendental mind held sacred, and to them the transcendentalists turned as to "monitors and angels," "guides, masters, friends."[2] This friendly attitude toward the Catholic mystics was rendered possible by the fact that in the Catholic concept of prayer there was no question of dogmas imposed by pope or council. Genuine prayer was, rather, the universal experience of all humanity, from the ignorant Negro slaves of the South, to men of learning and virtue prominent in every Christian and non-Christian religion.[3]

In their discussions on prayer, the transcendentalists examined every aspect of it: its prerequisites, its fundamental features, and its results in the person

87

who prayed well. For each of these, they invariably adverted to the Catholic

mystics as examples eminent in the field.

First of all, for a genuine life of prayer, the transcendentalists selected

certain qualities as absolutely essential: tender devotion and piety, faith, love,

trust, freedom, and an attraction for spiritual things. Again and again their

writings direct attention to these qualities as predominant in such saints as Ber-

nard of Clairvaux, Catherine of Siena, Joan of Arc, Teresa of Avila, Anselm,[4] and

above all Augustine of Hippo. They were especially fond of citing Augustine's

Confessions as a model of inwardness and relish for spiritual realities, and of

perfect love and confidence "casting itself on the infinite tenderness" of God.[5]

As still more perfect exemplars of the life of man with God they looked to Thomas

a Kempis[6] and above all to a man who might be called the canonized saint of the

transcendentalists, Francois de Salignac de La Mothe Fenelon, Archbishop of Cambrai

during the age of Louis XIV.

Fenelon was probably introduced to the transcendentalists by the wife of one

of their own number, Mrs. Charles Follen, who translated selections from his writings

in 1829. Channing picked up the book and gave it wide notice by his rather lengthy

commentary, "On the Character and Writings of Fenelon," although he himself had be-

come familiar with the Archbishop much earlier. Fenelon's name thereafter appears

repeatedly in the transcendentalists' writings, particularly wherever reference is

made to the qualities of soul requisite for true inward greatness.[7]

These and other Catholic mystics[8] not only possessed the prerequisites for

prayer; they also succeeded in attaining to the deepest level of that experience

of God which was the cherished goal of the transcendentalists. To seek the divine

Spirit in all things, to be filled with the idea of the Holy, to be absorbed in

God, to listen to his voice, to meet him, be familiar with him, commune with him

in the soul--these were the "noble aspirations" which they found exemplified in

the prayer of the great Catholic mystics.[9] Such experiences of spiritual realities

constituted the loftiest aim of the inner life, life in its ultimate human and divine fulness.[10]

Finally, as further proof of the divineness of a life with God, the transcendentalists again turned to the Catholic mystics for evidence of the abundant fruit that a life of prayer could produce: beauty of soul, an intuitive knowledge of God and man, joy, wisdom, and profound inward peace.[11]

Enraptured though they thus obviously were with the Catholic mystics, the transcendentalists nonetheless sounded a note of warning about the risks involved in an indiscreet pursuit of a life of prayer. The more practical and service-oriented among them pointed to the gospel for confirmation of their conviction that the truest love of God lay less in the private piety of the Catholic mystic than in active deeds of charity. A few of them judged the preference for a life of contemplation to be sheer indolence, while other regarded the effort to withdraw into an exclusive love for God as deceptive. Others condemned it as egotistical and unnatural and as a self-indulgent flight from neighborly concern and common sense.[12]

Even their beloved Fenelon came in for some share of blame under this head. For Fenelon, they were well aware, had been censured by the Church for extremes of quietism, and this "heresy" all the transcendentalists except Jones very carefully avoided.[13] This rare instance of their concurrence with the Church's pronouncements was due to their concept of the goodness of human nature, outward as well as inward. Thus, though they could admire Fenelon and/ his feminine counterpart Madam Guyon as "the purest and holiest of human beings," and could extol their virtues endlessly,[14] they could only admire the extremes of such virtue from afar. And some found that they too were forced to condemn quietism overtly as a "disease."[15] Yet even this error in Fenelon they never failed to cite with delicacy and a certain reluctance. Channing spoke the mind of many in this regard by his remark: "When a good man errs, we almost reverence his errors."[16]

About the many nameless mystics who lived out their devotion to God in the

prayerful atmosphere of monasteries and convents, the transcendentalists were likewise somewhat ambivalent. At one time Clarke could view the growth of the monastic
system as a wave of spiritual power springing from those who longed for a purer
faith. At another he censured monasticism as the outgrowth of an exaggerated search
for the well-being of one's own soul.[17] Emerson found the "taking of the veil" at
one time pathetic and misguided, at another inspiring.[18] Alcott possessed a rather
childlike curiosity on being invited to a ceremony of veiling, which he called a
spectacle and a show. Yet he felt obliged later to acknowledge the "virtues" of
the Sisters of Mercy whose ceremony he had witnessed.[19]

At the very least the transcendentalists thought of the monastic or religious
life as a waste and a failure.[20] At worst, they objected to the painful and harsh
asceticism with which the history and present practices of monasticism seemed replete. Their Puritan strain forced a few of them to admire the discipline and
sanctity which they observed in the Church's doctrine and practice of self-denial,[21]
but the majority followed the transcendental evaluation announced by Channing:
"Self-crucifixion, then, should it exclude self-reverence, would be anything but
virtue."[22] Brownson charged that the Church, by what he supposed was its insistence on the dichotomy between soul and body, had through asceticism perpetuated
the myth of the evil of matter. In thus arguing for the corruption of one element
in human nature, the Church was in effect denying reverence to the whole--a point
of cardinal importance to a transcendentalist.[23] Less specifically, but entirely
in keeping with their exaltation of human nature, the other transcendentalists
denounced the severer forms of Catholic asceticism as demeaning, fanatical, and
inhuman.[24] Osgood summed up their characteristic opinion by dismissing what he
believed to be the Catholic view of the saintly man, the monk: a "spectral being
dead to earth," who gloried in punishing his corrupt body. In place of this image,
Osgood asked that all "champions of Spirit and Life" look to another kind of saint,
one who embodies every transcendental value:

> We behold at once a man among men, striving to connect all the
> uses of this world with the sanctions of a better,--recognizing
> beauty and consecration in all the works of God,--giving society,
> government, literature, labor, religion, all their due, and
> earnest to serve God in all things....He looks upon Christ as
> the image of God...and endeavors in all things to revere God thus
> manifested. He is a man of prayer....He keeps his body free from
> intemperate excess, his soul free from evil passions. He walks
> as a friend and brother, speaking the truth in love....[25]

Of all the aspects of Catholic asceticism which the transcendentalists

chose to discuss, none came under heavier attack than that of celibacy. Again

beginning with Channing, they directed a good deal of fervor toward discrediting

a practice which they maintained conflicted diametrically with their lofty notions

of human life.

We rarely find the transcendentalist acknowledging his own weakness or

failures, rarely asking for prayers, for light, or for strength. His humility

was of another sort: he gloried in the greatness and beauty of all his powers,

powers that were not his own, but that were bestowed upon him by an all-loving and

all-wise creator. Hence it was inconceivable for him that any could advocate--still

less submit to involuntarily[26]--total abstention from any created good, above all

any which comprised his own divinely human nature. He can consequently be found

frequently denouncing celibacy as observed in the Catholic Church. It was, he

argued, contrary to the gospel, unnatural and degrading,an error and a curse, a

sacrifice of manhood and an insult to woman.[27] "So sacred is nature that it can-

not be trampled on with impunity," warned Channing, indicating his entirely nega-

tive understanding of the monk's vow.[28] Some of the transcendentalists, moreover,

could not conceive of the monastic life as anything but what Newcomb called the

"organized enemy of mankind," since by its supposed depreciation of the family, it

did more than any other institution to undermine society.[29] Further, a man or

woman "cut off from the human race" and "doomed" to celibacy and asceticism was

sure to live a life of narrowed and obscured intellect, a life joyless and morbid,

and worst of all, a life laden with corruption and the grossest hypocrisy.[30]

Yet only to the extent that the monk seemed to despise the divine elements within nature and the world was he an object of the transcendentalists' disapproval. To despise the world was to despise God, cautioned Clarke, for the world was full of God. Yet he recognized that a Catholic monk may live apart from the world and not despise it. And, contrariwise, a Protestant might live within the world and practice a kind of austerity that denied all the joy and glory and beauty of nature, genius and art.[31] Within the atmosphere of the Catholic monastery and the celibate life the transcendentalist could often find, vividly embodied, the fruits of some of his highest hopes and dreams, particularly those of piety, solitude and peace. Bartol warned against disparaging peaceful and pious cloisters as belonging only to the middle ages. What a state of "poverty and emptiness" we are left in, he lamented, when such values are today discarded in favor of material progress and prosperity. Even Parker noted the contrast between the material-minded men of his day and the poor country priest he met in France, who "labors on all his life, in celibacy and silence, perhaps a man of genius, no doubt of learning;...."[32] With less idealism, and in what was undoubtedly a moment of frustration with an over-abundance of "company, business, [and] household chores," Emerson commented wearily that perhaps "the Roman Church with its celibate clergy and its monastic cells was right." The burden of maintaining his household he saw as a task which could only "untune and disqualify" him for writing, and the quiet of the cloister never seemed so alluring.[33]

It was not all frustration, however, that made Emerson see advantages in the existence of monasteries and convents. He and other transcendentalists occasion-ally classified them as a welcome refuge or retreat for other reaons as well. For Emerson they could be asylums for both the intellectual in pursuit of knowledge and the "stricken" in pursuit of rest. From another angle he saw convents as places of refuge for women, as a kind of protest against the degradation of their sex until the day should come when a genuine and lofty form of love should again find its place in the world. For Parker, the monastic asylum was one for the weak, who could not cope with the "fever" of the world, while Bancroft praised its usefulness as a shelter for the preservation of "old world truths: that would renew humanity" in a decaying society.[34] In all these ways, the transcendentalists saw the religious state as a fitting protest and antidote for society's ills. More positively, they noted time and again how beneficial to society were the contributions of the religious orders of the middle ages, and to a lesser extent, those of the present day.[35]

But these benefits were principally functional. Only a very few passages can be found in the transcendentalists' writings in which they pierced through to a more authentic understanding of the monastic system's primary thrust. The concept of either the individual or the system as "consecrated" or "dedicated" is one rarely grasped by them. Parker, in what was toward the end of his life a rarely open and perceptive moment, did touch more directly upon the transcendental heart of the matter. He judged the entire monastic system to be an outgrowth of the central aspect of man's innermost consciousness: his desire for union with God. This understanding of monasticism as embodying the principle of communion with God is also touched upon for a brief moment by a handful of the other transcendentalists.[36] But for the most part their recognition of the principle at work is confined to this or that individual, never to the system. The few instances noted here represent the rare occasions when they were able to concede a place of equal merit to an institutionalized religious life, the life of monastic and celibate orders.

DEVOTIONAL OBSERVANCES

Many of the men and women whom the transcendentalists looked to as models of prayer and communion with God were canonized Catholic saints. If the transcendentalists could recognize this noblest of attainments in these men and women, could

they also accept the Catholic's "devotion" to the saint as such? They approached
this subject with caution, for, they warned, such devotion could go to excess.
Their critical comments on what may be called the institutionalization of devotion
to the saints were given for the same reasons as those on the institutionalization
of religion--it could conceal God, not reveal him. Devotion to the saints, they
objected in the first place, could issue in a kind of polytheism or new mythology.[37]
This, obviously, would by its very nature minimize the honor which belonged to God
alone, since it would be "interposing inferior sanctities between the soul and
the All-holy."[38] As for the saints acting as intercessors with God, the transcendentalists for the most part thought that this was not only unnecessary, but un-
imaginable. They chided the Catholic for expecting too much of the saints' power,
and for hiding immoral deeds behind the protection of one saint or another.[39]
Particularly when devotion to the saints included veneration of relics and images,
they felt that here was a clear sign that the honoring of saints amounted to
superstition and idolatry.[40]

In further from another point of view, this Catholic practice offered the transcendentalist a ready-made framework for his devotion to the divine in the human.
The Protestant churches, charged Brownson, had "driven the Divinity out of his
works, and placed him beyond the reach of the heart....But the Catholic Church,
in permitting the invocation of saints...has recognized and given it, consciously
or unconsciously, her sanction. We have done great disservice to religion by
dethroning the saints...." He and other transcendentalists, while keeping at a
distance from direct prayer to the saints, commended the practice of recognizing
them as symbols of "the beauty of holiness," and occasionally admitted themselves
awe-struck in the presence of the saints' remains.[41]

In further encouraging veneration of the saints the transcendentalist reminded his readers that all believers are saints, all are holy. He noted that
the Catholic Church was, in this realm at least, no respecter of persons, for in

her canonizations she paid no regard to earthly rank or riches.[42] In an aside,
Hedge reproached the Church at length for omitting the more "genial" types of
saint--the sincere, the frank, the cordial, the lover of fun.[43] But it was ordinarily only on the basis of personal holiness or moral living that both Catholic
and transcendentalist held up a man or woman for special veneration. In this the
transcendentalist was often in almost perfect accord with the Church's assessment
of what constituted genuine nobility in man. He looked to the Catholic saints,
then, for example and inspiration in his own search for the perfect life.[44]

Besides turning to individual saints for inspiration, some of the transcendentalists adopted the Church's belief in a "communion of saints." Their desire
for a universal order of mankind, in which all would become what some of the
saints were, made this one of the few Catholic doctrines acceptable to them. It
was an altogether suitable vehicle in which to conceive their hopes for a better
world. William Henry Channing depicted the doctrine as a light that had continued
to burn brightly through the medieval night of superstition and oppression. He
eloquently urged his reader to accept the spiritual fellowship that this belief
in "the incessant interworking of the whole Church Triumphant with the whole
Church Militant" could afford. After Hecker became a Catholic, he claimed that
the doctrine of the communion of saints, which the Catechism of the Council of
Trent had introduced to him, had supplied him with the weightiest historical
argument for the Catholic Church. Even the sceptical Parker apprized this
Catholic belief as "beautiful to the feelings, not like the cold wordy rubric of
the Protestants."[45]

All that the transcendentalists had to say in favor of devotion to the
saints in general, they repeated in a particular way about the Virgin Mary. Although they occasionally referred to Catholic "worship" of Mary, ordinarily
this was used only in the loosest sense, connoting simply a profound and pious
devotion.[46] About the only real disagreement with Catholics that they had in

the area of devotion to Mary was regarding the doctrine of the Immaculate Conception. Yet even here it was not so much a rejection of the meaning of the doctrine itself, as an objection to the Church's right to formulate it.[47] Bartol alone, with characteristic transcendental reverence for the innate goodness in all men, offered an evaluation of the doctrine itself. "What a biting satire," he wrote, "to suppose in human history incorrupt conception but once...a superstitious miracle in what should be a common event,...."[48] This perspective of universal human goodness was the only one from which the transcendentalists could accept "devotion" to Mary at all. Their Unitarian orientation toward a profound reverence for Christ as the most "divine" of men they readily extended to the veneration of other human beings. Particularly did it extend to that other "heavenly" person, the one who, almost on a par with Christ, could embody their entire conception of human-divine perfection. Some even looked to her as a final human ideal. Their observations on her modesty, meekness, purity, and tenderness often evoked in them transports of admiration for the "celestial loveliness" in her that reflected both the complete woman and the divinized race.[49] Certain of their casual references to Mary in poems, prayers and addresses are echoes of the traditional Catholic conception of the "Virgin Mother," the serene and lowly "Madonna," the bride of the Holy Spirit.[50] As a complement to these notions, some of them actually addressed Mary as an object of their prayer.[51]

Within the transcendental framework then, Mary was both an example of moral perfection and the most accurate summation, next to Christ, of the close identification of God and man. Going a step further, many of the transcendentalists held her up as a remarkable expression of the infinite perfections of God himself. The Protestant conception of God they felt was incomplete; it was too remote, too barren of the warmth of compassion and the joy of love. Parker especially found the harsh Calvinist God wholly lacking in perspective, and often in his own formulation of prayer and in his discussions of the divine nature, he referred grandly to God as "the Father and Mother of all."[52]   Other transcendentalists

applied this insight to their evaluation of the Catholic religion as superior to

the Protestant in this regard.   They argued that through retention of the "femi-

nine" characteristics of the Godhead in their devotion to Mary, Catholics exhibited

a better understanding of the nature of God himself.[53]   The transcendentalists

consequently found little difficulty in occasionally drawing spiritual nourishment

from the Catholic image of the Virgin Mother.   For them her image became a delicate

symbol of what they depicted in lyrical terms their loving and gentle God to be.[54]

Besides devotion to the saints, the transcendentalists examined every other

manifestation of personal piety among Catholics: veneration of images--especially

the crucifix[55]--the use of holy water, rosaries, incense, and various practices

for gaining indulgences.   All such usages they judged acceptable in any case where

they could detect a humanizing or spiritualizing element coming through the sensi-

ble form.[56]   They rejected these, however, where they felt the absence of warmth

or personal piety.   In such cases a legalistic or superstitious formalism seemed

to be but a cloak for the neglect of moral livng and of   "the plain, hard duty

of self-cleansing."[57]   Yet they judged that on the whole, Catholicism demonstrated

an intensity of personal piety more adequately and on a far wider scale than did

Protestantism.[58]   They were deeply impressed whenever they witnessed throngs of

Catholic worshippers, rich and poor alike, kneeling daily side by side in the

European shrines.[59]

Our group commended Catholics too for a more appropriate observance of Chris-

tian feasts and Sundays.   In their more idealistic moments, they regarded special

observances and holy days as out of character with a genuine respect for the sanc-

tity of every day and every season.   Thoreau, for example, wondered that the com-

memoration of insignificant events should take precedence over "the annual pheno-

mena of...life."   Bartol made a similar observation, but in later years when he

was re-examining some of his earlier beliefs, he reversed himself with the comment:

"All days are holy;...[yet] suppose we begin with one? God is everywhere; but, lest ignorant creatures think him nowhere,...let Protestant service and Romish mass [of a Sunday] remind them he is at least somewhere." Others were also willing to concede that sameness can produce indifference until a better world should come. Until then, the spirit of celebration that they themselves endeavored to stimulate was better achieved by the observances of the Catholic Church than by any other. In a sermon entitled "The Christian Use of Sunday," Parker observed that Catholics had been more true to the sacred nature of each day by continuing to celebrate the Lord's Supper on week-days. But, he added, Catholics have also retained most faithfully the joyous, festive aspect of Sunday, forbidding as they do fasting, labor, or penance on that day. Clarke applauded the Catholic view of the Lord's Day as "a day of freedom, not of constraint, of joy, and not of gloom." He earnestly enjoined everyone else to do likewise.[60]

Other transcendentalists dipped into the Church cycle of feasts and found it rich in potential by reason of its "variety and power" and its recognition of a venerable and imitable past.[61] They saw a value particularly in the observance of such strictly Catholic celebrations as All Saints' and All Souls' Days. The latter day particularly interested Hedge. To him it seemed to be a fitting recognition of "the bond of fellowship of spirit" with the dead, a bond of communication with them which could never be dissolved. Clarke, in a sermon preached on the Sunday after All Souls' Day, described the feast as the only one which celebrated universal human brotherhood. He hailed it as a day intended not only for "the great and distinguished...the holy and happy alone; but for the unwise, the unhappy, the unholy also,--those whose present lives seem to be failures." The transcendentalist could see that in the celebration of this feast, the Catholic acknowledged what he himself nearly worshipped--the dignity of all men. As Clarke concluded: "It is a feast of Christian hope, of hope for all,--hope founded in the indestructible elements of the soul itself, as made by God, and made for himself."[62]

ART AS RELIGIOUS EXPRESSION

In addition to "devotions" and personal mystical prayer, the transcendentalists readily sanctioned another and equally significant mode of religious expression. In the various art forms of painting, sculpture, architecture, music, and literature they could see embodied a religious experience of a very valid kind. They looked to the arts in fact to perform a dual function--both to express and to evoke the natural religious sentiment in man. Since the "icehouse of Unitarianism"[63] offered no such instrumentality, the obvious place to seek it was in the mother of western religious art, the Catholic Church.

The masterpieces of Christian art elicited from the transcendentalists innumerable responses from various viewpoints, all, however, with definite religious overtones. They observed these works firstly from an aesthetic point of view; more importantly, as the reflection of human--and therefore divine--beauty; and above all, as both expression and inspiration in the worship of God.

Many of the transcendentalists were in a favorable position to comment upon the masterworks at first hand, having toured widely the cathedrals and galleries of Europe. With few exceptions they found themselves captivated by the inspired medieval genius that had covered Europe with its "flowers in verse and flowers in stone."[64] The immensity and beauty of the cathedrals cast over them a kind of spell, that even from a merely aesthetic point of view rendered them almost speechless with awe. They seemed to feel themselves unequal to the task of expressing adequately their admiration for the "sumptuous temples" whose "extraordinary beauty" and "endless delight" "astonish the eye" with their splendor and sublimity.[65] The basilica of St. Peter's in Rome, especially, they found breath-taking in its majesty, particularly when illuminated at night.[66] In glowing terms they praised the artistic skill of Raphael, Michaelangelo, DaVinci and the other geniuses in painting and sculpture whose works adorned the cathedrals and museums of Europe.[67] They remarked often on the stirringly beautiful music which could be heard within the cathedral walls and which they accepted as the cultural heritage of a more gifted age.[68] On occasion their comments on Dante and Tasso were also limited to an aesthetic appreciation.[69] And the Catholic liturgy too, was for them, a "gorgeous ritual" and an impressive composite of artistic ingenuity.[70] With perhaps a less than candid appreciation, Clarke summed up the purely aesthetic appeal of all the Catholic arts this way:

> The grand architecture and the splendid music; the processions of priests in their gorgeous robes and vestments; the mysterious ceremonies at the high altar, genuflexions, the smoke of incense, swinging of censers, elevation of the host, ringing of bells,--all is calculated to touch the imagination, like a solemn tragedy. There is something essentially dramatic in the whole ritual, and most people love the drama.[71]

For the transcendentalist, however, art was far more than merely an aesthetic affair. It must be remembered that for him art was a projection of the essential nature of all being in general, of man in particular, and of the divinity as it dwelt within the innermost being of each human person. To contemplate a work of art, therefore, was to contemplate the highest nobility within man. It was to unite oneself with sublimist beauty and truth, God himself.

The majority of observations made by the transcendentalist upon Catholic art give evidence of this religious orientation. In them we have a running commentary upon his concept of the true nature of art, and indeed upon much of his philosophy of the nature and end of the human person.

Since the function of art was to portray the "correspondences" between all things, the artist revealed the universal and primal spirit which underlay everything made by God. Geniuses like Dante and Michaelangelo had the power, by their use of artistic symbol, to release this spirit, this all-pervading "eternal fact" met in innumerable forms.[72] The "holy sights and sounds" of Catholic artistry Bartol likened to "cords of sacred association," that splendidly imprisoned men

to gaze through the narrow openings of the senses, upward to the sky. The music
of a high Mass they saw as an instrument through which heavenly truth was not reasoned out coldly to the understanding, but, as Dwight expressed it, "passed through
his very soul, like an experience." A Gothic cathedral and the ceremonies carried
on within could affirm "that it was done by us and not done by us," being done by
the universal spirit in man. This universal spirit explains by archetypes the
ground and nature of all history, whether of governments, nature, or the arts,
since their roots are in each individual man. Santa Croce and the Dome of St.
Peter's, therefore, "are lame copies after a divine model," where "brood the souls
of ages."[73]

Moreover, the universal spirit emanating from what is most profound in man
works through the giant cathedrals, or great religious music, or the classic
thoughts of a Dante to make these works the embodiment of man's aspirations for
unity and fellowship.[74] Thus is a cathedral the material counterpart of the soul,
the incarnation of his thoughts, the language of his heart. In the same way Dante
and Raphael are almost identified with the soul; the poet is the poem; and
Michaelangelo's statues are emblems sculptured not out of marble but out of
"spirit."[75]

Above all does the music of Catholic services reveal what words usually con-
ceal--the speechless light and vision of the soul. Dwight grew ecstatic in his
comments upon the power of medieval music and neo-classical Masses to reveal and
express the heart's deepest yearnings for a better world of harmony and peace.
Paradoxically, his appreciation of the most religious music of the Catholic Church
was in direct proportion to his rejection of its creed, though not its spirit.
In explaining his purposes for forming the Mass Clubs at Brook Farm, he remarked
that the music was "quite innocent of creed, except that of the heart and of the
common deepest wants and aspirations of all souls, darkly locked up in formulas,
till set free by the subtle solvent of delicious harmonies."[76]

For the transcendentalist, the best expression of the intuitions of the soul was created through an organic combination of all the arts. More than one found a model combination in the liturgy of the Catholic Church, which, through an appeal to all the senses simultaneously, awakened the noblest longings of human nature, and spoke of its deepest values.[77]

These values were, first of all, exalted sentiments and feelings: love, joy, hope, trust, exultation. The lofty shrines of Europe and their ceremonies and adornments not only expressed, but evoked these sentiments in the transcendentalist observer. Not for himself alone, but hopefully for all, they satisfied the "insatiable demand [for] harmony" that he found in the distraught person of contemporary man.[78]

Catholic art also mirrored other facets of divine beauty in the human person. In the "miracles" of sculpture, painting, music, and liturgy, as well as in the writings of a Manzoni or a Dante, the transcendentalists found juxtaposed every divine and human grace--tenderness, humility, strength, purity, and goodness and holiness of every sort.[79] They discerned in the organic arrangements of these arts the marriage of truth with beauty, and in this form did it seem to them that a divine humanity was best represented.[80]

Even more than aesthetic beauty, more than artistic correspondences with their own souls, the transcendentalists gloried in Catholic art as a manifestation of the Divine Person or Force itself. Looking at the purity of a face by Raphael, they could be instantly reminded that "here is a vessel of God."[81] "Beauty itself," reflected Bancroft in elaborating upon a remark of Michaelangelo, "is but the sensible image of the infinite." The correspondence here was not between the work of art and a human trait. Rather, as Emerson remarked of Dante, it consisted in the work of art as either an acknowledgment or a revelation of God.[82] In the Catholic liturgy of the Mass and the sacraments especially could the transcendentalists observe the lineaments of God penetrating the material and the human, and man partaking of the divine.[83]

Allusions to the divine only, without regard to its presence within the human, are innumerable. They offer a striking proof that the transcendentalists were not exclusively absorbed in the contemplation of themselves. They show these men and women as deeply religious, profoundly appreciative of any man's effort to confess an objective God and to worship him in accordance with the most central need of man's being. Perhaps for this reason, the transcendentalists possessed an unusual perception of the nature of divine worship as it expressed itself in the forms of Catholicism, particularly in the liturgical synthesis of the arts.

Before seeing how they observed the Catholic arts as worship, it might be well to notice how often the transcendentalists found the reverse--that Catholic artistry seemed wanting in this most crucial aspect of art's function. Some few of them found Dante confusing and unacceptable, particularly where he seemed to lose himself within the "dread converging circles of the pit," a symbol of the future of any man which they found wholly offensive.[84] Parker scoffed at some of the "medieval fictions" and wanton extravagance on which medieval sculptors had squandered their skill. And Cranch, alone among the transcendentalists, felt that the arts had been totally stifled by the Church's constricting beliefs.[85]

Negative observations on the power of Catholic art to honor God were centered mostly upon the liturgy. Since doctrinally the transcendentalists could not accept the notion of sacrament as the Catholic understood it, it is not hard to see why they could look upon its attendant ceremonies with a harshly critical eye. It is perhaps in this area that they display the greatest ambivalence. For while they could at certain times find the Catholic liturgy exceptionally meaningful, on numerous other occasions their bitter criticism comes close to the kind they ordinarily reserved for the Church's creed. Instances abound where they describe the Catholic liturgy as nothing more than artificial religiosity and empty ritualism; pageantry and mummery; formalism, manipulation and dumb show; a moral inanity; a smothering, pagan, sensual religion.[86] They reminded their readers that forms were nothing when faith had fled, and they sometimes questioned whether such faith ever permeated Catholic observance.[87] Even when they revelled in the inspiration provided by a cathedral, they preferred the inspirations of nature. As Thoreau reasoned, after praising the religious atmosphere of Notre Dame Cathedral in Montreal: "In Concord, to be sure, we do not need such. Our forests are such a church, far grander and more sacred."[88] Others, though surprisingly few, judged that better than any Gothic shrine for the worship of God was the temple of the heart, "the only temple he delights to fill."[89]

Transcendental criticism of Catholic ritual was most strident in reference to that symbol and sacrament in which they found neither artistic nor religious import--the sacrament of penance, or "Confession." In this practice they saw merely the ultimate error resulting from "the entire surrender of the understanding to a symbol."[90] They condemned it as a tool of unscrupulous priests for penetrating the secrets of families and of consciences and for the manipulation of political power.[91] Or at best, they judged it to be a practice calculated only to encourage repeated wrongdoing or puerile submission.[92] Only a small number of transcendentalists could see some value in Confession, though not as an instrument of worship. These could see its usefulness merely as a support for the needs of conscience and of universal human weakness.[93]

Despite this profusion of negative criticism about the place of Catholic art in worship, the transcendentalists' positive reactions are equally intense and numerous. Although committed to a rather personalist form of religion, they conceded the advantage of clothing the inward spirit with outward form. "Religion craves expression," insisted Hedge, "a permanent religion, a stated expression: a common religion, a common worship and common rites." If the individual felt no need for symbol and sacrament, Hedge judged the religious sentiment to be but imperfectly developed in that man. For, most of the transcendentalists agreed, sign and symbol, especially as made use of in the Catholic arts, were the noblest and surest indications of the inner life of worship. Emerson saw in the glorious temples constructed by human hands a vivid witness to the ineradicableness of the religious principle, and Parker viewed them as the tribute that art pays, as its fairest flower, to the religious element in all men. Most of the other transcendentalists at one time or another described them as magnificent structures that ageless piety had erected in its most beautiful forms in a spirit of reverential worship of God.[94]

Besides expressing man's worship, Catholic art had a matchless power to evoke it, to "call out the slumbering religious sentiment" in every man.[95] These "godly piles" were signs of a profound form of spiritual vision and faith in the loving presence of God within the Church. As such they were singularly calculated to arouse a sense of the divine presence in anyone who came near. It was the peculiar power of this living and embodied faith to lead any man to aspire to communion with that presence, in much the same way that the Gothic spires reached toward the heavens. "A Gothic cathedral like Antwerp or Strasburg," wrote Clarke in the language of "correspondences," "what is it but a striving upward of the soul to lose itself in God?"[96]

Numerous other references to Catholic art or liturgy as the "aspiration," the "soaring" of the soul toward God are to be found in the writings of the transcendentalists,[97] and they themselves were often affected by its power. Several of them wrote warmly of their own personal experiences when entering a cathedral alone or during a service, where they felt drawn to worship the presence of God strikingly brought home to them. During Emerson's first trip to Europe he wrote, "I yielded me joyfully to the religious impression of holy texts and fine paintings and this soothfast faith." Margaret Fuller likewise confessed: "Their spirit touched me, and I prayed too"; and Bancroft: "I threw myself on my knees." Similarly, Clarke in his Autobiography acknowledged: "As we enter these solemn

aisles a sense of religion enters the soul..., and for a few moments [we] feel
the presence of eternity." Again, after describing his impressions during a visit
to the Cathedral of Antwerp, he added: "I saw reverence on the faces of the worshippers. I was no longer lonely....I felt human hearts beating around me to the
same tone as mine; and I was in communion with those worshippers and with God."
Later he commented once more on the same spirit of fellowship that the Catholic
services had evoked in him: "Our minds were possessed by the same thought, and
one God was with us....I felt the presence of God....I prayed."[98]

In the most characteristic mode of transcendental reflection, a few of our
group philosophized that art actually had no other purpose than "to serve the gods,"
and that its mission was "entirely holy."[99] Here again the Catholic Church provided the model. No wonder the arts now languish, lamented Emerson; formerly the
Catholic Church had "turned them to continual account in its service," whereas
their entire scope in the contemporary world was mere exhibition. Or as Osgood
put it, since the days of the Protestant Reformation the convenant between art
and religion had be sundered.[100]

In attempting to realize again the essential relationship between art and
worship, many of the transcendentalists made elaborate proposals for a church
of the future which would incorporate all the best forms of Roman worship.[101]
Hedge, Judd, and William Henry Channing began immediately by adopting for use
within their own congregations portions of Catholic liturgy. In this endeavor
they confined themselves mainly within the sphere of music--the"natural species
of worship," as Emerson called it.[102] As we have seen, Dwight originated the Mass
Clubs as a musical enterprise for uplifting the soul through the great Masses.
The interest of others in the music of the Catholic liturgy is further evident in
their adoption of Catholic hymn texts for discussion and for various other purposes in their writings.[103]

The overall effect, then, of Catholic art upon the transcendentalists was to elicit their protest when it seemed to be abused, and their warm approbation when it seemed to fit their ideas on the nature of art. If for Clarke the unique strength of the Catholic Church was in its organization, for others it lay in the majestic manner in which that Church had used every human art and skill to draw men to the service of God. Judd summed up the sentiments of many of them when he wrote:

> How the old Romanists...loved their Church, and what a Church they
> made of it! how their painters painted for it, and their musicians
> composed for it, and their architects planned for it! what beauti-
> ful, what gorgeous needlework their women wrought for it! Look once
> a month between this city [Augusta,Maine] and Hallowell or Gardiner,
> of a Sunday, and see the Romanists, youths and children, old men and
> maidens,--in winter snows, or mire of March, or heat or midsummer,--
> trudging afoot to their church in this city! What is the reason?
> There are many, but the underlying reason is, they have a Church,
> they all belong to it, its history is theirs, its hopes are theirs;
> in all its majesty, in all its promise....[104]

                              * * *

The hopes, the majesty, the promise of the Church! Thus in their moments of enthusiasm could the transcendentalists capture from Catholicism a spirit that they sought for their own religion. But their anti-institutional stance prevented them from endorsing the "creeds and forms" of the Church as a whole. The creeds and certain of the forms of worship that seemed to them lifeless were a sign of the rigidification and institutionalization of what should be a free spirit. Clarke expressed his judgment clearly on this point:

> The vital impulse given by such men as Paul and Augustine embodies
> itself in institutions; expresses itself by symbolic ceremonies,
> and a rich worship;...speaks in words of burning force and sharpest
> precision; and then the spirit which has produced all this is lost
> sight of in reverence paid to its own work. Then men reverence
> forms, ceremonies, creeds, outward institutions;....[105]

Hence, he decided, the true church does not--cannot--consist in altars, priests, ritual, creed, doctrine.[106] For by this time these things, rather than revealing God, hid him. Rather than being a means for this ennobling of men in virtuous

living, they covered over an immoral life.[107] Cranch put the conflicting thoughts
of the other transcendentalists into bitter verse:

> And yet the priest, discordant mid accords,
>   With waste of words, half truth, half error mixed
> Thin homilies and theologic prayers,--
>   He only jarred the music, spread betwixt
> Nature and God a cloud that dimmed the sun,
>   And made the inspiring Church a vaulted tomb.[108]

Yet often the doctrinal and legalistic implications that could spoil a beautiful experience were also what gave it its deepest meaning. Since whether religion touched upon all areas of life was an important consideration for the transcendentalists, they could also warmly approve this Church. When they examined it as a totality, they sometimes found a Church that appealed not only to man's senses nor solely to his intellect, not exclusively to his moments of direct communion with God or service of man. The grandeur of this Church was, in fact, in its power to establish an intimate relation with the whole of life. Hedge and Parker were two who glimpsed the vision of this reality at one time or another. In an address before the Ministerial Conference of Boston Hedge expressed feelingly his admiration for the Catholic order:

> [The Catholic Church] does not dismiss its disciples at the door of
> the church, but follows them to their homes with its ordinances and
> its sacraments. It entwines itself with their whole existence, from
> the cradle to the grave, and even follows them beyond....It presides
> over their waking and their sleeping, over their business and their
> board, and over their very amusements, which it cares for with a
> thoughtfulness that considers and consults all the wants of earth-
> born man. At home and abroad its eye is upon them, its banner is
> over them, its symbols attend them.[109]

In a similar strain, Parker, before he turned bitter against the Catholic Church, wrote approvingly of the broad understanding which it exhibited for all types of persons, and of its ability to adapt itself to the needs of each. His remarks constitute the most sensitive transcendentalist response to the total system of Catholic belief and practice. In his opinion the Church had created an organization which was the most perfect the world had ever seen,

> with a policy wiser than any monarch had dreamed of, and which grew
> more perfect with the silent accretions of time; with address to
> allure the ambitious to its high places, and so turn all their energy
> into its deep wide channel; with mysteries to charm the philosophic,
> and fill the fancy of the rude; with practical doctrines for earnest
> workers, and subtle questions, always skillfully left open for men
> of acute discernment; with rites and ceremonies that addressed every
> sense, rousing the mind like a Grecian drama, and promising a parti-
> cipation with God through the sacrament; with wisdom enough to bring
> men really filled with religion into its ranks; with good sense and
> good taste to employ all the talent of the times in the music, the
> statues, the painting, the architecture of the temple, thus conse-
> crating all the powers of man to man's noblest work; with so much
> of Christian truth as the world in its wickedness could not forget.[110]

Ironically, this was the most positive and insightful synthesis of the Church ever

to be made by any of the transcendentalists. It was written by an erratic and

superficial scholar, in a rare moment of illumination when he succeeded in doing

what he had attempted to do in all of his voracious reading--absorb and synthesize

an enormously complex set of facts and ideals into a small and manageable package.

The other transcendentalists touched innumberable times here and there upon the

vast surface of the Catholic Church's wealth; none so broadly incorporated such

an immense quantity of knowledge nor so succinctly delivered his impressions

upon it.

Such then were the transcendentalists' opinions of the institutional Church.

Beyond these remarks on the Church's nature and identity, they had more to say.

They extended their commentary also to the Church's history, its development, its

place among other evolving religious systems and secular societies. Their con-

structs on these subjects were sometimes enlightened, sometimes shortsighted and

partisan, always vigorous. It is these concerns that we shall examine next.

[1]Broadly speaking the transcendental interest in prayer was an interest in mysticism. Most of them made some effort toward the study and practice of mysticism in both its Oriental and its Christian forms, and some wrote a great deal on the subject.

[2]Emerson to Elizabeth Tucker, February 1, 1832, in Emerson, Works, VII, 401; Clarke, Vexed Questions, p. 51. See also W.H. Channing, "A Confession of Faith," The Present, I (September, 1843), 9-10; Hedge, Sermons, p. 165. Bartol makes the surprising statement that while Free Religion--of which he was an advocate--frees us, it cannot feed us. For nourishment of his "religious nature," he felt he had to "flee" to King David, to St. Augustine, to the German and other mystics, from whom, though mixed with errors, he derived more than from the "refuse and ash-heap of the objector's laboratory" (Bartol, Rising Faith, p. 376).

[3]Clarke, Autobiography, p. 198; Clarke, Events and Epochs, pp. 293, 297; Clarke, Essentials, p. 22; Clarke, Slavery in the United States: A Sermon Delivered in Armory Hall, on Thanksgiving Day, November 24, 1842 (Boston, 1843), p. 9; Brownson, The Convert, p. 314; Eemrson, Works, VI, 204; ibid., VII, 401; Emerson, Journal B, 1835, in Emerson, JN, V, 78; Emerson, Journal Q, 1833, in ibid., IV, 84; Osgood, God with Men, p. 249; Osgood, The Coming Church, p. 19; Channing, Works, VI, 205; Parker, Discourse of Religion, p. 196; Parker, West Roxbury Sermons, pp.146-147.

[4]Emerson, Blotting Book II, 1829, in Emerson, JN, VI, 93-94; Emerson, Journals, 1849, VIII, 72; Emerson, Works, II, 123; ibid., XII, 193-194, 227; Marsh, in Aids to Reflection by Coleridge, p. ix; Clarke, Memorial and Biographical Sketches (Boston, 1878), p. 130, hereafter cited as: Clarke, Memorial Sketches; Clarke, Events and Epochs, pp. 146, 167-168, 280-281; Clarke, Ten Great Religions, p. 136; Clarke, "Joan of Arc," CE, LXV (July, 1848), 1-27; Clarke, Hour Which Cometh, p. 38; Clarke, Eleven Weeks in Europe, pp. 99-100; Clarke, "Buckle's History of Civilization," CE, LXXI (November, 1861), 383; Clarke, Christian Doctrine of Prayer, pp. 222-223; Parker, Ten Sermons, p. 363; Parker, "The Life of St. Bernard of Clairvaux, a Chapter Out of the Middle Ages," CE XXX (March, 1841), 1-41, hereafter cited as: Parker, "Life of St. Bernard"; Parker, Lessons from Matter and Man, p. 348; Osgood, "Christian Ethics," CE, XXIX (November, 1840), 173; Osgood, Studies in Christian Biography, pp. 168-212; "Joan of Arc," WM, II (November, 1836), 230-231; Hedge, Sermons, p. 165; Brooks, Songs and Ballads, Translated from Uhland, Koerner, Buerger, and Other German Lyric Poets, Specimens of Foreign Standard Literature, ed. George Ripley, XIV (Boston, 1842), 137-142; Fuller, Summer on the Lakes (Boston, 1844), p. 162; Fuller, Woman in the Nineteenth Century, and Kindred Papers Relating to the Sphere, Conditions, and Duties of Woman (Boston, 1855), hereafter cited as: Fuller, Woman, in The Writings of Margaret Fuller, ed. Mason Wade (New York, 1941), pp. 171, 218, hereafter cited as: Fuller, Writings.

[5]Hedge, "Life of St. Augustine," pp. 225-240; Clarke, Essentials, pp. 22-23; Clarke, Every-Day Religion, p. 428; Clarke, Common-Sense, p. 313; Osgood, Studies in Christian Biography, pp. 1-65; Parker, Ten Sermons, pp. 211-212; Bartol, Rising Faith, p. 376; Newcomb, as cited in Van Wyck Brooks, Flowering of New England, p. 246; Osgood, "German Hymns," CE, LXIX (September, 1860), 246; Osgood, "Christian Ethics," XXIX, 173; Thoreau, Journal, March 10, 1856, VIII, 203. Among many more, Emerson's letters, journals, and published works contain numerous indexed and unindexed references to St. Augustine.

[6]Ripley, Book Review of Materialism in Religion by Harwood, p. 270; Parker, Ten Sermons, pp. 211-212, 363; Clarke, "Sermon on Scolding," pp. 342-343; Clarke, Every-Day Religion, p. 459; Clarke, Events and Epochs, p. 281; Osgood, God with Men, p. 259; Bancroft, Poems, p. 36; Bancroft, Journal, January 1, 1822, in Howe, Life of Bancroft, I, 136; Bartol, Principles and Portraits, p. 70. Emerson's letters, journals and published works contain numerous indexed and unindexed references to aKempis.

[7]Channing, "Humility in the Investigation of Christian Truth," Christian Disciple, May, 1813, in Channing, Memoir, I, 369; Channing, "On Fenelon," pp. 165-215; Channing, Works, VI, 205. To cite a few of the many allusions to Fenelon in the other transcendentalists: Alcott, "Days from a Diary," The Dial, II (April, 1842), 421; Osgood, "Thoughts Upon Fenelon," in Gifts of Genius: A Miscellany of Prose and Poetry, by American Authors (New York, 1859), pp. 202-213; Osgood, God with Men, p. 259; Osgood, Mile Stones, p. 172; Osgood, The Coming Church, p. 19; Bartol, Rising Faith, pp. 53, 289; Follen, as cited in Peabody, Reminiscences of Channing, p. 266; Hedge, Prose Writers of Germany (New York, 1847), p. 441; Hedge, Sermons, p. 165. The letters, journals and published works of Emerson and Parker contain numerous indexed and unindexed references to Fenelon.

[8]Among others, these included:

Tauler: Bartol, Principles and Portraits, p. 70; Emerson to Parker, June 29, 1857, in Emerson, Letters, V, 80; Clarke, Events and Epochs, p. 281; Parker, Ten Sermons, p. 363; Hedge, Sermons, p. 165; Osgood, "Christian Ethics," XXIX, 173.

Madame Guyon: Fuller, Woman, p. 171; Bartol, Principles and Portraits, p. 303; Bartol, The Upper Standing. A Sermon Preached in the West Church, Boston, March 3, 1872 (Boston, 1872), p. 6; Osgood, Studies in Christian Biography, pp. 191-192, 205; Osgood, Mile Stones, p. 164; Clarke, Memorial Sketches, p. 130; Emerson, Journal B, January 7, 9, 1835, in Emerson, JN, V, 5, 7; Kirby, "Reminiscences of Brook Farm," p. 524.

Frederick Schlegel: Hedge, Hours with German Classics (Boston, 1886), p. 430; Osgood, Studies in Christian Biography, p. 2; Very, as cited in Edwin Gittleman, Jones Very: The Effective Years, 1833-1840 (New York, 1967), p. 148.

Meister Eckhart: Clarke, Events and Epochs, p. 280; Parker, Discourse of Religion, p. 392; Hecker to Brownson, April 9, 1844, as cited in Holden, Early Years of Hecker, p. 205.

Synesius: Emerson, Works, IV, 337; Hedge, "Synesius," UR, XXXI (March, 1889), 243-251.

Hugh of St. Victor: Parker, "Life of St. Bernard," p. 41; Parker, Ten Sermons, p. 363.

[9]Follen, Works, II, 261, 266; Alcott to Elizabeth Oakes Smith, in Alcott, Letters, p. 794; Bancroft, Poems, p. 36; Bartol, Upper Standing, p. 6; Bartol, Principles and Portraits, p. 70; Bartol, "The Preacher's Trail," Atlantic Monthly, XI (February, 1863), 211; Brownson, "Transient and Permanent in Christianity," p. 449; Brownson, Charles Elwood, p. 292; Channing, Memoir, I, 127; Channing, "On Fenelon," pp. 174, 185-186; Clarke, "Joan of Arc," p. 4; Clarke, Ten Great Religions, p. 136; Clarke, Events and Epochs, p. 297; Osgood, "Christian Ethics," XXIX, 172; Osgood, God with Men, pp. 249, 259; Osgood, Studies in Christian Biography, p. 203; Osgood, Mile Stones, pp. 164, 173; Osgood, "German Hymns," pp. 246, 254; Parker, Ten Sermons, p. 393; Parker, Discourse of Religion, p. 336; Hedge, Sermons, pp. 163-165; Hedge, Reason in Religion, p. 100; Hedge, "Life of St. Augustine," pp. 228, 239; Hedge, "Mohammedan Mysticism," UR, XXIX (May, 1888), 412, 414; Emerson, Journal B, January 7, 1835, in Emerson, JN, V, 5; Emerson, Blotting Book Y, 1830, in ibid., III, 193; Emerson, Journal E, December 26, 1840, in ibid., VII, 409; Emerson, Works, VI, 204; ibid., X, 205; Emerson, "Prayers," The Dial, III (July, 1842), 80-81. See also Kenneth Cameron, Index-Concordance to Emerson's Sermons. With Homiletical Papers, 2 vols. (Hartford, Connecticut, 1963), II, 668-692; this is an ingenious attempt on Cameron's part to trace, in detail, Emerson's thoughts on the divine in man to parallel passages in Fenelon.

[10]Carried to its logical fulfillment, such an aspiration would lead two of the transcendentalists into the Catholic Church--Brownson and Hecker, the latter a genuine mystic, the former a more practical sort of intellectual who yet traces to his study of Leroux's doctrine of communion the beginning of his conversion away from transcendentalism and to Catholicism (Brownson, "Liberalism and Socialism," BrQR, April, 1855, in Browson, Works, X, 527; Brownson, "Leroux on

Humanity," pp. 100-139).

[11]Channing, "On Fenelon," pp. 175, 181-183, 203-204; Emerson, Journal C, 1838, in Emerson, JN, V, 457-458; Emerson, Blotting Book PSI, 1830, in ibid., III, 207; Emerson, Encyclopedia, 1824-1836, in ibid., VI, 207, 207n; Emerson, Notebook T, 1843, in ibid., 383; Emerson, Works, VIII, 346-347; ibid., XII, 193-195; "Angelus Silesius the Cherubic Pilgrim," MQR, II (September, 1849), 474; Charles Lane, "Interior or Hidden Life," The Dial, IV (January, 1844), 374, 378; Parker, Lessons from Matter and Man, p. 342; Ripley, Philosophical Miscellanies, I, 213, 217-218; ibid., II, 269; Fuller, "The Great Lawsuit. Man versus Men. Woman versus Women," The Dial, IV (July, 1843), 38; Bancroft, Journal, January, 1822, in Howe, Life of Bancroft, I, 136; Bartol, "Preacher's Trial," p. 211; Bartol, Principles and Portraits, p. 70; Bartol, Discourses on Christian Spirit, p. 144; Bartol, Upper Standing, p. 6; Clarke, "Joan of Arc," pp. 1-27; Clarke, Christian Doctrine of Prayer, pp. ix-x, 53, 222-223; Clarke, Autobiography, p. 265; Osgood, "Christian Ethics," XXIX, 172; Osgood, Studies in Christian Biography, pp. 64, 188, 200-205; Osgood, "Thoughts Upon Fenelon," pp. 202-213; Hedge, Reason in Religion, p. 100; Hedge, "Synesius," pp. 243, 249; Alcott, "Days from a Diary," p. 421; Alcott, Sonnets and Canzonets (Boston, 1882), p. 67; Convers Francis, as cited in David A. Wasson, Beyond Concord: Selected Writings of David Atwood Wasson, ed. Charles H. Foster (Bloomington, Indiana, 1965), p. 42.

[12]Clarke, Events and Epochs, pp. 82-83; Brownson, "Leroux on Humanity," pp. 124-126; Bancroft, "Joseph II of Austria," NAR, XXXI (July, 1830), 19; Newcomb, Journals, September 13, 1866, p. 257; Thoreau, Journal, August 6, 1845, I, 375; Parker, Ten Sermons, pp. 287-288, 299; Parker, Discourse of Religion, pp. 260-261; Parker, Autobiography, pp. 359-260; Osgood, Studies in Christian Biography, pp. 138-141.

[13]Clarke, Events and Epochs, p. 297; Clarke, "Jones Very," 1839, in Selected Writings, ed. Hochfield, p. 221. In both these selections, Clarke draws the comparison between Fenelon and Very.

Quietism has been defined as absolute submission to the will of God, indifference to salvation, and an inclination toward passive contemplation that sets no value on service to others. A glimpse at Fenelon's life reveals that there is no basis for the charge that he did not believe in love and service directed toward his fellow men.

[14]Follen, Diary, November 27, December 13, 1827, in Follen, Works, I, 195, 214-215; Hedge, "Mohammedan Mysticism," p. 412; Hedge, Hours with German Classics, p. 100; Bartol, Discourses on the Christian Body, p. 170; Clarke, Events and Epochs, p. 282; Bancroft, History of the United States, 17th ed. (Boston, 1859), II, 344-345, 378; Channing to Joseph Blanco White, April 3, 1840, in Channing, Memoir, III, 359; Parker to Miss Patience Ford, June 15, 1841, in Weiss, Life of Parker, I, 447-448. See also Brooks, William Ellery Channing: A Centennial Memory (Boston, 1880), pp. 198-204. The Fruitlands library contained more than a dozen volumes by or about them (see Bronson Alcott's Fruitlands, comp. Clara Endicott Sears [Boston, 1915], p. 178). See also note 7 above.

[15]Convers Francis, Christianity As a Purely Internal Principle (Boston, 1836), p. 7; Channing, "On Fenelon," passim; Channing, introduction to the first edition of Channing, Works, I, xii; Osgood, "Thoughts Upon Fenelon," pp. 208-209; Parker to Miss Patience Ford, June 15, 1841, in Weiss, Life of Parker, I, 448.

[16]Channing, "On Fenelon," p. 175.

[17]Clarke, "The Right Seed," UR, XXII (November, 1884), 338; Clarke, Ten Great Religions, p. 25.

[18]Emerson, Journal Q, April 21, 1833, in Emerson, JN, IV, 71; Emerson, Works IX, 253.

[19]He took a boyish delight in recounting the fact of having dined afterwards with the Vicar General and some dozen priests and of being waited on by nuns

(Alcott to Mrs. Alcott, October 25, 1856, in Alcott, Letters, p. 206).

[20]Brownson, Charles Elwood, p. 212; Emerson, Works, XII, 48.

[21]Ripley, Book Review of The Early Jesuit Missions, trans. Rev. William Ingraham Kipp, 2 vols. (New York, n.d.), Harbinger, III (October 24, 1846), 316; W.H. Channing, "Revolution--Reaction--Reorganization," SA, I (July 21, 1849), 41; Channing, Papers, as cited in Rice, Federal Street Pastor, p. 298; Osgood "The Centenary of Spinoza," NAR, CXXIV (March, 1877), 287-288; Osgood, "Christian Ethics," XXX (May, 1841), 148.

[22]Channing, "On Fenelon," p. 194.

[23]Brownson, "Social Evils, and Their Remedy," BoQR, IV (April, 1841), 274-275; Brownson, New Views, pp. 14-15; Brownson, "Leroux on Humanity," p. 124. See also Osgood, Studies in Christian Biography, pp. 137-138.

[24]Fuller to New York Tribune, August 9, and December 30, 1847, in Fuller, At Home and Abroad, pp. 229, 271; Emerson, Wide World 7, 1822, in Emerson, JN, II, 8-9; Emerson, Journal D, 1839, in ibid., VII, 256; Emerson, Indian Superstition, p. 20; Parker, Ten Sermons, p. 386; Osgood, Studies in Christian Biography, p. 7; Hedge, Hours with German Classics, p. 439; Channing, "Letter on Catholicism," p. 274; Bancroft, History of the United States, II, 345; Hedge, "Christian Worship," Monthly Religious Magazine, X (October, 1853), 468-469.

[25]Osgood, God with Men, p. 267. See also his "St. Ambrose," p. 426. Osgood could at times see the paragons of the Catholic Church as fitting well within the framework of his transcendental model. To give only one example, more than half of his Studies in Christian Biography is devoted to Fathers of the Church and Catholic saints. But when trying to prove a point about spirit or letter, doctrine or life, he found them convenient victims for his vivid comparisons. This severe analysis of persons and ideas within strict categorical concepts--all light or all darkness--was a method which the transcendentalists frequently employed, whether in discussing history, religion, contemporary problems, or their own souls.

[26]Parker believed that Catholic men and women were sometimes forced into monastic celibacy against their will (Parker to Hannah Stevenson, August, 1852, as cited in Frothingham, Theodore Parker, p. 367; Parker, Sins and Safeguards, p. 184).

[27]Henry, About Men and Things. Papers from My Study Table Drawer (New York, 1873), p. 150; Clarke, Events and Epochs, pp. 82-83; Clarke, Steps of Belief, p. 245; Parker to Robert White, February 11, 1848, in Weiss, Life of Parker, I, 387-388; Parker, fragments, as cited in ibid., II, 27; Parker to Ripley, October 29, 1859, in ibid., p. 377; Parker, Ten Sermons, pp. 152, 288-289; Parker, Sins and Safeguards, p. 178; Parker, Rights of Man, p. 355; Parker, Theism, p. 235; Parker, Lessons from Matter and Man, p. 225; Bartol, Rising Faith, p. 130; Channing, "On Fenelon," p. 176; Channing to Ferris Pell, May 14, 1842, in Channing, Memoir, II, 324; Emerson, Journal D, August 28, 1838, in Emerson, JN, VII, 60; Osgood, "St. Ambrose," p. 425.

[28]Channing, Works, I, 300.

[29]Newcomb, Journals, September 13, 1866, p. 257; Judd, Birthright Church, p. 16; Osgood, The Hearth-Stone: Thoughts Upon Home-Life in Our Cities (New York, 1854), p. 30; Bartol, Rising Faith, p. 130; Channing, Works, I, 300; Channing, as cited in Peabody, Reminiscences of Channing, p. 159.

[30]Channing, as cited in Peabody, Reminiscences of Channing, pp. 131, 159; Channing, "On Fenelon," p. 176; Channing, Works, III, 143-144; Emerson, Notebook No. XVIII, 1821, in Emerson, JN, I, 258-259; Emerson, Siciliy, 1833, in ibid., IV, 131; Emerson, Italy, March, 1833, in ibid., pp. 138-139; Emerson, Works, VI, 227-228; Osgood, Hearth-Stone, pp. 30, 123-124; Osgood, Studies in Christian Biography, passim; Osgood, "Christian Ethics," XXIX, 166-170; ibid., XXX, 148; Parker, Sins and Safeguards, pp. 196-197; Parker, Lessons from Matter and Man, pp. 196-197; Parker, Discourse of Religion, pp. 448-449; Parker, "Life of St. Bernard," p. 10; Parker, Ten Sermons, p. 387; Parker to Ripley, October 29, 1859, in Weiss,

Life of Parker, II, 377; Peabody, _Record of a School: Exemplifying the General Principles of Spiritual Culture_ (Boston, 1835), p. 187; Thoreau, _Excursions_, pp. 15, 84; Ripley, Book Review of _Materialism in Religion_ by Harwood, p. 269; Henry, _About Men and Things_, p. 150; Bartol, _Rising Faith_, p. 130; Bancroft, _History of the United States_, passim; Brownson, _New Views_, pp. 15-16; Clarke, "Right Seed," p. 388; Kirby, "Reminiscences of Brook Farm," p. 525.

[31]Clarke, _Hour Which Cometh_, p. 141.

[32]Bartol, _Church and Congregation_, in a chapter significantly entitled, "Proportion," p. 330; Parker, Journal, 1844, in Weiss, _Life of Parker_, I, 217; Fuller, fragment, 1848, in _Memoirs of Margaret Fuller_, II, 295; Clarke, _Ten Great Religions_, p. 145; Brownson, "The Present State of Society," _Democratic Review_, July, 1843, in Brownson, _Works_, IV, 441; Bancroft, _Poems_, p. 59; Osgood, _Mile Stones_, p. 64; Osgood, "Christian Ethics," XXIX, 173; Emerson, Sicily, February 25, 1833, in Emerson, _JN_, IV, 126; Emerson, Journal E, 1840, in _ibid._, VII, 394-395.

[33]Emerson, Journal E, 1841, in Emerson, _JN_, VII, 420.

[34]Emerson, Journal E, 1841, in Emerson, _JN_, VII, 394-395; Emerson, _Journals_, 1848, VII, 534; Bancroft, _History of the United States_, 20th ed. (Boston, 1852), IV, 151; Parker, _Discourse of Religion_, pp. 379-380. The principal advantage, however, that Parker saw in the practice of priestly celibacy was a practical one: by their vows the monks were prevented from establishing a hereditary clerical aristocracy (Parker, "Life of St. Bernard," p. 8n; Parker, _Discourse of Religion_, p. 379).

[35]See below, Chapter V and VI.

[36]Parker, _World of Matter and Spirit_, pp. 241-242; W.H. Channing, "Ernest the Seeker," pp. 236-237; Clarke, _Steps of Belief_, p. 243; Clarke, _Ten Great Religions_, p. 145. Hedge, too, praised the system as an outgrowth of inner inspiration, but, with less of the transcendental overtone, he saw it as an inspiration derived from the gospel of Christ (Hedge, "Antisupernaturalism in the Pulpit," p. 153).

[37]Hedge, _Reason in Religion_, p. 252; Hedge, "Romanism in Its Worship," pp. 224-230; Parker to Rev. Mr. Senkler, January 22, 1860, in Weiss, _Life of Parker_, I, 374; Parker to Mrs. Ednah Cheney, December 31, 1859, in _ibid._, II, 404; Clarke, _Ten Great Religions_, pp. 28-29.

[38]Hedge, _Reason in Religion_, p. 252; Osgood, "Taylor's Lectures on Spiritual Christianity," _CE_, XXXI (January, 1842), 310; Fuller to New York _Tribune_, May 27, 1849, in Fuller, _Writings_, p. 504; Parker to Charles Ellis, January 29, 1840, in Weiss, _Life of Parker_, II, 413-414; Clarke, _Christian Doctrine of Prayer_, 174-175.

[39]Parker to John Manley, December, 1859, in Weiss, _Life of Parker_, II, 382; Fuller, Book Review of _Select Tales from Gesta Romanorum_ (New York, 1845), New York _Tribune_, May 31, 1845; Emerson, Journal B, 1835, in Emerson, _JN_, V, 94; Emerson to Abel Adams, May 28, 1833, in Emerson, _Letters_, I, 384-385; Emerson, _Works_, X, 114; Parker, Journal, March 3, 1844, in Weiss, _Life of Parker_, I, 211; Parker, _World of Matter and Spirit_, p. 270; Parker, _American Scholar_, p. 251; Francis, _Popery_, p. 15; Channing, _Works_, VI, 107; Clarke, _Vexed Questions_, p. 59; Clarke, "Christ and His Antichrists," p. 407.

[40]Channing, _Works_, I, 311; Channing, "Letter on Catholicism," pp. 165, 277; Clarke to Fuller, December, 1848, in _The Letters of James Freeman Clarke to Margaret Fuller_ (Hamburg, Germany, 1957), pp. 146-147, hereafter cited as: Clarke, _Letters_; Clarke, _Eleven Weeks in Europe_, p. 247; Fuller, "New Year's Letter from a Catholic Priest," New York _Tribune_, March 12, 1845; Fuller to New York _Tribune_, February 20, 1849, in Fuller, _Writings_, p. 488; Parker to Convers Francis, March 18, 1844, in Weiss, _Life of Parker_, I, 230; Parker, _Ten Sermons_, p. 94; Osgood, _Studies in Christian Biography_, p. 103; Hedge, "The Philosophy of Fetishism", _UR_, XV (March, 1881), 200-201; Hedge, "Christian Worship," p. 467; Hedge, "Romanism in Its Worship," pp. 224-226, 230; Francis, _Popery_, p. 15; Emerson to Abel Adams, May 28, 1833, in Emerson, _Letters_, I, 384-385; Bartol, "The Way to Find God, _MJAUA_, I (February, 1860), 50.

[41]Brownson, "The Secret of the Lord," BoQR, IV (July, 1841), 313; Hedge, "Philosophy of Fetishism," pp. 202-203; Parker to Dr. Lamson, December 31, 1843, in Weiss, Life of Parker, I, 225; Parker, Journal, March 3, 1844, in ibid., 210; Parker to Convers Francis, January 28, 1844, in ibid., 228.

[42]Clarke, Christian Doctrine of Forgiveness, p. 13n; Hedge, Reason in Religion, pp. 446-447; Parker to Convers Francis, January 28, 1844, in Weiss, Life of Parker, I, 228; Parker to Convers Francis, March 18, 1844, in ibid., p. 231; Bartol, "The Celebration of John Pierpont's Centennial Birthday," UR, XXIV (July, 1885), 20.

[43]Hedge, Reason in Religion, pp. 448-455.

[44]Dwight, "Music," Aesthetic Papers, May, 1849, pp. 25-26; W.H. Channing, "Ernest the Seeker," p. 57; John Greenleaf Whittier, "The Men of Old," SA, I (August 18, 1849), 97; Channing, Works, Complete Edition, pp. 1018-1019; Fuller, "Romaic and Rhine Ballads," The Dial, III (October, 1842), 147-148; Fuller to New York Tribune, August 9, 1847, in Fuller, At Home and Abroad, pp. 229-230, 232; Fuller, Diary, January 5, 1849, in Rostenberg, "Margaret Fuller's Roman Diary," p. 213; Fuller to Richard F. Fuller, January 25, 1849, in Fuller, At Home and Abroad, p. 241; Fuller to New York Tribune, December 2, 1848, in Fuller, Writings, p. 481; Bartol, Discourses on Christian Spirit, p. 209; Bartol, Rising Faith, pp. 62-63; Hedge, "Life of St. Augustine," pp. 225-240; Emerson, Works, X, 203; Osgood, "St. Ambrose," pp. 414-436; Clarke, Ten Great Religions, pp. 28-29; Clarke, Every-Day Religion, pp. 57, 296, 396; Clarke, Common-Sense, pp. 396-398; Parker, Discourse of Religion, p. 384; Parker, The Slave Power, ed. James K. Hosmer (Boston, n.d.), p. 300; Parker, Theism, p. 281; Parker to Convers Francis, March 18, 1844, in Weiss, Life of Parker, I, 231; Peabody, "Glimpse of Christ's Idea of Society," p. 217. See also above, Chapter I, note 1, and Chapter II and III, passim.

In addition to individual saints already mentioned, others cited favorably by the transcendentalists include Ignatius Loyola, Thomas More, Thomas aBecket, Agnes, Francis Xavier, Elizabeth, Nicholas, Charles Borromeo, Philip Neri, Francis of Assisi, Cecelia, Monica, Louis IX of France, and Francis de Sales.

[45]W.H. Channing, The Gospel of Today: A Discourse Delivered at the Ordination of T.W. Higginson, as Minister of the First Religious Society in Newburyport, Massachusetts, September 15, 1847 (Boston, 1847), p. 10; W.H. Channing, "The New Church," SA, II (February 2, 1850), 72-73; Hecker, "Dr. Brownson and Catholicity," Catholic World, XLVI (November, 1887), 225; Parker to Convers Francis, March 18, 1844, in Weiss, Life of Parker, I, 232-233. See also Channing, Works, VI, 206; Osgood, "Taylor's Lectures on Spiritual Christianity," p. 315.

[46]Clarke, Steps of Belief, p. 249; Clarke, Events and Epochs, pp. 39-40; Hedge, "Christian Worship," p. 467; Furness, "Nature and Christianity," CE, XLIII (July, 1847), 42; Fuller, "The Great Lawsuit," p. 22; Parker, World of Matter and Spirit, p. 81; Parker, Ten Sermons, p. 134; Parker to Convers Francis, March 18, 1844, in Weiss, Life of Parker, I, 231; Parker, American Scholar, p. 390; Bartol, Rising Faith, pp. 113, 172.

[47]Furness, Veil Partly Lifted, pp. 246-247; Parker to John Ayres, July 31, 1849, in Weiss, Life of Parker, II, 304; Parker, Transient and Permanent, p. 354; Clarke, Events and Epochs, pp. 163-164; Hedge, "Antisupernaturalism in the Pulpit," pp. 145-146.

[48]Bartol, Rising Faith, p. 122.

[49]Bartol, Rising Faith, p. 122; Bartol, Discourses on Christian Spirit, p. 184; Emerson, Sermon 13, December 25, 1827, as cited in Cameron, "History and Biography in Emerson's Unpublished Sermons," p. 113; Emerson, "Holiness," January 31, 1838, in The Early Lectures of Ralph Waldo Emerson, ed. Stephen E. Whicher, Robert E. Spiller, and Wallace E. Williams, 2 vols. (Cambridge, Massachusetts, 1964), II: 1836-1848, p. 351, hereafter cited as: Emerson, Early Lectures; Emerson, Works, VII, 176; ibid., XI, 413-415; Clarke, Steps of Belief, p. 249; Clarke, Ten Great Reli-

gions, pp. 28-29; Furness, "Nature and Christianity," p. 42; Furness, Remarks on the Four Gospels (Philadelphia, 1836), p. 75n; William Ellery Channing the Younger, "Christian Song of the Middle Ages," The Present, I (November 15, 1843), 136; Hedge, "Mythical Element in the New Testament," p. 173; Hedge, Ways of the Spirit, p. 78; Hedge, The Leaven of the Word: A Sermon Preached at the Ordination of Rev. Joshua Young, as Pastor of the New North Church in Boston, Thursday, February 1, 1849 (Boston, 1849), p. 5; Channing, Works, IV, 137; Channing, Works, Complete Edition, p. 1019; Channing, Conversation, 1825, as cited in Peabody, Reminiscences of Channing, pp. 130-131; Parker, Transient and Permanent, p. 393; Follen, Works, V, 147; Fuller, Woman, p. 137; Fuller, "Great Lawsuit," pp. 21-22, 26, 47; Fuller, Life Without and Within; or, Reviews, Narratives, Essays, and Poems, ed. Arthur B. Fuller (Boston, 1875), p. 247; Osgood, Hearth-Stone, pp. 27-43, 186, 215-216; Osgood, American Leaves, p. 376; W.H. Channing, "Confession of Faith," p. 7.

[50] Emerson, Works, XI, 413; Judd, Sermon, 1851, in Arethusa Hall, Life and Character of Reverend Sylvester Judd (Boston, 1857), p. 229, hereafter cited as: Hall, Life of Judd; Emerson, "Holiness," January 31, 1838, in Emerson, Early Lectures, p. 351; Osgood, Hearth-Stone, p. 61; Fuller, Woman, p. 131.

[51] Fuller to New York Tribune, March 21, 1849, in Fuller, At Home and Abroad, pp. 378-379; Fuller, Life Without and Within, p. 396; Emerson, Journal, 1826-1828, in Emerson, JN, III, 88; Emerson, Journal A, 1834, in ibid., IV, 258; Bartol, Pictures of Europe, p. 209; Parker, as cited in Weiss, Life of Parker, I, 45n; "La Madonna di San Sisto," The Present, I (December 15, 1843), 165.

[52] See for example, Parker, prayer, in Weiss, Life of Parker, II, 39-40; Parker, World of Matter and Spirit, p. 197; Parker, Autobiography, pp. 332-333, 382, 413; Parker, Sins and Safeguards, p. 48; Parker, Ten Sermons, p. 136; and many more. Clarke adopts the expression in Common-Sense, p. 414.

[53] Channing has the most extreme expression of this concept. In a personal letter, he wrote with some approval: "The actual deity of a large part of the Catholic world is a woman, 'the blessed Mary'" (Channing to the Misses Roscoe, July 7, 1824, in Channing, Memoir, III, 322). See also Cranch, "Symbolic Conceptions of the Deity," p. 247.

[54] Furness, Power of Spirit, p. 95; Furness, Story of the Resurrection, p. 147; Bartol, Rising Faith, p. 122; Bartol, Book Review of Sermons, by Hedge (Boston, 1891), pp. 329-330; Bartol, Principles and Portraits, pp. 50-51; Bartol, Radical Problems (Boston, 1872), p. 126; Hedge, Reason in Religion, pp. 342-344; Emerson, Works, XI, 628; Clarke, Steps of Belief, p. 249; Osgood, Hearth-Stone, pp. 29-30, 185-186.

Even where the Catholic veneration of Mary seemed to amount to adoration, they could sometimes justify the cult on the grounds that it was the worshipper's sincere way of "worshipping God in the beauty of holiness" (the expression is identical in Follen, Works, II, 199, and Hedge, Ways of the Spirit, pp. 81-82).

[55] Furness, who was particularly devoted to extolling the nobility of the human elements in the gospels, wrote: "The Madonna and the Crucifix,--to what myriads of suffering and dying men have these most human of symbols spoken of the Infinite Love!" (Furness, Power of Spirit, p. 95). Channing could honor the significance of the crucifix as "the emblem and witness of all-suffering love" (Channing, Works, Complete Edition, p. 997). Elsewhere, however, he complained of its use as injudicious (Channing, Works, IV, 205-206).

[56] Clarke, Steps of Belief, p. 255; Clarke, Go Up Higher, p. 82; Clarke, Eleven Weeks in Europe, p. 284; Hedge, Reason in Religion, pp. 30-31; Hedge, "Ecclesiastical Christendom," pp. 124-126; Bartol, "Celebration of John Pierpont's Centennial Birthday," p. 20; Bartol, Church and Congregation, pp. 318-319; Thoreau, Excursions, p. 14.

[57] Furness, Veil Partly Lifted, p. 4; Dwight, "On the Proper Character of Poetry and Music for Public Worship," CE, XXI (November, 1836), 259; Hedge,

"Romanism in Its Worship," pp. 228-240; Hedge, "Luther and His Work," pp. 810-811; Clarke, Christian Doctrine of Prayer, pp. 30-31, 160; Clarke, Steps of Belief, pp. 233, 250-255; Clarke, Eleven Weeks in Europe, p. 270; Clarke, "Christ and His Antichrists," p. 356; Brooks, Journal, April 1, 1866, in Brooks, Poems, Memoir, p. 83; Parker, Transient and Permanent, pp. 260-263; Channing, Sermon, in Peabody, Reminiscences of Channing, p. 196; Osgood, Studies in Christian Biography, p. 131; Francis, Christianity As a Purely Internal Principle, pp. 5-6; Francis, Popery, pp. 20-21; Bartol, "Person in Religion. An Address Delivered Before the Ministerial Union, March 9, 1868," MJAUA, IX (May, 1868), 163; Bartol, "Martin Luther," p. 523; Fuller, Life Without and Within, p. 251; Emerson, Sicily, 1833, in Emerson, JN, IV, 117.

[58]Clarke for one reproached the Protestants for this (see for example his "Christ and His Antichrists," pp. 406-408).

[59]Clarke, Discourse on the Aspects of the War. Delivered in the Indiana Place Chapel, Boston, on Fast Day, April 2, 1863 (Boston, 1863), pp. 7-8; Clarke, Eleven Weeks in Europe, p. 270; Clarke, "Christ and His Antichrists," pp. 407-408; Kirby, "Reminiscences of Brook Farm," p. 524; Cranch, Autobiography, September, 1848, in Scott, Life of Cranch, p. 151; Fuller, Life Without and Within, p. 338; Parker, Speeches, Addresses, and Occasional Sermons, 3 vols. (Boston, 1855), I, 219, hereafter cited as: Parker, Speeches; Hedge, "Ecclesiastical Christendom," pp. 124-125; Emerson, Sicily, 1833, in Emerson, JN, IV, 117.

[60]Thoreau, Journal, October 16, 1859, XII, 390; Bartol, Radical Problems, p. 85; Bartol, "Emerson's Religion," in The Genius and Character of Emerson. Lectures at the Concord School of Philosophy (Boston, 1884), p. 128; Parker, Transient and Permanent, pp. 243-247; Clarke, Vexed Questions, p. 135; Clarke, Hour Which Cometh, p. 106.

Parker, however, blamed the Catholic Church for having taken "unnecessary pains to promote fun and frolic on feast days, and he laid the Puritan reaction to this cause (ibid., pp. 250-251). Bartol also lamented that in some Catholic areas of Europe "the sabbath-day is a play-day" (Bartol, Pictures of Europe, p. 240).

[61]Osgood, The Coming Church, pp. 19-20; Parker, St. Bernard and Other Papers, ed. Charles W. Wendte (Boston, 1911), p. 162. Channing noted also the importance of the Catholic cycle of festivals for Negroes of "the Catholic islands" of the West Indies, where Sundays and festivals provided the only respite from excessive labor, and where thus a "superstition" was transformed into a blessing (Channing to [?], January 20, 1831, in Channing, Memoir, III, 141).

[62]Clarke, Hour Which Cometh, pp. 169-170. See also Osgood, Mile Stones, pp. 281, 290; Hedge, Sermons, pp. 302-303.

[63]Emerson, Journal N, 1842, in Emerson, JN, VIII, 218.

[64]Parker to Miss Cobb, February, [1860?], in Weiss, Life of Parker, II, 421.

[65]Parker, Journal, January 1, February, 1844, in Weiss, Life of Parker, I, 205, 208-209; Parker to Mrs. Ednah Cheney, December 31, 1859, in ibid., II, 404; Cranch, Journal, November 22, 1846, January 11, 1847, April 17, 1881, in Scott, Life of Cranch, pp. 116-117, 329; Cranch, "Letter on Traveling," WM, V (June, 1838), 183. Follen to Mr. McKay, January 2, 1837, in Follen, Works, I, 428; Brooks, Journal, 1866, in Brooks, Poems, Memoir, p. 89; Emerson to Cornelia Frances Forbes, January 20, 1877, in Emerson, Letters, VI, 302; Emerson, Journal Q, May 25, 1833, in Emerson, JN, IV, 74; Emerson, Sicily, 1833, in ibid., p. 131; Emerson, Italy and France, 1833, in ibid., p. 169; Emerson, Italy and France, June, 1833, June 9, 1833, in ibid., pp. 184, 190; Emerson, Journal London, 1848, in ibid., X, 271.

Whether or not Emerson possessed a genuine artistic sense seems to be the subject of controversy (see, for example, Edward Emerson, Notes, in Emerson, Works, I, xxii, and II, 442; Philip Rahv, "Two Visits," in Discovery of Europe: The Story of American Experience in the Old World, ed. Philip Rahv [Garden City, New York, 1960], p. 150; Franklin B. Newman, "Emerson and Buonarroti," New England Quarterly,

XXV [December, 1952], 525-535; Rusk, Life of Emerson, p. 300; Hopkins, Spires of Form, passim.). The majority of scholars contend that he had little. Nor was he a profoundly religious or spiritual man. Yet curiously enough, he evinced a far more penetrating understanding of the spiritual base of religious art than any of the other transcendentalists.

[66]Cranch, Journal, November 22, 1846, in Scott, Life of Cranch, p. 117 and passim; Cranch, Autobiography, Easter Sunday, April 4, 1847, in ibid., p. 117; Emerson, Italy, April 4, 7, 11, 1833, in Emerson, JN, IV, 155-158; Bartol, Church and Congregation, p. 261; Parker, American Scholar, p. 174; Fuller to Richard F. Fuller, January 19, 1849, in Fuller, At Home and Abroad, p. 430; Clarke,"Washington City in November," MJAUA, II (December, 1861), 554; Brooks, Journal, 1866, in Brooks, Poems, Memoir, pp. 74, 78-79; Brooks, Journal, April 1, 1866, in ibid., p. 84; Brooks, "Evening Chimes of Rome," in ibid., p. 122.

[67]Bancroft, Poems, p. 34; Emerson to Chauncy Emerson, April 16, 1833, in Emerson, Letters, I, 373; Emerson, Italy, March 31, April 17, 1833, in Emerson, JN, IV, 155, 160; Emerson, Journals, 1849, VIII, 33; ibid., 1851, X, 214; Emerson to Hermann Grimm, June 27, 1861, in The Correspondence of Ralph Waldo Emerson and Hermann Grimm, ed. Frederick William Holls (New York, 1903), pp. 58-59; Fuller to New York Tribune, May, 1847, in Fuller, At Home and Abroad, p. 224; Fuller, Woman, p. 138; Parker, Journal, January, 1844, in Weiss, Life of Parker, I, 204, 206; Parker, American Scholar, p. 84; Hedge, "Bartol's Pictures of Europe," CE, LIX (November, 1855), 435; Bartol, Rising Faith, p. 171; Bartol, "Christianity on Trial," UR, VII (February, 1877), 183-184; Channing, 1825, as cited in Peabody, Reminiscences of Channing, p. 96; Cranch, Journal, March 4, 1881, in Scott, Life of Cranch, p. 324; Cranch, The Bird and the Bell, pp. 277-282.

[68]Parker, Journal, January, March, 1844, in Weiss, Life of Parker, I, 206, 213; Cranch, Journal, January 11, 1847, April 17, 1881, in Scott, Life of Cranch, pp. 117, 329; Cranch, "The Concert and the Church," WM, VI (March, 1839), 340-341; Fuller to the New York Tribune, January, 1848, in Fuller, At Home and Abroad, p. 298; Brooks, Journal, April 1, 1866, in Brooks, Poems, Memoir, p. 81; Bancroft to Mrs. J.C. Bancroft Davis, October 4, 1868, in Howe, Life of Bancroft, II, 212; Emerson, Works, IX, 484; Emerson, Italy, March 31, April 3, 1833, in Emerson, JN, IV, 153-154.

[69]Emerson, Italy, April 17, 1833, in Emerson, JN, IV, 160; Emerson, Journals 1869, VIII, 33; Emerson, Works, II, 232; ibid., VII, 205; ibid., XII, 197, 290; Fuller, as cited by Emerson in Fuller, Memoirs, I, 344; Fuller, "Italy," November 18, 1845, in Fuller, Writings, p. 353; Fuller, Life Without and Within, p. 28; Bancroft, Literary and Historical Miscellanies (New York, 1855), pp. 139, 196, 521, hereafter cited as: Bancroft, Literary Miscellanies; Bancroft, Poems, pp. 47-49; Hedge, Prose Writers of Germany, pp. 268, 388; Bartol, Book Review of Sermons by Hedge, p.333; Newcomb, Journals, January 16, 1865, p. 107; Cranch, The Bird and the Bell, p. 8; Henry, "Tasso and the Alberti Manuscripts," New York Review, IX (October, 1841), 425; The Writings of Henry David Thoreau, vol. IV: Cape Cod and Miscellanies, p. 354; ibid., vol. II, Walden, p. 115. See also Sanborn, Life of Thoreau, p. 113.

[70]Channing, "Letter on Catholicism," p. 274; Emerson, Italy, April 5, 7, 1833, in Emerson, JN, IV, 156-157; Emerson to Fuller, January 7, 1843, in Emerson, Letters, III, 115-116; Emerson to Lidian Emerson, January 8, 1843, in ibid., pp. 117-118.

[71]Clarke, Steps of Belief, pp. 248-249.

[72]Emerson, Works, II, 361; ibid., VIII, 27.

[73]Bartol, Discourses on the Christian Body, p. 223; Dwight, "Music," p. 32; Emerson, Works, II, 11-12, 17; Brooks, "On Entering St. Peter's," in Brooks, Poems, Memoir, p. 121.

[74]Stetson, Two Discourses Preached Before the First Congregational Society in Medford: One Upon Leaving the Old Church; and One at the Dedication of the New (Boston, 1840), p. 50; Dwight, "The American Review's Account of the Religious Union of Associationists," The Harbinger, V (June 19, 1847), 30, hereafter cited as:

Dwight, "American Review's Account"; Emerson, Italy and France, May, 1833, in Emerson, JN, IV, 175; Emerson, Journal F, 1850, in ibid., VII, 499; Emerson, Works, XII, 244; Very, Poems and Essays, Complete and Revised Edition. With a Biographical Sketch by James Freeman Clarke and a Preface by Cyrus A. Bartol (New York, 1886), pp. 16-17, hereafter cited as: Very, Poems and Essays, Complete Edition; Ripley, "Christmas in Philadelphia," The Harbinger, VI (January 1, 1848), 69; Osgood, Mile Stones, p. 130; Hedge, "European Travel," CE, LIII (September, 1852), 255; Fuller, Life Without and Within, pp. 337-338.

[75]Emerson, Journal Q, June 10, 1833, in Emerson, JN, IV, 75; Emerson, Journal B, September 28, 1836, in ibid., V, 206; Emerson, Works, II, 359; ibid., III, 216-217; ibid., IX, 7; ibid., XII, 234; Parker, as cited in Frothingham, Theodore Parker, p. 206; Parker, Lessons from Matter and Man, p. 95; Bartol, Pictures of Europe, p. 321; Hedge, "European Travel," p. 255; Dwight, An Address Delivered Before the Harvard Musical Assoication, August 25, 1841 (no pub. [1843]), p. 16; Brownson, "Synthetic Philosophy," Democratic Review, January, March, 1843, in Brownson, Works, I, 105-106; Very, Poems and Essays, Complete Edition, p. 15; Marsh, Notes on Aesthetics, in Wells, Three Christian Transcendentalists, Appendix E, p. 189.

[76]Dwight, "Music As a Means of Culture," Atlantic Monthly, XXVI (September, 1870), 322; Dwight, "American Review's Account," p. 30; Dwight, "On the Proper Character of Poetry and Music for Public Worship," p. 262; Dwight, Address Delivered Before the Harvard Musical Association, p. 4; Dwight, "Music," pp. 32-33. See also Peabody, "Dorian Measure," p. 102; Osgood, American Leaves, p. 378. "The ear," observed William Henry Channing in commenting on a nun's choir, "is the finest avenue to the spirit" (W.H. Channing, "Ernest the Seeker," p. 235).

[77]See for example, Emerson, Journal Q, February, 1833, in Emerson, JN, IV, 84; Charles Lane, "Popular Music," SA, I (November 17, 1849), 311; Fuller, "Rev. William Ingraham's Christmas Holidays in Rome," New York Tribune, December 25, 1845.

[78]Emerson, Works, II, 21; Dwight, "American Review's Account," pp. 29-30; Dwight, "Music," p. 32; Dwight, "Our Dark Age in Music," Atlantic Monthly, L (December, 1882), 814; Dwight, "Letters from Europe," Dwight's Journal of Music, XIX (April 6, 1861), 5; Vesper Hymn by Archbishop John Hughes, in Osgood, Mile Stones, p. 208; Selections from the Catholic Breviary and Easter Vigil Liturgy, in ibid., 101-102; Clarke, Orthodoxy, p. 184 (Clarke comments here that the Catholic sacramental actions were from their evocative power, not their intrinsic power, more reliable for producing genuine Christianity in the soul than were the Protestant emotional revivals); Osgood, American Leaves, p. 377; Osgood, "St. Ambrose," pp. 429-430; Bancroft, Journal, November 26, 1821, in Howe, Life of Bancroft, I, 131-132; Emerson, Journals, 1857, IX, 137; Bartol, Pictures of Europe, pp. 321-322; Hedge, "European Travel," p. 255; Furness, Remarks on the Four Gospels, p. 75n; Furness, Story of the Resurrection, p. 141; Channing, Works, Complete Edition, p. 1019; Parker to Convers Francis, January 28, 1844, in Weiss, Life of Parker, I, 228.

[79]Dwight, "Music," p. 32; Dwight, "Letters from Europe," February 9, 1841, Dwight's Journal of Music, XVIII (October 29, 1860), 366; Osgood, "Christian Ethics," XXIX, 174; Cranch, Autobiography, 1848, in Scott, Life of Cranch, p. 125; Channing, Works, Complete Edition, pp. 1018-1019; Hedge, as cited in Long, Frederic Henry Hedge, p.28; Hedge, Sermons, p. 253; Hedge, "European Travel," p. 255; Bartol, Discourses on Christian Spirit, p. 184; Bartol, Pictures of Europe, p. 326; Fuller to [?], December 1, 1849, in Memoirs of Margaret Fuller, II, 310; Fuller to New York Tribune, December 17, 1847, in Fuller, Writings, pp. 430-431; Brooks, Simplicity of Christ's Teachings, p. 247; W.H. Channing, "Edwards and the Revivalists," p. 374; Emerson, Works, XI, 216; Emerson, Italy and France, May 21, June 9, 1833, in Emerson, JN, IV, 177, 190; Emerson, Journal A, 1834, in ibid., 258, 322; Emerson, Journal B, June 26, 1835, in ibid., V, 54.

[80]Hedge, "The Cause of Reason the Cause of Faith," p. 222; Hedge, Sermons,

p. 388. This was especially true when an artist's work appeared as an expression of his admirable life (Emerson, Works, XII, 234; Alcott, Journals, p. 56).

[81]Emerson, Journal D, August 17, 1838, in Emerson, JN, VII, 47; Bartol has the same emphasis on God in the face of the human Christ in DaVinci's Last Supper (Bartol, Pictures of Europe, p. 370).

[82]Bancroft, Literary Miscellanies, p. 489; Emerson, Journal E, 1839, in Emerson, JN, VI, 275.

[83]Hedge, Ways of the Spirit, pp. 354-355; Parker, Discourse of Religion, p. 384.

[84]Bartol, "Goethe and Schiller," in The Life and Genius of Goethe. Lectures at the Concord School of Philosophy, ed. Franklin B. Sanborn (Boston, 1886), p. 110; Bartol, Discourses on Christian Spirit, p. 183; Bartol, The Preacher, the Singer, and the Doer: Dewey, Longfellow, and Bertram (Boston, 1882), p. 4; Bartol, "Emerson's Religion," p. 125; Bartol, Book Review of Sermons by Hedge, p. 333; Bartol, "Martin Luther," p. 512; Newcomb, Journals, October 24, 1851,   December 28, 1863, pp. 95, 102-103; Clarke to Sarah Clarke, October 26, 1874, in Clarke, Autobiography, p. 349.

Emerson was ambivalent about Dante, coming to appreciate even his art, let alone his religiosity, but slowly. Yet according to Joseph C. Mathews, Emerson has 175 references to Dante (Mathews, "Emerson's Knowledge of Dante," University of Texas Studies in English, XXII [1942], 175).

[85]Parker to Dr. Lamson, January 4, 1844, in Weiss, Life of Parker, I, 225; Parker to Clarke, [1859 or 1860], in ibid., p. 152; Parker to Charles Ellis, January 29, 1860, in ibid., II, 413-414; Parker, Lessons from Matter and Man, p. 76; Parker, Theism, pp. 7-8; Cranch, The Bird and the Bell, p. 7.

[86]Newcomb, Journals, September 28, 1865, p. 277; ibid., April, 1866, p. 205; ibid., September 16, 1867, p. 267; ibid., July 10, 1870, p. 291; Emerson, Journals, 1859, IX, 243; ibid., April, 1863, p. 500; Emerson, as cited in Cabot, Memoir of Emerson, I, 262; Emerson, "Martin Luther," 1835, in Emerson, Early Lectures, I, 120; Parker, Ten Sermons, pp. 326,337; Parker to Convers Francis, January 28, 1844, in Weiss, Life of Parker, I, 228; Parker to Miss Cobb, January 1, 1860, in ibid., II, 405; Ripley, "Religion in France," p. 278; Bartol, Church and Congregation, pp. 119, 137; Bartol, Word of the Spirit, pp. 9-10, 64; Bartol, Reason and Rome in Education, p. 9; Bartol, Rising Faith, p. 287; Bancroft, Journal, as cited in Levin, History as Romantic Art, p. 100; Bancroft, "Joseph II of Austria," p. 19; Clarke, "The Bible," pp. 39-40; Clarke, Ideas of Paul, p. 118; Clarke, Church-going: Past, Present, and Future (Boston, n.d.), p. 4; Clarke, Steps of Belief, p. 256; Hecker, Diary, November 15, 1843, in Elliott, Life of Hecker, p. 111; Hedge, "Christian Worship," pp. 464-465; Hedge, "Romanism in Its Worship," pp. 223, 232, 235-240; Hedge, Martin Luther and Other Essays, p. 158; Brooks, Simplicity of Christ's Teachings, pp. 245-246; Osgood, God with Men, p. 51; Osgood, "Poet of Puseyism," p. 53; W.H. Channing, "Ernest the Seeker," p. 57; Dwight, Book Review of Pictures from Italy by Charles Dickens (New York, 1846), The Harbinger, III (June 20, 1846), 28; W.H. CHanning to Clarke, December 20, 1835, as cited in Frothingham, Memoir of William Henry Channing, pp. 115-118; Judd, The Church, pp. 6, 13, 247; Channing, Works, VI, 208; Channing, as cited in Peabody, Reminiscences of Channing, p. 99; Francis, Popery, p. 19.

Cranch's "The Bird and the Bell" (in Cranch, The Bird and the Bell, pp. 1-22), is a transcendental paean of praise to "the Bird"--all Nature--and a lament of its defeat by "the Bell"--the Church bells of Florence, with all that they symbolized of Catholic worship and belief:

                    ...in the race
        Of rival tongues the Bell outrang the Bird,-- (p. 3).
Cranch's "Through the Fields to St. Peter's" (ibid., pp. 88-94), carries the same theme.

[87]Alcott to Elizabeth Oakes Smith, December 30, 1879, in Alcott, Letters, p. 794; Clarke, Eleven Weeks in Europe, p. 270; Clarke, Steps of Belief, p. 261; Bartol, Discourses on Christian Spirit, p. 180; Bartol, Discourses on the Christian Body, pp. 222-225; Bartol, Sincerity. An Address Before the Essex Conference, February 28, 1872 (Boston, 1872), p. 19; Very, Poems and Essays, Complete Edition, p. 280.

[88]Thoreau, Excursions, p. 14. Thoreau's journals are replete with allusions to field and lake and forest as his church; telegraph-harp and bird as his organ and his preacher. In the same vein see also Bartol, Pictures of Europe, p. 349; Furness, as cited in Hedge, "Dr. Furness's Word to Unitarians," pp. 437-438; Emerson to Cornelia Frances Forbes, January 20, 1877, in Emerson, Letters, VI, 302; Cranch, The Bird and the Bell, pp. 1-22, 88-94. Bartol warned, however: "Grandly saying that the universe is God's temple, what does it signify if we do not prostrate ourselves therein?" (Bartol, Discourses on the Christian Body, p. 226).

[89]Very, Poems and Essays, Complete Edition, p. 75. See also Channing, Worship of the Father, p. 45; Emerson, Works, VI, 204. Emerson also hinted that house and hearth were his temple of worship (Emerson, Journal D, June 28, 1839, in Emerson, JN, VII, 291).

[90]Hedge, "The Cause of Reason the Cause of Faith," p. 212.

[91]Clarke, Hour Which Cometh, p. 5; Clarke, Steps of Belief, p. 229; Newcomb, Journals, September 13, 1866, p. 257; Emerson, Blotting Book, I, 1827, in Emerson, JN, VI, 47; Emerson, "Thoughts on the Religion of the Middle Ages," p. 403; Bancroft, History of the United States, 5th ed. (Boston, 1866), IX, 504; Channing, "Letter on Catholicism," pp. 165-167; Francis, Popery, p. 12; Osgood, "The Schleiermacher Centennial and Its Lesson," p. 190; Osgood, Hearth-Stone, p. 123; Osgood, "Christian Ethics," XXIX, 170.

[92]Kirby, "Reminiscences of Brook Farm," p. 525; Follen, Works, II, 252; Thoreau, Cape Cod, p. 461; W.H. Channing to Clarke, December 20, 1835, in Frothingham, Memoir of William Henry Channing, pp. 118-119; Parker to Convers Francis, March 18, 1844, in Weiss, Life of Parker, I, 232.

[93]Brownson, New Views, p. 13; W.H. Channing, "Edwards and the Revivalists," p. 374. Parker once described confessionals as "needed and beautiful in their time" (Parker, Discourse of Religion, p. 384). Clarke, in his commentary on the Catholic practice of Confession, always added that confession to any other human could have the same beneficial effects (Clarke, Steps of Belief, p. 228; Clarke, Deacon Herbert's Bible Class, p. 113; Clarke, Christian Doctrine of Forgiveness, pp. 133-135).

[94]Hedge, Sermons, pp. 168-169; Emerson, as cited in Cabot, Memoir of Emerson, I, 318; Emerson, Sicily, 1833, in Emerson, JN, IV, 124; Emerson, Works, III, 200; ibid., IX, 6-8; Parker, Transient and Permanent, pp. 339-340; Parker, Discourse of Religion, p. 28; Stetson, Two Discourses, pp. 43-46; Henry, The Gospel; a Formal and Sacramental Religion. A Sermon Preached at the Church of the Advent, in Boston, on the Sunday after Christmas, 1845 (Boston, 1846), pp. 5-8; Clarke, Christian Doctrine of Prayer, pp. 148-149; Judd, The Church, p. 136; Bartol, Discourses on the Christian Body, pp. 225-226; Bartol, Word of the Spirit, pp. 52, 65; Bartol, Pictures of Europe, pp. 179-211, in a chapter entitled, "Testimony of Art to Religion"; Fuller, Life Without and Within, p. 251; Fuller to New York Tribune, December, 1847, in Fuller, Writings, p. 423; Dwight, "American Review's Account," p. 30; W.H. Channing, "Ernest the Seeker," p. 57; Osgood, "Poet of Puseyism," p. 47.

[95]Emerson, Journal N, 1842, in Emerson, JN, VIII, 182; Parker, Discourse of Religion, pp. 380-381, 384; Parker to Convers Francis, January 28, 1844, in Weiss, Life of Parker, I, 228; Osgood, "German Hymns," p. 238; Dwight, "American Review's Account," p. 30; Hecker, Diary, April 17, 1843, as cited in Elliott, Life of Hecker, p. 61.

96Clarke, Ten Great Religions, p. 136; Emerson, Italy, March 17, 1833, in Emerson, JN, IV, 144; Emerson, Journal B, 1836, in ibid., V, 211; Emerson, Journal U, December 25, 1843, in ibid., IX, 59-60; Emerson, Works, VII, 56; Channing, Works, III, 174; Hedge, Ways of the Spirit, p. 310; Hedge, "The Historic Atonement. Sermon Preached at the Conference of Unitarian and Other Churches at Syracuse, New York, October 9, 1866," MJAUA, IX (April, 1868), 211; W.H. Channing, "Ernest the Seeker," p. 57; Judd, The Church, pp. 170-171; Bartol, Pictures of Europe, p. 188; Dwight, "Music," p. 32; Osgood, "The Real and the Ideal in New England," NAR, LXXXIV (April, 1857), 546; Osgood, Studies in Christian Biography, p. 192; Osgood, The Coming Church, pp. 13-14.

Touching more directly upon the heart of the Catholic belief, Osgood mused: "What was it that reared of old the Gothic cathedral? What but the Mass, the doctrine of the bodily presence of God...." (Osgood, God with Men, p. 255).

97Fuller to James Nathan, September 5, 1845, in Fuller, The Love Letters of Margaret Fuller, 1845-1846. With an Introduction by Julia Ward Howe. To Which Are Added the Reminiscences of Ralph Waldo Emerson, Horace Greeley, and Charles T. Congdon (London, 1903), p. 155; Fuller, Life Without and Within, p. 105; Osgood, The Coming Church, p. 13; Parker, World of Matter and Spirit, p. 244; Parker to Miss Hunt, November 16, 1857, in Frothingham, Theodore Parker, p. 468; Parker, "German Literature," The Dial, I (January, 1841), 328; Dwight, "Music As a Means of Culture," p. 322; Dwight, "Letters from Europe," Dwight's Journal of Music, XVIII (September 15, 1860), 199; Follen, Works, IV, 292-293; Bartol, Pictures from Europe, p. 186; Bartol, "Christ's Authority the Soul's Liberty," CE, LV (November, 1853), 325.

98Emerson, Sicily, 1833, in Emerson, JN, IV, 117; Fuller to New York Tribune, December 17, 1847, in Fuller, At Home and Abroad, p. 261; Bancroft, Journal, November 26, 1821, in Howe, Life of George Bancroft, I, 131; Clarke, Autobiography, p. 373; Clarke, Hour Which Cometh, pp. 293-294; Clarke, Eleven Weeks in Europe, pp. 271, 276.

Other transcendentalists wrote of similar experiences: Cranch, Autobiography, September, 1848, in Scott, Life of Cranch, pp. 150-151; Parker to Convers Francis, January 28, 1844, in Weiss, Life of Parker, I, 227; Brooks, "On Entering St. Peter's," in Brooks, Poems, Memoir, p. 121; W.H. Channing, "Ernest the Seeker," pp. 50-54; Thoreau, Excursions, pp. 12-13.

99Emerson, Journal B, 1835, in Emerson, JN, V, 58; Dwight, "Common Sense," UR, XXXIII (May, 1890), 401.

100Emerson, Journal B, 1835, in Emerson, JN, V, 58; Osgood, "Christian Ethics," XXX, 147-148.

101These will be discussed in Chapter VII.

102Emerson, "Hymn Books," October 2, 1831, in Young Emerson Speaks: Unpublished Discourses on Many Subjects, ed. Arthur Cushman McGiffert, Jr. (Boston, 1938), p. 146; [Hedge], Christian Liturgy for the Use of the Church (Boston, 1853); Hedge and Frederic D. Huntington, eds., Hymns for the Church of Christ (Boston, 1853); Hall, Life of Judd, pp. 284-285.

William Henry Channing actually adopted music from the great Catholic Masses for the opening services of the Religious Union of Associationists (see H.N. Hudson, "Religious Union of Associationists," The American Review, V [May, 1847], 492-493). In 1868 Alcott commented before the First Meeting of the Free Religious Association that Catholics were "stealing our thunder," and that the Association should return the action by beginning with "the highest instrumentality"--music (SHM, Review of Proceedings of the First Annual Meeting of the Free Religious Association, Held in Boston, May 28 and 29, 1868 [Boston, 1868], Radical, IV [November, 1868], 395-396).

103Osgood, Mile Stones, p. 68 (a hymn of St. Ambrose); ibid., p. 208 (a hymn of the then Archbishop of New York, John Hughes); ibid., p. 278 (a hymn of

Hildebert, twelfth century Archbishop of Tours); Osgood, "St. Ambrose," pp. 423-435; Osgood, "German Hymns," pp. 234-257; Osgood, Review of Lateinische Hymen und Gesange aus Mittelalter, deutsch, unter, Beibehaltung der Versmasse. Mit beigedrucktem lateinische Urtexte by G.A. Konigsfeld (Bonn, Germany, 1847), CE, LXV (November, 1848), 457-459; Emerson, "Hymn Books," October 2, 1831, in Young Emerson Speaks, p, 146. Brooks translated a great number of modern European classics, many of which contained Catholic selections.

[104]Judd, The Church, p. 98.

[105]Clarke, Christian Doctrine of Forgiveness, pp. 162-163. See also Osgood, God with Men, p. 255; Bartol, Pictures of Europe, p. 248.

[106]Clarke, Common-Sense, p. 434.

[107]Hedge, Ways of the Spirit, pp. 72-73; Hedge, "Ecclesiastical Christendom," p. 127; Parker to Convers Francis, March 18, 1844, in Weiss, Life of Parker, I, 232; Emerson, Works, X, 113.

[108]Cranch, The Bird and the Bell, p. 189.

[109]Hedge, "Ecclesiastical Christendom," p. 126.

[110]Parker, Discourse of Religion, pp. 380-381.

CHAPTER V

TRANSCENDENTALIST VIEWS OF HISTORY

Anyone who examines thoroughly the writings of the transcendentalists will observe that many of them possessed a keen interest in things historical, particularly in the field of religion. And anyone who probes deeply into their historical writings can also discover the patterns into which their reflections can almost always be classed. In order to determine precisely where the transcendentalists saw the Catholic Church as fitting into the stream of history--past, present, and future--it is first necessary to determine what those patterns were.

The patterns or theories or--loosely--philosophies of history within which the transcendentalists operated were broadly two--an ahistorical approach to the past; and a theory of progressive development. Contrary to common opinion, few of the transcendentalists actually held the first. But since its very articulate and almost sole spokesman was Emerson, it has come to be identified with transcendentalist thought.[1]

It is a fact that Emerson was interested in history. In 1836-1837 he delivered a series of ten lectures on the philosophy of history;[2] in some of his sermons he treated of the history of sectarianism in the early nineteenth century;[3] and in all his writings and lectures, he repeatedly alluded to living examples from the past. The kind of history that he was not interested in was the history of races and epochs as an organic development into the total now. His interest therefore was sure, but ahistorical, in the sense that he viewed history from a purely subjective point of view. This subjectivism was not a matter of seeing history as revolving around himself or as interpreted by him-self. Rather it was an approach that explained the past solely in terms of the individual human persons who made it up. "The roots of all things," he wrote in his essay entitled "History," "are in man....Everything must be explained from individual history, or must remain words."[4]

Emerson's first reason for studying men of the past was to glean an under-standing of the nature of man, to learn "what man can do...what man can suffer ...what he can believe."[5] Not only this, but in interpreting history thusly, he felt that each man should write his own history book, to see how he related to the facts of the past, and to discover the law of his own being. This law he could perceive not in the writings of historians, but by means of his own intuition.[6]

That the law of one's being was not totally unique to each individual is clear from Emerson's insistence upon the universality of the laws of nature that were thus intuitively perceived. Here his concept of correspondences comes into full play. He repeatedly alluded to the correspondences between historical fig-ures--"representative men"--and the men of his day, or better, man of his day. He insisted that there was no such generalization as "an age," but that all ages were epitomized by "a few profound persons," by the "power of minorities, and of minorities of one." What was an institution, but "the lengthened shadow of one man"? What was all history but biography? In the laws which these men revealed Emerson saw not the individual but the spirit of humanity. Thus "all history becomes subjective and repeats itself,...in each man's life."[7]

Applied to religion, such exemplars of humanity become the focal point of one's total strivings for a better life. "How needful is David, Paul, aKempis ...to our devotion!"[8] Unnecessary were the traditions in which they were em-bodied and the institutions which seemed to Emerson as the stagnation of the spiritual life.[9] The release of man's spiritual and moral life from these historical encumbrances was, therefore, an obligation. In fact, one of Emerson's best interpreters makes the rather absolute affirmation that Emerson's sole objective was the freeing of man's spirit from institutional Christianity, thereby enabling him to pursue union with God in his own soul.[10] This was the burden of his Divinity School Address of 1838, in which he charged historical Christianity with placing a formidable barrier between the soul and God. Much earlier, it had been the theme also of his well-known letter to his aunt, Mary Moody Emerson, in 1826. "It is wrong," he wrote her, "to regard ourselves so much in a historical light as we do, putting Time between God and us;...it were fitter to account every moment...as a revelation proceeding each moment from the Divinity to the mind of the observer...." Perhaps he best summed up his stance before the historical religious past when he concluded:

> We ought not therefore to have this mighty regard to the long antiquity of its [Christianity's] growth,...but to consider its present condition as a thing entirely independent of the ways and means whereby it came into that condition and neither seeing what it was nor hearing what it said to past generations, examine what it is and hear what [it] saith to us.[11]

Despite his ahistorical frame of reference, Emerson sometimes did view former ages in a more developmental light. He could not, of course, see the possibility of analyzing with any certainty the causal relationships of the past. But he did perceive at times that the religious past could be divided into historic eras and that it could be seen as the progress of man from dying religious forms to living ones.[12]

From this point of view, Emerson's theories of history overlap with those of the second school of transcendentalists. Their elaboration of their theory was far more extensive and systematic than was his. But like his, it was constructed from an almost entirely religious perspective.

All the transcendentalists were keenly interested and quite knowledgeable in the field of history, although Bancroft was the only professional historian among them. And all who delved with some expertise into the past were also strongly affected by the romantic tinge of progressivism. Bancroft was the exemplar par excellence of this romantic progressivist thought. With the help of others, he had begun to spread its ideas after a study tour in Germany in 1829. Along with him, the most significant of the transcendentalists in this work were Hedge, Clarke, and Brownson.

According to Bancroft, the story of his country and of all religious and secular history could be understood only in the light of the progressivist faith. The history of the United States which he produced in this faith turned out to be what R.W.B. Lewis has accurately described as a sort of epic myth, a narrative that was less an account than a celebration.[13] In 1838 Bancroft summed up the whole thrust of his thematic approach in an article that elaborated his thesis: "The irresistible tendency of the human race is to advancement."[14] All the labored efforts of his mammoth history were to prove this point, to prove especially that man had progressed steadily from tyranny--especially religious tyranny--to the liberty of Protestant American citizenship.

Bancroft believed that the total schema of universal history had unfolded in this pattern as a direct result of divine purpose. Unlike other romantic historians, he was powerfully influenced by a religious conception of time, and in this the other transcendentalists followed him. Brownson for one worked out minutely a providential theory of his own, although with Emersonian overtones he disclaimed the possibility of classifying the progress initiated by God as a science.[15]

Hedge, on the other hand, did try to see the providential plan as totally concordant with a scientific and even Hegelian dialectic and at the same time completely harmonious with the freedom of man's will. His first elaboration of such a theory came out in 1834, and his complete and rather air-tight exposition of it thirty-six years later.[16] Referring to the "true religion" of the middle

ages, he wrote in the earlier article: "Everything which is destined to have

permanent value shall be progressive in its development." By the last article,

he was combining the providential and scientific aspects by calling this theory

"the principle of divine necessity,--that is, of a natural law in historic pro-

cesses....The end of all study of the past is the discovery of law, that is, of

spirit, that is, of Deity in the facts studied."[17]

Other transcendentalists also contended more or less thoroughly for the pro-

gressivist nature of the past, especially as embodied in Christianity.[18] Among

them, Clarke gave the progressive past the most systematic treatment. Each of

his writings that touches upon the subject shows this orientation, many of them

being written expressly to demonstrate the theory from factual evidence.

The progressive theory of religious history was popular in scholarly and

romantic circles of the nineteenth century. In our religiously primed group it

found particular acceptance, since they hoped for historical justification for

their attempts at religious renewal. Simply stated, the concept was one of

development or evolution.[19] They described it variously as a "spiral movement,

at once revolutionary and progressive,..."; as the "unfolding" of God in the

soul of man; as "a process and not a finality," a process always advancing to

greater perfection, always incomplete and unfinished till the perfect day shall

come.[20]

Many of the transcendentalists interpreted this development as one religious

spirit permeating all religious forms. For some, the spirit could encompass only

a few basic truths, as residing permanently in the heart of man. Such was Par-

ker's naturalistic belief.[21] For others, it could include the entire religious

posture of man as caught up in the perennial and unchangeable truths of the

genuine Church of Christendom--in whatever form that Church may have taken

through the ages. It could even have been the form of paganism, but in no

matter what the guise, it was the "true church" if it contained the "truth" of
the church. Thus there was an historical continuity giving life to all phases
of Christianity, and linking the new with the old.[22] Even the ahistorical advocates, Emerson, Parker, and Alcott, opted for this historical continuity. On
separate occasions they each concurred with St. Augustine's statement that Christianity had existed from the beginnings of the human race.[23]

In what did the historical development of the true religion consist? How
was it recognized, and what was the transcendentalist evaluation of it? The
answers to these questions must be combed out of the enormous amount of analyzing and synthesizing that several of the transcendentalists did on the subject
in one way or another. Basically they agreed that, given certain stable elements, the developmental process of religion took place in a series of stages or
epochs. In Clarke's term, these periods were waves of spiritual power succeeding
one upon the other, each one purifying the last.[24]

Each of the transcendentalists had his own peculiar method and criteria for
dividing past history into its various epochs. Some of them constructed more
than one scheme, depending on their current need. Some peered far back into
prehistoric times; and some braved a prognosis far into the future to a stage
beyond transcendentalism.

Out of all these often rather belabored theories it is possible to piece
together a somewhat clear picture of the developmental theory of history that
was common to them all. Briefly--though the transcendentalists could rarely
force themselves to be brief--the stages of all history were synonymous with
the stages of religious history. They lined up as follows: fetishism;[25] paganism or polytheism;[26] Judaism or monotheism;[27] universal Christianity, or the so-
called classic deism of Christ, St. Paul, and the early Church;[28] papal Christianity, or Roman Catholicism;[29] Protestant Christianity and its various off-
shoots;[30] rational Christianity;[31] and lastly the era of the true and perfect

Church, variously described. For some, the truly liberal Christianity, or transcendentalism, was this perfect Church, although its full implementation was yet to be achieved.[32] But for a few, as they began to grow disillusioned with transcendentalism, the perfect Church was to come only in an era beyond even that.[33]

The process of this development consisted in each successive era witnessing a renewal of man's spirit by a throwing off of outmoded and burdensome elements from the immediate past. Accordingly, each religious institution or form is provisional, giving way to others when it has outlived its usefulness. The need for a new phase becomes apparent when the old religion hardens into creeds or despotism, and a new one grows out of it that "puts the soul again into the presence of God and his love."[34] The seed of the new is contained in the old, and by a process of selection and dialectical development, a new creation is born and man transformed once more.[35]

It is not our purpose to discuss the transcendentalists' comments on all of these phases of religious history. We have rather provided a summary exposition of the philosophical framework within which they made their contributions to historical and religious thought. Within this context we can now situate our examination of the judgments they passed upon the Catholic Church's position in time--past, present, and to come.

THE DEVELOPING PHASES OF ROMAN CATHOLICISM

In their study of the historical dimensions of the Catholic Church, the transcendentalists ordinarily began with what they considered its origins in the post-apostolic age. The Church of the New Testament they conceived of as the prototype not of the Catholic Church as such, but of a "truly catholic" Christianity. Specifically it was a prototype of Unitarianism and, by extension, of its liberal offspring, transcendentalism.[36] The "Romish Church" they saw only as a development of later centuries when the primitive gospel became systematized. Their comments on the rise of this Church can be neatly confined under two headings: 1) the evolution of Catholic theology; and 2) the development of a hierarchical church.

Many of the transcendentalists displayed a genuine interest in the process by which the doctrinal aspects of Catholicism became articulated. Only a few of the total group, however, undertook more than a cursory study of that historical process. In this endeavor, Hedge stands preeminent, just as Clarke is easily seen to be the most knowledgeable in the area of contemporary Catholic theology. This is not to say that Clarke did not write at length on the Church's antecedents. In fact, his writings on church history are more extensive than any of the others'. But his analysis of the process by which Catholic theology developed is not so acute nor so specific as Hedge's. Osgood is a close second to Hedge, particularly in the realm of contributions made by the Church Fathers, in whom he became interested as a result of the Oxford movement.

The transcendentalists' discussions on the development of Catholic theology is impressive for its broad, though admittedly incomplete, understanding of the various streams that fed it. To their study they brought a sometimes painstaking analysis of purely human and environmental factors in its evolution. But they also brought a faith vision, since those who provided most of the commentary on the subject were not only the most scholarly, but also the most religiously orientated.

The transcendentalist approach to this analysis was not by means of a scientific explication of the total picture. None of them, for example, attempted to provide a single unified study of all the forces that shaped that development. Nonetheless, it is possible to put together their ideas on all these factors and to show their total concept in that fashion.

According to the transcendentalists, the earliest influence which caused the Catholic Church to clarify, enlarge, "corrupt," or in any way modify the original primitive gospel was a complex of forces extraneous to it. Although they judged some of these as the "engrafting" of elements foreign to the spirit of Christianity, often such accretions were taken as necessary accompaniments of the age.

The first of these influences was derived from Jewish usages which the early Church was accustomed to by reason of its heredity. Clarke approved of these as being in accordance with human nature. Hedge, however, did not, as he felt they only carried on the law of righteousness.[37] More obvious were the pagan influences upon Christianity. Since for the transcendentalists, all religions carried an element of truth, these influences were acceptable. Clarke correctly recognized that "some of the early Christian Fathers called on the heathen poets and philosophers to bear witness to the truth." This time Hedge concurred.[38] Long before these remarks were written, Brownson in his search for the true church had seen the Catholic system as this compound of Judaism and paganism, and in keeping with his progressivism had pronounced it "immeasurably their superior." William Henry Channing, on the other hand, broke with the progressivist thrust by describing Catholic theology as nothing more than "ancient philosophy recast."[39]

Far more significant than outside influences, however, was the impact made by the "providential men" within the fold of the Church itself. The early Church Fathers, objects of the transcendentalists' keenest interest, were invariably interpreted in their role as contributors to the shaping of Catholic belief. Whether or not the transcendentalists accepted the truth of one or another of the doctrines so formulated, they acknowledged these thinkers as outstanding men of history. They gave credit to the Fathers for the brilliance of their minds, but above all for the power which they exerted upon the Church for centuries to come, a Church which adopted their crystallization of doctrine with little change.[40]

Most of the transcendentalists hailed St. Augustine as the Father of Roman

Catholic theology, the one who did more than any other to mold the "anthropology" of Christianity.[41] Further, in their theological discussions, whether Catholic or Protestant, they frequently called upon the witness not only of Augustine, but of the other "orthodox" teachers of the early Church: Irenaeus, Jerome, Basil, Tertullian, Athanasius, Chrysostom, Cyprian, Justin Martyr, Clement of Alexandria, Origen, Gregory of Nyssa, Ambrose, Gregory Nazianzen, and others.[42] A favorite among these seemed to by Chrysostom, whose doctrines appeared to the transcendentalists to be the most liberal.[43] The least distinguished in their roster was Jerome, who, though "a faithful mirror of the opinions, manners, and morals of his age," deserved honor perhaps as a translator, but not as a teacher. Jerome's "unnatural" way of life and irascibility of temperament caused him to lose favor with the benign transcendentalists.[44]

Our group was also impressed by the universality of the Church in absorbing the opinions of so many different temperaments in the development of its doctrine. Hedge summed up his admiration for this openness of the Church in the introduction to his study of St. Augustine: "The dreaming Oriental, the volatile Greek, the practical Roman, the impetuous Goth, the fiery African are all represented in its organism."[45] In this connection both he and Osgood held up the example of the early Church as an admirable instance of common fellowship that could thrive even in spite of differences.[46]

The Greek and Roman influences in this diverse constitution particularly occupied the minds of Clarke and Hedge. They took careful note of the differences between the two, pointing up mainly the legalistic spirit of the Latin Fathers, the free, liberal, and inquiring tradition of the Greeks, and the specific coloration that both these gave to the development of Catholic thought.[47] Clarke gave preeminence in this process to the Latin Fathers, making the bold assertion that it was the Roman mind that determined the course of western theology. The development of the doctrine of the atonement, which was preoccupying the pens of many Unitarians of the day, provided him with an accommodating example.[48]

The Greek Church, on the other hand, brought a different influence to bear upon the development of theology, one which the transcendentalists for the most part preferred.[49] About the only weakness they could find in the Greek Fathers was one that Clarke's sharply theological--and transcendental--mind observed. He faulted them for supplanting simple revelation to all men with particular insight to the advanced speculative believer. But even this Clarke could accept as part of the doctrine of progress at work. For he saw an asset in the materialistic tone which the Alexandrian school gave to the church. In the Greek speculations on God and Satan, angels and devils, heaven and hell, the church found a safe retreat from the opposite extreme of dreamy oriental spiritualism and idealism, thus saving a healthy realism for the church.[50]

Tertullian and Origen were the two great figures in whom the transcendentalists saw embodied the dichotomy between these schools. When the transcendental argument was in need fo a fitting example of the dogmatic and legal spirit of Catholicism, they cited the former. And whenever the need was for the "truest representative of Liberal Christianity," they cited the latter.[51]

Another factor which the transcendentalists noted in the development of Catholic theology was the religious leadership united in Church Councils. They left untouched none of the important Councils of the early centuries--Nicaea, Constantinople, Ephesus, Chalcedon.[52] In their theological writings they used these Councils with the same familiarity and freedom as they used the Fathers. Particularly useful in their discussions was the role the Councils played in the development of the doctrine of the Trinity and consequently those of the natures of Christ and of Mary.[53]

Most of the transcendentalists' comments upon the Councils are made with mixed sentiments of admiration and disapproval. Osgood sees in them the working of all the elements that have made Catholics "the strangely mingled empire that subsequent history reveals."[54] Hedge, while elaborating his theory of the development of theology through the agency of the Holy Spirit, still feels that the Councils' influence often brought about "an apparently willful divergence from the primitive faith."[55] This represents no inconsistency on his part, because he sees even willful divergence from truth as part of man's freedom within the providential purpose. In fact, he suggests that God's providence is nowhere more conspicuous than in the "final dictum" of the Councils respecting the nature of Christ. His reason is that in its successive declarations, the early Church clarified its own understanding, thus triumphing over the heresies that threatened its unity. "It was well for the Church and well for humanity."[56]

A few of the transcendentalists went beyond the early Councils and carried their discussion of doctrinal development through the high middle ages. Again they studied the Church Councils, as well as the scholastic method of the Church's most prominent teachers--Thomas Aquinas, Anselm, Peter Lombard, Abelard, Duns Scotus, and Bonaventure.[57] But for the most part their interest in the later development of doctrine was minimal.

What were the transcendentalists' conclusions about the method by which Catholic doctrine became solidified? It was hard for them to see anything in the end but the gradual divorce of reason from faith. Moreover, they occasionally questioned the Church's motives in formulating doctrine. They did agree that the presence of heresies demanded a clarification of the Church's stand. But they charged that the Church had all too often made its judgments on the basis of mere speculation or "opinion," for partisan advantage, or for expediency's sake.[58] Still, even Parker could acknowledge that false doctrines had been taught in good faith and in good faith received, and that the purpose of the scholastic system had been a praiseworthy one--to demonstrate to the intellect what was accepted by faith.[59]

If there had indeed been errors, how could their presence be reconciled with the sure progress of religion? Certainly Parker and Emerson were quick to point out these errors as falsification and absurdities, and to condemn the Church for not really developing. But these two did not have to defend a progressivist theory of history.[60] The others, however, usually found a way out of the dilemma by drawing out whatever good they perceived as coming from each error. The succession of theories of belief was not merely change from one error to another, but a sign of growth, springing out of the "matrix and nursery"[61] of early Christianity.[62] Hedge--and he alone--could even see in the developments of Catholic doctrine a sign that God was with it, his hand providentially guiding it, and his Spirit working even within concepts Hedge could not endorse.[63]

The other phase of Catholic development which the transcendentalists studied was the formation of its outward structure. Some treated of monasticism as the earliest organized form of life within the Church,[64] but their greater interest lay in the growth of the clerical and hierarchical classes.

Ordinarily the transcendentalists adopted the Protestant position on this subject--that the Church did not exist as an organized institution from the beginning.[65] Some contended that it was not part of the original plan for Christianity, that its later growth was only circumstantial. It evolved, for example, only as an answer to the need for a way out of the ignorance, barbarism and anarchy of the fourth and fifth centuries.[66] The form it took was also recognized as a product of the times. They saw the contemporary influence of Roman imperial organization upon its hierarchical structure, and the consolidation of temporal power as a result of the iconoclast controversy. Its influence burgeoned as a result of its control over, and support by, the monastic system, and later as a consequence of its missionary activity, especially in the New World.[67]

Above all, the transcendentalists observed that as the Church increased in strength, it gained in ambition and in its often learned and/or forceful appeals to the masses of ignorant men. The institutional Church, which in the beginning had been a social necessity, now seemed a vast, potent enterprise. Individually the Church leaders grew in the splendor and corruption of their lives and the extent of their authority. Their influence assured, they claimed arbitrary sway over the minds and consciences of men and over the government of entire nations.[68] What is more, the transcendentalists judged that as "religion" became a full-time profession among monks and clergy, the true Christian message became submerged. The simple moral living proclaimed by the gospel was relegated to the realm of unimportance. In its place, "new" concepts of virtue, holiness and genuinely exalted religion were separated from the masses of men and became the preserve of a spiritual elite. These spiritual leaders in turn imposed rigid doctrines and forms upon the rest of men.[69] Thenceforward the Catholic Church set itself up as the final arbiter in all matters spiritual and temporal. Once this theocracy was established, the transcendentalists could see nothing more in it than a final usurpation of the arrogant despotism which that same Church had once wrested from imperial Rome.[70]

THE CATHOLIC CHURCH IN ITS PRIME

These harsh judgments which the transcendentalists passed upon the development of the Church in the past were entirely in keeping with their anti-institutional bias. At the same time, however, they acknowledged that there was another side of the coin. Although they had little positive respect for the contemporary authority of the Catholic Church, they did perceive that its authoritative position in the past had had certain beneficial results. As Parker expressed it, by the high middle ages the Catholic Church had become "the Organized Religion of the civilized world, a new force in it both for good and evil,...."[71] Since the transcendentalists were in the habit of searching out the good in all religions, they set out to do justice in a particular way to the Church whose legacy they equated with the legacy of the entire middle ages. "Has it been utterly evil, and done no good for a thousand and half of years?" Bartol asked. "With all its corruption," Hedge reminded his readers, "there must be some sterling excellence in such a Church. There must be a good deal of truth and a good deal of virtue at the bottom of such success."[72]

Most of the transcendentalists approached the search for positive elements in the medieval Church with a little more optimisim than Parker displayed in his mildly condescending remark: "It was the best thing men had in those days: let us not grumble. Man is honest always, and does the best he knows how."[73] As a kind of basis for their discussion, they all agreed that the Catholic Church was the most powerful organization of the period. One attributes this position to its intense ecclesiastical consciousness, its sense of divine mission.[74] Others account for its remarkable power by reason of its highly disciplined and efficient hierarchical organization.[75] Still others place its vast influence in the individuals who exercised an unexampled leadership throughout the centuries of its glory--Ambrose, Gregory the Great, Leo the Great, Urban II, Bernard, Innocent III, and others.[76]

The contributions of such a Church the transcendentalists willingly conceded to be manifold. It brought order and peace to a continent troubled by the barbarian incursions.[77] It introduced unity and brotherhood to a society that had disintegrated after the collapse of Rome and the havoc wrought by the invaders.[78] It stayed the hand of the barbarian, feudal, or imperial despot, who would exploit the helpless and wreak injustice upon the poor.[79] It opened the way for rich and poor alike to advance with equal opportunity in the kingdom of God on earth.[80] In this way it became the seedbed of freedom and equality of rights for all, showing as it did the mighty of this earth that "there was something in the world higher than kings,...."[81] It contributed monasteries as

"Christian democracies," and the mendicant orders as "democrats in religion."[82] It offered in the works of mercy of all its religious orders compassion, hope and charity on an extensive scale to the poor, the needy and the helpless.[83]

If mercy, justice, and democracy were the medieval Church's contributions to the lowly, it had something too for the well-born. By its promotion of chivalry, no less than by its devotion to the Virgin Mary, it brought an enormous civilizing influence to the rough and powerful upper classes, and it won respect for woman and amelioration of her state.[84]

On the level of personal morality and holiness, the transcendentalists recognized some of their deeply cherished values among the most significant contributions of the medieval Church. Over and above the practical love of one's fellow man, the Church during that period had intensified the religious sentiment that they themselves held foremost--love of God and its manifestation in piety and faith.[85] By the Church's prayerful and sacramental care of every aspect of man's life,[86] by its insistent moral teaching and the example of its saints,[87] the Catholic Church added to the sum total of human goodness in the world. Thereby was that world brought closer to God and to its divinely appointed end of perfection. Everything, from the fervor of the Crusades[88] to the extremes of asceticism which, as we have seen, the transcendentalists rebuked--all gave signs of an age vibrant with zeal for the cause of God and holiness of life.

To these civilizing, moralizing, and spiritualizing aspects of the medieval Church, the transcendentalists added its numerous cultural contributions. All that was said above in Chapter IV on their appreciation of the literature, architecture, and music of the Catholic Church bears witness to their lively appreciation of the Catholic medieval genius. Moreover, some of them also noted that other arts of a civilization on the march were introduced in the Catholic age. Especially significant were the agricultural and scientific advances introduced by the monasteries, and mechanical devices such as the printing press, maritime instruments, and so on. All these advantages of a higher civilization were brought about by men whose powers of mind and body had been released by the Church from servility, and whose remarkable spiritual energies were freed to work for the good of the race.[89]

The lofty intellectual development of the middle ages was another area which impressed the transcendentalists. A few could at times value the celibate and dedicated state as one which enabled the monks to emancipate themselves from familial and worldly concerns and devote their full time to the love of God and man. Therefore did the monasteries and other religious centers turn into places of wealth and prestige. But more importantly they became nuclei for the preservation of ancient wisdom--whether religious or profane--and for the education and enlightenment of a world shrouded in the night of barbarism, ignorance, or feudal tyranny.[90]

In all these ways the Church's rich diversity proclaimed the "everlasting Gospel" of human progress and laid the foundation of modern civilization.[91] "What other age," asked Hedge, "has given so freely and so well?"[92] In grandiloquent prose William Henry Channing recapitulated the transcendental view of the entire complex of the Church's contribution to the world:

> Truly, the Church has been a quickening centre of modern civilization, a fountain of law and art, of manners and policy....Beautiful have been its abbeys in lonely solitudes, clearing the forests, smoothing the mountains, nurseries of agricultural skill amidst the desolating wars of barbarous ages, sanctuaries for the suffering. Beautiful its learned cloisters, with students' lamps shining late in the dark night as a beacon to wandering pilgrims, to merchants with loaded trains, to homeless exiles--their silent bands of high-browed, pallid scholars, watching the form of science in the tomb of ignorance where she lay entranced. Beautiful its peaceful armies of charity, subduing evil with works of love in the crowded alleys and dens of cities, amid the pestilences of disease and the fouler pestilence of crime, and carrying the sign of sacrifice through nations more barren of virtues than the deserts which harbored them.[93]

DECLINE OF THE CATHOLIC CHURCH

But civilization owes permanence to no form, however valuable. "Doomed by the divine law of progress to sure extinction," Clarke reasoned,[94] the Church must be on its way. Having accomplished its mission, it must go thence to die or to remain as an encumbrance of the earth. In keeping with this law, the Catholic Church first fell prey to some of the very errors it had supplanted, finally rendering itself ineffectual. Furthermore, by the end of the middle ages, the civil state had attained to as much learning and humanity as the Church. The state, in fact, seemed to the transcendentalists to have become more Christian than the Church, and the Church's ideal being thereby realized, it had now to step aside.[95] Its function passed on to newer hands, hands prepared by itself and as worthy to perform the task as the Catholic Church had been in the beginning.[96] As Hedge phrased it, during the ascendancy of the Catholic Church, "religion had but entered into its chrysalis, to prepare for a new and glorious liberty."[97]

In what did the errors that caused the decay of the Church consist, in the minds of the transcendentalists? Their opinion was that there were many of these errors, but all can be subsumed under the title of "absolutism," a concept entirely repugnant to their spirit of individualism. Their complaints against the Church under this head are almost without relief, though often following closely upon panegyrics to the glory of its medieval period. On this subject, Emerson and Parker reverse the positions they usually occupy. It is Emerson who has the most biting commentary on the late medieval Church's "unprincipled usurpation of the dearest rights of men." Parker's sharpest remark on the medieval Church, on the other hand, was relatively mild: "There was a time when the Spirit of Freedom dared not enter the domain of Theology. The Priest uttered the Anethema:

HE THAT DOUBTETH IS DAMNED, and Freedom fled away."[98]

This apparent restriction upon freedom in the high and late middle ages was what the transcendentalists most resented in the medieval Church, as in the contemporary one. In a minor way a careful scholar like Osgood was willing at least to admit that "some freedom of inquiry" had remained in the medieval Church.[99] But more often his colleagues selected as their heroes of the later middle ages thinkers who deviated most notably from the Church's basic beliefs--Abelard, Arnold of Brescia, Savonarola, Galileo.[100] The struggles of these men with the official Church Hedge commended as a "coalition of reason with faith in the war against authority."[101] With the exception of some of Thomas Aquinas, Anselm, and Bonaventure, the transcendentalists did not examime the large body of opinion expressed in the writings of any of the other brilliant figures of the high middle ages--John of Salisbury, Peter Lombard, the School of St. Victor, to name a few. They simply selected the challengers and concluded from these more notorious instances that the main problem of the medieval Church was its fear of learning and its objection to reason and free thought.[102]

With more justice, the transcendentalists also attacked the medieval Church for its approach to heresy. They lamented that the means used by it to stamp out "opinion" were the very same that had been used against itself in the early days of Christianity--force and persecution.[103]

As a result of this emphasis on individual freedom, we find the transcendentalists saying very little about the more immediate events leading up to the next phase of religious history--the Protestant Reformation. A few quips about "monk Tetzel" and "his indulgences" are about all they offer on the sequence of events.[104] Their primary interest in the Reformation lay in their interpretation of its meaning for personal freedom. In a few instances it was a question of freedom of conscience or religious liberty.[105] But in most cases their stress was on the Reformation as a harbinger of intellectual freedom, in whatever way this was expressed, as a liberation of the mind, or as a victory for reason, opinion or judgment.[106] With a more marked transcendental thrust, some of them expanded on the movement as the triumph of human rights, and the period when the individual came into his own.[107] Perhaps their most characteristic conception of the Reformation, however, was as a return to "personal experience."[108] They cautiously explained that this was not Luther's original intent, that his was only a revolt against "papal errors" and "priestcraft."[109] But since Luther had initiated this period, he remained a hero to every transcendentalist who attempted to comment upon the man himself.[110] The other reformers too were providential men, loyal to the God in their breast, not to the Church which the transcendentalists had so lately been extolling.

More important, however, than the immediate events of the persons involved, were the ultimate results of the great wave for which Luther was responsible. For Luther "shook the power of Rome, when Rome ruled the world." In an effusion of glowing optimism, the transcendentalists depicted the Reformation as the eruption of a new and living force into the world.[111] In sum, it was a force that paved the way of progress for religion and morals, for science and learning, and for democratic government, particularly in the United States.

The philosophy or theology of history that placed American democracy as the ultimate benefit of the Reformation was Bancroft's pet theory, one which others occasionally shared with him.[112] In Bancroft's multi-volume and immensely popular History of the United States, he set out to prove the progressivist theory of history as culminating in the formation of the American nation. This country he characterized as embodying the fulness of the concept of freedom of man in the social, religious, and civil domains. Carefully selecting an enormous quantity of facts beginning in pre-colonial times, Bancroft constructed a narrative that ostensibly offered the answer to what he called "the American question." With a penchant for over-simplification, he could put the whole question of his thesis thusly: "Shall the Reformation, developed to the fulness of Free Inquiry, succeed in its protest against the Middle Age?"[113] Hie entire history attempted to prove that it could, that English Protestantism and popular liberty could succeed against France and the Roman Catholic Church. The freedom-loving spirit of the American colonists he depicted as a quest for every human right, those rights which they had learned from their "Protestant" mother country. With a magnificent flourish he portrayed the final blow to the Catholic Church as begun by George Washington at the age of twenty-two, and emerging thence to engage all of Europe in the contest:

> There, in a Western forest, began the battle which was to banish from the soul and neighborhood of our republic the institutions of the Middle Age, and to inflict on them fatal wounds throughout the continent of Europe. In repelling France from the basin of the Ohio, Washington broke the repose of mankind, and waked a struggle, which could admit only of a truce, till the ancient bulwarks of Catholic legitimacy were thrown down.[114]

The ultimate consequences of Luther's movement, then, were far-reaching. Hedge epitomized in a few words its vast ramifications:

> The Protestant Reformation which he inaugurated is very imperfectly apprehended if construed solely as a schism in the church, a new departure in religion. In a larger view, it was our modern world, with its social developments, its liberties, its science, its new conditions of being, evolving itself from the old.[115]

As for the Catholic Counter-Reformation that followed close upon the Protestant revolt, the transcendentalists took little note of it. None of them adverted to the possibility of reform from within, with the exception of a nod or two from Clarke and Parker.[116] They do not touch upon it elsewhere except in refutation. Even those who had recognized the power of the doctrinal aspects of the Church to unfold no longer discerned any hint of further growth from within. About the only glance that the transcendentalists gave to the post-Reformation Catholic Church was in the direction of its often "desperate" measures to consolidate its diminished strength. In the Council of Trent, the Thirty Years' War, and especially the formation and operation of the Jesuits, they saw little more than reactionary force and continued corruption. As Brownson put it, "The Church could do nothing but cling to its old pretensions."[117]

The transcendentalists' evaluation of the Jesuits was ordinarily given with the severity typical of their day,[118] but there are several exceptions. Bancroft praises the Jesuits' intelligence and their educative ability. He even defends them for justifying tyrannicide and for holding allegiance to the extranational power of the pope. Both these factors he applauded as favoring the people against a despotic monarch.[119] A few of the transcendentalists also praised the Jesuit and other missionary efforts in New France. While not favoring their dogmatic teachings, those transcendentalists who alluded to them have only the highest encomiums for their courage, integrity, and religious zeal, and for the influence--though temporary--which they exerted over the Indians.[120]

In the main, however, the transcendentalists saw only black reaction in the post-Reformation Catholic Church. They pick at signs of its continuing intolerance of other creeds, and hold these up as typical instances of an on-going policy. In their few comments upon the Church of this period they select only those isolated events which support their theories of its decline--the revocation of the Edict of Nantes; the St. Bartholomew Massacre; the calculating or arbitrary motives and actions of Catholic leaders and allies--Charles II, James II, and above all Philip II and the Spanish conquistadors.[121]

Our group found additional proof for the decline of European Catholicism in the ensuing history of France. Bancroft attributes the corrosion of morals and the eruption of the French Revolution partly to the general decay of its institutions though partly also to the expulsion of the Jesuits. The withdrawal of this order, he claims, left education in a sorry state and led to a general scepticism and eventual atheism. Conversely, other transcendentalists blame

France's tragedy on the "bigotry" and indolence of the Catholic hierarchy.[122]

In general, then, the transcendentalists dismiss the post-Reformation Catholic Church to the ranks of the dead or dying, leaving little doubt as to its impact upon the future. To the new age the Catholic Church would have little to offer. The "childhood of Christianity" was over;[123] the providential mission of the Catholic Church was complete.

THE NEW RELIGIOUS AGE

Once the outmoded forms had been done away with, there still remained a task for religious history to perform. According to the transcendentalists she did not perform it well during the period of Protestantism. When all was said and done, the reformers' only genuine contribution to religion--although a mighty one--was the release of the human spirit from its "bondage to forms" and its "slavery" to papal authority. But Protestantism offered no new religion of the spirit in their stead. In Brownson's opinion, it was not even a religion, only Catholicism in a weakened guise.[124] Nor did it offer any new moral or theological insights.[125] What is more, it did not incorporate within itself the best principles and practices of Catholicism. These elements had instead been indiscriminately rejected by the impetuous zeal of the reformers. Was it not a great loss to have eliminated from the new churches devotion to the saints and the Virgin Mary; to have destroyed Christianity's "covenant" with the arts; and to have repudiated the spirit of renunciation and contemplation characteristic of monasticism?[126] Furthermore, rather than implementing the freedom of spirit that Luther had apparently initiated, Protestantism had only added a new spirit of conformity to creeds and confessions and a new intolerance of dissent.[127] In particular were some of the transcendentalists sensitive to British policies against Catholics on this score in Ireland, Acadia, and Scotland, and on England's own domestic scene.[128]

The transcendentalists had a great deal more to say about Protestantism, which it is not our purpose to discuss here--its practices and beliefs, its history, its current status. Their treatment of it outstrips in length and complexity anything they had to say about Catholicism. This was essential because they themselves were neo-protestants--new protestors against prevailing religious forms, forms which in their day and place were predominantly orthodox Protestant.

Following upon the decline of Protestantism, the transcendentalists' next historical epoch was the age of reason. This was a period that might have issued from the French reaction to the medieval church.[129] But more likely, to keep within their theoretical framework, it was the American reaction to a solemn and rigidified Protestantism. As such, some of them viewed Unitarianism as a definite advance upon Protestantism, since its great object, as was Luther's in another age, was freedom.[130]

Others saw that Unitarianism had had its day. Even its ardent spokesman, Channing, began toward the end of his life to question its vitality.[131] The transcendentalists in their prime of course looked to their own revived form of religion for a better way. But it must be remembered that most of them remained within the Unitarian fold, albeit in its liberal wing. Certainly Emerson could expostulate on Unitarianism's "pale negations" and its position as a cold, intellectual successor to the "self-denying, ardent" Church of the middle ages.[132] But at the same time, other transcendentalists were reflecting upon liberal Unitarianism as a synthesis of much of what was good in the religions of the past. Their dialectical theory of development was again at work. Even Emerson, looking aside from his ahistorical perspective for a moment, called the sum of the Catholic and Protestant ages "a time of seeds and expansions, whereof our recent civilization is the fruit."[133]

But no one seemed sure, and certainly the group had no consensus among themselves nor a large following among others. Clearly the transition to the perfect religion of the future was still in process; the time of utopia had not yet arrived.

What the perfect synthesis of the future religion was to be like in the transcendentalists' opinion remains to be seen. But first it is necessary to bring their considerations of Catholicism up to date. We have seen what they thought of the institutional Church and what they regarded as its place in the past. We shall next examine their commentary on the Catholic Church as they observed it in action in their own day.

NOTES

[1]"The transcendentalist," George W. Cooke asserted, "forgot the past or ignored it" (Cooke, Historical Introduction to the Dial, I, 14). Later historians have perpetuated this erroneous view. Stow Persons' statement is typical: "Unlike other romantics, the transcendentalists were preoccupied with the present and the future rather than with the past" (Persons, American Minds, p. 212). For the same interpretation, see also Robert Clemmer's elaborate discussion of the superiority of the Pennyslvania transcendentalists' historicism over the ahistorical intuitionism of the New England group, in his "Historical Transcendentalism in Pennyslvania," Journal of the History of Ideas, XXX (October-December, 1969), 579-592.

[2]See Edward Emerson, Notes, in Emerson, Works, II, 442.

[3]See Cameron, "History and Biography in Emerson's Unpublished Sermons, p. 113.

[4]Emerson, Works, II, 17.

[5]Emerson, Journal A, 1834, in Emerson, JN, IV, 339. Man reads the tables of history, he remarked elsewhere, not as "ultimate facts, but because they reveal that nature which he has and some of the secret passages of his thought" (Emerson, Early Lectures, II, 182).

[6]Emerson, Journal B, 1835, in Emerson, JN, V, 89.

[7]Emerson, Works, II, 10, 61; ibid., VI, 39; ibid., VIII, 219; Emerson to Chauncy Emerson, August, 1828, in Emerson, Letters, I, 246; Emerson, Journal B, 1835, in Emerson, JN, V, 78; Emerson, Journal D, 1839, in ibid., VII, 211.

[8]Emerson, "Religion," January 19, 1837, in Emerson, Early Lectures, II, 93-94. He had expressed exactly the same thought earlier in his Journal B, March, 1836, in Emerson, JN, V, 145.

[9]See Cabot, Memoir of Emerson, I, 262. See also, among others, Emerson, Journal LM, 1848, in Emerson, JN, X, 307.

[10]A. Robert Caponigri, "Brownson and Emerson," pp. 370-371.

[11]Emerson to Mary Moody Emerson, September 23, 1826, in Emerson, Letters, I, 174-175.
An ahistorical approach to the past, particularly with a view to eliminating historical accretions, may also be seen in Thoreau, Parker, and Alcott.

[12]Emerson, Journals, 1849, VIII, 77-78; Emerson, "George Fox," February 26, 1835, in Emerson, Early Lectures, I, 174; Emerson, "Human Culture," January 31, 1838, in ibid., II, 213; Emerson, Works, X, 217; Emerson, "Thoughts on the Religion of the Middle Ages," passim.

[13]Lewis, American Adam, p. 164.

[14]Bancroft, "Progress of Civilization," pp. 406-407.

[15]In his New Views of Christianity, Society, and the Church. See also Brownson, Book Review of History of the Colonization of the United States by George Bancroft, 2 vols. (Boston, 1841), BoQR, IV (October, 1841), 513; Brownson, "Benjamin Constant on Religion," pp. 63-69; Brownson, "Remarks on Universal History," Democratic Review, XII (June, 1843), 575-586. As a matter of fact, it was the logical extension of the historical dimensions of Christianity that helped lead Brownson into the Catholic Church.

[16]Hedge, "Everett's Phi Beta Kappa Address," CE, XVI (March, 1834), 1-21; Hedge, "The Method of History," NAR, XCI (October, 1870), 311-329.

[17]Hedge, "Everett's Phi Beta Kappa Address," p. 14. The same reference to the middle ages is expressed and expanded in Hedge, "The Churches and the Church," especially pp. 194-197; Hedge, "The Method of History," pp. 313-314.

[18]Follen, "Constant on Religion," American Quarterly Review, XI (March, 1832), 120; Henry, Considerations on Some of the Elements and Conditions of Social Welfare and Human Progress. Being Academic and Occasional Discourses and Other Pieces (New York, 1861), p. 165, hereafter cited as: Henry, Considerations on Human Progress; Judd, The Church, p. 95; Ripley, Introductory Note on Benjamin Constant, in Ripley, ed., Philosophical Miscellanies, II, 284. Parker too accepted Christianity as progressive and providentially ordered, but any attempt to classify its progression scientifically he felt was futile. After summarizing briefly a Roman Catholic philosophy of history, he objected: "To me it savours of arrogance to decide in matters that are too high for me..." (Parker, Journal, 1841, in Weiss, Life of Parker, I, 168).

[19]Otto von Bismarck on Bancroft, in Bismarck to Motley, September 19, 1869, as cited in Otto zu Stolberg-Wernigerode, Germany and the United States of America During the Era of Bismarck (Reading, Pennsylvania, 1937), p. 99, hereafter cited as: Stolberg-Wernigerode, Germany and the United States; Clarke, Ten Great Religions, p. 507; Clarke, "The New Theology," UR, X (October, 1878), 394; Hedge, "The Destinies of Ecclesiastical Religion," p. 12; Hedge, Ways of the Spirit, pp. 63-64; Hedge, Martin Luther and Other Essays, p. 185; Parker, Autobiography, p. 299; Parker, Journal, 1841, in Weiss, Life of Parker, I, 167; Brownson, "Mr. Emerson's Address," BoQR, I (October, 1838), 510-511; Brownson, "Philosophy of History," p. 419; Brownson, New Views, passim; W.H. Channing, "The Middle Class," SA, I (September 15, 1849), 171; W.H. Channing, "Christian Church and Social Reform," as cited in Brownson, "Channing on the Church," p. 169; Bartol, Word of the Spirit, pp. 65-66; Bartol, Church and Congregation, pp. 109, 112-113.

[20]Hedge, "Method of History," pp. 326, 329; Hedge to Bellows, April 22, 1856, in Wells, Three Christian Transcendentalists, p. 214; Hedge, "Ecclesiastical Christendom," pp. 128-130; Hedge, Leaven of the Word, p. 4; Clarke, Essentials, p. 37; Clarke, Ten Great Religions, p. 507; Channing, "Letter on Catholicism," p. 272; Furness, Power of Spirit, p. 97; Parker, Theism, pp. 126-130, 370; Brownson, Charles Elwood, p. 232; Brownson, "Leroux on Humanity," pp. 104-105; W.H. Channing, "New Church," p. 72; W. H. Channing, "Christian Church and Social Reform," as cited in Brownson, "Channing on the Church," p. 171.

[21]See Parker, Transient and Permanent, pp. 1-39, for his most thorough exposition of this theory.

[22]Bancroft, "Progress of Civilization," p. 407; Clarke, "Orestes A. Brownson's Argument for the Roman Church," pp. 231-232; Clarke, The Well-Instructed Scribe, or Reform and Conservatism, as cited in Brownson, "Reform and Conservatism," BoQR, January, 1842, in Brownson, Works, IV, 79. As Hedge put it, the Christian Church is a schoolmaster, and "the different forms of that Church are successive schoolmasters, to bring men to the true Christ--the wisdom and the power of God" (Hedge, "The Churches and the Church," p. 196. See also his "Destinies of Ecclesiastical Religion," where he calls "ecclesiastical continuity" the "method" of history [p. 8, and the entire article]).

[23]Emerson, "Natural Religion Universal and Sympathetic," p. 385; Parker, Discourse of Religion, p. 70; Alcott, Table-Talk (Boston, 1877), p. 99.

[24]Clarke, "Right Seed," p. 388.

[25]Parker, Discourse of Religion, pp. 39-51; Brownson, "Benjamin Constant on Religion," p. 66; Hedge, "Philosophy of Fetishism," pp. 194-197.

Source citations in notes 25 through 33 are to all these specifically as stages. On each of the stages the transcendentalists have innumerable other discussions that are not cited here.

[26]Parker, Discourse of Religion, pp. 51-80; Parker, Theism, pp. 126, 370; Parker, American Scholar, p. 390; Brownson, "Benjamin Constant on Religion," p. 66; Brownson, New Views, p. 17; Brownson, Charles Elwood, p. 232.

[27]Parker, Discourse of Religion, pp. 80-90; Parker, Theism, p. 370; Clarke, Orthodoxy, p. 3; Clarke, "New Theology," p. 394; Brownson, "Philosophy of History," p. 410; Brownson, Charles Elwood, p. 232; Hedge, "The Cause of Reason the Cause of Faith," p. 226.

[28]Parker, Theism, p. 370; Parker, Discourse of Religion, p. 366; Clarke, "New Theology," pp. 394, 402; W.H. Channing, "New Church," p. 72; W.H. Channing, "Christian Church and Social Reform," as cited in Brownson, "Channing on the Church," p. 169; Osgood, "Christian Ethics," XXIX, 164-167; Hedge, "Method of History," p. 312; Brownson, "Benjamin Constant on Religion," p. 66.
The transcendentalists identified their own roots more in this period than in any other.

[29]Osgood, "Christian Ethics," XXIX, 168-174; Clarke, "Ancient Christianity and the Oxford Tracts," WM, VIII (July, 1840), 136; Clarke, Orthodoxy, pp. 3, 334; Clarke, Steps of Belief, passim; Clarke, Essentials, p. 37; Clarke, "New Theology," pp. 394, 402; Parker, American Scholar, p. 390; Parker, Theism, pp. 126-127, 370; Parker, Journal, 1841, in Weiss, Life of Parker, I, 167; W.H. Channing, "New Church," p. 72; W.H. Channing, "Middle Class," p. 171; W.H. Channing, "Christian Church and Social Reform," as cited in Brownson, "Channing on the Church," p. 170; Hedge, "Method of History," p. 313; Hedge, Martin Luther and Other Essays, p. 158; Brownson, New Views, pp. 5, 16-17; Brownson, Charles Elwood, p. 232; Cranch, "Divine Authority," UR, XII (November, 1879), 477; Channing, "Letter on Catholicism," p. 272.

[30]Hedge, Martin Luther and Other Essays, p. 158; W.H. Channing, "Christian Church and Social Reform," as cited in Brownson, "Channing on the Church," p. 170; W.H. Channing, "New Church," p. 73; Clarke, "New Theology," p. 394; Clarke, "Right Seed," p. 388; Clarke, Orthodoxy, p. 3; Clarke, Steps of Belief, passim; Clarke, Vexed Questions, p. 55; Clarke, "Polemics and Irenics," pp. 170-174; Clarke, Essentials, p. 37; Clarke, "On the Positive Doctrines of Christianity," MJAUA, V (February, 1864), 51; Brownson, New Views, pp. 17, 22; Brownson, Charles Elwood, p. 232; Parker, American Scholar, p. 390; Parker, Theism, pp. 126-127, 370; Osgood, "Christian Ethics," XXIX, 164; Hecker to Brownson, September 6, 1843, in Henry F. Brownson, Orestes A. Brownson's Early Life, p. 337; Bancroft, History of the United States, passim; Cranch, "Divine Authority," p. 477; Channing, "Letter on Catholicism," p. 272.

[31]Channing, "Letter on Catholicism," pp. 271-273; W.H. Channing, "New Church," p. 73; W. H. Channing, "Christian Church and Social Reform," as cited in Brownson, "Channing on the Church," p. 172; Clarke, Steps of Belief, p. 274; Clarke, "Polemics and Irenics," p. 178; Cranch, "Divine Authority," p. 477; Hedge, Martin Luther and Other Essays, pp. 297-298, 311.

[32]W.H. Channing, "New Church," pp. 73-74; Clarke, "Orestes A. Brownson's Argument for the Roman Church," p. 247; Clarke, "Polemics and Irenics," p. 181; Clarke, "New Theology," p. 394; Clarke, "On the Positive Doctrines of Christianity," p. 52; Parker, Transient and Permanent, passim; Parker, Journal, 1841, in Weiss, Life of Parker, I, 168; Bartol, Word of the Spirit, p. 65; Hedge, Martin Luther and Other Essays, p. 158.
All of the transcendentalists at one time or another thought of transcendentalism as the true religion of the spirit, but not all placed it necessarily within an historically evolving context.

[33]Hedge, "Destinies of Ecclesiastical Religion," pp. 12-13; Hedge, "The Cause of Reason the Cause of Faith," p. 226; Brownson, "Benjamin Constant on Religion," p. 69; Cranch, "Divine Authority," pp. 477-478; Brooks, Simplicity of Christ's Teachings, p. 70.

[34]Clarke, "Right Seed," p. 388. See also Clarke, "New Theology," pp. 400-402; Brownson, Charles Elwood, p. 232; Cranch, "Divine Authority," p. 377; Bancroft, History of the United States, as cited in Levin, History as Romantic Art, p. 271; Hedge, "Christianity in Conflict with Hellenism," p. 22.

[35]Clarke, "New Theology," p. 394; Clarke, "Polemics and Irenics," pp. 169-184; Clarke, Orthodoxy, p. 3; Brownson, "Reform and Conservatism," p. 86; Brownson, New Views, passim; Hedge, "Method of History," p. 329 and passim.

[36]Osgood, "Christian Ethics," XXIX, 164, 168-174; Parker, Theism, p. 370; W.H. Channing, "Christian Church and Social Reform," as cited in Brownson, "Channing on the Church," pp. 169-170; W.H. Channing, "New Church," p. 72; Clarke, "New Theology," p. 402.

[37]Clarke, Ten Great Religions, p. 251; Hedge, Reason in Religion, pp. 322-323.

[38]Clarke, "Open Questions in Theology," CE, LXXX (January, 1866), 83-84; Clarke, Ten Great Religions, p. 312; Hedge, "The Cause of Reason the Cause of Faith," pp. 206-207.

[39]Brownson, Charles Elwood, p. 232; W.H. Channing, "Christian Church and Social Reform," as cited in Brownson, "Channing on the Church," p. 170.

[40]Hedge and Osgood were aware that the Catholic Church had not accepted the total concept of the Augustinian doctrine of sin and grace, at least as that doctrine had been canonized by Calvinism (Osgood, Studies in Christian Biography, p. 33; Hedge, "Life of St. Augustine," pp. 225, 238).

[41]Clarke, Essentials, pp. 20, 23; Clarke, Events and Epochs, pp. 138-141; Clarke, Christian Doctrine of Forgiveness, pp. 162-163; Clarke, "Open Questions in Theology," p. 84; Cranch, "Pelagian Controversy," WM, VI (April, 1839), 395; Hedge, "Method of History," pp. 302-303; Hedge, "Life of St. Augustine," pp. 225, 236 and passim; Hedge, Reason in Religion, p. 22; Brownson, "Leroux on Humanity," pp. 101, 103-105; Osgood, God with Men, p. 256; Osgood, Studies in Christian Biography, pp. 22, 26. Though unable to accept Augustine's teachings, Osgood, in particular, wrote warmly of his brilliance and his influence (see the two chapters on Augustine in his Studies in Christian Biography, pp. 1-65).

[42]References are too numerous to cite here. A few examples will suffice: Clarke, A Sketch of the History of the Doctrine of Atonement (Boston, 1845), pp. 7-9, hereafter cited as: Clarke, Sketch of Atonement; Clarke, "Open Questions in Theology," pp. 83-84; Osgood, Studies in Christian Biography, passim; Osgood, "St. Ambrose," passim; Hedge, "Life of St. Augustine," passim; Hedge, "Shedd's History of Christian Doctrine," pp. 571-573; Hedge, Ways of the Spirit, passim; Hedge, "Allen's 'Christian History,' a Review of Joseph H. Allen, Christian History in Its Three Great Periods (Boston, 1883)," UR, XXI (April, 1884), 339-343; Hedge, "Doctrine of Endless Punishment," pp. 115-118; Parker, Discourse of Religion, passim; Parker, Transient and Permanent, passim; Ripley, Letters on Infidelity, First Letter, pp. 51-52.

[43]Osgood praised Chrysostom's "exuberant fancy and liberal creed" (Osgood, Studies in Christian Biography, p. 82. See also Parker to Rev. S.J. May, November, 1851, in Weiss, Life of Parker, I, 321; Judd, The Church, p. 2).

[44]See Osgood's two chapters on Jerome in his Studies in Christian Biography, pp. 91-124. Hedge expressed "great respect" for Jerome (Hedge to Convers Francis, January 26, 1842, in Wells, Three Christian Transcendentalists, p. 203), and Osgood acknowledge that Jerome was the most learned man of his day (Osgood, Studies in Christian Biography, p. 94), applauding especially his work on the New Testament (ibid., pp. 110, 125-126).

[45]Hedge, "Life of St. Augustine," p. 225.

[46]Hedge, "Method of History," p. 312; Osgood, "The Church of the First Three Centuries," CE, LV (November, 1853), 373.

[47]Osgood, "Church of the First Three Centuries," p. 370; Hedge, "The Two Religions," CE, LXVI (January, 1859), 89-112; Hedge, Ways of the Spirit, pp. 86-87;

Clarke, Ten Great Religions, pp. 350-354.

[48]Clarke, Ten Great Religions, pp. 351-353; Clarke, Christian Doctrine of Forgiveness, p. 107; Clarke, Sketch of Atonement, pp. 5-6.

[49]Parker has nothing but praise for the treasures bequeathed from the Greek mind (Parker, "Matter's History of Gnosticism," CE, XXIV [March, 1838], 115-116). See also Osgood, "Church of the First Three Centuries," p. 370.

[50]Clarke, Ten Great Religions, p. 256.

[51]Osgood, "Christian Ethics," XXIX, 166; Hedge, "The Two Religions," pp. 100-103; Clarke, Orthodoxy, p. 372; Parker to Rev. Joseph H. Allen, October 29, 1849, in Weiss, Life of Parker, II, 379.

In this connection Hedge has an elaborate discussion of "two religions"--religions discerned not according to lines of sect, but according to their legal or liberal philosophical tendencies. He sees as a result of the western and eastern streams "a dual Christianity...the rigid and the fluid of Christian faith" (Hedge, "The Two Religions," pp. 89-112).

Hedge always liked to discover a dualism or a dialectical conflict and resolution wherever he could. His writings on church history display such a tendency in his comments upon Latin and Greek, Augustine and Pelagius, Dominic and Francis, Calvin and Arminius, the Pope and the Albigensians.

[52]Osgood, Studies in Christian Biography, pp. 8-9, 131; Osgood, "Church of the First Three Centuries," p. 374; Parker, Transient and Permanent, pp. 191, 194; Parker, Journal, 1841, in Weiss, Life of Parker, I, 168; Hedge, "Shedd's History of Christian Doctrine," pp. 573-576; Hedge, "Christianity in Conflict with Hellensim," p. 19; Hedge, Ways of the Spirit, p. 146; Hedge, Reason in Religion, pp. 236-239; Hedge, "Christian Worship," p. 467; Hedge, "Allen's 'Christian History,'" p. 340; W.D. Wilson, "The Unitarian Movement in New England," The Dial, I (April, 1841), 414; Bartol, "Emerson's Religion," p. 115; Judd, Birthright Church, p. 15; Ripley, Doctrines of Trinity and Transubstantiation, p. 11.

[53]See for example Hedge, "Shedd's History of Christian Doctrine," pp. 574-576; Hedge, Reason in Religion, pp. 236-241; Hedge, "Christian Worship," pp. 466-467; W.D. Wilson, "Unitarian Movement in New England," p. 414; Parker, Transient and Permanent, p. 194. See also Chapter III above.

[54]Osgood, "Church of the First Three Centuries," p. 374.

[55]Hedge, Leaven of the Word, p. 4; Hedge, Ways of the Spirit, pp. 63-77. Parker is the only other transcendentalist who refers to the Councils with derision. He wonders if anyone could ask for "a completer history of human folly and bigotry" (Parker, "Hollis Street Council," The Dial, III [October, 1842], 202-203).

[56]Hedge, Ways of the Spirit, pp. 76-77. See his discussion of free will and providence in "Method of History," pp. 315-317.

[57]Ripley, Doctrines of Trinity and Transubstantiation, p. 10; Hedge, Introduction to Essays and Reviews by Eminent English Churchmen, 3rd American ed. With an Appendix and a New Introduction Written Expressly for This Edition by Frederic Henry Hedge (New York, 1874), p. x, hereafter cited as: Hedge, ed., Essays and Reviews; Hedge, "Shedd's History of Christian Doctrine," p. 571; Hedge, Reason in Religion, p. 310; Hedge, "The Two Religions," pp. 93-94; Hedge, Ways of the Spirit, p. 72; Hedge, "Romanism in Its Worship," p. 240; Clarke, Events and Epochs, passim; Clarke, Sketch of Atonement, pp. 10-15; Clarke, "Inspiration of the New Testament," p. 161; Osgood, "Christian Ethics," XXIX, 170-173; Osgood, God with Men, p. 256; Brownson, The Scholar's Mission, 1843, in Brownson, Works, XIX, 73; Brownson, "Church Question," p.472; Parker to Rev. S.J. May, November, 1851, in Weiss, Life of Parker, I, 321; Parker, Ten Sermons, p. 174.

[58]See for example Emerson, Notebook No. XVIII, 1821, in Emerson, JN, I, 253; Hedge, "The Cause of Reason the Cause of Faith," pp. 206-208; Hedge, "Shedd's History of Christian Doctrine," p. 570; Hedge, Reason in Religion, p. 342; Osgood, Studies in Christian Biography, pp. 58, 134; Osgood, "St. Ambrose," pp. 420-423;

Furness, Veil Partly Lifted, pp. 245-246; Parker, Discourse of Religion, p. 362; Parker, Theism, pp. 130-133; Parker, Transient and Permanent, p. 194.

[59]Parker, Discourse of Religion, p. 376; Parker, World of Matter and Spirit, p. 146.

[60]Parker, Discourse of Religion, p. 362; Parker, World of Matter and Spirit, p. 146; Parker, The Philosophical Idea of God and Its Relation to the Scientific and Religious Wants of Mankind Now, 1858, in American Philosophic Addresses, 1700-1900, ed. Joseph Leon Blau (New York, 1946), pp. 667-668; Parker, Transient and Permanent, pp. 18-19; Parker, St. Bernard and Other Papers, p. 200; Parker, "Hennell on the Origin of Christianity," pp. 160-161; Parker, Journal, 1841, in Weiss, Life of Parker, I, 168; Emerson, Journals, 1854, VIII, 495; Emerson, Notebook No. XVIII, 1821, in Emerson, JN, I, 258-259; Emerson, Journal, 1826-1828, in ibid., 48; Emerson, "Thoughts on the Religion of the Middle Ages," p. 402. See also Cranch, "A Sign from the West," The Dial, I (October, 1840), 164; Furness, Power of Spirit, pp. 97-98; Channing, Works, Complete Edition, p. 997; Brooks, "Revelation of St. John," p. 393; Brooks, "Hedge's Reason in Religion," NAR, CI (July, 1865), 291.

[61]Hedge, "Christianity in Conflict with Hellenism," p. 22.

[62]See for example Clarke, Sketch of Atonement, p. 28; Clarke, "Ancient Christianity and the Oxford Tracts," p. 136; W.H. Channing, "New Church," pp. 72-73; Hedge, "The Churches and the Church," p. 196; Furness, Veil Partly Lifted, pp. 245-246; Osgood, Studies in Christian Biography, pp. 46-47; Henry, Endless Future of the Human Race, p. 22.

[63]Hedge, "Christianity in Conflict with Hellenism," pp. 14-15; Hedge, "Life of St. Augustine," p. 229; Hedge, Ways of the Spirit, pp. 76-77; Hedge, "Method of History," pp. 316-317; Hedge, "The Churches and the Church," pp. 196-197.

[64]Clarke, Events and Epochs, pp. 82-122; Osgood, Studies in Christian Biography, pp. 112-113, 121, 138; Hedge, "Historic Atonement," p. 110; Hedge, Ways of the Spirit, p. 109; Parker, Discourse of Religion, pp. 360, 379-380.

[65]Henry disagrees (Henry, Notes on General History by Guizot, p. 51).

[66]Brownson, "Benjamin Constant on Religion," pp. 68-69; Brownson, "Laboring Classes," p. 443; Emerson, "Thoughts on the Religion of the Middle Ages," p. 404; Clarke, Ten Great Religions, pp. 350-351; Bancroft, History of the United States (Boston, 1874), X, 63; Parker, Discourse of Religion, p. 378.

[67]Hedge, "Romanism in Its Worship," pp. 228, 238-239; Clarke, Ten Great Religions, p. 350; Osgood, Studies in Christian Biography, p. 138; Bancroft, History of the United States, X, 63.

[68]Emerson, "Thoughts on the Religion of the Middle Ages," p. 404; Emerson, Notebook XVIII, 1822, in Emerson, JN, I, 310-311; Emerson, Wide World 7, 1822, in ibid., II, 12, 17; Emerson, "The True Priesthood," Sermon 171, in Cameron, Index-Concordance to Emerson's Sermons, II, 667; Parker, Discourse of Religion, pp. 268, 357-358, 386-389; Parker, St. Bernard and Other Papers, pp. 318-319; W.H. Channing, "Christian Church and Social Reform," as cited in Brownson, "Channing on the Church," p. 170; Channing, A Discourse on Some of the Distinguishing Opinions of Unitarians, Delivered at Baltimore in 1819, 12th ed. (Boston, 1836), 46; Judd, Margaret, II, 32; Clarke, Orthodoxy, p. 334; Osgood, "Christian Ethics," XXIX, 165-167; Osgood, Studies in Christian Biography, p. 100; Henry, Notes on General History by Guizot, pp. 51, 120; Bancroft, History of the United States, X, 68-73; Hedge, "Historic Atonement," p. 110; Brownson, New Views, p. 15; Brownson, Charles Elwood, p. 250.

[69]Osgood, Studies in Christian Biography, pp. 138-139; Osgood, "Christian Ethics," XXIX, 165-169; Osgood, "St. Ambrose," p. 426; Hedge, "Historic Atonement," pp. 110-111; Parker, Discourse of Religion, p. 364; Clarke, Ten Great Religions, p. 506.

[70]Emerson, Notebook XVIII, 1822, in Emerson, JN, I, 308-311; Osgood, Studies in Christian Biography, p. 53; W.H. Channing, "Christian Church and Social Reform," as cited in Brownson, "Channing on the Church," p. 170; Bancroft, History of the United States, X, 69-73; Clarke, "New Theology," p. 402; Parker, Discourse of Religion, p. 369; Parker, Autobiography, p. 403; Hedge, "Christianity in Conflict with Hellenism," pp. 19-20; Hedge, Presidential Remarks, 36th American Unitarian Association Convention, Boston, May 28, 1861, MJAUA, II (July, 1861), 299; Brownson, An Oration Before the Democracy of Worcester and Vicinity, Delivered at Worcester, Massachusetts, July 4, 1840 (Boston, 1840), p. 10.

[71]Parker, Autobiography, p. 403.

[72]Bartol, Religion in Our Public Schools: A Discourse Preached in the West Church, Boston (Boston, 1859), p. 23n; Hedge, "Ecclesiastical Christendom," pp. 120-121; W.H. Channing, "The Judgment of Christendom," SA, I (October 27, 1849), 265.

The transcendentalists were rarely willing to use the expression, "dark ages," and then only qualifiedly. "In modern Europe," commented Emerson, "the Middle Ages were called the Dark Ages. Who dares to call them so now?" (Emerson, Works, VIII, 214). And Hedge wrote: "In the dark ages, emphatically so called, more was done for society than during the whole period of ancient history" (Hedge, "Everett's Phi Beta Kappa Address," p. 10. Hedge elaborates this thesis on pp. 10-15). See also Henry, Notes on General History by Guizot, p. 144; Osgood, Hearth-Stone, pp. 50-51.

[73]Parker, St. Bernard and Other Papers, p. 320.

[74]Hedge, "The Two Religions," pp. 105-106; Hedge, "Ecclesiastical Christendom," pp. 121-122.

[75]Osgood, God with Men, p. 56; Clarke, Ten Great Religions, pp. 29, 395; Clarke, "The Church,--As It Was, As It Is, As It Ought To Be," hereafter cited as: Clarke, "The Church,--As It Was," as cited in Brownson, "The Church As It Was," p. 184.

[76]Osgood, God with Men, pp. 55-56; Osgood, "St. Ambrose," passim; Brownson, Scholar's Mission, p. 73; Clarke, Christian Doctrine of Prayer, p. ix; Clarke, Events and Epochs, pp. 164-166; Parker, "Life of St. Bernard," passim; Parker, American Scholar, p. 134; Parker, Transient and Permanent, p. 324; Bancroft, Literary Miscellanies, pp. 23-24; Hedge, "Allen's 'Christian History,'" pp. 340-342; Hedge, "The Churches and the Church," p. 197; Hedge, "Ecclesiastical Christendom," pp. 122-123. See also other references to these leaders, above, passim.

[77]Clarke, Essentials, p. 37; Clarke, "New Theology," p. 402; Parker, Theism, p. 16; Hedge, "Allen's 'Christian History,'" pp. 340-342; Bancroft, History of the United States, X, 63; Brownson, Charles Elwood, p. 232; Brownson, "Church of the Future," p. 67; Osgood, Studies in Christian Biography, pp. 46-47; Henry, Notes on General History by Guizot, p. 136.

[78]Clarke, Essentials, p. 37; Clarke, Ten Great Religions, pp. 29, 350, 354, 391; Bancroft, History of the United States, X, 63-64; Hedge, "The Churches and the Church," p. 197; Brownson, New Views, p. 15; Channing, Sermon, 1825, as cited in Peabody, Reminiscences of Channing, p. 181.

[79]Emerson, "War," Aesthetic Papers, May, 1849, p. 40; Hedge, "The Churches and the Church," pp. 197-198; Hedge, Leaven of the Word, p. 13; Osgood, "St. Ambrose," pp. 422, 434; Clarke, "The Church,--As It Was," as cited in Brownson, "The Church As It Was," p. 185; Clarke, Ten Great Religions, p. 392; Clarke, Steps of Belief, p. 248; Brownson, "Church of the Future," pp. 66-68; Brownson, "Origin and Growth of Government," p. 348; Brownson, "Present State of Society," p. 442; Whittier, "The Men of Old," p. 97; Bartol, Church and Congregation, p. 21; Bancroft, History of the United States, I, 163; ibid., II, 257; ibid., V, 34; ibid., X, 69-75; Bancroft, "Progress of Civilization," p. 397; Parker, "Life of St. Bernard," p. 9; Parker, Autobiography, p. 42; Parker, Ten Sermons, p. 320; Parker,

Discourse of Religion, p. 384; Channing, _Works_, Complete Edition, p. 997; Channing, "On Fenelon," p. 180; Henry, _Considerations on Human Progress_, pp. 373-374; Francis, _Popery_, p. 19n.

[80]Parker, _Discourse of Religion_, pp. 381-382;Parker, "Life of St. Bernard," p. 9; Henry, _Considerations on Human Progress_, p. 374; Bancroft, "Progress of Civilization," p. 397; Brownson, "Church of the Future," pp. 67-68; Osgood, _The Coming Church_, p. 16; Brownson, Literary Notice of _Life of Cardinal Cheverus_ by Huen-Dubourg, p. 388.

[81]Clarke, _Orthodoxy_, p. 334. See also Osgood, _Studies in Christian Biography_, p. 47.

[82]Henry, _Consideration on Human Progress_, p. 374; Clarke, _Events and Epochs_, p. 98.

[83]Channing, Sermon, 1825, as cited in Peabody, _Reminiscences of Channing_, p. 181; Osgood, _Hearth-Stone_, p. 123; Osgood, _Studies in Christian Biography_, pp. 183-184; Hedge, "Everett's Phi Beta Kappa Address," p. 15; Henry, _Endless Future of the Human Race_, p. 61; Henry, _Considerations on Human Progress_, pp. 373-374; Brownson, "Church of the Future," p. 68; Clarke, _Ideas of Paul_, p. 17; Clarke, _Events and Epochs_, pp. 98, 112, 119, 121; Bancroft, _History of the United States_, V, 35, 48.

[84]Brownson, "Church of the Future," p. 67; Channing, _Works_, Complete Edition, p. 997; Hedge, "Everett's Phi Beta Kappa Address," p. 15; Hedge, "Feudal Society," _UR_, XXVIII (July, 1887), 8-12, 18;Hedge, "Historic Atonement,"p. 111; Furness, Nature and Christianity," p. 42; Osgood, _Hearth-Stone_, p. 50.

[85]W.H. Channing, "Call of the Present: No. 3," as cited in Hecker, _Questions of the Soul_, p. 220; Parker, _Social Classes_, p. 329; Parker, _Autobiography_, p. 42; Parker, _World of Matter and Spirit_, p. 85; Osgood, "Christian Ethics," XXIX, 173; Osgood, _Studies in Christian Biography_, passim; Henry, Notes on _General History_ by Guizot, p. 120; Hedge, _Sermons_, p. 163; Brownson, "Present State of Society," pp. 441-442; Brownson, "Church of the Future," p. 66; Clarke, "The Church,-- As It Was," as cited in Brownson, "The Church As It Was," p. 185; Clarke, _Steps of Belief_, p. 248; Clarke, _Ten Great Religions_, p. 353; Dwight, "Music," p. 32; Peabody, _Identification of Artisan and Artist_, p. 4.

[86]Clarke, "The Church,--As It Was," as cited in Brownson, "The Church As It Was," pp. 184-185; Henry, _Endless Future of the Human Race_, pp. 61-62.

[87]Parker, _Theism_, p. 16; Parker, Journal, March 3, 1844, in Weiss, _Life of Parker_, I, 210; Parker, _Sermons of Religion_, pp. 178-179; Parker, _Discourse of Religion_, p. 384; Parker, "Life of St. Bernard," pp. 39-40; Osgood, "Christian Ethics," XXIX, 173; Osgood, _Studies in Christian Biography_, passim; Brownson, "Church of the Future," p. 66; Emerson, Journal N, 1842, in Emerson, _JN_, VIII, 258; Channing, "On Fenelon," p. 178; Brooks, "The Faithful Monk," in _The Hark and the Cross: A Collection of Religious Poetry_, comp. Stephen G. Bulfinch (Boston, 1867), pp. 162-163; Clarke, _Events and Epochs_, pp. 165-166; Hedge, _Reason in Religion_, p. 442.

[88]Emerson, _Journals_, 1851, VIII, 230; _ibid._, 1863, IX, 559; Emerson to Charles Chauncy Emerson, August, 1828, in Emerson, _Letters_, I, 246; Emerson,Journal, 1826-1828, August 9, 1827, in Emerson, _JN_, III, 93; Emerson, Wide World 7, 1822, in _ibid._, II, 8-9; Clarke, _Events and Epochs_, p. 164; Clarke, "Buckle's History of Civilization," p. 392; Clarke, _Christian Doctrine of Prayer_, p. ix; Furness, _Power of Spirit_, p. 13; Thoreau, _Excursions_, pp. 205-206, 224; Thoreau, _Journal_, July, 1840, I, 158; _ibid._, II, 146; Thoreau, "Godfrey of Boulogne," in _Unpublished Poems by Bryant and Thoreau_ (Boston, 1907), pp. xxvii-xxviii; Bancroft, _Literary Miscellanies_, p. 100.

[89]Parker, _World of Matter and Spirit_, p. 85; Clarke, _Events and Epochs_, pp. 120-121; Henry, Notes on _General History_ by Guizot, p. 144; Henry, _Considerations_

on Human Progress, p. 374; Brownson, "Present State of Society," pp. 442-447; Hedge, "Everett's Phi Beta Kappa Address," p. 15; Hedge, "The Cause of Reason the Cause of Faith," p. 219.

90Brownson, Scholar's Mission, p. 85; Brownson, Literary Notice of Life of Cardinal Cheverus by Huen-Dubourg, p. 388; Hedge, "Everett's Phi Beta Kappa Address," p. 15; Parker, Discourse of Religion, pp. 377, 384; Parker, World of Matter and Spirit, p. 85; Parker, Theism, p. 16; Clarke, Common-Sense, p. 255; Clarke, Essentials, p. 37; Clarke, "The Church,--As It Was," as cited in Brownson, "The Church As It Was," p. 185; Henry, Notes on General History by Guizot, p. 144; Henry, Considerations on Human Progress, p. 374; Emerson, Notebook XVIII, 1821, in Emerson, JN, I, 278; Furness, Remarks on the Four Gospels, p. 21; Bancroft, History of the United States, IV, 151; ibid., V, 35; Osgood, The Coming Church, p. 16.

91Hedge, Sermons, p. 156; Brownson, "Church of the Future," p. 67.

92Hedge, "Everett's Phi Beta Kappa Address," p. 15.

93W.H. Channing, "Call of the Present: No. 3," as cited in Hecker, Questions of the Soul, pp. 220-222.

Another of the transcendentalists' summations of the Church's riches comes in the form of Henry's Compendium of Christian Antiquities, a description of the early Church's orders, rites, beliefs, churches, discipline, feast days, minor councils, and so on (Henry, A Compendium of Christian Antiquities: Being a Brief View of the Orders, Rites, Customs, and Laws of the Christian Church in the Early Ages [Philadelphia, 1837]).

94Clarke, Events and Epochs, p. 122.

95Brownson, Charles Elwood, pp. 232-233; Brownson, "Parker's Discourse," p. 509; Brownson, "Benjamin Constant on Religion," pp. 68-69; Brownson, "Church of the Future," pp. 68-69; Parker, Discourse of Religion, p. 390; Parker, Theism, p. 16; Parker, "Life of St. Bernard," pp. 15, 35-37; Clarke, "Orestes A. Brownson's Argument for the Roman Church," p. 244; Clarke, Events and Epochs, pp. 121-122; Clarke, Steps of Belief, p. 248; Clarke, The Well-Instructed Scribe, or Reform and Conservatism (Boston, 1841), p. 6; Clarke, "New Theology," p. 402; Clarke, Ten Great Religions, pp. 29-30; Clarke, "The Church,--As It Was," as cited in Brownson, "The Church As It Was," p. 186; Henry, Notes on General History by Guizot, p. 143; Hedge, "The Churches and the Church," p. 198; Bancroft, History of the United States, II, 257; Emerson, Notebook XVIII, 1822, in Emerson, JN, I, 311; S.G. Ward, "Letters from Italy," The Dial, I (January, 1841), 390.

96Parker described this preparation, and termed it "Lutheranism before Luther" (Parker, Discourse of Religion, pp. 390-391). Clarke too wrote of the "Luthers before Luther" (Clarke, Events and Epochs, pp. 213-239). See also Parker, Theism, p. 17; Clarke, Ten Great Religions, p. 145; Clarke, Steps of Belief, p. 248; Hedge, "Everett's Phi Beta Kappa Address," p. 15; Brownson, "Benjamin Constant on Religion," pp. 68-69.

97Hedge, "Everett's Phi Beta Kappa Address," p. 15.

98Emerson, "Thoughts on the Religion of the Middle Ages," p. 404; Parker, "Hennell on the Origin of Christianity," p. 137.

Parker's comments on historical aspects of the Church were made when he was in his prime, a time when he could ordinarily remain temperate about the Church.

99Osgood, "Christian Ethics," XXIX, 170.

100Hedge, "The Cause of Reason the Cause of Faith," p. 208; Parker, "Life of St. Bernard," pp. 27-31; Parker to Rev. Chandler Robbins, January 27, 1843, in Frothingham, Theodore Parker, pp. 170-171; Parker, Sermons of Religion, p. 179; Emerson, Journal B, 1836, in Emerson, JN, V, 228; W.H. Channing, "Ernest the Seeker," pp. 238-240; Clarke, Orthodoxy, p. 345; Clarke, "New Theology," p. 400; Clarke, Hour Which Cometh, pp. 5, 38; Clarke, Events and Epochs, pp. 213, 230-240.

101Hedge, "The Cause of Reason the Cause of Faith," p. 208.

[102]Hedge, "Method of History," p. 329; Hedge, "The Churches and the Church," p. 199; Parker, "Life of St. Bernard," p. 26; Clarke, Ten Great Religions, pp. 29-30; Clarke, "The Church,--As It Was," as cited in Brownson, "The Church As It Was," pp. 185-186.

[103]W.H. Channing, "Christian Church and Social Reform," as cited in Brownson, "Channing on the Church," p. 170; Clarke, "The Church,--As It Was," as cited in Brownson, "The Church As It Was," p. 186; Parker, Discourse of Religion, pp. 386-388; Parker, Ten Sermons, p. 235; Parker, Sermons of Religion, p. 179; Parker, Rights of Man, p. 443; Osgood, "Christian Ethics," XXIX, 169; W.T., "Religious Persecutions," WM, VI (November, 1838), 160-165; Cranch, "Pelagian Controversy," p. 396; Francis, Popery, p. 3; Hedge, Hours with German Classics, p. 357; Bartol, Church and Congregation, pp. 119, 136; Clarke, Every-Day Religion, pp. 73, 100.
For reasons that are unclear, the transcendentalists complained but mildly against the Albigensian and Waldensian crusades, reserving heavier fire for the Inquisition (Clarke, Events and Epochs, pp. 326-327, 336; Clarke, Common-Sense, p. 65; Clarke, Go Up Higher, p. 112; Hedge, "The Two Religions," p. 106; Channing, Works, VI, 56, 193; Channing, "Dangers of Liberality," p. 134; Channing to Joseph Blanco White, April 13, 1840, in Channing, Memoir, III, 361; Channing, Remarks on Creeds, Intolerance, and Exclusion, p. 17; Osgood, God with Men, p. 198; Osgood, Studies in Christian Biography, p. 202; Parker, Sins and Safeguards, pp. 31, 33-34; Parker, Lessons from Matter and Man, p. 142; Parker, American Scholar, pp. 386, 416-417).

[104]Parker, Theism, p. 263; Bancroft, History of the United States, X, 73; Osgood, God with Men, p. 198; Hedge, "The Churches and the Church," p. 198; Emerson, "Martin Luther," February 12, 1835, in Emerson, Early Lectures, I, 121.

[105]Parker, Rights of Man, p. 487; Parker, American Scholar, p. 184; Bancroft, History of the United States, II, 457; Hedge, "Method of History," p. 329; Hedge, "Luther and His Work," pp. 805, 817; W. H. Channing, "Christian Church and Social Reform," as cited in Brownson, "Channing on the Church," p. 171; Very, Sermon 60, as cited in Reeves, "Jones Very As Preacher," p. 20.

[106]Parker, American Scholar, p. 184; Parker, West Roxbury Sermons, p. 124; Brownson, Book Review of Workingman's Library, vol. I (Boston, 1833), The Unitarian, I (April, 1834), 171; Brownson, "Christianity and Reform," ibid., February, 1834, p. 57; Clarke, Ten Great Religions, pp. 29-30, 142-143; Clarke, Steps of Belief, pp. 274-276; Clarke, Events and Epochs, p. 273; Clarke, Christian Register, 1883, as cited in Williams, Rethinking the Unitarian Relationship with Protestantism, p. 3; Cranch, "The Unconscious Life," UR, XXXIII (February, 1890), 118; Brooks, "Erasmus," CE, XLIX (July, 1850), 87; Channing, Works, I, 66; Channing, Memoir, I, 415; Emerson, Wide World 7, 1822, in Emerson, JN, II, 17; Emerson, Journals, 1849, VIII, 78; Hedge, "Method of History," p. 329; Hedge, "The Cause of Reason the Cause of Faith," p. 210; Hedge, "Luther and His Work," pp. 805-806; Hedge, Hours with German Classics, p. 82; Hedge, "Romanism in Its Worship," p. 223; Osgood, "DeWette's Views of Religion and Theology," CE, XXIV (May, 1838), 167; W.H. Channing, "The Christian Church and Social Reform," as cited in Brownson, "Channing and the Church," p. 171; Bancroft, History of the United States, I, 274; ibid., IV, 280; ibid., X, 74-75.
According to Levin (History As Romantic Art, p. 97), "intellectual freedom was the meaning attached by Bancroft to the term, "justification by faith." A scanning of the references cited here bears this out.

[107]Hedge, "Luther and His Work," p. 805; Bancroft, History of the United States, IV, 152; Clarke, Ten Great Religions, p. 143; W.H. Channing, "Judgment of Christendom," p. 265.

[108]Clarke, Vexed Questions, p. 55; Clarke, Sketch of Atonement, p. 15; W.H. Channing, "Edwards and the Revivalists," p. 374.

[109]Clarke, "On the Positive Doctrines of Christianity," p. 52; Clarke, Ten Great Religions, p. 143; Clarke to Fuller, April 7, 1834, in Clarke, Letters, p. 76; Hedge, "Luther and His Work,"p. 817; Emerson, Wide World 10, March 23, 1823, in Emerson, JN, II, 109; Emerson, Wide World 6, 1822, in ibid., I, 151; Emerson, "Martin Luther," February 12, 1835, in Emerson, Early Lectures, I, 131; Cranch, "The Unconscious Life," p. 118; Henry, Notes on General History by Guizot, p. 266.

[110]Clarke, Essentials, pp. 23-24; Clarke, Christian Register, 1833, as cited in Williams, Rethinking the Unitarian Relationship with Protestantism, p. 3; Clarke, "Buckle's History of Civilization," p. 392; Clarke, Vexed Questions, p. 48; Cranch, "The Unconscious Life," p. 118; Emerson, "Martin Luther," February 12, 1835, in Emerson, Early Lectures, I, 119, 141-143; Emerson, "Human Culture," December 6, 1837, in ibid., II, 217 (Emerson has about thirty references to Luther in his writings); Furness, Power of Spirit, p. 3; Hedge, Hours with German Classics, pp. 69, 82; Hedge, "The Cause of Reason the Cause of Faith," p. 208; Hedge, "Luther and His Work," passim; Parker, Discourse of Religion, p. 398; Bartol, "Martin Luther," p. 515.

[111]Clarke, Eleven Weeks in Europe, p. 232; Clarke, "Buckle's History of Civilization," p. 392; Clarke, Essentials, p. 23; Emerson, "Human Culture," December 6, 1837, in Emerson, Early Lectures, II, 217; Osgood, "Schnaase's History of the Arts of Design," NAR, CXXIV (January, 1877), 146; Bancroft, History of the United States, II, 457; Hedge, "The Churches and the Church," p. 20; Brownson, "Christianity and Reform," p. 57; Channing, Memoir, I, 415; Francis, A Discourse Delivered at Plymouth, Massachusetts, December 22, 1832, in Commemoration of the Landing of the Fathers (Plymouth, 1832), p. 11; Thoreau, Journal, August 21, 1840, in Miller, Consciousness in Concord, p. 158.

[112]Hedge, "Romanism in Its Worship," p. 243; W.H. Channing, "Christian Church and Social Reform," as cited in Brownson, "Channing on the Church," p. 171; Parker, Nebraska Question, p. 9.

[113]Bancroft, History of the United States, IV, 277.

[114]Ibid., p. 118.

[115]Hedge, "Luther and His Work," p. 805.

[116]Clarke, Events and Epochs, pp. 255, 272; Parker, Book Review of The Ecclesiastical and Political History of the Popes of Rome, During the Sixteenth and Seventeenth Centuries by Leopold Ranke, trans. Sarah Austin, 3 vols. (London, n.d.), The Dial, I (October, 1840), 266; Clarke, Every-Day Religion, p. 422.

[117]Brownson, New Views, pp. 16-17; Judd, Margaret, II, 16-17; Judd, Philo, p. 76; Hedge, "Romanism in Its Worship," pp. 223-243; Hedge, Leaven of the Word, p. 4; Osgood, "Christian Ethics," XXX, 162; Bancroft, History of the United States, X, 82.

[118]"History of the Early Christian Missions in China," Extract, from Canton Register, WM, VI (March, 1838), 328-333; Bartol, Radical Problems, p. 141; Parker, St. Bernard and Other Papers, p. 150; Charles A. Dana, Book Review of The Jesuits and The Roman Church and Modern Society by M.M. Michelet and Quinet (New York, 1845), Harbinger, II (December 20, 1845), 29; Charles A. Dana, Book Review of Father Darcy by Mrs. Anne Marsh-Caldwell (New York, 1846), ibid., (September 12, 1846), 218; Osgood, "Christian Ethics," XXX, 162-163.

Clarke's discussion of the Jesuits in Events and Epochs (pp. 265-272) is a mixture of praise and blame, his favorable reflections ending with the comment: "They did great things for the world. They taught the arts of civilization to savages and then ruled them with a rod of iron..." (p. 271).

[119]Bancroft, History of the United States, III, 120; ibid., V, 15-16; ibid., VII, 28; ibid., X, 49-50. See also Francis, Errors in Education (A Discourse Delivered at the Anniversary of the Darby Academy in Higham, May 21, 1828 [Higham, Massachusetts, 1828], p. 22), where he depicts the characteristics of Jesuit educators that made them successful; and Channing, Memoir (II, 378), where he reasons that the very intelligence of the Jesuits awakened a similar intelligence fatal to their cause.

[120]Bancroft, History of the United States, I, 27; ibid., III, passim; ibid.,
V, 111; ibid., VIII, 417 (Bancroft repeatedly points out the prime influence of
the Jesuits in the geographic expansion and consolidation of New France); Fuller,
as cited in Howe, Margaret Fuller, p. 122; Ripley, Book Review of The Early Jesuit
Missions by Kipp, p. 316; Francis, Life of Sebastian Rale, passim; Clarke, Common-
Sense, p. 370; Clarke, Every-Day Religion, p. 42.
Thoreau's devotion to the Jesuits of New France is remarkable. See for exam-
ple, Thoreau, Journal, January 22, February 7, 1852, II, 218, 283; The Writings
of Henry David Thoreau, vol. III: The Maine Woods, passim; ibid., vol. IV, Cape
Cod, p. 232. For his prodigious reading in the literature of Catholicism in New
France, see Lawrence Willson, "Thoreau's Canadian Notebook," Huntington Library
Quarterly, XXII:3 (May, 1959), 199; Willson, "Thoreau and Roman Catholicism," pp.
160-172; Cameron, Companion to Thoreau's Correspondence, pp. 290-292. Thoreau's
manuscripts on the Indians contain 330 pages of extracts from the Jesuit Relations (see Albert Keiser, "Thoreau's Manuscripts on the Indians," Journal of English and Germanic Philology, XXVII [April, 1928]), 189).
The only exception to this universal praise of the Jesuit missionaries is
provided by Parker (Parker, American Scholar, p. 292).
[121]Clarke, Events and Epochs, pp. 329-349; Bancroft, History of the United
States, I, 24, 66-72, 170; ibid., II, 177, 257, 442-443; ibid., IX, 301-303;
ibid., X, 48; Bancroft, Introduction to Philip II of Spain by Charles Gayarre
(New York, 1866), p. iii; Channing, Works, VI, 176; Channing, Memoir, III, 361;
Brooks, A Poem Pronounced Before the Phi Beta Kappa Society at Cambridge, August
28, 1845 (Boston, 1845), p. 13; Bartol, Church and Congregation, p. 119; Parker,
American Scholar, pp. 208, 249-266, 337; Osgood, "Hugo Grotius and His Times,"
CE, XLII (January, 1847),9; Clarke, Every-Day Religion, p. 422.
[122]Bancroft, History of the United States, V, 3-5; ibid., VII, 28; ibid.,
IX, 506; Osgood, "Modern Ecclesiastical History," CE, XLVIII (May, 1850), 412;
Clarke, Events and Epochs, p. 349; Clarke, "Parton's Life of Voltaire," Atlantic
Monthly, XLVIII (August, 1881), 263-273; Bartol, Radical Problems, p. 141; Chan-
ning, Works, VI, 176; Channing to M.J.C.L. Simonde de Sismondi, April 16, 1835,
in Channing, Memoir, II, 390.
[123]Parker to Dr. Lamson, January 4, 1844, in Weiss, Life of Parker, I, 225;
Channing, "Letter on Catholicism," p. 272; Brownson, New Views, p. 7; Brownson,
Boston Reformer, July 21, 1836, as cited in Henry F. Brownson, Orestes A. Brownson's Early Life, p. 173; Bartol, Discourses on Christian Spirit, p. 20; Francis,
Popery, p. 25; Hedge, Ways of the Spirit, p. 89.
[124]Brownson, "Benjamin Constant on Religion," p. 69; Brownson, Charles
Elwood, p. 232.
[125]Hedge, Hours with German Classics, p. 69; Osgood, "Christian Ethics," XXX,
145-149.
[126]Channing, Works, Complete Edition, pp. 1018-1019; W.H. Channing, "Edwards
and the Revivalists," pp. 374-375; Osgood, "Christian Ethics," XXX, 145-149;
Hedge, Reason in Religion, p. 344.
[127]Among others, Clarke's works are replete with this complaint.
[128]Bancroft, History of the United States, I, 274-284; ibid., II, 437-438,
445; ibid.,III, 102; ibid., IV, 193-206; ibid., V, 60-77; ibid., VI, 526; Bancroft, Literary Miscellanies, p. 94; Spirit of the Age, passim; Judd, Margaret,
II, 115-116; Follen, Works, IV, 245, 284-293; Fuller to New York Tribune, September 30, 1846, in Fuller, At Home and Abroad, pp. 148-149; Emerson, Works, V, 216-
217; Henry, Notes on General History by Guizot, pp. 266-267.
[129]Hedge, "Destinies of Ecclesiastical Religion," pp. 11-12.
[130]Clarke, The Unitarian Reform (Boston, 1839), p. 7; Judd, The Church, p.
95; Hedge, "Ecclesiastical Christendom," pp. 131-132.

[131]Channing to Joseph Blanco White, September 18, 1839, in Channing, Memoir, II, 394; Channing to Rev. James Martineau, September 10, 1841, in ibid., 399.

[132]Emerson, 1878, Works, X, 204-205. He used the phrase, "empty negation of the Unitarian" many years before (Emerson, Journal B, March, 1836, in Emerson, JN, V, 145).

[133]Brownson, "Parker's Discourse," p. 510; Hedge, "The Churches and the Church," p. 199; Hedge, "The Two Religions," pp. 107-109; Emerson, Works, VII, 206.

CHAPTER VI

THE CONTEMPORARY CATHOLIC CHURCH

The transcendentalists examined the Catholic Church's position in the contemporary world from a two-fold perspective--the level of its prestige among the
nations of Europe, and the benefits that it accorded society, particularly in their
own New England towns. As to the first, we shall see that their judgments were
almost entirely in keeping with their theory that the contemporary world-wide Catholic Church had passed its prime of usefulness in the evolutionary process of society. Regarding the second, their data was meagre and their conclusions fragmentary.

THE STATUS OF EUROPEAN CATHOLICISM

Insofar as it is true that self-identity is largely achieved in terms of in-
terrelationships, the Catholic Church of the nineteenth century could be said to
have been searching, consciously and unconsciously, for a new and viable self-
image as the Christian instrument of the world's salvation. The French Revolution
had once and for all toppled the Church's position of worldly prestige in Europe,
and it was to be decades before its status in the new age would become clear. In
the meantime its struggles seemed agonizing. As the temper of its hopes fluctu-
ated, so also, whether in unison or in discord, did that of many of its observers.

That the Catholic Church of the nineteenth century was having problems of
this nature did not go unnoticed by the transcendentalists. On the European continent, in the British Isles, and in the United States, they found any number of
symptoms of the Church's struggle for identity which excited their comment.

The most obvious of the Church's contemporary problems in Europe was the situation of the papacy vis-à-vis the Italian unification movement. As spokesmen
for liberalism, the transcendentalists easily sided in this conflict with which-
ever force seemed to be raising the standard of freedom from the shackles of

absolutism, in whatever form. Consequently the arrival of Pope Pius IX on the Italian scene was greeted with enthusiasm by the two who witnessed his early years at first hand. Parker and Margaret Fuller placed great hope in the new pontiff, and both for the same reasons: his kindly face and the promise he seemed to herald of a new and freer Church. Parker gave public thanks from his pulpit upon the pope's election and both publicly and privately expressed a warm admiration for him.[1] On her part, Margaret Fuller in her letters from Rome to the New York Tribune expressed repeatedly her confidence in the "nobleness and tenderness" of the pope, and in his "large and liberal sympathies." Her glowing reports of the intoxication of the Italian people with the reforms he had already initiated reveal how far she shared their faith.[2]

Yet from the start, she feared that hope was premature.[3] As the months passed, her optimism turned to dismay at the pope's apparent failure. In the late spring of 1848, she wrote rather definitively: "Good and loving hearts that long for a human form which they can revere will be unprepared and for a time must suffer much from the final dereliction of Pius IX to the cause of freedom, progress, and of the war. He was a fair image, and men went nigh to idolize it; this they can do no more."[4] By the end she was referring to the pope's words as silly, bigoted, and ungenerous, and to his reign as one of absolute despotism.[5] True to her transcendental ideal, she turned instead to what she had once called "the good sense of the people" of Rome. In them she hoped to find a more successful agent than the pope had apparently been "in fashioning a new and better era for this beautiful injured land."[6]

Margaret Fuller was the most articulate of the transcendentalists on the subject of Italian liberalism, but she was not the only one. Parker, of course, could not refrain, on his second trip to Italy (1859-1860), from expressing to his friends his opinions about this "obstinate, conscientious, good man," whose ideas Parker dubbed "pre-medieval."[7] Far more cordial toward the pope's position was William Henry Channing. The weekly publication of his <u>Spirit of the Age</u> coincided with the most crucial months of the Italian revolution. A careful sifting of its articles on the subject discloses a dual view: all articles condemning the pope are written by contributers;[8] all written by the editor himself, while not in total agreement with the pope, display a profound sympathy for the pontiff's dilemma.[9] They show that Channing was the only transcendentalist to discover the historical dimensions of the problem. The temporal lands of the Church, he reminded his readers, were not the property of any pope, but the patrimony of the entire Church; consequently it was not the pope's prerogative to give them away.[10] The papacy was, as Parker phrased it with a flash of sympathy, "in an ugly fix just now,"[11] and it could count on Channing to see it as that.

As the papal position grew more untenable, the transcendentalists attempted to predict its future status. While Parker happily trumpetted Pius IX as the last of the popes--"I mean the last with temporal power"--Osgood warned that restoration at the point of French bayonets would prove more disastrous than a papal defeat. He added that the papal system inexorably led to its own overthrow anyway, and no man on its throne could ever hold the mastery over it.[12]

Even the spiritual power of the papacy seemed in jeopardy. Margaret Fuller deplored the departure of Catholicism's soul; Hedge referred to the pope now as "a mere ecclesiastical expression," and Parker gleefully compared the defunct religious life of Rome with that of the mummies of Egypt.[13] At length, with the defeat of France by Germany, Cranch celebrated the papacy's spiritual and temporal demise in verse:

> Unguarded by her Gallic sentinel,
> She loosely holds the keys of heaven and hell;
> Her Pope, whose thunders rattled west and east,
> Changed by a pen-scrawl to a harmless priest.[14]

Besides Margaret Fuller and Parker, the Church in Europe had another first hand observer from among the transcendentalists. George Bancroft, both more knowledgeable and more biased than any of the others about the situation, was in

a position to comment upon the fluctuations of Catholic power at close range.

While he was United States Minister to Prussia from 1867 to 1873, he made numer-

ous recommendations to his government about the Prussian situation, including its

struggles with the Church. All the religious and political governments surround-

ing Prussia and Germany Bancroft classed as wholly absolutistic; but the Bismarck-

ian regime, he was sure, was the harbinger of an American type democracy. He sup-

ported without question, therefore, all of Bismarck's programs, including the

Kulturkampf.[15] And he did all he could to urge the American government to support

Prussia at the expense of France.[16]

Bancroft's evaluation of the Church-state struggle in central Europe can be

condensed in what he surmised was a single conflict between the ultramontanists

and the freedom-loving people of the non-aristocratic classes.[17] It was solely

within the light of this unmixed contest that he approved or disapproved of most

of the major events and persons of the day: the pope and the papal dilemma;[18]

the Catholic politicians and clergy of Germany, France and Spain;[19] the Jesuits;[20]

the entanglements by France in the Roman question;[21] the Maximilian affair in

Mexico.[22]

The rigid stand Bancroft adopted on the scene left no more room for any of

the positive judgments that he had occasionally advanced in his History of the

United States. Still less did he maintain the open spirit of his youth. As a

student in Germany he had warmly approved the Catholic piety and progress he ob-

served there. And a little later he had proposed to write, with positive senti-

ments of approval, a political and religious history of Italy.[23] By the latter

years of his life, on the contrary, his transcendental broadmindedness had de-

serted him.

Bancroft was not alone in defining the Church's problems in Europe as a

struggle between political and religious freedom on the one hand, and ultra-

montane absolutism on the other. Clarke's historical objectivity failed him for
a moment when he responded by a lengthy attack to the decree of papal infallibility, the papal encyclical Quanta Cura, and its accompanying Syllabus of Errors of
Pope Pius IX. In short, Clarke linked to the one cause of "ultramontane or
Jesuit" intrigue, the revolt of Italy and Austria from the Church, the loss of
the pope's temporal power, the expulsion of Bourbon monarchs from their thrones,
and the separation of Church and state in Mexico. These Jesuitical intrigues he
compared to American support of the Fugitive Slave Law.[24] Nor could other transcendentalists of like mind abide this "ultramontane insolence."[25] When they made
any judgments upon the European problem of church and state, it was with this sin-
ister collusion in mind.[26] Where they saw no church-state conflict in a European
nation, as in Portugal and Spain, a few of them dismissed such nations as morally
corrupt and culturally retrogressive.[27]

Rarely did these difficulties experienced by the European powers discourage
the transcendentalists. Rather, their optimistic spirit read in them signs of
bright hope for the future of Europe. Was not the Catholic Church the enemy of
free and creative thought?[28] And was not the transcendental faith its champion?
There was cause, then, for rejoicing that in France and Germany especially, the
Catholic Church was dead or dying. The powers of reform there were on the ascendancy, and everywhere the Church's defectors were in the vanguard of intellectual,
cultural and scientific progress.[29] As early as 1849 Parker was celebrating the
Church's passing in Europe, depicting in brilliant contrasts the advent of a new
age:

> All over Europe...ecclesiastical establishments are breaking down.
> ...The old forms of piety, such as service in Latin, the withhold-
> ing of the Bible from the people, compulsory confession, the un-
> grateful celibacy of a reluctant priesthood--all these are protested
> against....By the new Constitution of France, all forms of religion
> are equal. Even Spain, the fortress walled and moated about, whither
> the spirit of the middle ages retired and shut herself up long since,
> ...even Spain fails with the general failure. British capitalists

buy up her convents and nunneries, to turn them into woollen mills.
Monks and nuns forget their beads in some new handicraft;...Meditative
Rachals, and Hannahs, long unblest, who sat in solitude, have now become like practical Dorcas, making garments for the poor; the Bank is
become more important than the Inquisition. The Order of St. Francis
d'Assisi, of St. Benedict, even of St. Dominic, is giving way before the
new order of Arkwright, Watt, and Fulton,--the order of the spinning
jenny and the power-loom. It is no longer books on the miraculous conception, or meditations on the five wounds of the Saviour, or commentaries on the song of songs which is Solomon's, that get printed there: but
fiery novels of Eugene Sue, and George Sand.[30]

REVERSION TO MEDIEVALISM

Obviously the transcendentalists were anxious to corroborate factually their

assessment of the old era in Europe as giving way under the penetration of the new.

Yet sometimes they found themselves faced with contrary evidence. For theirs was

the age of the romantic movement, a period highly favorable to the advancement of

many of the Catholic values which the transcendentalists were impatient to dismiss.

About the Catholic elements of the romantic movement as such, the transcen-

dentalists had very little to say. They were, like many of their European contem-

poraries, children of the Enlightenment. Romanticism, therefore, did not mean

acceptance of Catholicism. Where it did, as for a Frederic Schlegel or a Count

Stolberg, the transcendentalists could only deplore such decisions as a reversion

to medievalism.[31]

The kindred feeling of the American transcendentalists for European romanti-

cism thus had little to do with Catholicism. It was circumscribed within the

bounds of another facet of the movement--its element of "striving" or "aspiration"

for communion with the sacred in nature and in life.[32] Only Hedge and Osgood took

a somewhat serious look at the Catholic side of the movement, acknowledging its

writers to be at least reverent and instructive. Hedge went further, predicting

that this "Romeward" movement might well become the most significant reaction

against the irreligious style of the Enlightenment. He judged European Catholi-

cism differently from a Bancroft or a Parker. Far from being a dead or dying in-

stitution, the Catholic Church in Hedge's view was influential and strong. Unlike them, he estimated that among European intellectuals "the sceptics at most are reckoned only by hundreds, and believers by millions."[33] Clearly, here was a vast difference in transcendental opinion about the current state of the Catholic Church.

The renewal of British interest in Catholicism caught the attention of the transcendentalists a good deal more than did the romantic interest. A few years before Channing's death, he wrote several times to British friends, pressing them to forward him information on both the Oxford Movement and their own views of it.[34] Many of the other transcendentalists gave at least a passing glance to the movement, while three of them--Brownson, Hedge, and Osgood--pursued the subject more thoroughly. Whether superficial or profound, their comments on Tractarianism embody a single pattern, with two threads emerging.

The first area of consensus bears upon the meaning of the Oxford Movement for modern times. The transcendentalists were almost unanimous in declaring it to be a "relapse," a serious reversion to the past, a trend, for some, tantamount to a denial of centuries of religious development.[35] They were concerned that some of the best minds in England were adopting this reactionary program, and that the whole movement nearly amounted to a return to Rome.[36] But they fervently prophesied that it would never gain the masses and would die in its turn.[37]

The second point which the transcendentalists made about Oxfordism was that while its thrust was contrary to the trend of the age, somewhat paradoxically it was also a sign to them of a renewed faith and piety. It proved that men were revolting against the impious theories of modern philosophers, as well as agianst outward religious forms.[38] Brownson viewed the movement as a promising reaction against the loss of a profound sense of the church, a very hopeful sign, further, of the possibility of the unification of all Christendom. Because of these prospects, he and Hedge assessed the movement as one of the most significant of the century. Emerson looked to it as already uniting the churches in their "basic pillars," providing the only kind of religious unity that he believed necessary.[39] Religion, therefore, was in anything but a state of decay, and the future, while it would surely take a shape far different from Puseyism or Catholicism, was full of promise for true religion.[40]

From this point of view it can be said that transcendentalism in New England was an American counterpart of both the Oxford movement and the European romantic movement. Each of these was in search of the true Christianity--however defined --one not overlaid with centuries of accretions, one that appealed to the deepest aspiration for truth and for union with God. To a greater or lesser degree each looked backward to the Fathers of the Church and to the medieval ages of faith for confirmation of truth and for inspiration to piety. Finally, with the exception of a handful of individuals, each of the movements stood shy of accepting in toto the Catholic locus of these values, and each continued to maintain its own distinct form for incorporating them all.[41]

IRISH CATHOLICISM

Taking a look at another part of the contemporary world, the transcendentalists found less room for optimism and at the same time smaller scope for criticism of the Catholic position. Across the channel from England they saw small and oppressed Ireland as a far different kind of symbol of their own apsirations. Here it was not piety but freedom that was their central concern. They invariably sympathized with the plight of the Irish in their struggle against the established Church of England,[42] just as they sympathized, as we have seen, with Ireland's past. Curiously, however, Furness was the only one of our group to volunteer his congratulations on the passage of the Catholic emancipation act in 1829. He so identified himself with the Irish cause as to call the victory "a most gratifying instance of the success of our principles."[43] The silence of the other transcendentalists is perhaps explainable by the fact that they had not yet solidified their views by that date. By the time they did, it was clear that Irish emancipation was still very far from becoming a complete reality.

In addition to sympathizing with the cause of emancipation, Channing viewed favorably the positive contributions to "civilization and pure morals" which the Catholic Church in Ireland was rendering to its members there.[44] But on this side of the Atlantic it was another matter. By and large Irish immigrants offered the transcendentalists their only view of American Catholics as a group. What this view consisted in became a challenge to the viability of the transcendental principle of universality in the acceptance of all people of genuine "piety."

But this was a difficult ideal to achieve. The transcendental group was highly educated and exceptionally intelligent; the Irish were ignorant and lacking in all but the most basic elements of education.[45] The transcendentalists were verbally facile and expansive in thought; the Irish were manual laborers, busily engaged in eeking out a living.[46] The transcendentalists felt emancipated from authorities and beliefs that traditionally held sway in the Christian Churches; the Irish were devoted to their priests and loyal to their creed.[47] The transcendentalists were preoccupied with norms of morality; the Irish were given to drink and to the crimes of the dispossessed.[48]

Such was the gap that separated our group from the newly arrived Catholic population of the Boston, Concord, and New York areas. It was a gap difficult if not impossible to bridge. Parker above all could scarcely abide the differences between himself and this common herd. He tried to acknowledge that some of them were pious from conviction, but for the most part he maintained rather steadily that they were a people foolish enough to want a priest "with assumed authority to guide, or push, or drive them."[49] Yet he at least made an effort, along with a few of the other transcendentalists, to understand the root causes of the immigrants' shortcomings. They placed the blame therefore on the political and social status of the Irish both here and abroad, and on their heritage of social oppression and their current susceptibility to exploitation.[50]

Nonetheless it remained difficult for the transcendentalists to be on the side of the Irishman. But neither could they be wholly on the side of the Native American. Though the transcendentalists were sometimes tainted with a little nativism and provincialism themselves, they did speak out occasionally against the more radical abuses perpetrated by extreme anti-Catholic sentiment.

The burning of the Ursuline Convent in Charlestown in 1834 was the earliest overt action to stir the transcendentalists' indignation. Caleb Stetson was the first to decry the incident. In a lengthy sermon he denounced the Charlestown mob as lawbreakers who would deprive the nation of the last vestiges of civil and religious liberty. Even if the evils that some claimed to be lurking within the convent walls actually did exist, he could not countenance violence as the cure, even for "odious nunneries." He guaranteed that while he had a voice to speak, he would raise it against such treatment of a Catholic institution--for reasons of Christianity and in defense of the supremacy of the laws of the republic.[51] Channing, in terms redolent of a Fourth of July oration, condemned the act as an outrage against the city which had been "the metropolis of liberty to the whole earth."[52] "Better," he warned, "that twenty convents should rise than that one should be suppressed by brute force." With Bartol, he feared that such actions could but increase the formidable Catholic loyalties, and would be doing a favor only to Rome.[53]

Other instances of anti-Catholic sentiment early in our period evoked sporadic comment from the transcendentalists. Osgood condemned Maria Monk's Awful Disclosures[54] as "a tissue of lies." Both he and Cranch criticized "the whole school of Anti-Popery plotters" of this early period, notably Lyman Beecher, as useless and ineffective.[55] As for the riots and burning of Catholic churches in Philadelphia in 1844, only Brownson and William Henry Channing took the time to deplore them.[56]

Coming further into the strictly Nativist period, we see a little more action

on the part of the transcendentalists, though again their output is meagre and am-
bivalant. As early as 1835 Channing was worrying about "the profanation of the
suffrage" by its too easy access by immigrants and the evil that he feared would
result. Clarke once more fell short of his own preaching in this regard. At the
very time that Parker was rebuking the Nativists, Clarke accused the Catholics of
courting persecution by nursing and tending "their only American persecution,"
the burning of the Charlestown convent. A few years later we find him succumbing
to a racist dissertation on the obvious failings of the "Keltic blood."[57]

But other transcendentalists objected to Nativism, though mainly in the tone
of detached observers: Nativism is illogical, ineffective, immoral, narrow and
unloving. The best alternative is to let the immigrant come, to give him the benefit of freedom, and to have him thus learn the lessons that only America can
teach him.[58] "I am glad the Catholics come here," wrote Parker at the height of
the Nativist furor. "If, with truth and justice on our side, the few Catholics
can overcome the many Protestants, we deserve defeat."[59] Emerson displayed the
same sentiment earlier when he expressed--only to himself--his hatred of the narrowness of the Native American Party. He predicted with usual optimistic hope
for the future, that once this continent became the asylum of all nations, blindness would give way, and a new race and new religion would emerge from the composite.[60]

Bartol believed that that age was beginning already in 1867 when he praised
a colleague for requesting legislative compensation for the victims of the convent
burning of thirty-three years before. Some half dozen years later he announced
that love had finally triumphed. With the same strain of Emersonian optimism he
wrote: "Love lives, and vengeance dies. Yonder Somerville hill shows how Romanist and Rationalist agree at last that fine houses, better than charred and
mouldering walls, adorn the summit where the Catholic convent was burnt by a
Protestant mob."[61]

THE CATHOLIC RESPONSE TO THE NEEDS OF THE DAY

Did the transcendentalists object to Nativism only from principles of tolerance and expediency? Did they detect no positive good in the group that was the
object of the nativist abuse?

We have seen that even with the exception of the Irish immigrants, the transcendentalists had little direct contact with Catholics in their own New England
towns. Where they did check on the work of the contemporary Church around them,
they looked to it as a religious body that ought to have more or less the same
function that the transcendentalists themselves had--to be a facilitator of communion with God, of virtue, of morality, and of social amelioration. As people
devoted to the betterment of the race, they hoped that any organization calling
itself a church would work toward the same objectives.

Applying these norms to the Catholic Church, we have seen what the transcendentalists thought of it as an instrument of prayer. What they regarded as its
practical usefulness in contemporary society, however, is another matter.

"The joy of philanthropy is a high delight," wrote Theodore Parker, "worth
all the exaltation of St. Hugh, and the ecstasies of St. Bridget and St. Theresa."[62]
Thus was summed up the hierarchy of religious values that the more social-minded
of the transcendentalists held as a matter of course. And this was the test that
they often applied to the worth of the Catholic Church in their time. The "wise
and noble action " which Channing urged ought always to be united with "speculation"[63] was the touchstone of a realistic and vital religion. The transcendentalists found much of this kind of fruitfulness in the Catholic Church of the
middle ages, but often they felt hard-pressed to discover even traces of it in
their own day. Brownson early agreed with the Saint-Simonians that since Pope
Leo X the Church had neglected its mission to the poor classes and had leagued

itself with the wealthy and the tyrant. At best, it had so far overemphasized

the individual piety of its members as to capitulate to pietism and to ignore the

genuine love of God that expressed itself in works of true gospel charity. He

concluded therefore that the Christian ideal was embodied not in the Church, but

in the Saint-Simonian concept of the indefinite progress of humanity.[64] Social

progress was the fruit by which one would know the tree. Thus, reasoned Clarke,

if the Catholic Church were what she claimed to be--the true Christian Church--

Catholic countries ought to be far in advance of Protestant countries in "science,

art, literature; in comfort, wealth, population, longevity; in good government,

in the administration of justice, in the reform of criminals and vicious persons;

in general education; in charitable institutions; in private morality, purity of

manners, peaceful homes, general goodness." He applied these rigid and extensive

criteria, and he found the Catholic Church wanting.[65]

Where, for example, was the Catholic Church in the struggle for the freedom

of the American Negro slave? "Every sect," complained Parker in an address before

the New York Anti-Slavery Society, "numbers friends of freedom--except the Cath-

olic." And he asked his audience, "Do you know a Catholic priest that is opposed

to slavery? I wish I did." On the contrary, he wrote in the same year, "The

Catholic clergy are on the side of slavery." Both in public and in private, Par-

ker repeatedly made this charge.[66]

The only transcendentalist who seems to have noticed any efforts of Catholics

to work for the rights of the black race was Clarke, and this only after the Civil

War.[67] None of the transcendentalists noticed the expressions of regret for

slavery made by the Catholic Bishop of Philadelphia, Francis Patrick Kenrick, nor

the varying degrees of abolitionist sentiment adopted by such other well-known

Catholics as Daniel O'Connell; Father Edward Purcell, editor of the Catholic Tel-

egraph of Cincinnati; publicists Mathew Carey and David Broderick; and, latterly,

one of their own former colleagues, Brownson.[68] What is perhaps more remarkable is the absence of criticism on their part, except from Parker,[69] of any of the pro-slavery statements made by other leading Catholic persons, including the Brownson of the ante-bellum period.

In scrutinizing the Catholic Church's response to other oppressed classes of society, the transcendentalists were able to observe more signs of genuine "Christianity." Brownson of course, in his famous essay on "The Laboring Classes," early offered the classic example of the transcendental philippic against priestly oppression of the working man. In it he advised that only the destruction of the priestly class could usher in the era of the working class reform. Parker too employed some choice words excoriating the Church for its minimal achievements on behalf of the poor and destitute.[70]

But for the most part, the transcendentalists did recognize the charitable works that they witnessed as a practical part of Catholic Christianity. Channing more than once extolled the efforts of Bishop Cheverus on behalf of the poor of Boston. With obvious admiration he depicted the bishop walking through the streets "under the most burning sun of summer, and the fiercest storms of winter, as if armed against the elements by the power of charity."[71] Along with others, Channing and even the captious Parker found occasions to express their appreciation of the work of active religious orders, especially Sisterhoods. In the transcendental view these orders were engaged in rescuing the helpless and destitute in one of the "noblest" forms of piety--the works of mercy.[72] "Peaceful armies of charity," William Henry Channing called them. Brooks wrote a poem in honor of the nursing Sisters whom he had met, "sisters of mankind [who] do works of heaven." And Bartol remarked after a similar encounter, "Protestants have not only to teach, but learn of Catholics."[73] After William Henry Channing had given up all thought of becoming a Catholic, he continued to point to the Church for an unparalleled example of what must be done to achieve his hoped-for Christian commonwealth. "All that is good in Socialism," he wrote, "has been and is practised by Catholics now,--witness the Religious Brotherhoods and Sisterhoods in all ages. Who ever taught such lessons of charity to the rich, of humility to the haughty, of unlimited fraternity and equality, as Catholics?"[74]

In another vein, Elizabeth Peabody used a speech of "the great Cardinal," Nicholas Wiseman, to support her conception of the growing dignity of lowly work as artistic and ennobling. She hoped that the spread of this concept would introduce a new age of dignity for the common laborer based upon the Cardinal's tenets.[75]

As for the moral and strictly religious needs of the day, the transcendentalists could sometimes find Catholics in the vanguard, although not as often. Parker claimed that in seeking out the poor, the rude, and the "unfriended" for religious instruction, "the Catholics put us quite to shame."[76] He recognized particularly that in another age the Catholic Church had been mother to all the reform movements that were sweeping the United States in his day. In earlier centuries, he pointed out, "there was not a temperance society in the world; the Church was the temperance society. There was not a peace soceity; the Church was the peace society; not an education society; the Church opened her motherly arms to many a poor man's son...."[77] But he also criticized the Church's present emphasis, judging that it had by now taken on less of the moral and more of the strictly religious functions of so many of the other contemporary churches.

Regarding the matter of temperance, only two or three of the other transcendentalists took notice of the movement in Catholic ranks. William Henry Channing, with the help of his assistant editor, Ripley, did make the Spirit of the Age a vehicle for supporting the temperance crusade of Father Theobald Mathew.[78] Earlier, before the crusade had reached its peak, William Ellery Channing had devoted a portion of a Sunday evening sermon to extolling the merits of this man, whom Channing for the moment ranked above all the other heroes and statesmen of the day.[79] But apparently none of the other transcendentalists, moralists though they were, gave the crusade any thought. Still less did any of them seem to notice the outcry against Father Mathew that could be heard in many an Irish quarter of the nation!

Other topics of current needs in which the Catholic Church was involved are touched upon here and there by the transcendentalists. Hedge commends Pope Pius IX for his part in the peace movement by refusing to war against Austria; Bartol, Clarke, and Channing applaud the zeal for foreign missionary work displayed by the Catholic Church; and the pages of the Harbinger contain two items of interest only in that they attempt to show what seems to the editors to be a Catholic tendency toward associationism and thereby philanthropy.[80]

Perhaps the most inclusive transcendental tributes to the contemporary Catholic contribution are offered by Osgood and William Henry Channing, in two articles that were intended as a defense of the immigrants. The first was a portion of William Henry Channing's discussion of the Philadelphia riots of 1844; the second, Osgood' commentary on several current documents of Catholic interest.[81] Both these articles attempt to highlight the gifts of the Catholic immigrant, particularly the Irish, to the total well-being of American society. They lift the diggers of canals and layers of rails to the level of benefactors of mankind. Readers are reminded that the Irish culture brought over by the immigrant had a direct relationship with the Catholic culture of the medieval world; that Catholic churches, colleges, and libraries were at that moment rendering incalculable service to this country; that artistry, refinement, and goodness were all a part of the immigrant's character gracing their new land. The Irish, moreover, were a healthy antidote to the "ferocious socialism and Red-Republicanism" which seemed to be invading the land. More profoundly, the Irish Catholic had much to teach the American Protestant about "the worth of the divine life"--surely a concept ranking at the very heart of the transcendental ideal. And finally William Henry Channing could envision a choice role that these men and women would play in his Christian Commonwealth. Blending together a variety of characteristics, the immigrants would provide the seed for the universal brotherhood that he looked forward to in the coming age.

AMERICAN CATHOLICS AND EDUCATION

One of the most controversial issues of the day involving American Catholics was the subject of edcuation. Basically the issues were two. The first, lasting during most of transcendentalism's peak years, consisted in a debate between Protestants and Catholics over the use of the Bible in public schools. The second concerned the broader issue of a separate Catholic school system.

Bartol was the only transcendentalist who regarded the Catholic opinion on education significant enough to warrant discourses on both these subjects. First, he published in 1859 a studied argumentation in support of the Catholic opposition to the Bible reading as currently practiced in the public schools.[82] So earnestly did he handle his refutation of the arguments in favor of the practice, that he was accused of offering "an apology for Romanism." "Romanists," he retorted, "will hardly so consider it."[83] Nor did he agree with those who appraised the controversy as merely "an accidental affair, a momentary disturbance." On the contrary, to him it was a matter of principle. In the first place, he judged that it was the Protestant duty in the debate not to demonstrate "whether or how far in this affair the Catholics are wrong, but to be ourselves plainly and unchallengeably right." But this he felt himself bound to admit he could not do. In the bulk of the discourse he demonstrates the fact that the Protestant position was indeed challengeable, on seven counts: 1) enforced Scripture reading was opposed to the American principle of religious liberty; 2) such force helped the Romanist cause more than hindering it; 3) the law was worthy of being disobeyed for the same reasons that the Fugitive Slave Law was; 4) such power in the hands of the state was opposed to "the faith we all profess to hold" and was a direct imitation of the "worst characteristics of Rome herself"; 5) the excuse that Catholics are mere automatons anyway, with no real conscience, was specious and unfair; 6) fear of the papacy was no justification and would only make martrys of Catholics; 7)

lastly, the Golden Rule ought to be kept, "yes, even with Rome!"

The most telling argument for Bartol's position on the Catholic side was his

spirited defense of the transcendental philosophy of education. For the first pur-

pose of education, he recalled, was not the imparting of doctrine or even the

vocal acknowledgement of a God. No, education's main purpose was "to awaken the

faculties and kindle the spark of intelligence." In this way only could education

call forth from children their own willed service of God. Enforced Scripture read-

ing, then, should be--as the Catholics wished--discontinued.[84]

More briefly but in much the same way, Furness and Osgood had defended the

Catholic position some years previously. Opposed as they were to required "forms,"

they opted rather for "the substance, the principle, the living" power of religion.

In a more pragmatic than transcendental vein, they feared lest enforced submission

of children to the study of the Bible should render it a "dull task book."[85]

But the transcendentalists' words were drowned in the sea of polemics which

the Bible-reading question evoked. They made not so much as a ripple on the sur-

face of the controversy. Decades later a few of them tried again, when the issue

had taken another turn. The Catholic Church, strengthened by growing numbers,

had gone from a defense of its own version of the Bible in the public schools (or

no Bible at all there), to a defense of its own enforced school system. The ques-

tion at stake in this case therefore was a much larger one.

Again Bartol took up the pen to discuss the pro's and con's of the Catholic

argument, this time partially reversing his position.[86] Formerly he had sympa-

thized with Catholic fears regarding a correct understanding of the second com-

mandment, a pivot around which the Bible debate revolved.[87] But now he urges that

this basis for such a broad controversy was too paltry. The Catholic Church would

do far better to trust the simple word of the Book than the word of pope or cardi-

nal about its meaning. Formerly he had warned that none could accuse the Catholic of being an automaton, or of having no conscience of his own;[88] now he elaborates

on the insincerity of the Catholic and his superficial submission to "papal des-

potism."

Still, Bartol is broad enough to see merit in the Catholic argument for sep-

arate schools. He admits that the public schools have in a measure become "god-

less," though he blames the Catholic agitation against the King James Bible for

the elimination of piety in the public system. And he grants that Catholics have

as much right to establish their own schools as anyone else in the republic. But

he condemns them for their desire to segregate a portion of the body of Christ,

above all by inculcating "abject submission" to an arbitrary and unprogressive

rule.

The crux, however, of Bartol's argument lies as before in his transcendental

philosophy of education. But this time he applies it in defense against the Cath-

olic position. Religion and morality, he asserts, ought to be taught in any

school system, but not by way of indoctrination. Rather, it must be inculcated

by "the constant outpouring and imbibing between teacher and scholar" of the Chris-

tian spirit. Education must be the awakening by the sensitive teacher of what is

innate in the child--his "sense of awe in this wondrous world, of love for its un-

seen source." Herein lies Bartol's opposition to the Catholic school as he saw

it. For the Catholic system, he believes, does not tap effectively this innate

force, attempting rather to sustain it by "partisan dividing dogma." Bartol was

also consistent with the transcendental belief that Catholicism was opposed to

reason and science. With demanding rhetoric, he challenges the Catholic priest:

"Who and what is the Deity....[?] Whither, O priest...have you taken him away?

[For] reason is his voice, science is his tongue, myriad evolution in mind and

matter is his hand." He issues a call then, to do away with the "romanizing of

truth." Into the public school system must be introduced instead a kind of reli-

gion that the transcendentalists had themselves long ago adopted,"a religion of radiation, inspiration and refreshment for the soul."[89]

Clarke was the only other transcendentalist who attempted a defense of the public school system versus the Catholic.[90] Before the last quarter of the century, he had had nothing at all to say about Catholics and education. When the school question finally reached him, he used the occasion of another controversial issue to express his views on both. In his sermon attacking papal infallibility he assailed also the Catholic's methods of accepting all that that dogma implied --particularly through the Catholic system of education.[91]

Clarke was under the impression that American Catholics were determined to destroy the public school system.[92] Perhaps he gained this impression partly from Pope Pius IX's comments on school systems in the Syllabus of Errors, which Clarke cites incorrectly and condemns.[93] He was also of the opinion that the Catholic schools taught only doctrine and neglected almost entirely such basic subjects as reading and writing. Hence he turns his discourse on infallibility into a defense of his theory of the absolute necessity for literacy in a republic. This is a goal which Catholic schools, he claims, can never hope to achieve. With Protestant and trasncendental fervor he argues for continued separation of church and state. Where there is conflict between the two, he declares categorically that it is the private conscience which alone has the right to decide-- since "no danger attaches to the supremacy of private judgment." Here again the transcendentalist's unquestioning trust in individual widsom surfaces, and Clarke sounds the alarm against its submission to any other person, be he pope, priest, or politician. Obedience to the pope is what Clarke especially fears, for though Pius IX is "a good man, a benevolent man," he is a man living in the tenth century, who would retard the history of the world immeasurably. To submit to such a one, Clarke warns in an unusual display of apprehension, would be treason against the national life, as it would destroy the country's literacy! To all Catholics

who would commit such treason, Clarke issues an invitation to leave the country
and a plea not to attempt to overthrow the institutions of the nation that has so
far protected them.[94] Such a maneuver obviously does not represent Clarke at his
best, and probably the whole argumentation should not be taken too seriously. But
aside from Bartol's discussion, it is the only other transcendental statement on
the subject.[95]

Such were the views of the transcendentalists on the Catholic Church in specific areas of activity in the contemporary world. For a group of such fertile
and imaginative minds, theirs is, on the whole, a rather uninspired commentary.
Knowledgeable and opinionated in so many areas, the transcendentalists seem lacking in depth of insight into the Catholic situation of their day, especially in
their own homeland. Using this knowledge, they situated the Church within the
contemporary world, and then went on to assess its potential and to predict its
future. It is to this prognosis that we shall next turn.

NOTES

[1]Parker, Journal, March 3, 1844, in Weiss, Life of Parker, I, 210. See also Ednah Dow Cheney, Reminiscences of Ednah Dow Cheney (Boston, 1902), p. 119. The Harbinger rhapsodized poetically about the "day-dawn in Italy" (Anne C. Lynch, "Day-Dawn in Italy," Harbinger, VI [January 15, 1848], 81).

[2]Fuller to New York Tribune, October 18, 1847, in Fuller, Writings, p. 416. Hedge too had a firm confidence in the pope's early liberalism (Hedge, "Madame Ossoli's At Home and Abroad," NAR, LXXXIII [July, 1856],262 -263).

[3]See among others, her letter to the New York Tribune of October 18, 1847, in Fuller, Writings, p. 416, and one of the following spring when she wrote: "Italy is free, independent, and one. I trust this will prove no April foolery, no premature news; it seems too good" (April 1, 1848, in ibid., p. 447).

[4]Fuller to New York Tribune, May 7, 1848, in a letter dated and begun April 19, 1848, in ibid., p. 465.

[5]Fuller to New York Tribune, February 20, June 21, 1849, in ibid., pp. 491, 522.

[6]Fuller to New York Tribune, January, 1848, in ibid., p. 441; Fuller to New York Tribune, April 19, 1848, in ibid., p. 465. For more of Margaret Fuller's critical comments on Pius IX see all her letters to the New York Tribune, October, 1847-June, 1849, in ibid., pp. 416-522; Fuller to Ossoli, n.d., in Memoirs of Margaret Fuller, II, 297; Fuller to M.S., November 23, 1848, in ibid., p. 253; Fuller to a friend [December, 1848?], in Mason Wade, Margaret Fuller: Whetstone of Genius (New York, 1940), pp. 237-238; Fuller to New York Tribune, January, 1848, in Fuller, At Home and Abroad, pp. 298-299; Fuller to Ossoli, August 18, 1848, in Thomas Wentworth Higgenson, Margaret Fuller Ossoli (Boston, 1884), p. 250; Fuller, Diary, January 9, 31, 1849, in Rostenberg, "Margaret Fuller's Roman Diary," pp. 213, 216. Not only were her transcendental hopes dashed with the failure of the revolution, but some of her human hopes as well: her husband, the Count d'Ossoli, was a revolutionist.

[7]Parker to Dr. Cabot, February 3, 1860, in Weiss, Life of Parker, II, 417. See also, among others, his letters to: Charles Sumner, August 13, 1859, in ibid., p. 335; John Manley, December, 1859, in ibid., p. 381; Mrs. Ednah Cheney, December 31, 1859, in ibid., p. 405; Miss Cobb, January 1, 1860, in ibid., pp. 405-406; John Manley, January 6, 1860, in ibid., p. 407.

[8]Articles on Mazzini in SA, passim; "European Politics," ibid., I (July 7, 1849), 13; Charles A. Dana, "The European Revolution," ibid., August 18, 1849, pp. 97-98; Ripley, "European Affairs," ibid., August 18, September 1, October 20, 1849, pp. 109, 141, 252; Thomas L. Harris, "The Old Age and the New," ibid., II (January 5, 1850), 10-11; P.J. Proudhon, "Confessions of a Revolutionist," (excerpt), ibid., March 2, 1850, pp. 130-131.

[9]W.H. Channing, "Revolution--Reaction--Reorganization," SA, I (July 21, August 4, 1849), 41, 73; W.H. Channing, "Peter's Pence," pp. 24-25; W.H. Channing, "Mazzini and the Roman Republic," ibid., July 21, 1849, p. 42; W.H. Channing, "Talks on the Times: Socialist and Catholic," ibid., August 18, 1849, pp. 106-107; W.H. Channing, "War of Principles and the Principle of Peace," ibid., August 25, 1849, pp. 120-121; W.H. Channing, "Criticisms and Confessions," ibid., September 1, 1849, p. 136; W.H. Channing, "Church and State," pp. 152-153; Extract from the New York Tribune, in W.H. Channing, "Industrial Freedom," ibid., October 6, 1849, p. 219.

[10] W.H. Channing, "Talks on the Times," p. 106.

[11] The comment was included by Parker in a letter written shortly before his death, in which he first declared that he hoped for no good from the papacy, and wished none for it (Parker to Ripley, Shrove Tuesday, 1860, in Weiss, Life of Parker, II, 432).

[12] Parker, Social Classes, p. 296; Osgood, "Modern Ecclesiastical History," p. 431; Osgood, Life and Its Record in This Generation. An Anniversary Address Delivered Before the New York Genealogical and Biographical Society, April 11, 1878 (New York, 1878), p. 13; Osgood, God with Men, p. 55.

[13] Fuller, Diary, January 1, 5, 1849, in Rostenberg, "Margaret Fuller's Roman Diary," pp. 211-213; Fuller to New York Tribune, January, 1848, in Fuller, At Home and Abroad, p. 299; Fuller to [?], May 6, 1849, in ibid., pp. 434-435; Hedge, "Madame Ossoli's At Home and Abroad," p. 263; Parker, Transient and Permanent, pp. 412-413; Parker to John Manley, November 5, 1859, in Weiss, Life of Parker, II, 378; Parker, Journal, November 1, 1859, in ibid., p. 386; Parker to Professor Desor, December 7, 1859, in ibid., p. 389.

[14] Cranch, "Louis Napoleon," in Cranch, The Bird and the Bell, p. 212. See also Hedge, "The Cause of Reason the Cause of Faith," p. 225; Bancroft to Hamilton Fish, October 27, 1873, in U.S. Foreign Papers, 1874-1875, pt. 1, p. 431.

[15] Bancroft to Hamilton Fish, German Dispatches, IV, No. 532 (October 27, 1873), in Sister M. Philip Trauth, "The Bancroft Dispatches on the Vatican Council and the Kulturkampf," Catholic Historical Review, XL (July, 1954), 188, hereafter cited as: Trauth, "Bancroft Dispatches"; Bancroft to Fish, March 18, 1872, in U.S . Foreign Papers, 1872-1873, pt. 1, p. 188; Bancroft to Fish, June 17, 1872, in ibid., p. 190; Bancroft to Fish, May 26, 1873, in ibid., 1873-1874, pt. 1, pp. 290-291; Bancroft to Fish, December 1, 1873, in ibid., 1874-1875, pt. 1, pp. 434-435; Bancroft to Fish, December 15, 1873, in ibid., pp. 436-437.

[16] See for example, Bancroft to Fish, October 18, 1870, in Howe, Life of Bancroft, II, 245-247; Arnold Blumberg, "George Bancroft, France, and the Vatican: Some Aspects of American, French, and Vatican Diplomacy, 1866-1870," Catholic Historical Review, L (January, 1865), 490.

[17] Bancroft to Fish, German Dispatches, I, No. 304 (December 4, 1871), as cited in Trauth, "Bancroft Dispatches," p. 184; Bancroft to Fish, German Dispatches, IV, No. 532 (October 27, 1873), in ibid., p. 188; Bancroft to Osgood, February 21, 1868, in Howe, Life of Bancroft, II, 203; Bancroft to J.C. Bancroft Davis, September 4, 1870, in ibid., p. 240; Bancroft to Fish, October 18, 1870, in ibid., pp. 245-247; Bancroft to Fish, December 4, 1871, in U.S. Foreign Papers, 1872-1873, pt. 1, p. 187; Bancroft to Fish, March 18, 1872, in ibid., pp. 187-188; Bancroft to Fish, May 26, 1873, in ibid., p. 291; Bancroft to Fish, October 27, 1873, in ibid., 1874-1875, pt. 1, p. 431; Bancroft to Fish, March 30, 1874, in ibid., p. 437; Bancroft to Professor Nippoli, March 5, 1869, Bancroft Papers, MHS, in Levin, History As Romantic Art, p. 125; Bancroft to J.C. Bancroft Davis, September 7, 1870, J.S. Bancroft Davis Papers, in Henry Blumenthal, A Reappraisal of Franco-American Relations, 1830-1871 (Chapel Hill, North Carolina, 1959), p. 190.

[18] Bancroft to Hamilton Fish, March 18, 1872, in U.S. Foreign Papers, 1872-1873, pt. 1, p. 188; Bancroft to Fish, June 24, 1872, in ibid., p. 192; Bancroft to Fish, October 27, 1873, German Dispatches, IV, No. 532, in Trauth, "Bancroft Dispatches," p. 188; Bancroft to Fish, January 31, 1870, Prussian Documents, XVI, No. 66, in ibid., p. 180; Bancroft to Osgood, February 21, 1868, in Howe, Life of Bancroft, II, 203; Bancroft to Mrs. J.C. Bancroft Davis, October 4, 1868, in ibid., p. 213; Bancroft to Fish, July 23, 1870, in Blumenthal, Reappraisal of Franco-American Relations, p. 191; Bancroft to Fish, May 25, 1874, in Stolberg-Wernigerode, Germany and the United States, Appendix, p. 302.

[19]Bancroft to C.C. Perkins, June 12, 1869, in Howe, Life of Bancroft, II, 228; Bancroft to Hamilton Fish, April 28, 1873, in U.S. Foreign Papers, 1873-1874, pt. 1, p. 284; Bancroft to Fish, May 26, 1873, in ibid., pp. 290-291; Bancroft to Fish, December 8, 1873, in ibid., 1874-1875, pt. 1, pp. 435-436; Bancroft to Fish, April 27, 1874, in ibid., p. 445; Bancroft-Bismarck Interview, September 26, 1867, in Stolberg-Wernigerode, Germany and the United States, Appendix, p. 282.
Bancroft missed the insight perceived by another member of the diplomatic corps in Berlin, British Ambassador Odo Russell. In 1874 Russell wrote: "Bismarck's anti-church policy has compelled the German bishops to rally round the Pope and to suffer martyrdom for discipline's, obedience's, and example's sake" (as cited in Erich Eyck, Bismarck and the German Empire [New York, 1964, c. 1958], p. 208).
[20]Bancroft to Hamilton Fish, Prussian Documents, XVI, No. 66 (January 31, 1870), in Trauth, "Bancroft Dispatches," p. 180; Bancroft to J.C. Bancroft Davis, September 4, 1870, in Howe, Life of Bancroft, II, 240; Bancroft to Fish, October 18, 1870, in ibid., p. 246; Bancroft to Fish, June 17, 1872, in U.S. Foreign Papers, 1872-1873, pt. 1, pp. 190-191; Bancroft to Fish, June 24, 1872, in ibid., p. 192.
[21]Bancroft to J.C. Bancroft Davis, September 4, 1870, in Howe, Life of Bancroft, II, 240; Bancroft to Fish, October 18, 1870, in ibid., pp. 245-247; Bancroft to Fish, May 26, 1873, in U.S. Foreign Papers, 1873-1874, pt. 1, pp. 290-291.
French poet Victor Hugo responded to Bancroft's anti-French policy by honoring him in a poem, "À la France," with the words: "Cet autre, nomme' Grant, te conspue,/ et cet autre, nomme' Bancroft, t'outrage" (cited in Blumberg,"George Bancroft, France and the Vatican," p. 493n).
[22]Bancroft to Hamilton Fish, October 18, 1870, in Blumenthal, Reappraisal of Franco-American Relations, p. 197; Bancroft, Abraham Lincoln: a Tribute [1866] (New York, 1908), p. 51.
[23]Bancroft, "Studies in German Literature," 1824, in Bancroft, Literary Miscellanies, p. 109; Bancroft, Oration Delivered on the Fourth of July, 1826, at Northampton, Massachusetts (Northampton, 1826), p. 21; Bancroft to Jared Sparks, September 28, 1825, in "Correspondence of George Bancroft and Jared Sparks, 1823-1832. Illustrating the Relation Between Editor and Reviewer in the Early Nineteenth Century," ed. John Spencer Bassett, Smith College Studies in History, II (January, 1917), 101-102.
[24]Clarke, Peter at Antioch; or, the Vatican vs. Bismarck and Gladstone.... 1874. The title is misleading; Clarke makes no mention of Gladstone or Bismarck.
[25]The expression is Hedge's, a rare example of contemptuousness on his part. In this instance he used the term in a discussion of the Reformation period (Hedge, "Luther and His Work," p. 811).
[26]Peabody, ed., Crimes of the House of Austria Against Mankind. Proved by Extracts from the Histories of Coxe, Schiller, Robertson, Grattan, and Sismondi, with Mrs. M.L. Putnam's History of the Constitution of Hungary, and Its Relations with Austria, Published in May, 1850, 2nd ed. (New York, 1852), passim; Brooks, "Renan's Life of Jesus," p. 229; Ripley, "Town and Country Items," SA, I (November 24, 1849), 335; Parker to the Twenty-Eighth Congregational Society, June 25, 1859, in Weiss, Life of Parker, II, 301; Hedge, "Ecclesiastical Christendom," pp. 114-115.
The exception is again William Henry Channing, who sided with the opinion of the New York Tribune that the Jesuits were indeed causing all the trouble, but that the Jews had put them up to it (W.H. Channing, "Industrial Freedom," p. 219).
[27]Dwight, Book Review of Italy, Spain, and Portugal, with an Excursion to the Monasteries of Alcabaca and Batalha by William Beckford (New York, 1846), Harbinger, III (September 12, 1846), 217; Emerson, Works, I, 231-232; Channing,

Works, VI, 56; Parker, Theism, p. 26.

28Brooks, "Renan's Life of Jesus," p. 220; Emerson, Journals, 1868, X, 233-234; Parker to Rev. J.T. Sargent, September 18, 1859, in Weiss, Life of Parker, II, 354; Parker, Notes, August 7, 1859, in ibid., p. 327; Parker to Clarke, [1859?], in ibid., p. 337; Parker, Transient and Permanent, p. 410; Parker, St. Bernard and Other Papers, p. 148.

29Hedge, "The Cause of Reason the Cause of Faith," p. 225; Emerson, Works, X, 112; Channing, Works, V, 407-408; Channing, Address, 1820, in Channing, Memoir, I, 424; Channing to M.J.C.L. Simonde de Sismondi, June 6, 1831, in ibid., II, 386; Channing to de Sismondi, September 19, 1832, in ibid., p. 388-389; Ripley, "Religion in France," p. 278; Parker, Theism, pp. 30-32, 53-54; Parker to Convers Francis, July 12, 1844, in Weiss, Life of Parker, I, 244; Parker to the Twenty-Eighth Congregational Society, June 25, 1859, in ibid., II, 301; Parker, St. Bernard and Other Papers, pp. 148-150; Parker, Ten Sermons, p. 174.

30Parker, "The Spiritual Condition of Boston," 1849 sermon, in Parker, Social Classes, pp. 296-297. These were the words he chose to describe one of the "four great declensions in piety": 1) the Protestant Reformation; 2) modern philosophy, physics and metaphysics; 3) modern democracy; 4) and all modern societies. While his aim was to deplore the weakening of piety, he depicts this particular phase of it with obvious relish.

31Emerson, Works, VI, 208-209; Hedge, "Classic and Romantic," Atlantic Monthly, LVII (March, 1886), 315-316; Hedge, Hours with German Classics, p. 439; Osgood, Our Patriot Scholar, p. 12; Peabody, ed., Crimes of the House of Austria Against Mankind, p. 1; Brownson, "The Present State of Society," pp. 454-455.

32Hedge, Hours with German Classics, p. 430; Hedge, "Classic and Romantic," p. 316; W.H. Channing, Gospel of Today, p. 10; James Marsh, as cited in Nicholson, "James Marsh and the Vermont Transcendentalists," pp. 33-34.

33Hedge, "Ecclesiastical Christendom," pp. 112, 123; Hedge, "Classic and Romantic," p. 309; Osgood, Book Review of Symbolism by Moehler, p. 120; Osgood, Studies in Christian Biography, pp. 2, 5. See also W.H. Channing, Gospel of Today, pp. 9-10.

34Channing to Miss Aiken, January 15, 1839, in Correspondence of William Ellery Channing with Lucy Aikin from 1826 to 1842, ed. Anna Letitia LeBreton (Boston, 1874), pp. 327-328, hereafter cited as: Channing, Correspondence; Channing to Joseph Blanco White, September 18, 1839, in Joseph Blanco White, The Life of the Rev. Joseph Blanco White, Written by Himself; with Portions of His Correspondence, ed. John Hamilton Thom, 3 vols. (London, 1845), III, 95, hereafter cited as: Joseph Blanco White, Life; Channing to White, November 20, 1839, in Channing, Memoir, II, 395.

35Emerson, Works, VI, 208-209; ibid., X, 244; Brownson, "Present State of Society," pp. 454-455; Newcomb, as cited by Johnson, ed. in Newcomb, Journals, p. 79; Channing to Joseph Blanco White, September 18, 1839, in Joseph Blanco White, Life, III, 95; Osgood, "Modern Ecclesiastical History," p. 431; Osgood, "The Schleiermacher Centennial and Its Lesson," pp. 189-190; Osgood, "The Nemesis of Faith," CE, XLVII (July, 1849), 95; Osgood, "Taylor's Lectures on Spiritual Christianity," p. 317; Osgood, Our Patriot Scholar, p. 12; Hedge, "The Cause of Reason the Cause of Faith," p. 213; Hedge, "Classic and Romantic," pp. 315-316; Hedge, "Ecclesiastical Christendom," pp. 112-113; Hedge, ed., Essays and Reviews, xiii; Clarke, "Ancient Christianity and the Oxford Tracts," p. 136; Clarke, "Christ and His Antichrists," p. 359; Parker, Theism, p. 31; Parker, Transient and Permanent, p. 175.

Hedge and Osgood both revered the recollections the Tractarians brought to mind, comparing them to visits to Gothic or ancient ruins. But "a Gothic ruin is a thing to visit," wrote Hedge, "not to imitate" (Hedge, "The Churches and the Church," p. 194; Osgood, "Poet of Puseyism," pp. 46-47, 54). Elsewhere Hedge referred to American Gothic churches as "practical anachronisms" (Hedge "Classic and Romantic," pp. 315-316. See also his "Ecclesiastical Christendom," p. 113).

[36]Hedge, ed., Essays and Reviews, pp. xiii, xvii; Hedge, "The Churches and the Church," p. 153; Hedge, "Ecclesiastical Christendom," pp. 115, 123; Parker, Theism, p. 31; Parker, American Scholar, p. 329; Parker, Book Review of Rest in Church, by Furlong Elizabeth Shipton Harris (London, 1848), MQR, I (June, 1848), 392; Parker to Convers Francis, October 18, 1843, in Weiss, Life of Parker, I, 223; Brownson, "Church Question," p. 466. Channing called the movement "the popish explosion at Oxford" (Channing to Joseph Blanco White, September 18, 1839, in Joseph Blanco White, Life, III, 95; Channing to Lucy Aiken, January 15, 1839, in Channing, Correspondence, p. 327).

[37]Osgood, Studies in Christian Biography, p. 141; Hedge, ed., Essays and Reviews, p. xvii; Parker, Social Classes, p. 298; Parker, Book Review of Rest in Church by Harris, p. 392; Parker, "Hennell on the Origin of Christianity," p. 161.

[38]Osgood, Studies in Christian Biography, pp. 2,5; Brownson, "Church Question," p. 475; Channing to Joseph Blanco White, November 20, 1839, in Channing, Memoir, II, 395; Channing, as cited in Renan, "Channing the the Unitarian Movement in the United States," p. 11; W.H. Channing, "Call of the Present: No. 3," p. 150; W.H. Channing, as cited in Frothingham, Memoir of William Henry Channing, p. 290; Parker, Theism, p. 31; Parker, Transient and Permanent, p. 175; Parker to Convers Francis, October 18, 1843, in Weiss, Life of Parker, I, 223.

[39]Brownson, "Church Question," pp. 470, 474-475, 467-468; Brownson, The Convert, p. 161; Hedge, "The Churches and the Church," p. 193; Emerson to Edward Bouverie Pusey, [1871?], in Emerson, Letters, VI, 192. See also Hecker to his family, March 1, 1844, in Holden, Early Years of Hecker, pp. 108-109; W.H. Channing, Gospel of Today, pp. 9-10.

[40]Parker to Convers Francis, October 18, 1843, in Weiss, Life of Parker, I, 223; Channing to Joseph Blanco White, November 20, 1839, in Channing, Memoir, II, 395.

As they drew nearer to the Catholic Church, Brownson and Hecker became more and more convinced that the Anglican Church could in no way claim to be a branch of the true church, that its separation from Rome was schismatic, and that adherence to the true high church meant adherence to Roman Catholicism (Brownson, "Bishop Hopkins on Novelties," BrQR, July, 1844, in Brownson, Works, IV, 527-542; Brownson, Letter to The Pathfinder, May 9, 1843, reprinted in Cameron, Companion to Thoreau's Correspondence, p. 34; Hecker to Brownson, April 9, 1844, in Holden, Early Years of Hecker, p. 205). For some time, Hecker had found the choice between the two to be the one thing preventing his decision (Hecker to Brownson, March 15, 1844, in Holden, Early Years of Hecker, p. 201; Hecker to Brownson, April 9, 1844, in ibid., p. 205).

[41]Osgood was the only one of our group to notice a decided similarity between transcendentalism and the Oxford Movement. But he was definitely opposed to the outward pageantry of the high church movement. In an article in which he mainly commends the Oxford poets for their piety and beauty, he offers an implied criticism of what he regards as an extreme variation of the transcendental theme: The Oxford Movement, he complains, "is transcendentalism carried beyond nature and connected with glorious buildings and ancient rites, instead of blue skies and holy instincts" (Osgood, "Poet of Puseyism," p. 54).

[42]Parker, Theism, p. 31; Parker, Rights of Man in America, pp. 199-202; Parker, Social Classes, p. 279; "Causes of the Present Condition of Ireland," MQR, III (June, 1850), 304-337; Channing to William Rathbone, February 28, 1840, in Channing, Memoir, III, 285; Emerson, Works, V, 376-377; Emerson, Sea, September, 1833, in Emerson, JN, IV, 240; "The Right to Labor," SA, I (July 21, 1849), 75; Ripley, "European Affairs," ibid., July 21, November 17, 1849, pp. 46, 317; Book Review of Ireland As I Saw It: The Character, Condition, and Prospects of the

People by William S. Balch (New York, n.d.), ibid., February 23, 1850, p. 116.

[43]Furness, A Discourse, Preached in the First Congregational Unitarian Church, on the Morning of the Lord's Day, May 24, 1829. Occasioned by the Recent Emancipation of the Roman Catholics Throughout the British Empire (Philadelphia, 1829), pp. 7-18.

[44]Channing, Works, VI, 37.

[45]Parker to Rev. J.T. Sargent, September 18, 1859, in Weiss, Life of Parker, II, 354; Parker, Social Classes, p. 279; Clarke, "True Theology," p. 45; Fuller, as cited in Higginson, Margaret Fuller Ossoli, p. 214; Thoreau, Journal, December 12, 1851, III, 135.

[46]"Reform Movements: Irish Emigrant Protection Scoieties," SA, II (February 2, 1850), 78; Thoreau, Journal, September 24, 1851, III, 17; ibid., September 1, 1853, V, 411; Thoreau, Walden, pp. 59-60, 226-231; Thoreau to Emerson, October 17, 1843, in Thoreau, Correspondence, ed. Walter Harding and Carl Bode (New York, 1958), p. 146; Emerson to Thoreau, September 8, 1843, in ibid., p. 137; Emerson, Works, X, 206; Osgood, "Americans and the Men of the Old World," p. 8; Osgood, "The German in America," CE, LI (November, 1851), 351.

[47]Parker, "The Material Condition of the People of Massachusetts," CE, LXV (July, 1858), 53; Parker, St. Bernard and Other Papers, p. 336; Parker to Rev. J.T. Sargent, September 18, 1859, in Weiss, Life of Parker, II, 354; Fuller, as cited in Higginson, Margaret Fuller Ossoli, p. 214; Emerson, Works, I, 320; ibid., X, 206; Osgood, "Americans and the Men of the Old World," p. 8; Osgood, "The German in America," p. 351; Furness, "The Character of Christ," CE, XV (January, 1834), 277.

[48]Parker to J.T. Sargent, September 18, 1859, in Weiss, Life of Parker, II, 354; Parker, Autobiography, p. 343; Parker, Rights of Man, p. 358; Parker, Social Classes, pp. 279-281; Parker, "Material Condition of the People of Massachusetts," pp. 52-54; Parker, Sins and Safeguards, p. 338; Parker to F.E. Parker, April 15, 1858, in Weiss, Life of Parker, I, 397; Fuller, "The Irish Character," New York Tribune, July 15, 24, 1845, as summarized by Vivian Hopkins, Emerson Society Quarterly, LV:26 (1969), 26; Thoreau, Journal, September 1, 1853, V, 411; Osgood, "Americans and the Men of the Old World," p. 8.

William Bean asserts that Parker's and others' fear of pauperism, crime, etc., in the immigrants was not sufficient to explain the prevalent anti-Irish feeling. In "Puritan Versus Celt" (New England Quarterly, VII [March, 1934], 74-89), he tries to show that the Puritan hostility to the Celts was largely due to political causes.

[49]Parker, Theism, pp. 33-34. See also Parker, Transient and Permanent, p. 410; Osgood, "Americans and the Men of the Old World," p. 8.

[50]Parker, "Material Condition of the People of Massachusetts," p. 53; Parker, Rights of Man, p. 357; Parker, St. Bernard and Other Papers, p. 336; Fuller, as cited in Higginson, Margaret Fuller Ossoli, p. 214; Fuller, "Irish Character," as summarized by Hopkins, p. 26; Channing, Journal, n.d., in Channing, Memoir, I, 234; Clarke, "True Theology," p. 45; Osgood, "The German in America," p. 351; W.H. Channing, "The Philadelphia Riots," Phalanx, I (May 18, 1844), 133-135.

[51]Stetson, A Discourse on the Duty of Sustaining the Laws, Occasioned by the Burning of the Ursuline Convent. Delivered at the First Church in Medford, Sunday, August 24, 1834 (Boston, 1834), pp. 4-16.

[52]Charlestown was a suburb of Boston.

[53]Channing, Sermon, October, 1834, in Channing, Memoir, III, 247-249; Channing, "Letter on Catholicism," p. 276; Bartol, Religion in Our Public Schools, p. 8.

[54]Maria Monk, Awful Disclosures of the Hotel Dieu Nunnery of Montreal (New York, 1836).

[55][Osgood], "Monthly Record," WM, II (November, 1836), 287; Osgood, "Debates on the Roman Catholic Religion," p. 63. Cranch's only criticism of "popery-phobia"

sprang from his objection to what he called its "extreme ultraism and narrowness of spirit" (Cranch, "Concert and the Church," p. 339).

[56]W.H. Channing, "Philadelphia Riots," pp. 133-135; Brownson, "The Presidential Nominations," BrQR, July, 1844, in Brownson, Works, XV, 488n (Brownson's complaint, though he was near joining the Catholic Church, rested on the defense of minority rights).

[57]Channing to Lucy Aiken, June 22, 1835, in Rice, Federal Street Pastor, pp. 207-208; Parker, Rights of Man, [1854], pp. 357-358; Clarke, "Polemics and Irenics," [1854], p. 167; Clarke, "Buckle's History of Civilization, [1861], pp. 386-387.

[58]"An Alarm," Harbinger, V (July 3, 1847), 58; Osgood, "Americans and the Men of the Old World," p. 11; Henry, Considerations on Human Progress, p. 403; Emerson, Journal Y, 1845, in Emerson, JN, IX, 299; Parker, "Material Condition of the People of Massachusetts," pp. 53-54; Parker, Rights of Man, pp. 357-358; Fuller, as cited in Higginson, Margaret Fuller Ossoli, p. 214.

[59]Parker, Rights of Man, [1854], pp. 357-358.

[60]Emerson, Journal W, 1845, in Emerson, JN, IX, 192; Emerson, Journal Y, 1845, in ibid., p. 299.

[61]Bartol, In Remembrance. Address, on the Occasion of the Death of Charles Greely Loring. Delivered in the West Church (Boston, 1867), p.17; Bartol, Radical Problems, pp. 376-377.

[62]Parker, Ten Sermons, p. 299.

[63]Channing to [?], July 13, 1842, in Channing, Memoir, III, 397.

[64]Brownson, The Convert, pp. 93-94; Brownson, "Leroux on Humanity," pp. 103-105, 124-126.

Parker' impatience with the pietism of the Catholic Church is reflected in his hopes for the effectiveness of his review, the Massachusetts Quarterly. While the journal was in the planning stages, he wrote that by means of this liberal periodical, the better minds of the day would terrorize the ultramontanists, making them see that they were no longer living in the middle ages, and "that they are not to be let alone dreaming in the garden of Eden, but are to buckle up and work" (Parker to Charles Sumner, n.d., as cited in Gohdes, Periodicals of Transcendentalism, p. 159).

[65]Clarke, Steps of Belief, pp. 267-268.

[66]Parker, "An Anti-Slavery Address," 1854, in Parker, Rights of Man, p. 167; Parker, Boston Evening Telegraph, July 2, 1854, as cited in Bean, "Puritan Versus Celt," p. 82; Parker, "The Rights of Man in America," 1854, in Parker, Rights of Man, p. 357; Parker to Rev. J.T. Sargent, September 18, 1859, in Weiss, Life of Parker, II, 354; Parker to Charles Sumner, August 13, 1859, in ibid., p. 382; Parker, Slave Power, p. 280; Parker, Nebraska Question, p. 70.

In Massachusetts the Catholics, mostly immigrants, were generally considered pro-slavery; in the South they were believed to be abolitionist. According to William G. Bean, the conviction in New England that the immigrants were against the anti-slavery cause became apparent in 1854 (Bean, "An Aspect of Know Nothingism--The Immigrants and Slavery," South Atlantic Quarterly, XXIII [October, 1924], 321).

[67]In a passing allusion, Clarke refers to the cooperation of Unitarians with Catholics in the Freedman's Aid Society after emancipation (see extract from his sermon at the National Conference of Unitarian and Other Christian Churches, April 4, 1865, in Clarke, Autobiography, p. 265).

Historian Bancroft quoted Bossuet in support of slavery (Bancroft, History of the U.S., X, 346), but he also has a discussion of the efforts of the medieval Church, particularly Pope Alexander II, "the guardian of the oppressed," and other popes to end the slave trade and even slavery itself (ibid., I, 163-164, 172).

[68]Brownson was a defender of slavery until the outbreak of the Civil War, when he took up the fight for total emancipation on the grounds that the war justified it (see Bean, "Puritan Versus Celt," pp. 76, 79-80; Madeleine Hooke Rice, American Catholic Opinion in the Slavery Controversy [Gloucester, Massachusetts, 1964, c. 1944], p. 152).

[69]In his Discourse of Religion, Parker quoted Bishop John England of Charleston, South Carolina, in proof of the contention that "the Catholic Church has been the uncompromising friend of slavery" (p. 383).

[70]Brownson, "Laboring Classes," [1840], passim; Parker, Theism, p. 177; Parker, Autobiography, pp. 359-360; Parker, Social Classes, pp. 324-325; Parker, Ten Sermons, p. 363. W.H. Channing and Hecker on one occasion also wondered about the Catholic's seeming preference for passive forms of religion (see Hecker, Diary, n.d., in Elliott, Life of Hecker, p. 117 [Holden in Early Years of Hecker, p. 196n, dates the entry January, 1844]; W.H. Channing, "Anniversary Week," Harbinger, I [June 21, 1845], 28).

[71]Channing, "On Fenelon," pp. 178-179.

[72]Channing, "Letter on Catholicism," p. 163; Channing, as cited in Peabody, Reminiscences of Channing, p. 99; Peabody, "The World's Need of Woman," CE, LXIX (November, 1860), 435-436, 438, 447; Osgood, Studies in Christian Biography, p. 207; "The French Clergy," from a correspondent of the Manchester Examiner, Harbinger, VI (April 29, 1848), 201-202; W.H. Channing, "Call of the Present: No. 3," p. 151; W.H. Channing, "Heaven Upon Earth," ibid., April 1, 1844, p. 422; W.H. Channing, "Ernest the Seeker," p. 52; Hecker to Brownson, January 21, 1844, in Henry F. Brownson, Brownson's Early Life, p. 509; Bartol, Reason and Rome in Education, p. 6; Bartol, Pictures of Europe, p. 78; Bartol, Discourses on the Christian Body, pp. 331-332; Emerson, Italy and France, May 12, 1833, in Emerson, JN, IV, 172; Emerson, Italy, 1833, in ibid., p. 138; Parker, Ten Sermons, p. 252; Parker to Convers Francis, March 18, 1844, in Weiss, Life of Parker, I, 232-233; Parker, Social Classes, p. 330; Parker, World of Matter and Spirit, p. 81; Fuller to New York Tribune, [December?], 1847, in Fuller, Writings, p. 425; Fuller, Life Without and Within, p. 324.

[73]W.H. Channing, as cited in Hecker, Questions of the Soul, p. 222; Bartol, Rising Faith, p. 318; Brooks, "The House of Mercy," 1871, in Brooks, Poems, Memoir, pp. 173-174. Brooks had had a successful operation for a growing blindness. In the poem he praises the Daughters of Charity at Carney Hospital, South Boston, as "angels, who with gentle feet...carry twofold light to darkened rooms,/ To darkened eyes and many a lowly heart."

It is hard to understand why Clarke had almost nothing to say on the subject of Catholic works of charity. We do know that later in his life he held weekly meetings to discuss such questions as, "What is doing here for animals?...for young men?...for street-boys?...for infants?...for the poor?" These gatherings were attended by Catholic and Protestant, orthodox and Unitarian. Thus, Clarke reported, "the lion at these meetings has lain down with the lamb," in an effort to overcome denominational barriers on behalf of the poor (Clarke, Autobiography, pp. 338-339).

[74]W.H. Channing, "Talks on the Times," p. 107.

After Sophia Ripley became a Catholic, she discovered several appropriate avenues through which she could exercise the transcendental urge to uplift the poor and the destitute. She spent the remaining years of her life working in hospitals and prisons and assisting the Good Shepherd Sisters of New York in their work with delinquent girls.

[75]Peabody, Identification of the Artisan and Artist, pp. 3-42.

[76]Parker, Sins and Safeguards, pp. 283-284. This is taken from a sermon on poverty which Parker delivered in 1849. But in the same year he complained that he had heard that the Catholic clergy did little to remove immorality in Boston

(Parker, Social Classes, pp. 276-277).

77Parker, Theism, p. 16.

78"Arrival of Father Mathew: Welcome to the City," SA, I (July 14, 1849), 30; "Father Mathew at Work," ibid., July 21, 1849, p. 47; James Redfield, "Character of Father Mathew," ibid., July 21, 1849, p. 60; Ripley, "Town and Country Items," ibid., July 21, 1849, p. 63; Ripley, "Father Mathew in Brooklyn," ibid., p. 64; "Arrival of Father Mathew in Boston," ibid., August 4, 1849, p. 79; Ripley, "Father Mathew,"ibid., August 11, 1849, p. 93; Ripley, "Festival to Father Mathew," ibid., August 11, 1849, p. 93; "American Affairs," ibid., December 29, 1849, pp. 408-410.

79Channing, Works, pp. 106-107.

80Hedge, "The Nineteenth Century," CE, XLVIII (May, 1850), 379; Bartol, Reason and Rome in Education, p. 6; Clarke, Orthodoxy, p. 36; Channing, "On Fenelon," p. 180; "The Catholics and Associationists," Harbinger,III (July 25, 1846), 102-103; Ripley, "The Catholics and Associationists," ibid., September 5, 1846, pp. 193-194.

81W.H. Channing, "Philadelphia Riots," [1844], pp. 133-134; Osgood, "Americans and the Men of the Old World," [1855], pp. 8-9. Osgood's article is a discussion of three publications: Select Speeches of Kossuth (1854); Speech of Hon. E. Brooks on the Church Property Bill. The Papal Power in the State, and the Resistance to This Power in the Temporalities of the Church, As Recently Seen in the United States and Europe. In the Senate of New York, March 6, 1855; The Church Property Question. Letter from Archbishop Hughes, in Relation to the Petition of St. Louis Church, Buffalo, and to Mr. Putnam's Anti-Catholic Church Property Bill (New York, March 28, 1855).

82Bartol, Religion in Our Public Schools.

83Ibid., appended Note, p. 23.

84A year later Bartol defended the Catholic position from another point of view. In a warning against the idolatry of Book or image, he declared himself in sympathy with the Catholic sensitivity to the correct translation of the second commandment, a crucial point in the controversy (Bartol, "Way to Find God," p. 50).

85See Alvan Lamson, Review of Religion, a Principle, Not a Form: A Discourse Delivered on the Lord's Day, March 17, 1844, in the First Congregational Church, in Reference to the Question Concerning the Use of the Bible in the Public Schools by Furness (Philadelphia, 1844), CE, XXXVI (May, 1844), 431; Osgood, "Education in the West," pp. 205-206. Osgood's article was a report on the meetings of a professional teachers' organization, in which the active participants were both Catholics and Protestants (see above, p. 54n).

86Bartol, Reason and Rome in Education [1879].

87Bartol, "Way to Find God," [1860], p. 50.

88Bartol, Religion in Our Public Schools [1859], pp. 12-13.

89Bartol, Reason and Rome in Education, pp. 4-17.

90Long before the question became a controversial one, Parker, in a sermon entitled, "The Perishing Classes of Boston," [1846], had also endorsed a proposal for separate Irish schools, as a plan "large and noble" (Parker, Speeches, I, 216).

91Clarke, Peter at Antioch [1874], pp. 7-10.

92See his charges on this score in Clarke, "Wanted, a Statesman!" Old and New, II (December, 1870), 649; Clarke, Steps of Belief, p. 269. In "True Theology," Clarke admits that the Catholics' fear of heretical books and teachers is at least consistent with their theology (p. 46).

93Clarke, Peter at Antioch, p. 7.

94Clarke, Peter at Antioch, pp. 7-10.

95An additional comment is provided by Henry, who in a brief review supports the proposed constitutional amendments of 1876 that would deprive the states of power to support schools run by religious groups (Henry, "Spear's Religion and the State," <u>NAR</u>, CXXIV [March, 1877], 319-320).

Georgiana Kirby in "Reminiscences of Brook Farm," (V, 525), contends that Brook Farmers discussed the Catholic detestation of the public school system, but this is undoubtedly an anachronism.

CHAPTER VII

THE CATHOLIC RELIGION OF THE FUTURE

THE CONDITION OF CONTEMPORARY CHRISTIANITY

Although the transcendentalists were critical of the Catholic Church's waning capacity for good, they did not dismiss it entirely as a remnant of a bygone age, one whose future was empty of possibility.

There seem to have been two schools of thought among the transcendentalists on the matter of the Catholic Church's potential. Sometimes the two divergent opinions were held simultaneously by one person. The first was that although the Church ought to have been receding according to the evolutionary pattern, in actuality it was still a strong and potentially dangerous adversary. The second opinion was that no danger lay within its fold, and this for one of two reasons. Either it was indeed still powerful but held no threat to the more liberal and free-thinking religions of the day; or else it was disintegrating from within, and--from without--the spirit and conditions of the age were against it.

Most of the transcendentalists were of the first opinion at one time or another. Among them Clarke most often sounds the alarm. Again and again he points out the many forces which still sustained "this great institution." Not only did the Roman Catholic Church seem to sum up all the great inspirations of the past; it appeared to be carried along by those forces even in the present day. Hedge expressed both his own and Clarke's thought along these lines when he wrote that the Catholic Church's continued vitality was owing to its having been deeply impregnated with "the spirit of the living God...poured out upon this Church in the days of her youth." This spirit, though now no longer given to that Church, would continue to supply it with "fulness and breadth" for a long time to come. The public opinion of the world, they both warned, was wrong in underrating the power of the Catholic Church and in thinking that it must soon expire. On the contrary, it was stronger today than ever before, the strongest church, Hedge added, in all Christendom, and "the strongest organized force on the globe."[1]

To support their contention Clarke and Hedge took several opportunities to enlarge upon certain significant factors maintaining the Church in power. First they dwelt on the Church's own peculiar traits: its lack of contentiousness within; its certainty of possessing the truth and its refusal to compromise; its thorough organization and the influence it exerted through the hierarchy, the pope and the councils; its confidence in its destiny and its sense of divine right; and its ability to convince its members of the proximity of God and Christ in the Eucharist. Secondly they pointed up those characteristics which the Catholic Church shared with Protestant sects but in which it excelled: humanity, faith, piety, gentleness, love, holiness; the power of proselytizing; the construction of beautiful churches and the accumulation of funds; its political and social influence; its appeal to the senses over the intellect; its emphasis upon worship over theology; its skillful use of all that is noble in the arts; and, in sum, its relation to "the whole of life."[2]

Many of these points are found scattered throughout their writings and those of the other transcendentalists, as we have seen. In these latter instances, however, it was their express purpose to demonstrate the power and steady advance of the Catholic Church in her "path of empire." The conclusion seemed obvious: the Church was indeed a threat to all liberal religion and even to free institutions. "The danger of the Church," wrote Clarke after depicting the spirit of virtue in Catholicism, "is that this beautiful religious spirit may be sacrificed to the power and growth of the organization." The Church will, he feared, make use of the religious freedoms granted to it in America to destroy those very freedoms. That, he concluded, "is her expectation, her determination, her purpose."[3]

Other transcendentalists concurred with the evaluation of the Church as a power "still in the ascendant...still majestic."[4] Nevertheless, only Parker

shared any of Clarke's alarm, classing Catholicism second among the four great

perils faced by his country.[5] The others expressed their misgivings only when

they perceived either a resurgence of papal power or a numerical growth in the

Church's members.[6] In these instances, although their manner appears brave, their

apprehension is apparent. Bartol, for example, contended that the Catholic move

to take over America through its public schools would fail in the end. With an

air of confidence he warned Catholics that "to assail any great and generous free-

dom among us is to spit on the wind." But as Clarke had done before him, he ad-

monished those who were building up an ecclesiastical oligarchy that they had

better emigrate of their own free will. He admitted at the same time that the

intent of his discourse was to be a warning to his colleagues: "The great wheel

at Rome, turning mightily without noise, sets in motion a million ecclesiastical

cogs;...."[7]

At other times the transcendentalists were more optimistic, though cautiously

so. Even when they enlarged upon the power of the Catholic Church and berated the

"seductions of that sorceress" or the "subtle activity of her agents,"[8] they added

that actually there was no ground for alarm. Wrote Bartol, "There are no indica-

tions as far as I can see, that the papacy is ever to invade our Canaan so as to

possess the land. If Jesuits contrive, let them be observed; if they encroach,

let them be repelled. But fear them, let us not!"[9]

More frequent than such admonitions, however, were spirited expositions of

all the signs of Catholic weakness. "How foolish it is," wrote Clarke in an earli-

er and more optimistic mood, "to suppose that any one denomination is to swallow

up all the rest!" If the Catholic Church had been unable to hold its own against

Luther in the sixteenth century, it was idle to hope that it would regain suprem-

acy in the nineteenth. Not only had its own strength declined since then, but now

it was opposed by both Protestant and Greek Churches and by the spirit of the times.[10]

The transcendentalists' assumption that the signs of the times were in direct opposition to Catholicism was based on their analysis of the popular mind. Everywhere, they asserted, the informed intellect was emancipating itself from what Alcott referred to as "the sway of tradition, authority, usage." Everywhere it was adopting the more progressivist orientation of a mind liberated from the past.[11] In this vein perhaps the most noteworthy effort in the transcendental defense against the encroachments of the Catholic Church was Channing's "Letter on Catholicism," which appeared in the Western Messenger in 1836. During this decade Lyman Beecher had begun his tour of the eastern states, warning Americans of the insidious spread of Catholicism in the west. Simultaneously, Clarke began to worry about the same matter, though less overtly. Not until 1880 did he announce that as editor of the Messenger, he was the one who had instigated the Channing letter.[12]

Channing's lengthy statement was a dissertation on the dangers of Catholicism, its evils and its strengths. All these dangers he dismissed as "not very formidable,"[13] since for all its power, the Catholic Church was opposed to the "true spirit of the times." The current progress of society and of the individual was evidence of "a natural movement of the soul." Catholicism, therefore, must fall before this inevitable evolution. In eloquent transcendental prose Channing settled all doubts and fears by reminding his readers of some basic realities:

> The great foe of the Romish church is not the theologian....It is human nature waking up to a consciousness of its power, catching a glimpse of the perfection for which it was made, beginning to respect itself, thirsting for free action and development, learning through a deep consciousness that there is something diviner than forms, or churches, or creeds, recognizing in Jesus Christ its own celestial model...; here is the great enemy of Catholicism.

Channing admitted that there was danger in the growing influence of the Church in the west,especially when Protestant sects were divided among themselves. But

this he adverted to only by way of encouragement to a certain unity.[14] Privately,
he expressed more concern. He saw that society was indeed in great danger, that
divided churches could not prevail, and that the one, powerful, united Church of
Catholicism could be triumphant. To prevent this catastrophe he did not advocate
tangible unity among the Protestant sects, nor preachments against the materialism
he saw infecting Unitarianism.[15] Neither did he believe that the European political revolutions were sufficient, though he did regard them as Catholicism's death
knell. In the last analysis, he advised, there was but one way to oppose Catholicism successfully. "Spread just, natural, ennobling views of religion. Lift
men above Catholicism, by showing them the great spiritual purpose of Christianity."[16] Such a religion was, obviously, the liberal form of Unitarianism of which
he was the grandest spokesman.

Pure, spiritual, transcendental religion constituted also the basic argument
of the others who felt secure against the blandishments of the Catholic Church.
They employed few statistics[17] or syllogisms, and a modicum of polemics or nativist diatribes. Almost their entire thrust lay in their unbounded hope in the
"true" religion of the soul. They too pointed up the "current of our time" as a
sure warrant for their sanguine faith that the "medieval" church could not last,
no matter who said otherwise.[18] In a review of Tocqueville's Democracy in America,
Osgood wrote that he was aware that many others besides the author believed in the
tendency of democracy toward Catholicism. But he added, "no great array of names
will make us believe, that our land of liberty is ever to be the seat of Papal
Supremacy." "What avails it," Channing asked a Philadelphia congregation, "that
this or another church summons to its aid fathers, traditions, venerated usages?
The spirit, the genius of Christianity is stronger than all these....I have no
alarm."[19]

Besides being contrary to the spirit of the times and to the spirit of transcendentalism triumphant, Catholicism held within itself the seeds of its own

decay. This assumption of the transcendentalists has become apparent in their ideas about the place of the Church in history and in the contemporary world. It appears also as an evident frame of reference in many of their other allusions to the Church. In these they took for granted that the Church no longer had life, health, or creativity, and that its time had come and gone. They described the Church in vivid metaphors as decrepit and in ruins, a toothless lion, a mere rind or empty shell. Or it was a dry and barren tree, struck with blight, its fruit overripe and rotten.[20] "The once powerful church," exulted Parker, "no longer sits the heir of all the ages, and the queen of civilization."[21]

This assessment of the Catholic Church's potential was not made within a vacuum but within the context of a total world picture. And with it was made an evaluation of the entire state of Christianity. The transcendentalists looked around them and found that it was not only the Catholic Church which was failing mankind; so were the Protestant Churches; so was Unitarianism. They found that theirs was a period of "unsettling of old creeds,"[22] when men were casting about for a new and viable religion. They commented often on what they observed as a widespread longing for an alternative to the "frigid utilitarianism" of recent decades.[23] Some of them detected prophetic signs of life in attempts of various kinds to restore the "palmy days" of religion, to search out higher ideals, and to fill the hungry and relieve the poor.[24]

With less confidence, others supposed the religious spirit of the day to be fading:[25] churches are empty; sects are divided; religion is rejected by men of science; authority and custom are flaunted; "incredulity verges on despair."[26] "We think we can defy any crisis, any teacher, any Providence...." complained Emerson.[27] Moreover, personal piety was turning cold; investigation bearing the fruits of skepticism and denial, or, conversely, of a "miserable eclecticism"; and spirituality giving way before materialism.[28] Even Unitarianism is despaired of by its chief patron, Channing. It lacks vitality, he admitted to a friend, because it was founded on a negative principle of rejection and it possessed therefore no deep religious principle. He implied further that the movement had early been paralyzed by a material philosophy, and toward the end of his life he saw little hope for it.[29]

Even Emerson, the patron saint of transcendental optimism, often shared this pessimistic view, one which developed in him more strongly in his later years. Hardly enthusiastic for the future of religion, groping himself, he confessed that he could not see "how the Great God prepares to satisfy the heart in the new order of things." It seemed to him as if there had to be a period of much doubt and much waiting before any clear vision of the future of religion could be perceived.[30]

OPTION FOR A NEW SYNTHESIS

The liberal, democratic, scientific spirit of the age, then, seemed hopeful; its religious spirit less so. Yet in the main the transcendentalists were not daunted. Above all things they confided in the spirit of man. And the majority of them, either intermittently or in well-defined patterns, held rather consistently to the belief that the perfect church of the future would eventually emerge. Progressivists and transcendentalists all, they accepted what Osgood called "the prerogative accorded to every age," namely, the right of each era to reinterpret its beliefs according to its "personal convictions and...providential position."[31] The mid-nineteenth century reinterpretation of belief was, of course, the transcendental faith. Our group spent much verbiage in speculating on that faith _per se_, and in some cases implementing the ways in which it could become a widespread reality.

What part did the Catholic Church play in these speculations? Was there no future for it except in monstrous conquest of its adversaries or in corrosion from within? A few of the transcendentalists saw another eventuality, that if the Church could accept change according to a liberal faith, perhaps there was

hope for it.[32] There could even be the possibility that, given a radical departure from its ecclesiastical, formal, and immoral ways, it would providentially
absorb all other churches--and in that case, it should.[33] A small number of them
even detected signs that the Church was indeed, quietly and almost imperceptibly,
becoming more progressive, or at least so were some members within it.[34]

More to their purpose, however, was a different context for the Church's
utility in times to come. While in their idyllic plans for the future of religion
the Catholic Church as such played no role, portions of its style and belief did.
In examining what their concepts of the "Church of the Future" were, we shall see
to what extent they could incorporate within it various features of Catholicism
which they approved.

The fundamental prerequisite for the new church was that it should be based
on a unity of all faiths. On this score the transcendentalists are unanimous.
Their earnest hope was that, evidence to the contrary, differences of opinion need
not continue to divide men. Indeed, they could be the source of a rich variety, a
pleasing diversity within the one church, providing for religion a new and splen-
did synthesis for the benefit of man.

The synthesis emerging from a union of all churches would be grounded in two
basic elements. The first was what constituted for the transcendentalists "genuine religion." In their minds, there was a "central Christianity" which all religions embodied, and which united them all in a faith that alone could be termed
"catholic."[35] For some, it could never be the catholicity of the Church of Rome.[36]
It would rather be a catholicity that was genuinely universal, one that in the
Church of the Future would unite diversity of custom with fellowship of spirit.[37]
For others, the Church of Rome was the best exemplar of the kind of universality
they wanted. Channing declared, a year before he died, that he honored the Catholic Church for one thing--that it clung to the idea of a universal church. His
nephew and others of our group referred numerous times to that Church as

exemplifying most perfectly--at least in theory--the "catholic" ideal. Perhaps

the kind of universality which the transcendentalists wished to emulate is most

clearly delineated in Clarke's description of the Roman Church's catholicity.

Late in his life he wrote: "The power of the Roman Catholic Church amid all its

errors and abuses, is that it retains the idea of a common life from which all

individual life must grow....The true church, or brotherhood of all saints, medi-

ates the love of God." Earlier, Bartol had written from another perspective:

"It is the grandest praise of the Roman communion, that with all its corruptions

and tyrannies, it has so largely succeeded in vindicating to itself as character-

istic the title Catholic, after Christian the highest epithet, best naming the

bond between the human and the divine." These aspects of communion were the ones

which the transcendentalists were most eager to attain.[38]

The second element in which the union of all churches was to be grounded was

equally important. The new Church was to be a composite of whatever of truth

could be culled from each religion or sect. The transcendentalists were convinced

that the traces of truth found in every religious system--Catholic, Protestant,

Etruscan, Oriental, African--were valuable, and that they ought to be incorporated

into the future church.[39] Almost all of them favored this convergence, each in his

own way calling repeatedly for cooperation and the breaking down of theological

and historical barriers.[40] Some few of them went further, actually initiating

this kind of "future church" among their own congregations, or at least detailing

the manner in which it could be realized.

Brownson was the first to come forth with a particular form of unification.

In 1836 he issued an appeal for such in his New Views of Christianity, Society

and the Church. "The time has come," he announced, "for a new church, for a new

synthesis of the elements of the life of humanity." The vital life of his cen-

tury having been broken down by spiritualism and materialism, there were only two

alternatives left for society: either to dispense with all religious teaching, or to build a new church. The mission of the new church would be to reconcile the spiritualist and materialist tendencies of the age. This it would do by exploiting another characteristic of the times--the tendency toward association. With these as basic elements--material and scientific progress, spiritual aspiration, and communion among all members of society--he organized his Society for Christian Union and Progress. His goal was eventually to incorporate all classes, all sects, all areas of life--politics, industry, finance, the arts, the family, the church.[41]

Brownson abandoned this idealistic project by 1840, when he realized it was having no other effect than to create another sect.[42] From 1842 to 1844 he turned instead to the existing Christian churches, admonishing them to unite--perhaps by means of a general council--within the fold of the true "catholic church" which they already constituted, although in splintered fashion.[43] He began by calling for "catholicism without the papacy." But as he came to acknowledge that the Roman Church would have to be included, he urged communion under the pope as a purely spiritual leader. Finally, he accepted the Catholic Church itself as the only way to insure that the future church would be one, catholic, inspired, and supreme--the four qualities he had selected as essential to the true church.[44]

Hedge was another who had ideas about what the bases of a united church should be. He did not found a church himself, but he did outline carefully the form it ought to take. As did Brownson, Hedge believed that the first task was to "knit the severed parts, to restore the broken communion." But unlike Brownson's method of balancing matter and spirit, Hedge would reconcile liberty for the individual with a "unity of wills and authority of wills united." The power generated by such a reconciliation would restore the communion of all society in what he called the Broad Church. Such a church would satisfy what Bartol described as Hedge's "innate tendency" to catholicity. The Broad Church would indeed be a catholic one, taking as it would the best components of Christian Churches from every point on the compass: the stability and conservatism of the east; the mobility

and progress of the west; the inner life and idealism of the north; and the exter-

ior productiveness, ritualism, symbolism, and ecclesiastical organization of the

south, that is, the Catholic Church.[45]

It is not to be expected that Clarke would be silent on the matter of a

united church of the future. The Church of the Disciples which he created in

Boston in 1841 was established with a view to carrying out the purposes of Christ

--to found "an association,--a united body, whose principle of union would be

faith in him;...." Thus Clarke's church would be broadly based, built solely as

it was on belief in Christ. His aim for the future was to form a "comprehensive

church," a judicious blend of all the best elements of Catholicism, Protestantism,

Unitarianism, and transcendentalism--all harmonizing in a perfect synthesis evolv-

ing out of the historical past.[46]

Reference has already been made to the proposals for unity made by William

Henry Channing. In some ways even more broadly conceived than the others, the

Socialist Christian Commonwealth envisioned a total reorganization of society,

"a union of virtuous, intelligent, happy brotherhoods, the earth over."[47] What

he once referred to as the "New Church of Universal Unity"[48] would reconcile union

with freedom and church with state, and would satisfy in an organic manner the

longing of the age for spiritual unity. In addition this church would combine the

best elements of revivalism, naturalism, and Catholicism. The result would be an

era of "Combined Order" in which man seeks God, God comes down to man, and men

relate to one another in "all-uniting goodness."[49]

FEATURES OF THE NEW CHURCH

With the philosophy of unity or communion as a base for their new church,

the transcendentalists turned attention to the components which they would select

from various religions and sects. Of these, we shall discuss only the ones which

have either a positive or a negative relation to the Catholic Church.

The first constituent of the future church pertains to organization. It might be suspected that in this regard the new church was to be wholly spiritual. But this is only partially true. Freedom, of course, was one of the hallmarks of all the transcendentalists. They would hardly need to tell us that this would be characteristic too of their ideal church. Hence they would naturally reject anything like a hierarchy. Rather than incorporating a clerical authority, Osgood, for one, urged that "the Church of the Future must be the free development of the mind and heart of the future, under divine influence." Or, as Hedge phrased it, the church would be under "one federal Head, who is invisible."[50] Next they affirmed the authority of their own souls, hearts, and free minds as superior to any Catholic authority. The future, they advised, would do well to rely on this higher warrant.[51] Once this concept had become an actuality, the distinction between priesthood and laity would disappear, "since the good everywhere are priests." If any priesthood at all were to remain, it would be entirely spiritual in function.[52] All traces of "theocracy," prophesied Parker, were doomed. "The glorious liberty of the children of God is to be the final result of all."[53]

On the other hand, not all the transcendentalists believed that liberty and visible authority were entirely incompatible. Some recognized that in a future church both freedom and some kind of outward organization could be desirable. As they searched for a model, Clarke and Hedge in particular were most impressed by the grand organization they discovered in the Roman Church. But the Catholic Church had obtained unity at the sacrifice of freedom; the Protestant Church, liberty and progress without union. The Church of the Future would have to combine both.[54] Further, the unity might have to be purchased by some submission to an ecclesiastical hierarchy or priesthood, until a truly spiritual race should appear.[55]

Ahead of Hedge in opting for an external church was Brownson. Like the others, he did not see the usefulness of detailing its structure, but he did

develop a far more elaborate argumentation on its behalf. The associationist-
reformist temper of this particular transcendentalist led him to decide that the
human race had, since the time of the Reformation, seen enough of individualism.[56]
His Church of the Future would definitely be affected by his judgment that men had
erred in fragmenting the church and robbing it of a unifying and authoritative
principle. In sum, his ideal church would be genuinely catholic and authoritative
in all matters touching upon human life. The faith of millions, not the tyranny
of a pope, would be the substructure of such a church. It would have a creed, but
a creed binding "in foro conscientiae," not by external force. Its beliefs would
be written not in this or that confession book, but "in the very heart of this
century."[57] It would be a church with the right of interpretation and judgment,
a right held not by an individual or a hierarchy, but by "the CHURCH." This church
would speak, as the Roman Church falsely claimed to speak, in the name of Christ.
It would discipline and instruct, inspire love and union in mankind, and spread
the kingdom of God on earth.[58]

If a part of this seems something like a description of the Roman Catholic
Church, it is. But, added Brownson, it is a description of what that Church was
"to a great extent," only until the time of Pope Leo X. Since then, he alleged,
that Church had been a church in the wilderness. Before it could become again
"the real body of the Lord," it must be totally transformed.[59]

As early as 1839 Brownson declared that if it came to a choice, his preference was for submission to the Catholic Church in matters of belief and conscience
rather than to the Protestant. But he was still too much of a transcendentalist
to submit to either an infallible Catholic pope or an infallible Protestant Bible.
It was rather the Quaker faith that appeared to him the most sure--submission to
the infallibility of the Spirit of God within the human soul. "To this the Christian would must come at last, and then the Church really universal , the true
Catholic Church, be constituted."[60] Obviously, the less like the Catholic Church

in organization a future church might become, the more transcendental such a church could be.

Another feature of the new church was that it would have to be oriented toward the betterment of the race, as the transcendentalists themselves were. William Henry Channing's Socialist Christian Commonwealth is an obvious case in point. It was to promote this ideal that he published his weekly, The Spirit of the Age, in 1849-1850. A decade previously, Brownson had anticipated much the same notion of a "Christian Commonwealth." His commonwealth was to be a Christian state, to replace the Church he had founded in 1836.[61] In it the work of worship would go on, but not only in the usual manner of Sabbath exercises. Rather, the traditional forms of worship would at best be but a preparation for the real worship of God in external acts of charity.[62] Furness expressed this aspect of the church in figurative terms. The true Church of the Future, he predicted, will turn away from

> the dry and mouldering symbols of the past...; its new ceremonial shall be the acts and labors and sacrifices of earnest and living men, relinquishing property, popularity, and life itself, when the need is, for freedom and for humanity; that Church whose High Mass is a cup of cold water given to the panting fugitive at the risk of fine and imprisonment, and whose hymns and prayers and liturgies are the daily offices of human love faithfully discharged.[63]

Hedge's comments on this transcendental dream of Furness's were calculated to bring his readers down to earth. Such an ideal church, beautiful as it was, would have to wait a more favorable day. Until then, the earthly church, with all its imperfections, its ministry, and its symbols, would have to remain "schoolmaster" to bring us thither.[64]

Not that Hedge was opposed to a social facet in the new church. On the contrary, its obligations to society were, in his mind, even more challenging and idealistic than were those of Brownson and Furness. The charge he laid on this "practical Christianity" was a vast one:

> ...to remove all the obstructions which lie in the way of such a life
> [of liberty and progress], all social evils and abuses--war, slavery,
> oppression in all its forms,--to break every yoke, to undo every bur-
> den, to put away all sin. In a word, reform, the regeneration of so-
> ciety in the Christian image,--this is practical Christianity.

Such would be the true church, and it would be Catholic and Protestant in one.[65]

The transcendentalists clearly recognized the medieval Church as a model of
this type of Christianity. Osgood urged that the new church even surpass the "old
Catholicism" in this respect. Brownson likewise looked back to the pre-Reformation
church as described by Saint-Simon for an ideal type of progressive and humanitarian "Christian democracy." Going back in history still further, Brownson held up
for imitation what he envisioned St. Augustine's City of God to be--the Religion
of Humanity as well as the Religion of God. Thus would all society and all association be holy, all be for the worship of God, and all legislators and civil
rulers be ministers at his altar.[66]

A third feature of the Church of the Future would be its power to transform
all of mankind by first transforming each individual from within. The transcendentalists consequently preached the cultivation of a personal holiness as the
most distinguishing characteristic of the highest progressive forms of religion.
No more would there be a dichotomy between matter and spirit, nor would matter be
considered somehow evil, as both Calvinists and Catholic ascetics had seemed to
think it was. Rather, everything--body and soul, matter and spirit, would be
"holy to the Lord." The cultivation of morality and holiness of life would super-
sede the theological disputation and dogmatism so characteristic of both Protestant and Catholic. And the practice of virtues common to the religious beliefs
of all mankind--Catholic included--would become universal. Humility, justice,
truth, and love would flourish, just as they had--or, as some might say, had not
--among the Grecian saints and the saints of Rome, the Catholic and the Protestant, the laborer and the priest.[67]

Of all these virtues, love was to be the supreme force by which the whole

Christian body could be healed. Love is the end of all, and catholicity the means; but Love, recalled Brownson, is Christ.[68] In this emphasis we come more to the heart of the transcendental message. Christ was the center, whether as God or as the perfect man who leads to God and to communion with God in the soul. This was the goal of all the transcendentalists, and therefore of all their churches of the future, however conceived and by whatever means.[69] A Brownson would at one time state that such an aspiration toward love could be found in any Christian Church of the present--Catholic, Presbyterian, Congregationalist, Anglican; in Boston, New York, Oxford, or Rome--and that it only needed to be tapped. At another time he and others could single out the Catholic Church as the exemplar par excellence of this virtue. "Protestant countries may have a higher worldly civilization," Clarke noted, "more education and intelligence, more manufactures and commerce, but Catholic countries have more humanity and reverence, a more habitual piety, more gentle manners. If Protestants have more knowledge, Catholics have more love."[70] Here at the peak of the pinnacle was love in its supremest form--love of God or piety.

One of the basic elements of genuine piety, however, Catholics did not possess. To the transcendentalists, "not Jesus alone, but every spirit in human form is divine."[71] To spread this concept was, they believed, a cherished part of the mission of liberal Christianity.[72] As far as the Christian churches had limited divinity to the person of Christ, they had erred. The Church of the Future would rectify this weakness and organize the worship of God in all men. True, the new church would have to build first upon a profound "belief in the invisible," such as was found in the Catholic Church,[73] but it would not end there. The true religion would worship God wherever he manifested himself, whether in nature or in Providence; whether in Christ or in the human soul and all its faculties.[74] Certainly no transcendental church would be complete or true to itself without this integral dimension in its faith.

Transcendental piety so understood was to have in the future church certain forms of external manifestation. These visible expressions would constitute a fourth element in the new church. Here again the Catholic model provided a standard. What most of the transcendentalists had experienced of Catholic practices led them to enlist many of these in the service of their new churches.

It is true that some of them were opposed, though not always consistently, to adopting Catholic architecture, music, and ritual for the Church of the Future. They seemed to believe that Catholic art should be admired but not imitated, and that the time when such forms were useful had passed. But their comments are few and mild.[75] The more articulate spokesmen for the new churches--and even Emerson, who offered no specific program for the future--were of another mind. Clarke's handbook for his Church of the Disciples, for example, lists congregational worship as one of the "methods" which the Church had already adopted. While the forms of such worship were still Protestant and Unitarian, Clarke in his handbook stated that he would eventually borrow from Catholic worship all that was beautiful in its art and ritual.[76] He believed that one reason why Sunday church attendance had fallen off in Protestant sects was that the "sacramental motive" had been done away with. A solution to the probelm would be to restore a richer spiritual life to church observance.[77] This could best be done by emulating the religious aesthetic he had witnessed in Catholic countries. "There is something there for the eye, ear, and heart, as well as for the intellect. Cannot we do the same?"[78]

Clarke also selected for his Church certain Catholic feast days, including those of All Saints and All Souls. In fact, he adopted from Catholicism anything else he could think of to incorporate the "sentiment of worship" and the "womanly and affectionate side of life" which he felt the Catholic Church so strongly exhibited. These facets of Catholicism he enlisted by way of complement to the "manly" and intellectual side borrowed from Protestantism. Lastly, he hoped that at some future date the new churches would imitate the Catholic practice of leaving church buildings open all day, without stipend, for rich and poor alike to enjoy the artistic riches and to refresh their souls.[79]

Though less systematic, other transcendentalists approved the adaptation of Catholic art and liturgy for the future. Dwight, of course, championed the prodigal use of great music as he had heard it in Catholic cathedrals. He put his whole hope for religious unity in this one transcendental means of uniting what was in the hearts of all men. The music of the great Catholic Masses, he argued, belongs not only to the Catholic Church, but

> to every soul who can respond to it....It belongs to humanity, to the one church universal which is not yet,....It speaks to hearts,...to that which all men have in common, and in cherishing which resides our only hope of unity, our only hope of ever seeing a truly catholic and universal church.[80]

Osgood, on the other hand, his tastes always simpler, preferred cheerful and popular hymns such as introduced into the church by St. Ambrose, rather than music like the sombre chants of the medieval Catholic ceremonial. His proposals for the use of other Catholic art were also more moderate, though sometimes inconsistent. In his early years he could not agree with Clarke, Brownson, and Emerson, who were asking for a transferral of European cathedral architecture to the future churches of America.[81] Among these, Emerson wondered how anyone who had been in a Catholic cathedral could ever have devised such a deformity as a pew. More to the point he wanted the architects of America to adopt the paint, marble, and stone of the European cathedral, to replace the "mean edifices" he was used to in New England. Brownson, for his part, stated unequivocally that the church of the future would press into its service poetry, painting, sculpture, music, architecture—all the fine arts. In this it would follow not the Protestant churches with their excessive "rationalism," but the Catholic Church of the past, which knew well how to appeal to the deepest sensibilities of love and inspiration in man.[82]

Osgood later came round to this point of view. He even went a step further and urged the adaptation of the Catholic usage of the centrality of the altar rather than the pulpit, as well as the introduction of feast days. Their purpose, he argued, would be sublime--to aid, by their solemnity, tenderness, variety, and power, man's striving for communion with the divine.[83]

The transcendentalist who more than any other hoped to add the richness of Catholic liturgy and artistic symbolism to the future church was Hedge. "A church," he mused, "requires a ritual, requires symbols and sacraments,--something outward as the exponent and medium of ecclesiastical life." The most valuable example of such a ritual Hedge found in the Catholic Church. He first cautioned against adoption of the "tropical luxuriance" of either its liturgy or its authority. Yet barring this, he strongly urged that everything "proper" in the Catholic way of symbol and rite be retained for the true church to come.[84]

Thus the transcendental church of the future. It would not involve, as some have implied, a purely romantic, individualistic kind of religion. And it would manifest more organic unity and more visible expression than one might expect. But its doctrine was freedom from doctrine, its sanctions private conscience, and its ritual as arbitrary and as free ranging as the tempers of its sponsors. At its core would be the transcendental faith, the simplicity of whose essence would be, in Clarke's expression, "...my brother man, bowed before my father, God"--God at the head, and man, "greater than the Temple, greater than its liturgy, prayers, its priests, its ritual," standing at his feet.[85]

Such was the mixture that the chief enthusiasts continued to hope for through every vicissitude. Very early in the career of transcendentalism, Brownson analyzed the era as an age of religious anarchy. But undismayed, he labelled the confusion a "transition-state," one which must give way to a new religious form "which all will love and obey."[86] Later Judd used the Catholic Church as warrant for a similar confidence. "If Romanism, with all its errors and wrongs, can build up such a Church, what cannot Unitarianism, or pure Christianity, do...?...[On] a Unitarian or Liberal basis we can rear as glorious and goodly a Church as any the world has seen."[87]

Of all the optimists, Bartol invariably expressed the most sanguine faith. In almost Teilhardian periods he declared that the present age of fearful unbelief was only part of the "sublime process, in the light of growing science and experience, not of dissolving, but enlarging, the idea of God." This, he prophesied, "was to be the religious glory of the coming age,--a better idea of God!"[88] At the conclusion of transcendentalism's peak decade he delivered a statement of utopian dreams which perhaps best condenses the euphoric transcendental hope:

> Such is already the process and commencing triumph of our religion. As it goes on, roots of bitterness, the growth of ages, will more and more decay, the habits of the race itself be changed, social evils vanish, common goods be established and multiplied, the garden of the Lord reappear with no narrow Oriental bounds, and the fruit of the Spirit be in all his tabernacles with his children. Freedom and love, inclination and will, fellowship and duty, the Protestant and the Catholic, man with man, and mankind with God, shall be one.[89]

[1]Clarke, Orthodoxy, pp. 30-36; Clarke, Steps of Belief, p. 200; Clarke, "True Theology," p. 40; Hedge, Reason in Religion, pp. 307-308; Hedge, "Ecclesiastical Christendom," pp. 116-122.

[2]Hedge, "Ecclesiastical Christendom," pp. 112-134; Hedge, Reason in Religion, pp. 307-308; Clarke, "True Theology," p. 40; Clarke, Orthodoxy, pp. 30, 35-36; Clarke, Steps of Belief, pp. 200-201; Clarke, Peter at Antioch, pp. 4-5.

[3]Hedge, "Ecclesiastical Christendom," p. 121; Clarke, Peter at Antioch, pp. 4-11; Clarke, Steps of Belief, pp. 201-202.

[4]Osgood, Studies in Christian Biography, pp. 89-90.

[5]The other perils he listed as slavery, devotion to riches, and the denial of a Higher Law (Parker to Rev. J.T. Sargent, September 18, 1859, in Weiss, Life of Parker, II, 354; Parker, Rights of Man, pp. 344, 354-358).

[6]See among others mentioned above, Parker, World of Matter and Spirit, p. 68; Clarke to Fuller, December, 1848, in Clarke, Letters, pp. 146-147; Fuller to New York Tribune, January 10, 1848, in Fuller, At Home and Abroad, p. 281; Alcott, as cited in S.H.M., Review of Proceedings of the First Annual Meeting of the Free Religious Association, pp. 395-396; Emerson, Journals, 1859, IX, 242-243; ibid., 1868, X, 233-234; Emerson to Clough, May 17, 1858, in Emerson-Clough Letters, ed. Howard F. Lowry and Ralph L. Rusk (Cleveland, 1934), #31; Bartol, Religion in Our Public Schools, p. 17; Channing to Joseph Blanco White, July 29, 1836, in Channing, Memoir, II, 373-374; Channing to White, September 18, 1839, in ibid., pp. 376-377; Channing to Miss Aiken, December 31, 1829, in Channing, Correspondence, p. 43.

[7]Bartol, Reason and Rome in Education, pp. 6-7, 13.

[8]Hedge, "Ecclesiastical Christendom," p. 116; Bartol, Religion in Our Public Schools, p. 17.

[9]Bartol, Religion in Our Public Schools, pp. 18-20. See also Hedge, "Ecclesiastical Christendom," pp. 116-117, where he predicts that the Catholic Church may outnumber every other Church in America, but if it does it would have to be under the providence of God and consequently have to undergo radical modifications first.

See also other moderate exhortations to caution, as for example, Bartol, "Jesus and Jerusalem: or Christ the Saviour and Civilizer of the World," QJAUA, IV (July 1, 1857), 419-420; Hedge, "Romanism in Its Worship," p. 243; Osgood, "Americans and the Men of the Old World," p. 10; Osgood, "Taylor's Lectures on Christian Spirituality," pp. 317-318; Osgood, "Debates on the Roman Catholic Religion," pp. 62-63; Judd, Margaret, II, 99-100; Judd, The Church, p. 95.

[10]Clarke, Essentials, pp. 90, 92-93; Clarke, "Polemics and Irenics," p. 169.

[11]Alcott, "Tablets," Radical, II (November, 1866), 178; Ripley, "Religion in France," pp. 278-279; Parker, Slave Power, p. 136; Parker, World of Matter and Spirit, pp. 75-76; Channing, Memoir, I, 424.

[12]Clarke, Address, April 7, 1880, in Channing Centenary, p. 86.

[13]Channing, "Letter on Catholicism," p. 270. At this time Osgood too reckoned, from observation during his year's stay at Louisville as associate editor of the Western Messenger, that Catholicism was not making any alarming progress there, and he warned the nativists that provoking it could only help its cause. Leave it to itself, he advised, and it will die (Osgood, "Debates on the Roman Catholic Religion," pp. 61-64).

[14]Channing, "Letter on Catholicism," pp. 271-273.

Clarke was pleased about the effects of Channing's letter. It was republished in at least two other periodicals, and the demand for copies of it was great enough to warrant separate reprints (see Clarke, "Monthly Record," WM, II [December, 1836], 356; Clarke, ibid., III [February, 1837], 501).

[15]Channing to Joseph Blanco White, July 29, 1836, in Channing, Memoir, II, 373-374; Channing to White, September 18, 1839, in ibid., p. 394; Channing to Lucy Aiken, December 31, 1829, in Channing, Correspondence, p. 43.

[16]Channing, "Letter on Catholicism," pp. 271, 276.

[17]Bartol did make some general references to the Statistical Atlas of the United States, based on the ninth census of 1870, noting the facts only that the proportion of Catholics to Protestants was narrow in most of the country, was half the population of the southwest, and one-fourth that of the large cities of Massachusetts and New York (Bartol, Reason and Rome in Education, p. 13). Without giving his source, Parker cited the fact that of every thirteen Catholics coming to America, only four remained in the Catholic Church (Parker, Theism, p. 34).

[18]Stetson, "A Discourse on the Duty of Sustaining the Laws," p. 13; Bartol, Word of the Spirit, pp. 65-66; Bartol, Reason and Rome in Education, p. 6; Channing to Joseph Blanco White, September 18, 1839, in Channing, Memoir, II, 376-377; Channing to Mrs. Joanna Baillie, April 5, 1857, in ibid., p. 393; Clarke, "Monthly Record," WM, II (December, 1836), 356; Hedge, ed., in Essays and Reviews, xiii; Parker, as cited in Frothingham, Theodore Parker, p. 206.

[19]Osgood, Book Review of Democracy in America, Part Second, by Alexis Tocqueville (Paris, 1840), CE, XXIX (September, 1840), 106; Channing, Works, VI, 220.

[20]Parker, Transient and Permanent, p. 346; Parker, St. Bernard and Other Papers, p. 149; Parker, Theism, passim; Parker, Ten Sermons, p. 174; Parker to the Twenty-Eighth Congregational Society, June 25, 1859, in Weiss, Life of Parker, II, 301; Parker to Ripley, October 29, 1859, in ibid., p. 376; Parker, Journal, November 1, 1859, in ibid., p.386; Ward, "Letters from Italy," [The Dial], p. 391; Brownson, "Parker's Discourse," p. 510; Brownson, New Views, pp. 5, 36; Brownson, "Benjamin Constant on Religion," p. 69; Brownson, "The Church Question," p. 472; Hedge, Reason in Religion, pp. 307-308; Furness, Power of Spirit, p. 107; Bancroft to Hamilton Fish, Prussian Documents, Vol. 16, No. 66, January 31, 1870, in Trauth, "Bancroft Dispatches," p. 180; Cranch, The Bird and the Bell, pp. 10, 15-16; Channing, Conversation, [1825?], as cited in Peabody, Reminiscences of Channing, p. 154; Channing to M.J.C.D. Simonde de Sismondi, June 16, 1831, in Channing, Memoir, II, 386; Fuller, as cited in Memoirs of Margaret Fuller [no source given], I, 247; Fuller to New York Tribune, January, 1848, in Fuller, At Home and Abroad, p. 299; Bartol, Pictures of Europe, pp. 238-239, 249; Clarke, "Orestes A. Brownson's Argument for the Roman Church," p. 244; Clarke, "New Theology," p. 400; Clarke, Discourse, January 23, 1845, as cited in Bolster, James Freeman Clarke, p. 154; Clarke, Orthodoxy, p. 36; Francis, Popery, p. 25; Emerson, Universe A, 1822, in Emerson, JN, I, 389; Emerson, Works, X, 227; Thoreau, Journal, August 19, 1851, II, 403-404; W.H. Channing, "Call of the Present: No. 3," p. 151.

[21]Parker, World of Matter and Spirit, p. 85.

[22]Cranch, "Divine Authority," pp. 465-466, 477-478; Bartol, "Permanence in Religion and in Preaching: Orville Dewey's Autobiography, Letters, and Collected Works," UR, XXI (March, 1884), 193; Parker, World of Matter and Spirit, pp. 75-76; Brownson, "Benjamin Constant on Religion," p. 69; Brownson, "Channing on the Church and Social Reform," p. 171; Brownson, New Views, p. 28; Emerson, Works, I, 142.

[23]Brownson, New Views, p. 28; Emerson, Works, VI, 389-390.

[24]W.H. Channing, Gospel of Today, p. 24n; Hedge, "The Cause of Reason the Cause of Faith," pp. 225-226; Parker, Theism, pp. 52-53; Emerson, Journals, 1849, VIII, 78.

[25]Emerson, Journals, 1859, IX, 203; Emerson, Works, I, 142; ibid., X, 205; Hedge, "Antisupernaturalism in the Pulpit," p. 153; Parker, Theism, p. 368; Judd, Philo, passim.

[26]Emerson, _Journals_, 1863, IX, 559. See also Emerson, _Works_, X, 205.

[27]Emerson, _Journals_, 1863, IX, 559.

[28]Judd, as cited in Hall, _Life of Judd_, pp. 264-265; W.H. Channing, "Anniversary Week," p. 28; Cranch, "The Unconscious Life," p. 110; Brownson, _Scholar's Mission_, p. 80; Brownson, Editorial, _Boston Reformer_, July 1, 1836, in Henry F. Brownson, _Brownson's Early Life_, p. 167; Brownson, "Church Unity and Social Amelioration," _BrQR_, July, 1844, in Brownson, _Works_, IV, 519; Alcott, _Journals_, January, 1837, p. 385.

[29]Channing to Joseph Blanco White, September 18, 1839, in Joseph Blanco White, _Life_, III, 95.

[30]Emerson, _Works_, VI, 389-390; Emerson, _Journals_, 1863, IX, 559.

[31]Osgood, _The Coming Church_, p. 6.

[32]Clarke, _Orthodoxy_, p. 279; Clarke, _Peter at Antioch_, p. 4; Clarke, _Steps of Belief_, p. 205; Brownson, "Education of the People,"_CE_, XX (May, 1836), 166.

Parker was ambivalent about the Church's possibilities for survival. Though he many times referred to it as dead or dying, and declared categorically that it would not change because it could not (Parker, "Material Condition of the People of Massachusetts," p. 54), he wondered privately whether its "terrible unity" would not cause it to outlive all other Christian churches (Parker to Convers Francis, March 18, 1844, in Weiss, _Life of Parker_, I, 233).

[33]Hedge, "Ecclesiastical Christendom," pp. 117, 127, 131; Hedge, "The Cause of Reason the Cause of Faith," p. 225.

[34]Bartol, "Jesus and Jerusalem," p. 420; Ripley, "Religion in France," p. 280; Francis, _Popery_, pp. 8-9; W.H. Channing, "Heaven Upon Earth," p. 422; Hedge, "Luther and His Work," p. 817; Brownson, _Gospel Advocate_, VI (March 15, 1828), 88, as cited in Sveino, _Orestes A. Brownson's Road to Catholicism_, p. 36.

[35]Osgood, "Debates on the Roman Catholic Religion," p. 62; Osgood, _God with Men_, p. 249; Hecker to his family, March 1, 1843, in Holden, _Early Years of Hecker_, pp. 108-109; Fuller, _Papers on Literature and Art_, 2 parts (New York, 1846), Part II, pp. 161, 173; Clarke, _Essentials_, p. 29; Clarke, _Every-Day Religion_, pp. 308-309; Hedge, Reason in Religion, p. 49; Hedge, "Count Zinzendorf and the Moravians," _UR_, XXV (January, 1886), 4; Bartol, _Radical Problems_, pp. 216, 227; Parker, _Discourse of Religion_, p. 70; Parker, _Theism_, p. 244; Dwight to his sister, May, 1839, in Cooke, _John Sullivan Dwight_, pp. 32-33; Emerson, Journal Q, 1833, in Emerson, _JN_, IV, 84; Emerson, Journal B, 1835, in _ibid._, V, 57; Cranch, "Divine Authority," p. 468; Channing, _Works_, IV, 90; Alcott, _Table Talk_, p. 99; Alcott, _Journals_, August 24, 1873, p. 440.

[36]Francis, _Popery_, p. 13; Osgood, "The Church of the First Three Centuries," p. 374; Osgood, "Doctrine of the Holy Spirit," pp. 321-322; Osgood, "Hugo Grotius and His Times," p. 29; Hedge, Presidential Remarks [American Unitarian Association, 1860], p. 305; Hedge, "The Unitarian Denomination: Its Advantages and Mission," _QJAUA_, III (October 1, 1855), 5; Hedge, "The Churches and the Church," pp. 194-195; Channing, _Works_, VI, 209.

[37]Osgood, _The Coming Church_, p. 24; Osgood, "The Practical Study of the Human Soul," _CE_, LXIII (November, 1857), 348; Osgood, _Studies in Christian Biography_, motto for title page; Brownson, "Church of the Future," p. 71; Hedge, Address, 1849, as cited in Williams, _Rethinking the Unitarian Relationship with Protestantism_, p. 20; Hedge, ed., _Essays and Reviews_, p. xviii; Cranch, "Sign from the West," pp. 170-171; Clarke, "The Essence of Christianity," _UR_, IV (December, 1875), 601; Brooks, _Simplicity of Christ's Teachings_, p. 70; Judd to All the Clergy of Augusta, Maine, April 9, 1842, in Hall, _Life of Judd_, p. 197.

[38]Channing, _Works_, VI, 206; W.H. Channing's articles in _The Spirit of the Age_ and _The Present, passim_; W.H. Channing, _Gospel of Today_, p. 35; Clarke, _Ten Great Religions_, p. 503; Clarke, _Essentials_, p. 98; Clarke, "Essence of Christianity," p. 600; Bartol, _Church and Congregation_, pp. 2-3, 12; Hecker, Diary, April 28,

1843, in Elliott, Life of Hecker, p. 64; Hedge, "The Cause of Reason the Cause of Faith," p. 225.

[39]See among others Clarke, Events and Epochs, p. 241; Clarke, Essentials, pp. 94, 98; Clarke, Go Up Higher, p. 161; Clarke, "Polemics and Irenics," pp. 170-171; Clarke, Ten Great Religions, p. 493; Bartol, Rising Faith, p. 318; Bartol, Christ the Way, p. 7; Thoreau, Walden, p. 115; Parker, Transient and Permanent, p. 299; Emerson, Journal Y, 1845, in Emerson, JN, IX, 299; Emerson, Journal CD, July 10, 1847, in ibid., X, 105-106; Emerson, "Self-Culture," September 5, 1830, in Young Emerson Speaks, ed. McGiffert, p. 102; Emerson, Works, X, 227; Follen, Preface to his unpublished and incomplete Religion and the Church, in Follen, Works, V, 258; Parker, Theism, pp. 13, 18; Parker, Autobiography, p. 315; Channing, Works, VI, 205; Cranch, "Symbolic Conceptions of the Deity," pp. 247-248.

[40]Examples are too numerous to cite. Of the minor transcendentalists, two who deal with the question in their unique literary genre are Very, in his poem, "On the Great Divisions of the Christian Church, The Catholic, the Protestant, and the Greek," in Very, Poems and Essays, Complete Edition, p. 281, and Judd in his two-volume novel, Margaret: A Tale of the Real and the Ideal, Blight and Bloom.

The Unitarian par excellence held this unity as one of his fondest hopes. "I desire," wrote Channing, "to escape the narrow walls of a particular church." For him, there should be only one church, "grander than all particular ones... spread over all lands, and one with the church in heaven,..." (Channing, Memoir, II, 402).

[41]Brownson, New Views, pp. 22-28, 32, 43. See also Hecker to Brownson, October 16, 1843, in Holden, Early Years of Hecker, p. 185.

[42]See Brownson, "Free Religion," The Catholic World, November, 1869, in Brownson, Works, III, 418.

[43]See for example, Brownson, "The Church Question," pp. 477-479, 482.

[44]Brownson, "Parker's Discourse," [1842], pp. 488-510; Brownson, Conversation, [1842?], as cited in Henry F. Brownson, Brownson's Early Life, pp. 460-461.

[45]Hedge, Leaven of the Word, p. 14; Hedge, "The Broad Church," 1860, in Hedge, Sermons, pp. 150-170; Bartol, Book Review of Sermons by Hedge, p. 330.

The term "Broad Church" was also used by Henry, but in a less precise sense. For him it meant a church comprehensive and tolerant, a church "respecting the honest conviction of serious men" (Henry, About the Bishop's Declaration on Baptism, pp. 29-30).

[46]Clarke, "The Church,--As It Was," as cited in Brownson, "The Church As It Was," pp. 181, 191; Clarke, "Polemics and Irenics," pp. 163-184.

In the discussion which followed Clarke's delivery of "Polemics and Irenics," he was criticized for his unorthodox approach. His reply is typical of the dynamic and even existential character of transcendentalism: "It was said that, instead of going to the Gospel to find the truth, I recommended going to different sects, and taking from each whatever opinion seemed agreeable. I recognize the living Church, in all its branches, as the best interpreter of the Gospel" (ibid., appended note, p. 184).

[47]W.H. Channing, "Call of the Present--No. 2--Science and Unity," The Present, I (November 15, 1843), 78.

[48]W.H. Channing, "Talks on the Times: Socialist and Catholic," p. 107.

[49]W.H. Channing, "Peter's Pence," p. 25; W.H. Channing, Gospel of Today, pp. pp. 8-11, 25; W.H. Channing, "Heaven Upon Earth," p. 422; W.H. Channing, "Christian Church and Social Reform," as cited in Brownson, "Channing on the Church," p. 172; W.H. Channing, "The Judgment of Christendom," SA, I (October 27, 1849), 264-265. See his articles in SA, passim, for the socialistic orientation of this new Christian commonwealth.

Evidence of other transcendentalists' hopes for breaking down denominational barriers may also be found, but none of these represents a comprehensive program.

For most it was a case of mere rhetoric. Two minor exceptions where specific action is projected come from Alcott and Convers Francis. Alcott opened his Temple School to all faiths and even tried to bring in a Catholic pupil ("Description of Mr. Alcott's School," Extract from a letter, WM, I [October, 1835], 223). He was unsuccessful (see Shepard, ed., in Alcott, Journals, p. 38). Convers Francis proposed to Parker a "World Bible" of religious sayings of historical figures as widely varied as Confucius, aKempis, and the German transcendentalists (as cited in Wasson, Beyond Concord, p. 42). This kind of unification, however, can hardly be called a church.

50Osgood, The Coming Church, p. 23; Hedge, "Unitarian Denomination," p. 5.

51Bartol, Character, p. 23; Osgood, "Schleiermacher Centennial and Its Lesson," pp. 189-190; Ripley, "Religion in France," pp. 278-280; Clarke, "Christ and His Antichrists," pp. 358, 398-399; Furness, as cited in Hedge, "Dr. Furness's Word to Unitarians," p. 437; Channing to M.J.C.L. Simonde de Sismondi, December 19, 1832, in Channing, Memoir, II, 389.

52W.H. Channing, "Anniversary Week," p. 28; Brownson, "Nature and Office of the Church," BrQR, April, 1844, in Brownson, Works, IV, 492; Brownson, "Laboring Classes," passim; Brownson, "Church of the Future," pp. 74-75; Clarke, "Orestes A. Brownson's Argument for the Roman Church," p. 247; Clarke, "The Church--As It Was," as cited in Hutchison, Transcendentalist Ministers, p. 145; Francis, Popery, p. 16; Hedge, "The Churches and the Church," p. 204; Osgood, "Practical Study of the Human Soul," p. 348.

53Parker, Nebraska Question, pp. 14-15.

54Clarke, Ideas of Paul, p. 390; Clarke, Essentials, p. 98; Clarke, "Essence of Christianity," p. 600; Clarke, Steps of Belief, pp. 219, 281-282; Hedge, "The Churches and the Church," pp. 200-204; Hedge, "The Two Religions," passim. The reconciliation of unity and freedom was also to be a primary thrust of William Henry Channing's Christian Commonwealth.

55Osgood, God with Men, pp. 54-55; Hedge, "Dr. Furness's Word to Unitarians," p. 438; Hedge, Sermons, p. 57; Hedge, "Ecclesiastical Christendom," p. 131; Hedge, "Destinies of Ecclesiastical Religion," p. 14.

56Brownson, "Parker's Discourse," p. 489.

57Ibid., p.508.

58Ibid., pp. 488-510; Brownson, "Present State of Society," pp. 455-456.

59Brownson, "Parker's Discourse," p. 510; Brownson, "Present State of Society," p. 455.

60Brownson, Literary Notice of Life of Cheverus by Huen-Dubourg, pp. 388-389; Brownson, in a series of lectures, 1842-1843, as cited in Henry F. Brownson, Brownson's Early Life, pp. 383-384. Later as Brownson shifted his sympathies toward the Catholic Church, he for a time decided that the Quaker Church was the end, the Catholic Church the means (Brownson, Christian World, [1842?], as cited in ibid., p. 465).

61Brownson, "Laboring Classes," [1840], pp. 437-438; Brownson, The Convert, p. 110.

62Brownson, "Laboring Classes," [1840], p. 438. As Brownson put it in "Church of the Future" (p. 72), worship was not to be in "idle hymns and idler ceremonies," but in "those substantial acts of piety and love which really do tend to the melioration of the condition of all men."

63Furness, as cited in Hedge, "Dr. Furness's Word to Unitarians," p. 437.

64Hedge, ibid., p. 438.

65Hedge, "The Churches and the Church," p. 203. He referred to this church as "the Catholic Protestant Church of Christian union and Christian progress" (ibid., p. 204).

66Osgood, The Coming Church, p. 17; Brownson, "Leroux on Humanity," p. 101; Brownson, The Convert, pp. 93-94; Brownson, "Church of the Future," p. 72.

[67]Brownson, "Social Evils, and Their Remedy," p. 275; Brownson, "Leroux on Humanity," pp. 125-216; Francis, Popery, pp. 12-13, 26; Emerson, Works, VI, 214; Emerson to Anna Barker Ward, May 5, 1859, in Emerson, Letters, V, 144; Emerson, Journal Q, 1833, in Emerson, JN, IV, 84; Parker, World of Matter and Spirit, pp. 80-81; Parker, A False and True Revival of Religion. A Sermon Delivered at Music Hall, Boston, on Sunday, April 4, 1858 (Boston, 1858), p. 8; Parker, Ten Sermons, p. 49; Parker to Miss Cobb [February, 1860?], in Weiss, Life of Parker, II, 421; Bartol, Reason and Rome in Education, p. 18; Channing, Works, III, 166; Channing to M.J.C.L. Simonde de Sismondi, June 16, 1831, in Channing, Memoir, II, 386; W.H. Channing, as cited in Frothingham, Memoir of William Henry Channing, p. 290; Cranch, "Divine Authority," p. 468; Cranch, "Sign from the West," pp. 170-171; Dwight to his sister, May, 1839, in Cooke, John Sullivan Dwight, pp. 32-33; Osgood, "Hugo Grotius and His Times," p. 29; Hedge, "Christianity in Conflict with Hellenism," pp. 21-22; Fuller, Papers on Literature and Art, Part II, p. 173; Ripley to [?], n.d., as cited in Codman, Brook Farm, p. 287.

This reliance on a naturalistic form of religion was regarded by Emerson as a reaction against the cant and monachism of the Christian, and specifically Catholic, Church. Clarke considered it rather a sign that despite all their differences, the "universal diffusion of love, righteousness, and truth" was at the bottom of the religion of Catholic and Protestant, orthodox and liberal alike (Emerson, Journals, 1849, VIII, 78; Clarke, "On a Recent Definition of Christianity," p. 3; Clarke, Steps of Belief, p. 287).

[68]Brownson, "Church Question," p. 480.

[69]Clarke, "The Church--As It Was," as cited in Hutchison, Transcendentalist Ministers, p. 146; W.H. Channing, "The New Church," p. 74; Bartol, Christ the Way, passim; Bartol, Discourses on the Christian Body, p. 196; Judd, Margaret, II, 256; Parker, World of Matter and Spirit, p. 90.

[70]Brownson, "Church Question," pp. 481-482; Brownson, New Views, passim; Clarke, Orthodoxy, p. 36; Clarke, Eleven Weeks in Europe, pp. 270-271; Clarke, Steps of Belief, p. 257; Clarke, Vexed Questions, pp. 59-61; Clarke to the Church of the Disciples, December 4, 1852, in Clarke, Autobiography, p. 198; Clarke, Sermon extract, April 4, 1865, in ibid., p. 265; Channing, "On Fenelon," p. 180; Parker to Convers Francis, March 18, 1844, in Weiss, Life of Parker, I, 232.

[71]W.H. Channing, "New Church," p. 74.

[72]Hedge, "Christianity in Conflict with Hellenism," p. 22; Brownson, "Church of the Future," pp. 63-64. Clarke's and Bartol's works frequently reflect this orientation also.

[73]Hedge, "The Two Religions," p. 109; Hedge, Reason in Religion, p. 49; Hedge, Ways of the Spirit, p. 310; Clarke, Common-Sense, p. 370; Clarke, Essentials, p. 29; Bartol, Rising Faith, p. 318.

[74]Brownson, "Church of the Future," pp. 63, 71-73; Osgood, The Coming Church, pp. 7-8.

[75]Bartol, Radical Problems, pp. 113-114; Francis, Popery, p. 25; Parker, Ten Sermons, pp. 337, 340; Parker, Autobiography, p. 17; Parker, World of Matter and Spirit, p. 210; Channing, "On Fenelon," p. 180; Osgood, The Coming Church, p. 16.

[76]Clarke, Church of the Disciples in Boston, pp. 24-25. The other "methods" are The Social Principle (cooperation) and The Voluntary Principle (ibid., pp. 18-24).

[77]Clarke, Church-Going, Past, Present, and Future, pp. 5, 11.

[78]Clarke, Steps of Belief, p. 257; Clarke, Christian Doctrine of Prayer, pp. 154-157.

[79]Clarke, Church of the Disciples in Boston, pp. 22-23; Hour Which Cometh, pp. 169-170; Clarke, Steps of Belief, pp. 257, 281-282; Clarke, fragment, July, 1882, in Clarke, Autobiography, p. 373; Clarke, The Experiment of a Free Church; Its Difficulties and Advantages [Boston, 188?], p. 1; Clarke, Vexed Questions, p.

208. William Henry Channing, Emerson, and Margaret Fuller approved this practice also (see among others, Emerson, Sicily, 1833, in Emerson, JN, IV, 117; Emerson, Journal London, 1848, in ibid., X, 271; W.H. Channing, "Ernest the Seeker," pp. 53-56; Fuller, Life Without and Within, pp. 337-338). But the elder Channing opposed the open church as "foreign to our habits" of praying in privacy (Channing, "Letter on Catholicism," pp. 276-277).

80Dwight, "The American Review's Account," p. 30. See also Dwight, "Music As a Means of Culture," p. 331.

81Osgood, "St. Ambrose," pp. 429-432; Osgood, "The Second Service in Our Churches," MJAUA, VI (December, 1865), 542; Osgood, "Taylor's Lectures on Spiritual Christianity," pp. 317-318.

82Emerson, Sicily, 1833, in Emerson, JN, IV, 117-118, 131; Emerson, Italy, March 17, 1833, in ibid., p. 144; Emerson to William Emerson, March 23, 1833, in Emerson, Letters, I, 369; Brownson, "Church of the Future," p. 74. William Henry Channing was of the same mind (see Frothingham, Memoir of William Henry Channing, p. 115).

83Osgood, The Coming Church, pp. 13-14, 19-20; Osgood, "Schleiermacher Centennial and Its Lesson," p. 185.

84Hedge, Sermons, pp. 168-169. His Christian Liturgy for the Use of the Church [1853], is a book based primarily on Catholic tradition, and his Hymns for the Church of Christ [1853], contains, among many others, fifty-eight hymns borrowed from Catholic sources.

Hedge so often urged the preservation of whatever was rich in the Catholic liturgy, that his friends thought he might become a Catholic (Cooke, Historical Introduction to The Dial, II, 70).

William Henry Channing too preferred that "sublime art" and perfect ritual be a goal of the Future Church. For these he pointed to the Catholic example as providing the direction toward a still more glorious church ([W.H. Channing], "Mr. [Henry] Channing's Lecture," Harbinger, I [November 15, 1845], 367-368; W.H. Channing, "Anniversary Week," p. 28).

85Clarke, Common-Sense, p. 443.

86Brownson, "Benjamin Constant on Religion," p. 69. Brownson had many more transitions to go through first himself--the date was 1834.

87Judd, The Church, p. 98.

88Bartol, Word of the Spirit, p. 46.

89Bartol, Discourses on Christian Spirit, p. 53.

CHAPTER VIII

TRANSCENDENTALIST AND CATHOLIC

CATHOLICISM IN THE LIVES OF THE TRANSCENDENTALISTS

From what has been said, it is clear that for some of the transcendentalists, Catholicism's only impact was by way of speculation. For others, it took a more practical form in their adoption of certain aspects of its piety and wisdom. For still others, Catholicism eventually became a way of life.

The transcendentalists' most overt flirtation with Catholicism took place at Brook Farm. The liberal view of religion and sectarianism held by all the Brook Farmers made it possible to accept in their membership persons of many faiths-- Jewish, Protestant, Catholic and Unitarian. Their stress upon an intelligent and sensitive approach to religion rendered them capable of dismissing previous prejudices and accepting from one another all that seemed genuine in the religions of their companions.[1] Not the least of these was the Catholic faith.

We have seen that the Brook Farmers manifested a decided interest in Catholic reading material and in Catholic music. Besides cultivating an intellectual and aesthetic appreciation, some of them adopted various Catholic usages as a practical part of their daily living. Reminiscences written by former residents at the farm allude to a handful of these: the appearance of rough wooden crosses and pictures of the Madonna and other saints; the "rattling of rosaries under aprons";[2] the serving of fish on Fridays; attendance at Catholic services down the road in Boston; and particularly, discussions on the spiritual, doctrinal, and practical nature of Catholic belief and observance.[3] The high priest of these dabblers in Catholicism was Charles King Newcomb, "young Fra Carlo," as Emerson called him.[4] King's serious interest in becoming a Catholic and a priest began as early as 1838 when he studied Catholicism under a seminary professor. Later, at Brook Farm, he adopted many Catholic observances as his own. According to the editor of his journals, he was with difficulty dissuaded from taking the final step, but he never lost interest. Till the end of his life he continued, though with a high degree of ambivalence, to be attracted to Catholic services.[5]

There were a few boarders at Brook Farm who took more than an outside interest in the Catholic Church. Some half dozen were Catholics already, and either during or after the Brook Farm years, their number at least doubled. After a year or more of preparation, five of the "original transcendentalists," as one of the Brook Farmers described it some thirty years later, "kneeled before the altar to surrender the last iota of their spiritual independence."[6] The total number was closer to ten, if we include Brownson.[7] Though never a resident, Brownson was a frequent visitor to the farm, and his son, Orestes Jr., attended school there. Of these converts, three deserve particular attention--Hecker, Brownson, and Mrs. Ripley.

The wife of Brook Farm's founder was a singularly educated woman, one keenly interested in both the personalist and the social dimensions of religion. She took up the study of Catholicism at Brook Farm, reading first Dante, then devotional works such as Fenelon and St. Catherine, and finally the Fathers of the Church in the original Greek.[8] Undoubtedly too, the influence of numerous intellectual and spiritual conversations with Hecker and Brownson had much to do with her attraction to the Catholic Church.[9] She did not, however, take any definitive action openly while at the Farm, lest such a radical departure from her husband's philosophy prove harmful to his enterprise. But as soon as the Farm failed, she embraced the Catholic faith.[10] The rest of her life, until her death in 1861, she spent in works of a charitable nature--in hospitals, in prisons, and with the Good Shepherd Sisters in New York, whose work with delinquent girls she helped to establish there.[11] Her husband, while he could not share her convictions, did everything he could to make her new life possible. At the end he had the sacraments of the Church brought to her and a requiem Mass arranged in accordance with her wishes.

The irony of the final sequence is that it took place within a Catholic Church which had formerly housed the Unitarian pulpit where her husband had preached.[12]

More within the area of our concern is the conversion to Catholicism of Orestes Brownson. We have already seen some of the fields of religious thought through which his mind played. They have provided some inkling of the often painful philosophical route through which Brownson's mind wound its way to the Catholic Church. Without following that _transitus_ in detail, we will make a few observations on it, as seen in the light of his own apologetic.

The mass of material which Brownson's pen produced in working his way toward truth attests to the sincerity of his search and the dynamism he brought to the task. For our present purpose it is possible to trace, through this wide body of material, the areas of transcendental belief which he slowly discovered were incompatible with genuine truth. Over against these we can place the contrary Catholic assertions which he reluctantly found himself obliged to adopt. By means of this brief survey, we can agree with most of his biographers that every step of his pilgrimage led inexorably though unconsciously to the Catholic Church.[13]

Probably the most basic transcendental concept which Brownson had to grapple with was that of the divinity of man. After a long struggle he came to the conclusion that he had no choice but to reject the extremes of subjectivism held out by the German and French transcendentalists, one after another of whom he had adopted. Once he came to the realization that the subject who knows is distinct from the object known, he saw his way clearly to all the ramifications of such a theory. Then began in earnest his journey out of idealism and into Catholicism. One by one he replaced transcendental beliefs with Catholic ones. For the divinity of humanity and the unity of all natures, he would place separate and distinct natures and forms, especially the objective person of God. For man as the measure of truth and goodness, therefore, he would place the authority of history and tradition, particularly as embodied in an objective organism. For sectarianism and excessive individualism he would place organic unity. For the motivation of social and humanitarian reform, he would place the religious dynamic of inner renewal of man's soul as the driving force for such reform. For the human mind as the seat of innate truth, he would place the mind as instrument through which truth can be perceived. For the immediate apprehension of the divine, he would place the mediation of Christ as the way to communion with the separate and distinct God. And finally, Nature he would not replace, but would embellish it with the supernatural --the revelation and grace of God.[14] As he renounced the first of each of these couples, he saw that its opposite lay ready at hand.[15] The only thing was to embrace it.

Yet he hesitated. He knew little of Catholicism. Until he made up his mind to reject all radical philosophies, he had read very few Catholic authors.[16] Not through them did he make his way to Catholicism, but mainly through the French philosophers, particularly Pierre Leroux. The latter's concept of communion he later explained as the natural counterpart of the Catholic concept, both of them separating subject and object. Thus negatively did he turn from a subjective religion. But the Catholic Church itself did not seem a welcome place. For a time he demurred, while acknowledging nevertheless that that Church was the possessor of the truth for which he had been searching and the unity that he craved. "I recoiled," he wrote later, "and set my wits to find out, if possible, some compromise, some middle ground on which I could be faithful to my Catholic tendencies without uniting myself to the present Roman Catholic Church."[17]

For a period of several months his compromise took the form of his "Catholicism without the papacy."[18] But his writings were getting too Catholic. Rumors spreading abroad, he felt obliged to defend himself in the opening pages of his new review, Brownson's Quarterly. "There is no truth," he insisted, "in the report that I have joined, or am intending to join, the Roman Catholic Church." This statement he published in January of 1844,[19] a few short months before he determined to enter the gate where his logic had led him.

By March Brownson was writing to Hecker, "My own feelings and convictions, in spite of my struggles to the contrary, carry me to the Catholic Church, and I foresee plainly that I must sooner or later become a member of it." But with what had by now become characteristic hesitance, he added, "I seek, however, to maintain my position for the present."[20] The "present," nevertheless, did not last much longer. At the end of May he sought and obtained an interview with Benedict Joseph Fenwick, the Catholic Bishop of Boston. Here he met another obstacle. When he voiced his fear of adopting a system of belief which seemed to exclude the salvation of Protestants, the Bishop did not attempt to mollify him.[21] But this was his last stumbling block. Shortly afterwards he placed himself under the instruction of the more friendly coadjutor Bishop John Fitzpatrick. A week later Brownson wrote to Hecker to inform him of the decision: "I can be an alien no longer,...."[22] The July issue of his Review made the announcement public:

> We have no wish to disguise the fact,--nor could we, if we would,-- that our ecclesiastical, theological, and philosophical studies have brought us to the full conviction, that, either the church in communion with the See of Rome is the one holy catholic apostolic church, or the one holy catholic apostolic church does not exist. We have tried every possible way to escape this conclusion, but escape it we cannot.[23]

On October 20 of the same year, Brownson was administered conditional baptism by Bishop Fitzpatrick and thus entered upon the last stage of his pilgrimage. His work was by no means done; he was to become Catholicism's foremost American polemicist for the three or more decades that lay ahead.

Brownson's closest friend at Brook Farm, and probably the only one who genuinely understood him, was Isaac Hecker. Although Hecker's stay at the farm was short-lived--less than a year--he seems to have made a name for himself there by his mystical temperament and his earnest search for truth and inner peace. More sensitive and intuitive than Brownson, Hecker arrived at convictions about the

Catholic Church simultaneously with Brownson and outwardly along much the same path. The two read, studied and discussed Fenelon, Pascal, and the German philosophers together. When it came to a final step for Hecker, he could look back at his friendship with Brownson and reflect often that it was Brownson who was the master. To him Hecker believed he owed the opening up of channels that led eventually to the Catholic Church. He acknowledged that he owed more to Brownson than to any other man--Brownson, his Father, Brother, Friend.[24]

Despite the influence of the older man over Hecker, the latter did not accept the Catholic faith upon his word alone. Strictly speaking, he did not accept it on Brownson's word at all. Brownson's importance for Hecker was owing to the fact that he cleared the path on which Hecker could walk. But it was Hecker's own path. His motivation in joining the Church partially coincided with Brownson's, but it was mainly the product of his own original thinking. In later years, Hecker wrote of the philosophical and religious judgments on which he and Brownson concurred: the general scepticism of the day, the weakness of the Emersonian stance, the personal force of a concrete and therefore Catholic Christianity. Moreover, they both rejected what Hecker termed the nineteenth century's "intellectual disease," subjectivism. And they both accepted the supernatural nature of religion and the authoritative necessity of the Church.[25] Yet these were not deciding factors for Hecker as they were for Brownson, important though Hecker considered them to be. Rather, Hecker became convinced of Catholicism in a manner that corresponded more with the forces of his own temperament. For Hecker had a passionate love for both God and man. He had been a radical socialist for a number of years, attempting to better the conditions of the Boston working class. When he saw that he was accomplishing little, he tried joining the utopias of Brook Farm and Fruitlands. When these too failed to satisfy, he decided that the only way he could hope to change the world was through membership in one or another organized church.

In 1843, while he was a resident of Brook Farm, Hecker first came upon the

Catholic doctrine which was to determine his whole future life. It was the doctrine of the brotherhood of man--which he dearly cherished--expressed in Catholic
terms as the communion of saints. As he wrote later, "It alone was to me a heavier
weight on the Catholic side of the scales than the best historical argument which
could be presented."[26] From that point onwards, Hecker's reflections disclose his
attraction for the Church to have been directed primarily by two of his transcendental longings--the desire for unity and harmony in one's own person and with the
universe; and the desire for the betterment of the whole human race. In this regard, as early as the spring of 1843 he wrote a transcendental meditation in praise
of the Church:

> The Catholic Church alone seems to satisfy my wants, my faith, life, soul.
> These may be baseless fabrics, chimeras dire, or what you please. I may
> be laboring under a delusion. Yet my soul is Catholic, and that faith
> responds to my soul in its religious aspirations and its longings. I
> have not wished to make myself Catholic, but it answers on all sides to
> the wants of my soul. It is so rich, so full. One is in harmony all
> over--in unison with heaven....[27]

But heaven and inner harmony alone were not the goal. "I would always have those
higher and diviner ideas in all our spheres of activity," he wrote Brownson, "that
I would never forget that the kingdom of Heaven is to be established upon Earth."
Whatever church he would eventually join, it would have to be the one which would
best satisfy these two aspects of his concept of true religion.[28]

Like Brownson, Hecker gradually worked himself to the position that the
longed-for unity would have to be embodied in an authoritative church. In the beginning, his mental gymnastics on the subject were too typically transcendental
to make any concrete sense. "Catholicism," he acknowledged early in 1843, "is solidarity; Protestantism is individuality....We want neither the authority of History nor of the Individual; neither Infallibility nor Reason by itself, but both
combined in Life. Neither Precedent nor Opinion, but Being--...."[29] It took him
another year to untangle his thoughts on the matter. At length, in the spring of

1844 he settled in favor of "the voice of the universal church," rejecting an excessive reliance on individual judgment as "fatal to real progress."[30]

Hecker's obstacles in deciding to join the Catholic Church were also in large part different from those of Brownson. The Protestant denominations he could not abide, finding them fanatic and bigoted.[31] By degrees, he came to the realization that the true Church could be embodied only in its Catholic "phase"--whether Anglican or Roman.[32] The choice between these two--or neither of them--conditioned his struggle for about the same period during which Brownson was opting for Catholicism without the papacy. But Hecker's transcendentalism stood in the way. His diary entries during this period reveal that, while his mighty colleague was roaring out to the public the latest refinement of a Brownsonian catholicism, Hecker's sensitive spirit was passing through a siege of anguish. Only a week before he remonstrated against Brownson's latest compromise as illogical--if you believe the Catholic Church to be true, you are obliged to join it[33]--Hecker asked his diary plaintively:

> What shall I say? Am I wrong? Should I submit and give myself to that which does not engage my whole being? The [Catholic] Church is not to me the great object of life....What shall I say?...Is not the true way for me to go in that wherein I feel that I exist? Is it not best for me to live my own nature rather than to attempt to mould it like some object?[34]

Hecker's other diary entries at this time also show his preoccupation with an ardent search for the will of God and a communion with the divine that would still his inner unrest. A first definitive step in this quest came at the time of his rejection of individualism. He decided to become a priest. This decision gave him at last a peace that he had not experienced during any of the evanescent stages through which he had passed.[35] He still did not know which of the two Catholic communions to join, but he was clear that transcendentalism no longer held out any hope for him. In a letter written to his family he confided his disillusionment: "I have had a few words with Emerson....He and his followers...are heathens in thought and profess to be so....They are the narrowest men, and yet think they are extremely 'many sided.'"[36]

"I am a Catholic," he wrote to Brownson about the same time, announcing his intention of calling on the Catholic bishop of New York, John J. Hughes. The purpose of the call, he explained, was to inquire further into the matter that he had so recently been discussing with an Anglican divine.[37] Yet after the interview, he was still writing to his diary and to his friend, "But I am not prepared...."[38]

By June, however, the conflict was over. After again turning the alternatives over and over in his mind, he decided to make the move. Two days after receiving word of Brownson's decision, Hecker went to Boston for interviews with Brownson, Bishop Fenwick, and Bishop Fitzpatrick. He too then placed himself under Bishop Fitzpatrick for instruction.[39] At last the inner turmoil came to an end. "Never," he confided to his diary, "have I felt the quietness, the immovableness, and the permanent rest that I do now. It is inexpressible."[40] Hecker had indeed found a permanent resting place. He went on to beomce a Catholic priest and founder of the Paulist congregation, dedicated to the winning of Americans in an American way to the Catholic faith.

TRANSCENDENTAL REFLECTIONS ON THE CATHOLIC OPTION

When Brownson continued his visits to Brook Farm after joining the Catholic Church, he found a variety of responses awaiting him. Most were quite negative. "He out-Heroded Herod in his fierce adherence to the creed he had espoused," wrote one resident years later.[41] Though the account where this remark appears is a biased one, it probably reflects the truth. As a later biographer explained it, his "iron mind" and his habit of pulverizing an opponent with his formidable argumentation made everyone uncomfortable. "His was the offense of being remorselessly logical."[42] Another colleague published a rebuke for this kind of declamation in the Harbinger:

The great difficulty, now as ever, with Mr. Brownson is, that he sees
only one truth at a time, or rather one side or aspect of truth, which
he is driven to assert as the whole and only truth in the universe....
The absolute is his forte. His God is absolute, his Church is absolute, his metaphysics is absolute, and all his reasonings and statements
are absolute.[43]

Hecker's analysis of the animosity engendered by the crusading fervor of the Catholic Brownson is perhaps most incisive. As a friend who could see both Brownson's
and his opponents' views with remarkable precision, Hecker expressed the dual perspective thus: "He [Brownson] defeats but will never convince an opponent....No
one loves to break a lance with him, because he cuts such ungentlemanly gashes.
He is strong and he knows it."[44]

As a matter of fact, not many of the transcendental group evinced any desire
to break a lance with the Catholic Brownson. Parker, for example, never offered
any vendettas to the misguided Brownson; he had too much respect for the man.
Over a year before Brownson announced his decision, Parker sensed that he seemed
to be tending toward the Catholic Church. Still respectful of both Brownson and
the Church, Parker evaluated the possibility with the simple remark, "God bless
him, wherever he is! He has a hard head."[45] Even in the last years of Parker's
life, when he judged the Church mercilessly, he could not refrain from tempering
his criticism of Brownson with praise for his genius. In one of the last articles
he wrote for the Christian Examiner, Parker took the opportunity to prophesy the
death of the Catholic Church owing to its unwillingness to sponsor change, and in
an aside described Brownson thus:

Mr. Brownson is the most distinguished Catholic in America, a man of
very large intellectual talents, great power of acquisition, and the
facile art to reproduce in distinct and attractive forms. He is powerful in speech, as with the pen, having also an industry which nothing
daunts, or even tires. But compare the Democratic Brownson, fighting
--(his life was always a battle, is, and will be)--fighting for liberty,
for man and woman, with the Catholic Brownson, the "Saint Orestes" of
some future mythology![46]

Neither did William Henry Channing have any denunciation in his store for Brownson. Channing continued to regard Brownson with favor even after the latter took him on in masterly form, refuting point by point Channing's developmental thesis of Christian history.[47] In a sermon delivered more than fifteen years after their acquaintance at Brook Farm, Channing discoursed at length on what he judged to be the finest examples of the religious types of his day: for Naturalism, Emerson; for orthodoxy, Henry Ward Beecher; and for Catholicism, Orestes A. Brownson.[48]

Only one transcendental mind felt both obligated and able to enter the public arena for debate with the formidable Brownson. Clarke was this courageous soul. In private, Clarke attempted to dismiss playfully the rash of conversions to Catholicism which he witnessed taking place in Boston.[49] But beginning in 1848, and continuing spasmodically for the next quarter century, certain pages of book and periodical fairly dance with charges and counter-charges; iron-clad argumentation and brilliant, incisive demolition; politeness and sarcasm; cool logic and warm contempt. For Brownson felt equally obliged, especially since he had come from the transcendental ranks, to do his part in the on-going debate. Everything remotely anti-Catholic that came from the pen of the erudite spokesman of the liberal creed, Brownson felt compelled to refute. It is an interesting game to trace the duels of these two champions, to speculate on why it sometimes took Clarke five years to reply, and to note, with satisfaction or chagrin, that Brownson always seemed to have the last word.[50]

The only other transcendentalist who had anything to do with the Catholic Brownson was Ripley. But Ripley firmly declined to lock horns with "absolute reason," as he described Brownson after receiving a theological challenge from him.[51] The one other disagreement they had on the subject of Catholicism occurred a decade later. Brownson's determination to advance all things Catholic forced him to demand that Ripley employ Catholic writers for the Catholic articles in

Ripley's sixteen-volume New American Cyclopedia.[52] Ripley consented, employing

the same policy for articles on other religious faiths. But Brownson complained

again. Engaging persons of all faiths, he reasoned, implied on Ripley's part an

equal acceptance of them all![53] This time Brownson received no reply.

But Ripley could not dismiss all his Catholic intimates so easily. Both his

wife and Hecker seem to have sustained great hopes for Ripley's eventual option

for the Catholic Church. Ripley did manifest some interest in Catholic worship,

especially in the early years of his wife's Catholicism. But he feared, at least

in Brownson's and Hecker's opinions, for his job and for his reputation.[54] Accord-

ing to Hecker's account, Ripley's friends were so hostile toward the Church that

they refused to send for Hecker to administer the last rites to Ripley, though

the latter had previously requested this of Hecker.[55]

Hecker's choice of the Catholic faith put a few other of his transcendental-

ist friends on the spot as well. Bancroft seems silent on the matter, until he

could write Hecker a warm word of praise for the erudition which Hecker displayed

in his first book, Questions of the Soul.[56] As with some of the Brook Farmers in

their interest in the Catholic Church, however, Bancroft's was exclusively an

aesthetic appreciation.

As for Alcott, at whose Fruitlands Hecker had boarded for two brief terms, it

was even less than a matter of aesthetics. It was little more than curiosity.

When Emerson pressed Alcott to get an explanation from Hecker for his Catholicism,

Hecker retorted simply with, "Mr. Alcott, I deny your inquisitorial right in this

matter." That was the end of the inquisiton, by Alcott at least.[57] Later there

seem to have been two or more meetings of a more cordial nature. The first was a

chance meeting at the Astor Library, followed by a warm invitation from Hecker

for Alcott to meet his brother priests. Alcott's comments on the incident are

rather indifferent,[58] as are most of his on the Catholic Church. The only other

encounters were when Hecker spoke in Concord on a subject that could have answered all the inquisitorial questions Alcott and Emerson might have asked.

Hecker's topic on these occasions was, "Why I Became a Catholic." Alcott brings

a mixture of insight and ignorance to his journal entry after the first lecture:

"I find little difference of faith between his and mine. I would have mine in

fresh fair forms, without his historic accompaniment."[59]

A more difficult adversary was Hecker's closer friend, Thoreau. The latter's

quarrel with Catholicism was more ardent than was Alcott's.[60] Entirely in keeping

with his position, Thoreau's reaction to Hecker's option came in an outburst:

"What's the use of your joining the Catholic Church? Can't you get along without

hanging onto her skirts?"[61] Thoreau was not one to hang onto the skirts of any

institution, but Hecker, with less than his usual perception, would try to make

him see the light. With a sense of the providential nature of his mission, Hecker

on the day before his baptism wrote to Thoreau. Avoiding any mention of the rea-

son for his proposed trip to Europe--to study for the priesthood--Hecker urged his

friend to accompany him.[62] Thoreau, however, penetrated the ruse and declined.

His reply was mild and perhaps a little wistful:

> I am strongly tempted by your proposition...but the fact is, I cannot
> so decidedly postpone exploring the Farther Indies....the other day
> for a moment I think I understood your relation to that body [the
> Catholic Church]; but the thought was gone again in a twinkling....I
> am really sorry that the Genius will not let me go with you....[63]

Hecker tried again two weeks later, but Thoreau still declined,[64] and Hecker re-

treated for the time being. He was disappointed but not discouraged, until after

the failure of two more attempts to convince his friend that Catholicism offered

fulfillment for both their aspirations. Writing from Holland nearly two years

later, Hecker got straight to the point without any subterfuge:

> My interest in your greatest welfare compels me to write you a few lines,
> perhaps they may aid in your progress. I have found my centre and of
> course my place in the Roman Catholic Church....
>   Though now my friend within cloistered walls [,] in my cell I am

infinitely freer than I was when beating the air on Concord cliffs....
We don't want the middle ages, but we want its inspiration. It is here,
my friend, it is here. Mon Dieu could you see and feel it once.[65]

Two years later Hecker made a final futile attempt, appealing again to Thoreau's
obvious intoxication with freedom: "I would like marvelously to free your soul
by placing it in the light of Catholicity that hectic dissension has robbed it
of...."[66]

But Thoreau could not buy his package, and Hecker turned his efforts to a
larger world. This arena Hecker could and did influence through his congregation
and through its organ, The Catholic World. Years later, through its pages Hecker
expressed his disillusionment and perhaps bitter disappointment with Thoreau when
he wrote: "He was the only man among the transcendentalists that allowed their
theories the fullest play in him, and the incompleteness and failure of his life
cannot be concealed by all the verbiage and praise of his biographers."[67]

EMERSON'S PROBLEM

Only one more of the transcendentalists had anything to say about the decisions of their friends to enter the Catholic Church. This was Emerson, second
only to Thoreau in his disapproval of attachment to any outward form or organization. His reactions to his friends' choice of Catholicism are carefully recorded
in his journals. By tracing these chronologically, we can distinguish the pattern
of his response. With this established, it is possible to determine more or less
clearly what his overall feeling for lived Catholicism really was.

Emerson's first acquaintance to embrace the Catholic faith was a young Boston
girl, Abby Adams. His reaction was rather condescending, both toward the girl and
toward her friends and family who were alarmed at her fancy. For the girl, he
judged, was still a child in need of experience. Perhaps the beautiful forms and
humane spirit of the Catholic Church would awaken her religious nature. He encouraged her to go on in her intention, regardless of opposition, and to suck the
orange of Catholicism thoroughly for whatever it could give her.[68]

But Emerson was not so amenable two years later when it came Hecker's turn. When his and Alcott's inquest of Hecker's motivation failed, Emerson must have continued to puzzle over the matter. He later posed to Hecker a leading question: "Mr. Hecker, I suppose it was the art, the architecture, and so on in the Catholic Church which led you to her?" We do not have Emerson's reaction to Hecker's reply, but we can guess that it failed to satisfy. For Hecker simply offered a terse defense worthy of the style of Emerson himself: "No; but it was what caused all that."[69]

The _piece de resistance_ for Emerson came, however, four years later, when the next one to go the way of Hecker turned out to be a close friend of Emerson's, Anna Barker Ward. This time his letters and journals on the subject bleed with sorrow. Not now did he urge an uneducated and simple young thing to learn something from the Church. For Anna was of pure blood, intelligent and highly educated. Instead of pointing up for her the beautiful forms of Catholicism, as he had for Abby Adams, he pleaded with her. Could she not have said, as he would have done, "Look, I do without your rococo"? But he could not dissuade her, and the depth of his melancholy is revealed in his despairing submission: "My low and lonely sitting here by the wayside is my homage to truth, which, I see, is sufficient without me;...."[70]

To his friends he confided his grief,[71] but to none with more pathos than to Anna herself: "What if you go away, & stay away, & try to hide yourself farther away from me in the seclusions of opinion--you have ever been to me a dear & enshrined person...."[72] For it was, after all, as Emerson always maintained, only matters of opinion that separated churches, and these differences looked to him so frivolous: "How supremely unimportant the form, under which we celebrate the justice, love, & truth, the attributes of the Deity & the soul!"[73] Yet for Anna to choose one of these forms was far from a frivolous matter, and indeed supremely important to him.

Emerson remained disconsolate over this event. Perhaps because of it we can understand his refusal, a few years later, to help Hecker secure a hall in Concord to deliver his address on Catholicism. In a polite and superficial dialogue, he simply told Hecker that no one was interested in theological questions these days, though Hecker saw through the excuse. Privately Emerson lamented the fact that Hecker's "whimsies"--his choice of Catholicism--had served to end their friendship once and for all. For once such men as Hecker speak of their whims, "they are not the men we took them for, and we do not talk with them twice." Probably Emerson had at this point reached the nadir of his bias, as it was surely the most arrogant position which this liberal and genial transcendentalist could adopt. "I doubt," he concluded with hopeless irritation, "if any impression can be made on Father Isaac."[74]

The following year Emerson was still despondent. He expressed disgust at "this running into the Catholic Church" by the young, though he acknowledged with regret that there was nothing to offer them in its stead. Again a decade later we find him referring to a new Catholic in the Ward family as another fatality falling upon it.[75] Thus, contrary to an assertion of Richard Birdsall,[76] it would seem that even in later years, Emerson did continue to lose his serenity over the subject of Catholicism.

What basically was at the root of Emerson's problem with the Church? Was it, as Birdsall implies,[77] a bitterness over Anna Ward's conversion, over this "chance-wind" that had made "a foreigner" of her?[78] Or was his dejection over her choice and that of others symptomatic of a dilemma that lay deeper within him, perhaps at the very core of his self-constituted religion?

For there were elements in transcendentalism that were irreconcilable, at least in the extreme and perhaps least inconcistent form of it that might be called Emersonianism. The paradox lay in the fact that Emerson was a sheer intuitionist and at the same time he was in a very real way a sensist. Though he looked first within his own soul for the meaning of man and the universe, he looked with equal alacrity to all the most pregnant of visible things and persons: the physical world, the men of brilliance of the past, and the artistic products of their genius, particularly their religious genius. In each of these he saw "Thought's interior sphere" gladly doing a partial bit of the work that the "vast soul" planned universally in and through them all.[79]

We have seen that Emerson found the religious aesthetic of the Catholic Church to be among the paramount expressions of such a spirit. In Italy, in Baltimore, in Philadelphia, in New Orleans, in St. Augustine, he found himself irresistibly attracted to the Catholic churches, to all in them that delighted his senses and stirred his spirit. "It is well for my Protestantism," he wrote to his wife from Baltimore, "that we have no Cathedral in Concord....I should be confirmed in a fortnight." "And today," he declared to Margaret Fuller at the same time, "I detest the Unitarians and Martin Luther and all the parliament of Barebones." "The Unitarian church," he concluded to his wife, "forgets that men are poets."[80] When in Rome especially, that master of English prose often could not find words adequate to describe the effect the place had upon him. As he put it once: "Ah great great Rome! it is a majestic city!...And yet I would give all Rome for one man such as were fit to walk here, & could feel and impart the sentiment of the place."[81] When he did find words, as for example in commenting on a Vatican work of Michaelangelo, it was often only to show how powerful an aid religious art was to him in learning to express, as he phrased it, "the divinity that haunts me."[82]

There was inherent in this fascination with the Church of Rome an insoluble dilemma--Emerson's repulsion was as great as his attraction. Early in his life even the art sometimes repelled him, and he described the cathedral in St. Augustine as "full of great coarse toys."[83] Yet he returned to the cathedral,[84] and to more and more cathedrals, until he learned what was for him their message. "When I went to Europe," he wrote later, "I fancied the great pictures were strangers;

some new unexperienced pomp and show." But when he arrived in Rome he met the contrary of what he had anticipated:

> I saw that the picture was the reverse of all this...& itself pierced directly to the simple & true; that it was familiar & sincere; that it was the old eternal fact I had met already in so many forms,--unto which I lived; that it was the plain You & Me I knew so well,--had left at home in so many conversations...that fact I saw again in the Academia of Naples..., & yet again when I came to Rome & to the paintings of Raphael, Angelo, Sacchi, Titian, & Leonardo da Vinci.[85]

By this time Emerson had worked through his theory of the universal correspondence of all things. Here in the Roman Catholic Church he saw these many forms exquisitely shaped to give expression to that theory. Yet at the same time he saw the "old eternal fact" expressed so clearly in the You and Me, that he decided that travelling to the Vatican and Milan and Paris was as "ridiculous as a treadmill." He had all the riches he needed; they were in himself.

Moreover, Emerson found much to dissatisfy and even disgust him in the Catholic Church--its "superstition," its pomp and formalism, its hierarchical stucture, its dogmatism. But even some of its faults he found praiseworthy: "The Catholic Church," he confided to his journal, "is...every way superior [to the Protestant]. It is in harmony with Nature, which loves the race and ruins the individual."[86] Perhaps in this enigmatic transcendental view, Emerson felt himself most at one with the Catholic Church as he saw it, since, individualist though he was, he nonetheless admitted: "I like man, but not men."[87]

Emerson's ambivalence was further complicated by his dilemmas as to what to do about the Church. At one time or another he could bring himself to acknowledge the "colossal theologies" of Christianity and other religions as necessary for the human mind. He could appreciate, though from afar, the men who had "organized their devout impulses or oracles into good institutions"--specifically the Catholic, Anglican, and Calvinistic Churches. But for the most part he despised theological or institutional systems and for that matter any system at all. At one time he could with bravado apply his theory of compensation to the foolish fear of Catholicism that he saw spreading around him.[88] But as the complexities of his dilemma grew and he saw the power of the Church to attract new followers, he feared for the thin alternatives which "the other side" had to offer. He deplored the historical accidents that had "nailed us to the north wall of opposition, and foreordained us to be pale Protestants, Unitarians, freesoilers, abolitionists." He lamented the fact that even stoicism, a form of religion so attractive to the cultivated, had now "no temples, no academy, no commanding Zeno or Antoninus...[and] pure Ethics is not now formulated and concreted into a cultus, a fraternity, with as-semblings and holy days, with song and book, with brick and stone."[89] This obser-vation on "pure" religion's failure to supply the needed supports for human nature was written in 1863, a date well removed from the apex of Emersonian transcenden-talism. By then the only thing he could offer in lieu of these buttresses was "the moral sentiment." By then Emerson had reduced religion to morality.

In the transcendental hey-day it was not so. While Emerson had no final solu-tion--and never would construct one--he firmly replied to the dilemma back in 1839 with his poem, "The Problem." The opening lines express the predicament involved in his ambivalent attitude toward the enticing elements of the Church:

> I like a church; I like a cowl;
> I love a prophet of the soul;
> And on my heart monastic aisles
> Fall like sweet strains, or pensive smiles;
> 5   Yet not for all his faith can see
> Would I that cowlèd churchman be.
>
> Why should the best on him allure,
> 8   Which I could not on me endure?[90]

The remaining fifty-four lines of the poem fail to answer the question posed. But they provide at least the rationale for his chosen alternative to the cowled churchman. It is perhaps his most lyrical exposition of the transcendental doc-trine in which all Nature is priestified and all craftsman's art adopted by

Nature to do the same. No need then for clerical priest or prophet, nor for church or ceremony. The vast Over-soul, in its ceaseless "fiery Pentecost"[91] burns through all these magnificent channels to do the priestly work of inspiring the mind of man.

The answer however did not satisfy, and it palled in the end. In later years Emerson relied less on intuition and more on forces of morality, evolution, and even of church-attendance.[92] This prince of transcendentalists could with as much reason as Hecker be called Ernest the Seeker, since all his life he sought for truth but never seems to have found it to his satisfaction. Late in their lives, Brownson estimated that Emerson had come as near to it "as one can who is so unhappy as to miss it." Brownson found particular pathos in Emerson's supposed mournful admission of failure in a line from his poem, "The Sphinx," where Emerson wrote, "Each answer is a lie."[93] As early as 1847 Brownson predicted that Emerson's transcendental illusion would vanish. In the triumphant tone of one who has been through the stages of search and has come to the promised land, Brownson wrote of him:

> He loves and wooes nature, for he fancies her beauty and loveliness
> emanate from the divinity of his own being....It is he that gives the
> rose its fragrance....But the illusion does not last. He feels, after
> all, that he is a man, only a man; and the enigma of his own being...
> torments him, and from his inmost soul cries out, and in no lullaby
> tones, for a solution. But, alas! no solution comes;....

In the same year, Bartol, who had little use for Emerson's "immense self-respect," described the latter's "stricken and struggling stoicism" as a "voice of consolation [which] dies away in a wail." After Emerson's death Bartol was still dismissing the Emersonian solution as vacuous: "Emerson charges 'pale negations' on the Unitarian order," he wrote. "But he was as pale as the rest."[94]

Before this image, the vision of Emerson as sanguine and self-confident begins to fade. It is ironic that the man who possessed in himself an intense longing for God had in the end to submit silently to an unacknowledged defeat. As he grew older the genius within spoke less and less often; the brilliant illuminations which he had accustomed himself to wait for came but rarely. He who had

sought his ultimate greatness from the daemon within his own breast--in a spirit

of self-reliance, in an implicit trust in Nature and the divinity of it, and in

an impersonal Over-soul that pervaded all--was to see his fondest hopes unrealized.

The burden of his situation can be detected in occasional remarks of his, even

early in his life. One of the best examples of this may be seen in his comments

during a visit to the Baltimore cathedral. He had become enthralled with the cath-

edral's organic fusion of the arts which best represented the correspondences in

all Nature. After rhapsodizing on its perfection, he concluded with a remark of

bitter pathos: "Ah! that one word of it were true!"[95]

Emerson's failure to find the God he was seeking is best explained from these

early days, in the determined stance he took toward the divinity of his own self-

hood. Even amid the enchantment of the Catholic genius he found in Italy, he had

written in 1833: "Here's for the plain old Adam, the simple genuine Self against

the whole world."[96] This centrality of the Self was the one thing he never lost

sight of in the years to come, until it became near divine. The god he sought,

then, was only a human being after all, and it was the only god he ever found.

Emerson's ambivalent attitude toward the Catholic Church was shared by many

of the transcendentalists, though possibly to a lesser degree. In this connection

Channing's remark is telling: "...we ought not to doubt that among the corruptions

of the Catholic Church there are rich relics of primitive truth."[97] Perhaps here

we have the keynote of the transcendental attitude toward Catholicism. Seekers

after perfection, they perceived in the Catholic Church an uncanny mixture of

light and shadow. Its richness was combined with corruption, its sublime beauty

with decay, its fearful authoritarianism with universal adaptibility. None of

them who grew astonished at its powerful influence neglected to express also exas-

peration at its obvious conservatism. None who ever noted its holiness failed to

comment as well on its immorality. None who became captivated by its aesthetic inspiration could overlook entirely its pompous display. Before the Church they stood in a kind of awe at elements they regarded as grossly material but profoundly divine; rigidly doctrinnaire and repressive, but tenderly human, creative, and alive. In brief, in the Catholic Church they discovered both the weakness and strength of earth, and the power and glory of heaven.[98] In their simplistic enthusiasm for utopian goals, they could not accept such a complex force in its totality; there was no room for it in the transcendental ideal.[99]

THE TRANSCENDENTAL CATHOLIC

Thus far did the transcendentalist accept the Catholic. But what of the Catholic acceptance of the transcendentalist? What of their areas of convergence?

We have not here attempted to examine any of the nineteenth century Catholic polemical literature—except some of Brownson and Hecker—written in immediate response to transcendentalism. Nor can we offer an exhaustive analysis of the similarities between the two faiths. Yet a few comparisons are in order.

It perhaps needs no saying that as Catholics, Brownson and Hecker were the first to see in transcendentalism an affinity with Catholicism. Brownson acknowledged his surprise when he first learned that articles of his, written during the period of his transition out of transcendentalism, were being reprinted in the Catholic press.[100] It soon became natural for him to draw comparisons between transcendentalism and Catholicism. These at first were far from flattering to the former, as he pursued his usual ironclad logical and polemical method. In fact, even as late as 1870 he was declaring that the transcendentalists, who had begun by attempting to distinguish between the transient and permanent in Christianity, had ended by losing both.[101]

Hecker likewise began his trek away from the transcendental faith by denouncing the transcendentalists as "heathens" and "the narrowest of men." In a diary entry of 1844 he drew an unflattering picture of the typical member of that group: a man of nerve and no blood, of self-reliance and no love, "a dissecting

critic--heartless, cold," whose church was nature and whose god was himself.[102]
But once he joined the Catholic Church, Hecker quickly took up the transcendental
tools he had abandoned.

First, he thought that the Fourierist movement, because of its humanitarian
goals, would be the means of opening the eyes of the Brook Farmers to Catholic
principles. He even displayed a sparkle of transcendental naivete by asserting
that the Brook Farm experiment, with its Fourieristic inclination, was Ripley's
apprenticeship for the Catholic priesthood.[103] But he very soon became more realistic, using as bait instead the more cherished tenets of the transcendental camp.
These he would show as having their chiefest home in the Catholic Church. We have
seen one example of this in his efforts with Thoreau, where he played up the Catholic inspiration and love of inner freedom. Thenceforward his appeal to the transcendentalists would be made from the springboard of Nature. His first book Questions of the Soul was addressed principally to them. In it he alludes to every
transcendental value, citing with approval Channing's tribute to human sentiment
as opposed to despised external "forms":

> We were not born
> To sink our finer feelings in the dust;
> And better to the grave with feelings torn,
> So in our steps stride truth and trust
> In the great love of things, then to be slaves
> To forms,....[104]

The Catholic Hecker saw nothing objectionable whatever in this revered doctrine
of transcendentalism. He utilized it, along with an appeal to the natural use of
reason, as the cornerstone of his book. Without any qualification he declared
that for any man "to corrupt, to enfeeble, or to abandon" the natural and God-
given instincts and faculties of the soul is spiritual suicide and is the only
sin.[105]

The groping Seeker of Brook Farm days[106] was now writing with a mature certitude, and though by this time a Catholic priest, he had by no means changed

radically. In the same vein he wrote to Anna Barker Ward that what was further needed was a book which would show "that Christian perfection does not require one to close his eyes to the beauties of nature, nor is foreign to the duties of common life, nor exacts the renunciations of human relations....that humility is not abjection, mortification not destruction, nor obedience servility."[107] The Catholic priest could hardly have touched more sensitively the kernel of the transcendental grudge against Catholicism.

Nearly a quarter century after joining the Catholic Church, Hecker was still stressing likeness rather than differences in the two faiths. This is clear from the remark made by Alcott after hearing Father Hecker lecture: "I find little difference of faith between his and mine."[108] A decade later we find Hecker lighlighting transcendental values again, though now as mere echoes of the Catholic tradition of all ages--human reason, the dignity of the soul, and the worth of man. All of these, he notes, were specifically elaborated by Thomas Aquinas and recently confirmed by the Vatican Council. Here in Catholic philosophy could be found "every truth which the transcendentalists so enthusiastically proclaimed in speech, in poetry, and prose." To the transcendentalists who missed this insight, he applied with a sense of particular justification Sterling's lament, "Oh wasted strength!"[109] For statements such as these, Hecker was more than once censured by the Protestant press as a rationalist and a transcendentalist.[110] But he never swerved in his belief in the transcendental core of affinity with Catholicism.

Brownson acknowledged Hecker's use of the transcendental theme of the nobility of man as both genuine and felicitous. For the most part, Brownson himself continued--much to Hecker's dismay[111]--to maintain a militant anti-Protestant position in most of his own writings. But he did take more than one opportunity to admit his candid preference for the transcendental view of human nature over the Protestant.[112] On one occasion he even outdid Hecker, in his very praise of the man, in a lyrical defense of the transcendental aspects of Catholicism. Hecker,

Brownson wrote,

> does not ask them [transcendentalists] as a preparation for grace, to
> abjure reason, stifle the affections, suppress nature; but recognizes
> in reason, love, nature, a preamble to Catholicity, and insists on Cath-
> olicity only as adapted to all the wants of nature, to heal its wounds,
> illumine its darkness, to solace its grief, to strengthen its weakness,
> to elevate it to its union with God, the True, the Beautiful, the Good;
> the end, and the beatitude of the soul.[113]

Indeed, both Brownson and Hecker went so far as to affirm that transcendentalism
is itself the road to Rome.[114]

Early in his studies for the Catholic priesthood Hecker was led to smile at
how far the utopian experiment at Fruitlands had fallen short of what had existed
for centuries in the Catholic Church.[115] But he did not lose his respect for the
effort. Nor did he tire of demonstrating to the transcendentalists, as well as to
every other American, that their ideals could most easily be attained in the Catholic Church. This was the entire aim of the congregation of Paulist priests which
in 1858 he founded and in which he labored as the guiding spirit for thirty years.

There have been a few others who, after Hecker, have attempted to perceive
affinities between transcendentalism and Catholicism. Who would not agree with
them that Thoreau and Walden exemplify the monastic, Franciscan, and Theresian
preference for the dignity of human life, the reverence for simple things, and the
joy of poverty and detachment?[116] A few authors have observed other areas of consensus within the two faiths. These include their emphasis upon the immanence and
providence of God, the freedom of man's will, the ultimate triumph of good, the
value of symbol, the sacramental aspects of nature as revelatory of the divine,
the sense of unity in all things, the capacity of man for transcendent truth, and
the all-inclusive centrality of the religious principle.[117] All these elements
are as basic to traditional Catholic thought as they are to transcendentalism.
Less within the mold of tradition, we see other students finding distinct transcendental overtones in the Catholic attraction for a Teilhardian progressive

cosmology.[118]

Over and above mere speculation, perhaps Brownson and Hecker were not the
last to experience for themselves the confluence of transcendental and Catholic
streams. In many liberal Catholics of today we can find further parallels between
the two faiths. Certain contemporary Catholic authors, for example, echo in
almost identical phrases the transcendental consternation with Church or world
and the transcendental beliefs and hopes for mankind. Catholic authors may be
seen doing historical traces of the periods when their Church was willing to in-
tegrate the positive content of all religions into its theology and cosmology, and
of when and why this openness diminished. They can be found sketching the development of the Church, especially of doctrine, in somewhat the same way as the transcendentalists did in their theories of history. Many among them are urging the
Church to greater holiness and to a reaffirmation of the primitive gospel principles of reverence, love, and prayer.

Catholic authors of today do still more that would have pleased a transcendentalist. They clarify the nature of the Church as composed of all its members,
not just the hierarchy. They question the use of force by the medieval Church.
They center attention upon the intellectus agens in man as his spirit acting as
inner light. They focus upon the solidarity of men and the responsibility of the
individual for the social good of all. They warn against Baroque excesses and reliance upon externals, to the exclusion of the inner dynamisms these forms are
meant to reveal. They call urgently for social justice and enlist in every movement for the melioration of society. They reaffirm the sacredness of the secular.
They speak of the search for God in the heart of every substance and as the Ground
of Being. They discern a kind of incarnation of God in every man, in every deed,
and in the interrelatedness of things. They find man's central religious problem
to be within his own being and his personal quest for union with God. They see
music as entering into the substance of prayer, and poetry as providing an

experience of the universal and the transcendent, and they experiment with all the arts as supplying the thrust and the environment for worship. They possess a dynamic ecumenical orientation unknown to the nineteenth-century Catholic. And finally, they search, even as the transcendentalists searched, for an aggiornamento of the vital religious spirit within every man and within all of society.[119]

Even portions of the documents of the Second Vatican Council (1963-1965) can read like a transcendental declaration of faith. The Council acknowledged the values in non-Chrisitan religions and confirmed the ecumenical movement toward Christian unity. It stressed the importance of a "noble beauty" for the liturgy in preference to "sumptuous display," repeatedly expressing concern that exterior worship should be the manifestation of the interior, and should not give way to formalism. With a shift toward a religious humanism, it refurbished the dignity of the priesthood of the laity, and reaffirmed freedom of conscience and the nobility of the human person.[120]

Furthermore, both responsibly and irresponsibly, many Catholics today are moving toward a freer faith, one less tied to tradition, to hierarchy, to "forms," to dogmas. They look for a faith more imbued with the romantic and transcendental exaltation of the individual and his own peculiar inspirations, together with an overt disregard or denial of his sinfulness. While this option on the part of today's Catholic sometimes lacks the transcendentalists' profoundly Godward thrust --ours is not the "God-ridden epoch"[121]--it does have definite parallels with the nineteenth-century movement.

One major area where, until recently, it has been difficult to detect many transcendental overtones in twentieth-century Catholicism is in the area of hope --that urgent, joyous, confident enthusiasm for a future bright with possibility. Ironically, here the transcendentalist is a nascent Catholic. In few other areas does Catholic tradition coincide more precisely with that of the transcendentalist than in an unbounded trust in the future perfection and happiness of the race.

The locus of the respective paradises of Catholic and transcendentalist may differ, but their certitude about the nature of mankind's ultimate fulfillment remains essentially the same. For both Catholic and transcendentalist, man's final completion will come in consummate union with God and with his brothers--in perfect "love to God and love to man."[122]

NOTES

[1] See John Thomas Codman to a friend, June 9, 1845, in Codman, Brook Farm, pp. 269-270; Codman, in ibid., pp. 167-168.

[2] Kirby, "Reminiscences of Brook Farm," Old and New, V (May, 1872), 524.

[3] Ibid., III (April, 1871), 429; ibid., IV (September, 1871), 356-357; ibid., V (May, 1872), 523-526; Kirby, Years of Experience, pp. 109, 118, 158-159; Swift, Brook Farm, p. 116; Ora Gannett Sedgwick, "A Girl of Sixteen at Brook Farm," Atlantic Monthly, LXXXV (March, 1900), 402.

Mrs. Kirby's accounts are highly spiced with her own anti-Catholic bias. This, in Holden's view, may be due to the fact that her close friend of Brook Farm days, Isaac Hecker, had later become a Catholic (Holden, Early Years of Hecker, p. 112n).

Van Wyck Brooks describes the Brook Farmers as "bursting with profane passions for...the Church of Rome" (Brooks, Life of Emerson, [1932], p. 105), but Swift declares that the interest in Catholicism at Brook Farm was not so great as has been alleged, particularly by Mrs. Kirby (Swift, Brook Farm, [1899], p. 116).

[4] Emerson to Fuller, July 27, 1840, in Emerson, Letters, II, 319.

[5] See Newcomb, Journals, passim; Johnson, ed., in Newcomb, Journals, pp. 14, 38, 86, 205; Kirby, Years of Experience, pp. 158-159; Kirby, "Reminiscences of Brook Farm," III, 429; Swift, Brook Farm, pp. 116, 200.

[6] Kirby, "Reminiscences of Brook Farm," V, 526.

[7] John T. Codman, who went to Brook Farm himself at the age of seventeen, puts the number at "some four and possibly more" (Codman, Brook Farm, p. 246), and Frothingham at "half a dozen perhaps" (Frothingham, Transcendentalism in New England, p. 355). But it is possible to name eight: Anna Mitchell lists Mrs. Ripley, Hecker, Brownson, George Newcome, and Buckley Hastings, the purchasing agent for the Farm (Mitchell, "The Brook Farm Movement Viewed through the Perspective of Half a Century," Catholic World, LXXIII [April, 1901], 30); Swift and Sedgwick name Mrs. Ripley's niece, Sarah F. Stearns, who later entered a convent (Swift, Brook Farm, p. 75; Sedgwick, "Girl of Sixteen at Brook Farm," p. 402); and Henry F. Brownson supplies the names of two ministers at the Farm in whose conversion his father was instrumental--William J. Davis and George Leach (Henry F. Brownson, Orestes A. Brownson's Middle Life: From 1845 to 1855 [Detroit, 1899], p. 96). To these might be added a ninth, Orestes Brownson, Jr., who in later years joined the rest of his family in the Catholic Church.

[8] Burton, "Sophia Dana Ripley," pp. 40-42; Annette Driscoll, "Brook Farm Convert," Ave Maria, XXXI (June 7, 1930), 709-710.

[9] Sedgwick and, probably following her, Burton, claim that Hecker's presence at Brook Farm gave Mrs. Ripley the impetus toward Catholicism (Sedgwick, "Girl of Sixteen at Brook Farm," p. 402; Burton, "Sophia Dana Ripley," p. 41), while Henry F. Brownson alleges that distinction for his father (Henry F. Brownson, Orestes A. Brownson's Middle Life, p. 96).

[10] Charles Crowe places her private adherence to the Church in 1846 (Crowe, George Ripley: Transcendentalist and Utopian Socialist [Athens, Georgia, 1967], p. 224); Burton cites 1847 as the year Hecker, then in Europe, received a letter announcing her intent (Burton, "Sophia Dana Ripley," p. 42); and Frothingham gives as the year "1848, about autumn" (Octavius Brooks Frothingham, George Ripley [Boston, 1882], p. 236).

[11] Alcott to Mrs. A. Bronson Alcott, October 25, 1856, in Alcott, Letters, p. 206; Burton, "Sophia Dana Ripley," p. 342.

Throughout these years, Hecker, first a Redemptorist and then a Paulist priest, was her spiritual guide (Holden, Early Years of Hecker, p. 128).

[12]Burton, "Sophia Dana Ripley," p. 342; Driscoll, "Brook Farm Convert," p. 711; Frothingham, George Ripley, p. 239.

[13]Maynard believes that Brownson was consciously tending toward Catholicism, ever since he rejected Presbyterianism (Maynard, Orestes Brownson, p. 108). But this hardly seems possible.

[14]See for example Brownson's several articles in BrQR, on Kant, Fichte, Hegel; Brownson, "Leroux on Humanity," p. 119; Brownson, "R.W. Emerson's Poems," BrQR, April, 1847, in Brownson, Works, XIX, 190; Brownson, "Transcendentalism," passim; Brownson, The Mediatorial Life of Jesus, A Letter to Reverend William Ellery Channing, 1842, in Brownson, Works, IV, 140-172; Brownson, "Parkerism," p. 233; Brownson, The Convert, p. 139; Brownson, "Protestantism Ends in Transcendentalism," p. 127; Brownson, "Parker's Discourse," pp. 488-510; Brownson, "Church Question," p. 475; Brownson, "No Church, No Reform," BrQR, April, 1844, in Brownson, Works, IV, 501-510; Brownson, "Reform and Conservatism," p. 97; Brownson, "The Mission of Jesus," 1843, as cited in Brownson, The Convert, p. 155; Brownson, "Emerson's Prose Works," p. 437; Brownson, "Schmucker's Psychology," Democratic Review, October, 1842, in Brownson, Works, I, 22; Brownson to Hecker, June 6, 1844, in Holden, Early Years of Hecker, p. 223; Brownson, "The Transcendental Road to Rome," BrQR, XIII (January, 1856), 94, 95.

[15]Brownson, "Parker's Discourse," p. 510; Brownson, "The Mission of Jesus," as cited in Henry F. Brownson, Brownson's Early Life, pp. 458-460, and in Schlesinger, A Pilgrim's Progess, pp. 174-175; Brownson, "No Church, No Reform," pp. 510-511; Brownson, "Church Question," pp. 475-476; Brownson to The Pathfinder, May 9, 1843, in Cameron, Companion to Thoreau's Correspondence, p. 34; Brownson, The Convert, pp. 148-149.

For the best accounts of Brownson's struggles toward the light, see his own writings, particularly The Convert (Van Wyck Brooks in The Flowering of New England [p. 249], called this in 1940 the best account yet written about the spiritual cross-currents of the 1840's and 1850's), and those mentioned in note 14 above. For good studies on one or more aspects of this religious pilgrimage, see Lapati, Orestes A. Brownson; Schlesinger, A Pilgrim's Progress; Maynard, Orestes Brownson; Raemers, America's Foremost Philosopher (Washington, D.C., 1931); Sveino, Orestes A. Brownson's Road to Catholicism; Hecker, "Dr. Brownson and Catholicity"; Hecker, "Dr. Brownson in Boston"; Hecker, "Dr. Brownson's Road to the Church," Catholic World, LXVI (October, 1887), 1-11; Ryan, "Orestes A. Brownson," pp. 98-120; Caponigri, "Brownson and Emerson"; Fitzsimons, "Brownson's Search for the Kingdom of God"; J. Fairfax McLaughlin, "A Study of Dr. Brownson," Catholic World, LXXVII (June, 1903), 310-319. The first volume of the Brownson biography by his son is biased but useful (Henry F. Brownson, Orestes A. Brownson's Early Life).

[16]Lapati states that till this time Brownson had read only the Catechism of the Council of Trent and Milner's End of Controversy (Lapati, Orestes A. Brownson, p. 39).

[17]Brownson, The Convert, p. 159.

[18]Brownson, "Parker's Discourse," pp. 488-489. And see above, p. 202. Hecker saw the illogic in this kind of proposition. After hearing Brownson describe the anomaly in a sermon, Hecker wrote: "I confess the sermon was wholly unsatisfactory to me....If you grant that the Roman Catholic Church is the true Church, there is, to my thought, no stopping place short of its bosom" (Hecker to his mother, May 9, 1843, in Elliott, Life of Hecker, p. 65).

[19]Brownson, "The Church," BrQR, I (January, 1844), 15.

[20]Brownson to Hecker, March 11, 1844, as cited in Maynard, Orestes Brownson, p. 137.

[21]Brownson's account of the interview, as cited in Henry F. Brownson, Brownson's Early Life, pp. 472-473.

[22]Brownson to Hecker, June 6, 1844, in Holden, Early Years of Hecker, p. 223.

[23]Brownson, "Sparks on Episcopacy," _BrQR_, July, 1844, in Brownson, _Works_, IV, 559.

[24]Hecker, "Dr. Brownson and Catholicity," p. 235; Hecker to Brownson, March 9, 1844, in Henry F. Brownson, _Brownson's Early Life_, p. 512; Hecker to Henry F. Brownson, April 17, 1876, in Holden, _Early Years of Hecker_, p. 81; Hecker Memorandum, n.d., in Elliott, _Life of Hecker_, p. 179.

[25]Hecker, "Dr. Brownson in Boston," [1887], pp. 469-472; Hecker, "Dr. Brownson's Road to the CHurch," [1887], pp. 6-11; Hecker, "Dr. Brownson and Catholicity," [1887], pp. 226-234.

[26]Hecker, "Dr. Brownson and Catholicity," p. 225.

[27]Hecker, Diary, April 24, 1843, in Elliott, _Life of Hecker_, p. 63.

[28]Hecker to Brownson, March 15, 1844, in Henry F. Brownson, _Brownson's Early Life_, p. 515.

[29]Hecker, Diary, April 28, 1843, in Elliott, _Life of Hecker_, p. 64.

[30]Hecker to Brownson, March 15, 1844, in Henry F. Brownson, _Brownson's Early Life_, p. 515.

[31]Hecker to his brother John, May 30, 1843, in Holden, _Early Years of Hecker_, p. 145.

[32]Hecker, Diary, June 5, 1843, in _ibid_.

[33]See above, p. 249, note 18.

[34]Hecker, Diary, April 28, 1843, in Holden, _Early Years of Hecker_, p. 144.

[35]Hecker, Diary, March 17, 1844, in _ibid._, p. 201

[36]Hecker to Brownson, March 15, 1844, in Henry F. Brownson, _Brownson's Early Life_, p. 515; Hecker to his family, April 24, 1844, in Holden, _Early Years of Hecker_, p. 231.

[37]Hecker to Brownson, March 15, 1844, in Henry F. Brownson, _Brownson's Early Life_, p. 516.

[38]Hecker, Diary, March 22, 1844, in Elliott, _Life of Hecker_, p. 137; Hecker to Brownson, March 25, 1844, in Henry F. Brownson, _Brownson's Early Life_, p. 519. Hecker's first biographer lays his indecision to the sternness of "discipline" he found in Bishop Hughes (Elliott, _Life of Hecker_, p. 143). Elliott was a Paulist priest, who took the occasion to rebuke American Catholics for their "extreme view of the primary value of highly-wrought discipline," and suggested that people with less discernment than Hecker regarding the essential liberty of the Church were being held away by such an emphasis (_ibid._).

[39]Schlesinger oversimplifies the case when he states that as soon as Brownson's intentions were known to Hecker, the latter put himself under instruction too (Schlesinger, _A Pilgrim's Progress_, p. 182).

[40]Hecker, Diary, June 13, 1844, in Elliott, _Life of Hecker_, p. 154.

[41]Kirby, _Years of Experience_, pp. 146-147.

[42]Maynard, _Orestes Brownson_, pp. xxiii, 117.

[43]Parke Godwin, "Mr. Brownson on Association," _Harbinger_, VI (January 15, 1848), 84.

[44]Hecker, Diary, June 29, 1845, in Maynard, _Orestes Brownson_, p. 143.

[45]Parker to Miss Healey, April 4, 1843, in Weiss, _Life of Parker_, I, 353.

[46]Parker, "Material Condition of the People of Massachusetts," p. 54.

[47]Brownson, "Channing on the Church," [1849], pp. 137-206.

[48]W.H. Channing, as cited in Clarke, "Washington City in November," [1861], p. 559.

[49]He wrote to Margaret Fuller, then on assignment in Italy: "If you do not soon return we shall be all Catholics. Helen Davis has just been reconciled to the church....I expect Joe Angier will follow....Brownson occupies his time in worshipping the bone of a saint,..." (Clarke to Fuller, December, 1848, in Clarke, _Letters_, pp. 146-147).

[50]A few of the more deliberated instances of these controversies may be found in the following:

Clarke, The Church,--As It Was, As It Is, As It Ought To Be, March 15, 1848 (Boston, 1848); Brownson, "The Church,--As It Was, Is, and Ought To Be," [July, 1848], pp. 179-196.

Brownson, "Church vs. No Church," BrQR, April, 1845, in Brownson, Works, V, 331-389; Clarke, "Orestes A. Brownson's Argument for the Roman Church," [March, 1850], pp. 227-247 (a commentary on BrQR of January, 1844, to January, 1850); Brownson, "The Christian Examiner's Defense," BrQR, July, 1850, in Brownson, Works, VII, 197-229.

Clarke, Steps of Belief, or Rational Christianity Maintained Against Atheism, Free Religion, and Romanism, [1870]; Brownson, "Steps of Belief," [December, 1870], pp. 378-399.

[51]Ripley, as cited in Crowe, George Ripley, p. 225.

[52]Ripley and Charles A. Dana, ed. (New York, 1858-1863).

[53]See Henry F. Brownson, Orestes A. Brownson's Later Life: From 1856 to 1876 (Detroit, 1900), pp. 132-134.

[54]Hecker, Memorandum, January 23, 1885, in Elliott, Life of Hecker, p. 90. See also Crowe, George Ripley, p. 238.

[55]Hecker, Memorandum, January 23, 1855, in Elliott, Life of Hecker, p. 90. Elliott asserts that Hecker loved Ripley best of all the transcendentalist group (Elliott, ibid.)

[56]Bancroft to Hecker, March 14, 1855, in Holden, Early Years of Hecker, p. 177.

[57]Hecker, as cited in an unsigned and undated memorandum, in Elliott, Life of Hecker, p. 89. The incident took place shortly after Hecker joined the Catholic Church.

[58]Alcott to Mrs. A. Bronson Alcott, October 10, 1865, in Alcott, Letters, p. 200.

[59]Alcott, Journals, June 21, 1868, p. 391. There seem to have been two such lectures. Hecker indicates that one took place during the war (Hecker, as cited in an unsigned and undated memorandum, in Elliott, Life of Hecker, p. 89). His biographer adds that it was delivered in 1862 in a church (Elliott, ibid. Emerson had refused to help Hecker secure a hall; Alcott had promised to secure one, but did not [Hecker, as cited in an unsigned and undated memorandum, in ibid.]). The Alcott journal entry has 1868 and refers to a lecture as having taken place in the Town Hall. Both indicate that the subject was the same. The evidence seems to be that Alcott attended both, while Emerson did not.

Hecker relates another chance meeting during which Alcott displayed a flicker of interest in the Church, but nothing seems to have come of it (Hecker, Diary, March 5, 1888, in ibid., p. 81).

[60]Historians are not in agreement as to the nature and extent of Thoreau's opposition to Catholicism. Walter Harding, for example, describes Thoreau as violently anti-Catholic (Harding, A Thoreau Handbook [New York, 1959], p. 58), while Frank Buckley regards Thoreau's portrayals of the Irish as significant for their unique freedom from religious and political bias (Buckley, "Thoreau and the Irish," New England Quarterly, XIII [September, 1940], 400). Each of the views is needed to modify the other.

[61]Thoreau, undated memorandum, in Elliott, Life of Hecker, p. 89.

[62]Hecker, Diary, July 30, 1844, in Walter Harding, The Days of Henry David Thoreau (New York, 1965), p. 164; Hecker to Thoreau, July 31, 1844, in E.H. Russell, "A Bit of Unpublished Correspondence Between Henry Thoreau and Isaac Hecker," Atlantic Monthly, XC (September, 1902), 372.

[63] Thoreau to Hecker, August 14, 1844, in Russell, "Bit of Unpublished Correspondence Between Henry Thoreau and Isaac Hecker," pp. 372-373.

[64] Hecker to Thoreau, August 15, 1844, in ibid., pp. 373-374; Thoreau to Hecker, n.d., in ibid., p. 374.

[65] Hecker to Thoreau, May 15, 1847, in Harding, Days of Henry David Thoreau, p. 166.

[66] Hecker to Thoreau, Summer, 1849, in ibid.

[67] Hecker, "Thoreau and New England Transcendentalism," Catholic World, XXVII (June, 1878), 296. The article is extremely harsh on both Thoreau and transcendentalism. Two months previously Hecker published a somewhat milder attack on Emerson (Hecker, "Ralph Waldo Emerson," Catholic World, XXVII [April, 1878], 90-97). What precipitated these articles is unclear.

[68] Emerson, Journal N, 1842, in Emerson, JN, VIII, 181-182; Emerson to William Emerson, August 11, 1842, in Emerson, Letters, III, 78-79.

[69] As cited in an unsigned and undated memorandum, in Elliott, Life of Hecker, p. 89.

[70] Emerson, Journals, 1859, IX, 242-244.

[71] Emerson to Clough, May 17, 1858, in Emerson-Clough Letters, #31; Emerson to Samuel Gray Ward, August 10, [1859?], in Emerson, Letters, V, 169.

[72] Emerson to Anna Barker Ward, May 5, 1859, in Emerson, Letters, V, 142-143.

[73] Ibid., p. 144.

[74] Emerson, Journals, 1862, IX, 467-468; Hecker, as cited in an unsigned and undated memorandum, in Elliott, Life of Hecker, p. 89. Curiously, Emerson's journals were silent on the matter of Hecker's conversion when it took place nearly twenty years previously.

[75] Emerson, Journals, April, 1863, X, 500; Emerson to Lidian Emerson, January 4, 1872, in Emerson, Letters, VI, 194.

[76] Richard D. Birdsall, "Emerson and the Church of Rome," American Literature, XXXI (November, 1959), 280.

[77] Ibid., passim.

[78] Emerson to Anna Barker Ward, draft, from typescript journals for 1859-1860, in Emerson, Letters, V, 143n. The terms do not appear in the final letter, May 5, 1859, in ibid., pp. 142-143.

[79] See, among others, his poems, "The Problem," "The World-Soul," "The Sphinx," "The Solution"; and his essays, "The Poet," "The Over-Soul," and "Circles."

[80] Emerson to Lidian Emerson, January 8, 1843, in Emerson, Letters, III, 117-118; Emerson to Fuller, January 7, 1843, in ibid., p. 116.

[81] Emerson to Charles Chauncy Emerson, April 16, 1833, in ibid., I, 374.

[82] Emerson, "Lecture on the Tests of Great Men," 1835, as cited in Hopkins, Spires of Form, p. 216.

[83] Emerson, Memorandum, 1827, in Emerson, JN, III, 116.

[84] Emerson, Memorandum, February 25, 1827, in ibid., p. 117.

[85] Emerson, Journal D, 1839, in ibid., VII, 222.

[86] Emerson, Journal GH, 1847, in Emerson, JN, X, 178.

[87] Emerson, Journal O, 1846, in ibid., IX, 378.

[88] Emerson, Works, IV, 4; ibid., X, 203. Of the fears of the age, including the fear of Catholicism, Emerson wrote: "Nemesis takes care of all these things, balances fear with fear, eradicates nobles with upstarts, supplants one set of nobodies with another set of nobodies" (Emerson, Journal GH, 1847, in Emerson, JN, X, 143-144.

[89] Emerson, Journals, 1857, IX, 114; ibid., April, 1863, IX, 500.

[90] Emerson, Works, IX, 6. According to Thoreau, the poem was written in 1839 in immediate reaction to the preaching of Barzillai Frost (cf. a notation by Thoreau on a transcript copy of "The Problem" [see Kenneth Cameron, "Emerson, Thoreau, Parson Frost, and 'The Problem,'" Emerson Society Quarterly, VI (1957),

16]), who was a continual spiritual irritant to Emerson. But the dilemma was not a new one. Emerson's public rejection of institutional Christianity had come the previous year with his Divinity School Address. Shortly after it he expressed his perplexity on this matter privately: "It is very grateful to my feelings to go into a Roman Cathedral, yet I look as my countrymen do at the Roman priesthood. ...I find an unpleasant dilemma in this, nearer home. I dislike to be a clergy-man and refuse to be one. Yet how rich a music would be to me a holy clergyman in my town. It seems to me he cannot be a man, quite & whole. Yet how plain is the need of one, & how high yes highest is the function....Something is wrong I see not what" (Emerson, Journal D, 1838, in Emerson, JN, VII, 60).

91Emerson, "The Problem," in Emerson, Works, IX, 8.

92According to both Bartol and Emerson's daughter, Emerson attended church regularly in his later days (see "The Errancy of Emerson," The Catholic Review, XXII [August 19, 1882], 122; Rusk, Life of Emerson, p. 499).

93Emerson, Works, IX, 24; Brownson, "Emerson's Prose Works," [1870], pp. 433-435. Brownson misinterprets the line. In the poem, written in 1841, Emerson dem-onstrates that each answer that one receives merely from the senses is a lie; the whole of truth is contained only in nature's oracle within.

94Brownson, "R.W. Emerson's Poems," p. 192; Bartol, "Poetry and Imagination," CE, XLII (March, 1847), 258-259; Bartol, "Unitarian Idea and Situation," p. 197. Hecker rendered an equally unequivocal judgment: "Against [the teaching of Thomas Aquinas on the necessity of revelation] Mr. Emerson protested, set up human reason, ...and with varying consistency assailed revelation and exaggerated human self-sufficiency in all his writings, both verse and prose; with occasional misgivings wrung from him by the sorrows of human infirmity, which human reason had no power to console" (Hecker, "Two Prophets of This Age," Catholic World, XLVII [August, 1888], 685).

95Emerson to Fuller, January 7, 1843, in Emerson, Letters, III, 116.

96Emerson, 1833, as cited in Introduction to Emerson, JN, IV, xiii.

97Channing, Works, Complete Edition, p. 1018.

98Some individual studies which each discuss both positive and negative as-pects of the Catholic Church are the following: Parker, Discourse of Religion; Hedge, "Ecclesiastical Christendom"; Hedge, "The Churches and the Church"; Chan-ning, "Letter on Catholicism"; Channing, "On Fenelon"; Clarke, Steps of Belief; Clarke, Orthodoxy; Clarke, Vexed Questions; and many others of Clarke.

99The dichotomy between the theoretical openness of the transcendentalists, as compared with its absence in fact, is highlighted in their attitude toward Margaret Fuller. Once she had married an Italian Catholic and had her infant bap-tized in his Church, they grew very uncomfortable about her new status. A com-mentary by Joseph Krutch in this regard, though a bit harsh, exposes the extent of their inability to accept Catholicism in their real lives: "At best, most of the New England transcendentalists accepted a carefully edited version of the universe from which many phenomena were expunged with all the fussy fastidiousness of any other proponent of Victorian propriety. At worst they complacently read into the universe whatever they liked to think they had found there and they gave authority to whatever prejudices they most cherished by calling them 'higher laws.' Thus, though few objected to Margaret Fuller's accepting the universe, a great many, it appears, objected to her accepting Count Ossoli--on the assumption, apparently, that neither Italians nor Catholics were part of the universe as New England had chosen to define it" (Joseph Wood Krutch, Henry David Thoreau [New York, 1948], pp. 190-191).

100Brownson, The Convert, p. 156.

101Brownson, "Emerson's Prose Works," p. 438.

102Hecker to his family, April 24, 1844, in Holden, Early Years of Hecker, p. 231; Hecker, Diary, June 14, 1844, in Elliott, Life of Hecker, p. 155.

[103]Hecker to Brownson, April 6, 1844, postmarked July 6, 1844, in Henry F. Brownson, Brownson's Early Life, p. 525.

[104]Channing, as cited in Hecker, Questions of the Soul, [no source given], p. 12.

[105]Hecker, Questions of the Soul, p. 16.

[106]The title of William Henry Channing's article, "Ernest the Seeker," was applied to Hecker by reason of the intensity of his search.

[107]Hecker to Anna Barker Ward, November 2, 1860, as cited in Birdsall, "Emerson and the Church of Rome," p. 276.

[108]Alcott, Journals, June 21, 1868, p. 391.

[109]Hecker, "Transcendental Movement in New England," [1876], pp. 529-532. The article is a review of Frothingham's Transcendentalism in New England, [1876].

[110]See Brownson, "Transcendental Road to Rome," p. 88.

[111]"...the best minds of New England," Hecker wrote the year before his death, "were ripe for the study of the essential truths of Catholicity from a point of view of reason and its natural aspirations, and Dr. Brownson should have been the pioneer of a large movement among them" (Hecker, "Dr. Brownson and Bishop Fitzpatrick," p. 6). This was written a decade after Brownson's death.

[112]Brownson, "Questions of the Soul," pp. 541, 544; Brownson, "Transcendental Road to Rome," pp. 88-96.

[113]Brownson, "Transcendental Road to Rome," p. 96.

[114]Hecker, "Transcendental Movement in New England"; Hecker, Questions of the Soul; Brownson, The Convert; Brownson, "Transcendental Road to Rome." Sveino goes further and sees Brownson's very Catholicity as a "'transfigured' transcendentalism" (Sveino, Orestes A. Brownson's Road to Catholicism, p. 314).

[115]Hecker to Thoreau, May 15, 1847, in Holden, Early Years of Hecker, p. 178n.

[116]Harold C. Gardiner, "Era of the Half Gods," p. 10; Michael F. Moloney, "Henry David Thoreau, 1817-1862: Christian Malgré Lui," in Gardiner, ed. American Classics Reconsidered, pp. 202, 205-206.

[117]Robert C. Pollack, "A Reappraisal of Emerson," Thought, XXXII (Spring, 1957), 126-131; Gardiner, "Era of the Half Gods," pp. 4-11; Shuster, Catholic Spirit in America, pp. 58-61; Ryan, "Orestes A. Brownson," p. 117.

[118]Francis E. Kearns, "Emerson and the American Catholic Scholar," Emerson Society Quarterly, XXXIX (1965), 66; John J. McAleer, "Transcendentalism and the Improper Bostonian," ibid., p. 76.

[119]A sampling of twentieth century Catholic spokesmen whose writings carry one or more of these emphases are: Charles Peguy, Paul Claudel, Pierre Teilhard de Chardin, Gabriel Marcel, Henri Bremond, Jacques Maritain, Romano Guardini, Jean Danielou, Etienne Gilson, Maruice Blondel, Francis Thompson, George Bernanos, Karl Adam, Karl Rahner, Hans Urs von Balthasar, Yves Congar, Marie-Dominique Chenu, Henri DeLubac, and many others.

[120]Declaration on the Relationship of the Church to Non-Christian Religions; Decree on Ecumenism; Constitution on the Sacred Liturgy; Dogmatic Constitution on the Church; Declaration on Religious Freedom; passim.

[121]See above, p. 1.

[122]Parker's phrase (see above, p. 12).

BIBLIOGRAPHY

The following listing includes only those items which were useful for this study. The transcendentalist writings here named represent less than half their total output.

I INDIVIDUAL TRANSCENDENTALISTS

AMOS BRONSON ALCOTT

Alcott, Amos Bronson. "Days from a Diary," The Dial, II (April, 1842), 409-437.

_____. The Journals of Bronson Alcott. Selected and edited by Odell Shepard. Boston: Little, Brown and Company, 1938.

_____. The Letters of A. Bronson Alcott. Edited by Richard L. Herrnstadt. Ames, Iowa: The Iowa State University Press, 1969.

_____. "Philosophemes," Journal of Speculative Philosophy, IX (April, July, 1875), 190-209, 245-263.

_____. Sonnets and Canzonets. Boston: Roberts Brothers, 1882.

_____. Table-Talk. Boston: Roberts Brothers, 1877.

_____. "Tablets," Radical, II (November, 1866), 177-179.

* * *

"Description of Mr. Alcott's School," Western Messenger, I (October, 1835), 223-225.

Sanborn, Franklin B. and Harris, William T. A. Bronson Alcott: His Life and Philosophy. 2 vols. Boston: Roberts Brothers, 1893.

Sears, Clara Endicott (comp.). Bronson Alcott's Fruitlands. With Transcendental Wild Oats by Louisa May Alcott. Boston: Houghton Mifflin Company, 1915.

Shepard, Odell. Pedlar's Progress: The Life of Bronson Alcott. Boston: Little, Brown and Company, 1937.

GEORGE BANCROFT

Bancroft, George. <u>Abraham Lincoln; a Tribute</u>. New York: A. Wessels Company, 1908.

_____. "Correspondence of George Bancroft and Jared Sparks, 1823-1832. Illustrating the Relation Between Editor and Reviewer in the Early Nineteenth Century." Edited by John Spencer Bassett, <u>Smith College Studies in History</u>, II (January, 1917), 65-143.

_____. <u>History of the United States, from the Discovery of the American Continent</u>. 10 vols. Boston: Little, Brown and Company. Vols. 1-2, 17th ed., 1859; vol. 3, 20th ed., 1868; vol. 4, 20th ed., 1852; vol. 5, 1852; vol. 6, 1854; vol. 7, 3rd ed., 1858; vol. 8, 6th ed., 1860; vol. 9, 5th ed., 1866; vol. 10, 1874.

_____. "Joseph II. of Austria," <u>North American Review</u>, XXXI (July, 1830), 1-26.

_____. "Last Moments of Eminent Men," <u>North American Review</u>, XXXVIII (January, 1834), 116-134.

_____. <u>Literary and Historical Miscellanies</u>. New York: Harper and Brothers, 1855.

_____. <u>Oration Delivered on the Fourth of July, 1826, at Northampton, Massachusetts</u>. Northampton: T. Watson Shepard, Printer, 1826.

_____. <u>Poems</u>. Cambridge, Massachusetts: The University Press, 1823.

_____. "Progress of Civilization," <u>Boston Quarterly Review</u>, I (October, 1838), 389-407.

* * *

Blumberg, Arnold. "George Bancroft, France, and the Vatican: Some Aspects of American, French, and Vatican Diplomacy, 1866-1870," <u>Catholic Historical Review</u>, L (January, 1965), 475-493.

Blumenthal, Henry. <u>A Reappraisal of Franco-American Relations, 1830-1871</u>. Chapel Hill: University of North Carolina Press, 1959.

Eyck, Erich. <u>Bismarck and the German Empire</u>. New York: W.W. Norton and Company, 1964 [c. 1958].

Howe, M.A. DeWolfe. <u>The Life and Letters of George Bancroft</u>. 2 vols. New York: Charles Scribner's Sons, 1908.

Levin, David. <u>History As Romantic Art: Bancroft, Prescott, Motley and Parkman</u>. New York: Harcourt, Brace and World, 1959.

Nye, Russell B. <u>George Bancroft: Brahmin Rebel</u>. New York: Alfred A. Knopf, 1944.

Rathbun, John W. "George Bancroft on Man and History," Transactions of the Wisconsin Academy of Sciences, Arts and Letters, LXII (1954), 51-73.

Stolberg-Wernigerode, Otto zu. Germany and the United States of America During the Era of Bismarck. Reading, Pennsylvania: The Henry Janssen Foundation, 1937.

Trauth, Sister M. Philip. "The Bancroft Dispatches on the Vatican Council and the Kulturkampf," Catholic Historical Review, XL (July, 1954), 178-190.

U.S. Congress. House. Papers Relating to the Foreign Relations of the United States, 1872-1873, Part 1; 1873-1874, Part 1; 1874-1875, Part 1. Washington: Government Printing Office, 1873, 1873, 1874.

Wade, Mason. "The Literary Historians: The Brahmins Contemplate the Past." American Classics Reconsidered: A Christian Appraisal. Edited by Harols C. Gardiner, S.J. New York: Charles Scribner's Sons, 1958.

CYRUS AUGUSTUS BARTOL

Bartol, Cyrus Augustus. "The Bible," Unitarian Review, XIX (January, 1883), 30-52.

_____. Book Review of Sermons by Frederic Henry Hedge (Boston, 1891), Unitarian Review, XXXVI (November, 1891), 325-337.

_____. "The Celebration of John Pierpont's Centennial Birthday," Unitarian Review, XXIV (July, 1885), 14-21.

_____. Character: The Man and the Physician. A Sermon Preached in the West Church, Boston, Sunday, December 9, 1877. Boston: A. Williams and Company, 1878.

_____. Christ the Way. A Sermon Preached at the Ordination of the Reverend George M. Bartol, As Minister of the First Church of Christ, in Lancaster, Massachusetts, Wednesday, August 4, 1847. Lancaster: Ballard and Messinger, 1847.

_____. "Christianity on Trial," Unitarian Review, VII (February, 1877), 182-191.

_____. "Christ's Authority the Soul's Liberty," Christian Examiner, LV (November, 1853), 313-338.

_____. Church and Congregation: A Plea for Their Unity. Boston: Ticknor and Fields, 1858.

_____. "Discourse on Dr. Mayhew," in The West Church and Its Ministers: Fiftieth Anniversary of the Ordination of Charles Lowell, D.D. Boston:Crosby, Nichols, and Company, 1856.

_____. A Discourse, Preached in the West Church, on Theodore Parker. Boston: Crosby, Nichols, Lee and Company, 1860.

_____. Discourses on the Christian Body and Form. Boston: Crosby, Nichols, and Company, 1852.

_____. Discourses on the Christian Spirit and Life. 2nd ed. revised, with an introduction. Boston: Crosby and H.P. Nichols, 1850.

_____. "Emerson's Religion," in The Genius and Character of Emerson. Lectures at the Concord School of Philosophy. Boston: James R. Osgood and Company, 1884.

_____. "Goethe and Schiller," in The Life and Genius of Goethe. Lectures at the Concord School of Philosophy. Edited by Franklin B. Sanborn. Boston: Ticknor and Company, 1886.

_____. "Hedge's Reason in Religion," Christian Examiner, LXXIX (July, 1865), 84-95.

_____. In Remembrance. Address, on the Occasion of the Death of Charles Greely Loring. Delivered in the West Church. Boston: Printed for the Society, 1867.

_____. "Jesus and Jerusalem: or Christ the Saviour and Civilizer of the World," Quarterly Journal of the American Unitarian Association, IV (July 1, 1857), 405-429.

_____. "The Key of the Kingdom," The Monthly Religious Magazine and Independent Journal, XXII (July, 1859), 1-22.

_____. "Martin Luther," Unitarian Review, XX (December, 1883), 509-523.

_____. "Ministry at Large," Christian Examiner, XXV (November, 1838), 219-227.

_____. "Modern Skepticism," Christian Examiner, XLIX (November, 1850), 317-341.

_____. "The Nature of Knowledge--Emerson's Way," in Concord Lectures in Philosophy: Comprising Outlines of All the Lectures at the Concord Summer School of Philosophy in 1882; with an Historical Sketch. Collected and arranged by Raymond L. Bridgman. Cambridge, Massachusetts: Moses King, 1883.

_____. "Our Fellowship," in The West Church, Boston. Commemorative Services on the Fiftieth Anniversary of Its Present Ministry and the One Hundred and Fiftieth of Its Foundation, on Tuesday, March 1, 1887. With Three Sermons by Its Pastor. Boston: Damrell and Upham, 1887.

_____. "Permanence in Religion and in Preaching: Orville Dewey's Autobiography, Letters, and Collected Works," Unitarian Review, XXI (March, 1884), 193-207.

_____. "Person in Religion. An Address Delivered Before the Ministerial Union, March 9, 1868," Monthly Journal of the American Unitarian Association, IX (May, 1868), 153-165.

_____. Pictures of Europe, Framed in Ideas. 2nd ed. Boston: Crosby, Nichols, and Company, 1856.

_____. "Poetry and Imagination," Christian Examiner, XLII (March, 1847), 250-270.

_____. The Preacher, the Singer, and the Doer: Dewey, Longfellow, and Bertram. Boston: A. Williams and Company, 1882.

_____. "The Preacher's Trial," Atlantic Monthly, XI (February, 1863), 206-212.

_____. Principles and Portraits. Boston: Roberts Brothers, 1880.

_____. Radical Problems. Boston: Roberts Brothers, 1872.

_____. Reason and Rome in Education. A Sermon Preached at the West Church, Boston, Sunday, November 23, 1879. Boston: George H. Ellis, 1879.

_____. Religion in Our Public Schools: A Discourse Preached in the West Church, Boston. Boston: Ticknor and Fields, 1859.

_____. "Representative Men," Christian Examiner, XLVIII (March, 1850), 314-318.

_____. The Rising Faith. Boston: Roberts Brothers, 1873.

_____. Sincerity: An Address Before the Essex Conference, February 28, 1872. Boston: Reprinted from the Radical for May, 1872.
_____. "Theological Changes," Unitarian Review, XIII (April, 1880), 289-302.

_____. "The Tidings," in The West Church, Boston. Commemorative Services on the Fiftieth Anniversary of Its Present Ministery and the One Hundred and Fiftieth of Its Foundation, on Tuesday, March 1, 1887. With Three Sermons by Its Pastor. Boston: Damrell and Upham, 1887.

_____. "The Unitarian Idea and Situation," Unitarian Review, XXVI (September, 1886), 193-206.

_____. The Upper Standing. A Sermon Preached in the West Church, Boston, March 3, 1872. Boston: Leonard C. Bowles, 1872.

_____. "The Way to Find God," Monthly Journal of the American Unitarian Association, I (February, 1860), 49-58.

_____. The Word of the Spirit to the Church. Boston: Walker, Wise, and Company, 1859.

* * *

Bellows, Henry Whitney, "Bartol's Discourses on the Christian Body and Form," Christian Examiner, LIV (January, 1853), 103-123.

CHARLES TIMOTHY BROOKS

Brooks, Charles Timothy. "Erasmus," Christian Examiner, XLIX (July, 1850), 80-100.

_____. "German Hymnology," Christian Examiner, LXIX (November, 1860), 402-415.

_____. "Hedge's Reason in Religion," North American Review, CI (July, 1865), 288-291.

_____. A Poem Pronounced Before the Phi Beta Kappa Society, at Cambridge, August 28, 1845. Boston: Charles C. Little and James Brown, 1845.

_____. Poems, Original and Translated by Charles Timothy Brooks, with a Memoir by Charles W. Wendte. Selected and edited by W.P. Andrews. Boston: Roberts Brothers, 1885.

_____. "Renan's Life of Jesus," North American Review, XCVIII (January, 1864), 195-233.

_____. "The Revelation of St. John," Christian Examiner, XLIV (May, 1848), 386-403.

_____. Schiller's Homage of the Arts, with Miscellaneous Pieces from Rückert, Freiligrath, and Other German Poets. Boston: James Munroe and Company, 1846.

_____. Simplicity of Christ's Teachings, Set Forth in Sermons. Boston: Crosby, Nichols, and Company, 1859.

_____. (trans.). Songs and Ballads Translated from Uhland, Korner, Burger and Other German Lyric Poets. Vol. XIV of Specimens of Foreign Standard Literature. Edited by George Ripley, 14 vols. Boston: James Munroe, 1842.

_____. William Ellery Channing: A Centennial Memory. Boston: Roberts Brothers, 1880.

* * *

Klenze, Camillo von. Charles Timothy Brooks, Translator from the German, and the Genteel Tradition. Boston: D.C. Heath and Company, 1937.

ORESTES A. BROWNSON

Since Brownson's thought evolved through several rather well-defined stages, and since his attitude toward transcendentalism changed radically, it is useful to single out the precise periods when various statements of his were made. For this reason, pertinent items contained in his collected works are listed separately.

Brownson, Orestes Augustus. "Aspirations of Nature," Brownson's Quarterly Review, October, 1857, in Brownson, Works, XIV, 548-577.

_____. "Bancroft's History of the United States," Brownson's Quarterly Review, October, 1852, in Brownson, Works, XIX, 382-418.

_____. "Benjamin Constant on Religion," Christian Examiner, XVII (September, 1834), 63-77.

_____. "Bishop Hopkins on Novelties," Brownson's Quarterly Review, July, 1844, in Brownson, Works, IV, 527-542.

_____. Book Review of History of the Colonization of the United States by George Bancroft, 2 vols. (Boston, 1841), Boston Quarterly Review, IV (October, 1841), 512-518.

_____. Book Review of Workingman's Library. Vol. I (Boston, 1833), The Unitarian, I (April, 1834), 170-177.

_____. "Channing on the Church and Social Reform," Brownson's Quarterly Review, April, 1849, in Brownson, Works, X, 137-206.

_____. Charles Elwood, or, The Infidel Converted, 1840, in Brownson, Works, IV, 173-316.

_____. "The Christian Examiner's Defense," Brownson's Quarterly Review, July, 1850, in Brownson, Works, VII, 197-229.

_____. "Christianity and Reform," The Unitarian, I (February, 1834), 51-58.

_____. "The Church," Brownson's Quarterly Review, I (January, 1844), 9-17.

_____. "The Church, As It Was, Is, and Ought To Be," Brownson's Quarterly Review, July, 1848, in Brownson, Works, VII, 179-196.

_____. "Church of the Future," Boston Quarterly Review, January, 1842, in Brownson, Works, IV, 57-78.

_____. "The Church Question," Brownson's Quarterly Review, January, 1844, in Brownson, Works, IV, 461-483.

_____. "Church Unity and Social Amelioration," Brownson's Quarterly Review, July, 1844, in Brownson, Works, IV, 512-526.

_____. "The Church vs. No Church," Brownson's Quarterly Review, April, 1845, in Brownson, Works, V, 331-389.

_____. The Convert, or Leaves from My Experience, 1857, in Brownson, Works, V, 1-200.

_____. "Education of the People," Christian Examiner, XX (May, 1836), 153-169.

_____. "Emerson's Essays," Boston Quarterly Review, IV (July, 1841), 291-308.

_____. "Emerson's Prose Works," Catholic World, May, 1870, in Brownson, Works, III, 424-438.

_____. "Free Religion," Catholic World, November, 1869, in Brownson, Works, III, 407-423.

_____. "The Laboring Classes," Boston Quarterly Review, III (July, October, 1840), 358-395, 420-510.

_____. "Leroux on Humanity," Boston Quarterly Review, July, 1842, in Brownson, Works, IV, 100-139.

_____. "Liberalism and Socialism," Brownson's Quarterly Review, April, 1855, in Brownson, Works, X, 526-550.

_____. Literary Notice of Life of Cardinal Cheverus, Archbishop of Bordeaux, Formerly Bishop of Boston, Massachusetts by J. Huen-Dubourg. Translated by E. Stewart (Boston, 1839), Boston Quarterly Review, II (July, 1839), 387-389.

_____. The Mediatorial Life of Jesus. A Letter to Rev. William Ellery Channing, 1842, in Brownson, Works, IV, 140-172.

_____. "Mr. Emerson's Address," Boston Quarterly Review, I (October, 1838), 500-514.

_____. "Nature and Office of the Church," Brownson's Quarterly Review, April, 1844, in Brownson, Works, IV, 484-495.

_____. New Views of Christianity, Society, and the Church, 1836, in Brownson, Works, IV, 1-56.

_____. "No Church, No Reform," Brownson's Quarterly Review, April, 1844, in Brownson, Works, IV, 496-512.

_____. An Oration Before the Democracy of Worcester and Vicinity, Delivered at Worcester, Massachusetts, July 4, 1840. Boston: E. Littlefield, 1840.

_____. "Origin and Ground of Government," Democratic Review, 1843, in Brownson, Works, XV, 296-404.

_____. "Parkerism, or Infidelity," Brownson's Quarterly Review, II (April, 1845), 222-249.

_____. "Parker's Discourse," Boston Quarterly Review, V (October, 1842), 385-512.

_____. "The Philosophy of History," Democratic Review, May, June, 1843, in Brownson, Works, IV, 361-423.

_____. "The Present State of Society," Democratic Review, July, 1843, in Brownson, Works, IV, 423-460.

_____. "The Presidential Nominations," Brownson's Quarterly Review, July, 1844, in Brownson, Works, XV, 484-493.

_____. "Protestantism Ends in Transcendentalism," Brownson's Quarterly Review, July, 1846, in Brownson, Works, VI, 113-134.

_____. "Questions of the Soul," Brownson's Quarterly Review, April, 1855, in Brownson, Works, XIV, 538-547.

_____. "R.W. Emerson's Poems," Brownson's Quarterly Review, April, 1847, in Brownson, Works, XIX, 189-202.

_____. "Reform and Conservatism," Boston Quarterly Review, January, 1842, in Brownson, Works, IV, 79-99.

_____. "Remarks on Universal History," Democratic Review, XII (June, 1843), 569-586.

_____. "Schumucker's Psychology," Democratic Review, October, 1842, in Brownson, Works, I, 19-57.

_____. The Scholar's Mission, 1843, in Brownson, Works, XIX, 65-87.

_____. "The Secret of the Lord," Boston Quarterly Review, IV (July, 1841), 308-320.

_____. "Social Evils, and Their Remedy," Boston Quarterly Review, IV (April, 1841), 265-291.

_____. "Sparks on Episcopacy," Brownson's Quarterly Review, July, 1844, in Brownson, Works, IV, 558-567.

_____. "Steps of Belief," Catholic World, December, 1870, in Brownson, Works, VIII, 378-399.

_____. "Synthetic Philosophy," Democratic Review, December, 1842, January, March, 1843, in Brownson, Works, I, 58-129.

_____. "The Transcendental Road to Rome," Brownson's Quarterly Review, XIII (January, 1856), 81-102.

_____. "Transcendentalism," Brownson's Quarterly Review, 1845, 1846, in Brownson, Works, VI, 1-113.

_____. "Transient and Permanent in Christianity," Boston Quarterly Review, IV, (October, 1841), 436-474.

_____. "Truth Not Dangerous," Boston Quarterly Review, III (April, 1840), 167-181.

_____. "Two Articles from the Princeton Review, Concerning the Transcendental Philosophy of the Germans, and of Cousin, and Its Influence on Opinion in This Country," Boston Quarterly Review, III (July, 1840), 265-323.

_____. The Works of Orestes A. Brownson. Edited by Henry F. Brownson. 20 vols. Detroit: Thorndike Nourse, 1882-1887.

* * *

Brownson, Henry F. Orestes A. Brownson's Early Life: From 1803 to 1844. Detroit: H.F. Brownson, Publisher, 1898.

_____. Orestes A. Brownson's Latter Life: From 1856 to 1876. Detroit: H.F. Brownson, Publisher, 1900.

_____. Orestes A. Brownson's Middle Life: From 1845 to 1855. Detroit: H.F. Brownson, Publisher, 1899.

Caponigri, A. Robert. "Brownson and Emerson: Nature and History," New England Quarterly, XVIII (September, 1945), 368-390.

Fitzsimons, Matthew A. "Brownson's Search for the Kindgom of God: The Social Thought of an American Radical," Review of Politics, XVI (January, 1954), 22-36.

Gilhooley, Leonard. Contradiction and Dilemma: Orestes Brownson and the American Idea. New York: Fordham University Press, 1972.

Godwin, Parke. "Mr. Brownson on Association," Harbinger, VI (January 15, 1848), 84.

Hollis, C. Carroll. "Brownson on George Bancroft," South Atlantic Quarterly, XLIX (January, 1950), 42-52.

Kirk, Russell (ed.). Selected Essays by Orestes Brownson. Chicago: Henry Regnery Company, 1955.

_____. "Two Facets of the New England Mind: Emerson and Brownson," The Month, n.s., VIII (October, 1952), 208-217.

Lapati, Americo D. Orestes A. Brownson. New York: Twayne Publishers, 1965.

McLaughlin, J. Fairfax. "A Study of Dr. Brownson," Catholic World, LXXVII (June, 1903), 310-319.

Maynard, Theodore. Orestes Brownson: Yankee, Radical, Catholic. New York: T. Macmillan Company, 1943.

Raemers, Sydney Albert. America's Foremost Philosopher. Washington, D.C.: St. Anselm's Priory, 1931.

Ryan, Alvan S. (ed.). The Brownson Reader. New York: P.J. Kenedy and Sons, 1955.

_____. "Orestes A. Brownson, 1803-1876: The Critique of Transcendentalism." American Classics Reconsidered: A Christian Appraisal. Edited by Harold C. Gardiner, S.J. New York: Charles Scribner's Sons, 1958.

Schlesinger, Arthur, Jr. A Pilgrim's Progress: Orestes A. Brownson. Boston: Little, Brown, and Company, 1939.

Sveino, Per. Orestes A. Brownson's Road to Catholicism. New York: Humanities Press, 1970.

WILLIAM ELLERY CHANNING

Channing, William Ellery. Correspondence of William Ellery Channing with Lucy Aikin from 1826 to 1842. Edited by Anna Letitia LeBreton. Boston: Roberts Brothers, 1874.

_____. "Dangers of Liberality," The Christian Disciple, III (May, 1815), 133-136.

_____. A Discourse on Some of the Distinguishing Opinions of Unitarians, Delivered at Baltimore in 1819. 12th ed. Boston: Leonard C. Bowles, 1836.

_____. Discourses, Reviews, and Miscellanies. Boston: Charter and Hendee, 1830.

_____. "Letter on Catholicism to the Editor of the Western Messenger [1836]," in Channing, Works, II, 261-287.

_____. Letter on Creeds, &c. London: Smallfield and Son, 1839.

_____. Memoir of William Ellery Channing. With Extracts from His Correspondence and Manuscripts. By William Henry Channing. 3 vols. Boston: American Unitarian Association, 1848.

_____. "On the Character and Writings of Fenelon," 1829, in Channing, Discourses, Reviews, and Miscellanies, pp. 165-215.

_____. Remarks on Creeds, Intolerance, and Exclusion. Boston: James Munroe and Company, 1837.

_____. "Thoughts on Poverty," The Christian Disciple, IV (April, 1816), 117-122.

_____. The Works of William Ellery Channing. 6 vols. Boston: James Munroe and Company, 1841-1843.

_____. The Works of William Ellery Channing, with an Introduction. New and Complete Edition, Rearranged. To Which Is Added The Perfect Life. Edited by William Henry Channing. Boston: American Unitarian Association, 1886.

_____. The Worship of the Father: A Service of Gratitude and Joy. Boston: James Munroe and Company, 1838.

* * *

Bellows, Russell Nevins (ed.). The Channing Centenary in America, Great Britain, and Ireland. A Report of Meetings Held in Honor of the One Hundredth Anniversary of the Birth of William Ellery Channing. Boston: George H. Ellis, 1881.

Brown, Arthur W. Always Young for Liberty: A Biography of William Ellery Channing. Syracuse, New York: Syracuse University Press, 1956.

_____. William Ellery Channing. New York: Twayne Publishers, 1961.

Edgell, David P. "A Note on Channing's Transcendentalism," New England Quarterly, XXII (September, 1949), 394-397.

_____. William Ellery Channing. Boston: The Beacon Press, 1955.

Ladu, Arthur I. "Channing and Transcendentalism," American Literature, XI (May, 1939), 129-137.

Patterson, Robert Leet. The Philosophy of William Ellery Channing. New York: Bookman Associates, 1952.

Renan, J. Ernest. "Channing and the Unitarian Movement in the United States, A.D. 1780-1842." Leaders of Christian and Anti-Christian Thought. Studies in Religious History and Criticism. First Series. London: Mathieson and Company, 1895.

Rice, Madeleine Hooke. Federal Street Pastor: The Life of William Ellery Channing. New York: Bookman Associates, 1961.

Warner, Louis H. "Channing and Cheverus: A Study in Early New England Tolerance," The Christian Register, May 4, 1939, pp. 296-299.

Wright, Conrad. The Liberal Christians: Essays on American Unitarian History. Boston: Beacon Press, 1970.

WILLIAM HENRY CHANNING

Channing, William Henry. "Call of the Present--No. 2--Science of Unity," The Present, I (November 15, 1843), 73-80.

_____. "Call of the Present; No. 3.--Oneness of God and Man," The Present, I (December 15, 1843), 145-155.

_____. "Christian Socialists," Spirit of the Age, I (July 7, 1849), 8-10.

_____. "Church and State," Spirit of the Age, I (September 8, 1849), 152-153.

_____. "The Church of God with Us," Spirit of the Age, I (December 1, 1849), 344-345.

_____. "A Confession of Faith," The Present, I (September, 1843), 6-10.

_____. "Criticisms and Confessions," Spirit of the Age, I (September 1, 1849), 136.

_____. "Edwards and the Revivalists," Christian Examiner, XLIII (November, 1847), 374-394.

_____. "Ernest the Seeker," The Dial, I (July, October, 1840), 48-58, 233-242.

_____. The Gospel of Today: A Discourse Delivered at the Ordination of T.W. Higginson, As Minister of the First Religious Society in Newburyport, Massachusetts, September 15, 1847. Together with the Charge, Right Hand of Fellowship, and Address to the People. Boston: William Crosby and H.P. Nichols, 1847.

_____. "Heaven Upon Earth," The Present, I (April 1, 1844), 411-425.

_____. "Industrial Freedom," Spirit of the Age, I (October 6, 1849), 218-219.

_____. "The Judgment of Christendom," Spirit of the Age, I (October 27, 1849), 264-265.

_____. "Mazzini and the Roman Republic," Spirit of the Age, I (July 21, 1849), 42-43.

_____. (ed.). The Memoir and Writings of James Handasyd Perkins. Boston: William Crosby and H.P. Nichols, 1851.

_____. "The Middle Class," Spirit of the Age, I (September 15, 1849), 169-171.

_____. "The New Church," Spirit of the Age, II (February 2, 1850), 72-74.

_____. "Peter's Pence," Spirit of the Age, I (July 14, 1849), 24-25.

_____. "The Philadelphia Riots," Phalanx, I (May 18, 1844), 133-135.

_____. "Revolution--Reaction--Reorganization," Spirit of the Age, I (July 21, August 4, 1849), 40-42, 72-74.

_____. "Talks on the Times: Socialist and Catholic," Spirit of the Age, I (August 18, 1849), 106-107.

_____. "Thanksgivings and New-Year Wishes," The Present, I (January 15, 1844), 225.

_____. "The War of Principles and the Principle of Peace," Spirit of the Age, I (August 25, 1849), 120-121.

* * *

Frothingham, Octavius Brooks. Memoir of William Henry Channing. New York: Houghton, Mifflin and Company, 1886.

"Mr. Channing's Lecture," The Harbinger, I (November 15, 1845), 367-368.

JAMES FREEMAN CLARKE

Clarke, James Freeman. "Ancient Christianity and the Oxford Tracts," Western Messenger, VIII (July, 1840), 136-137.

_____. Anti-Slavery Days. A Sketch of the Struggle Which Ended in the Abolition of Slavery in the United States. New York: John W. Lovell Company, 1883.

_____. Autobiography, Diary and Correspondence. Edited by Edward Everett Hale. New York: Negro Universities Press, 1968 [c. 1891].

_____. "The Bible." Unitarian Affirmations: Seven Discourses Given in Washington, D.C., by Unitarian Ministers. Boston: American Unitarian Association, 1879.

_____. "Buckle's History of Civilization," Christian Examiner, LXXI (November, 1861), 374-399.

_____. "Christ and His Antichrists. An Address to the Alumni of the Divinity School, Cambridge, July, 1861," Monthly Journal of the American Unitarian Association, II (August, September, 1861), 349-361, 397-411.

_____. The Christian Doctrine of Prayer. An Essay. Boston: American Unitarian Association, 1854.

_____. The Christian Doctrine of the Forgiveness of Sin; An Essay. Boston: American Unitarian Association, 1867.

_____. Church-going: Past, Present, and Future. Boston: American Unitarian Association, n.d.

_____. The Church of the Disciples in Boston. A Sermon on the Principles and Methods of the Church of the Disciples. Delivered Sunday Morning and Evening, December 7, 1845. Boston: Benjamin H. Greene, 1846.

_____. Common-Sense in Religion: A Series of Essays. Boston: James R. Osgood and Company, 1873.

_____. Deacon Herbert's Bible Class. Boston: George H. Ellis, 1890.

_____. "A Defense of Jones Very's Sanity by the Reverend James Freeman Clarke, and Poems Published in The Western Messenger But Not Included in Any Edition of Jones Very's Works," Western Messenger, VI (March, 1839), 308-314.

_____. Discourse on the Aspects of the War, Delivered in The Indiana Place Chapel, Boston, on Fast Day, April 2, 1863. Boston: Walker, Wise, and Company, 1863.

_____. Eleven Weeks in Europe; and What May Be Seen in That Time. Boston: Ticknor, Reed, and Fields, 1852.

_____. "The Essence of Christianity," Unitarian Review, IV (December, 1875), 590-601.

_____. Essentials and Non-Essentials in Religion. Six Lectures Delivered in the Music Hall, Boston. Boston: American Unitarian Association, 1877.

_____. Events and Epochs in Religious History: Being the Substance of a Course of Twelve Lectures Delivered in the Lowell Institute, Boston, in 1880. 3rd ed. Boston: Ticknor and Company, 1887.

_____. The Experiment of a Free Church; Its Difficulties and Advantages. [Boston, 188?].

_____. Go Up Higher; or Religion in Common Life. Boston: Lee and Shepard, 1887.

_____. The Hour Which Cometh and Now Is: Sermons, Preached in Indiana-Place Chapel, Boston. Boston: Walker, Wise, and Company, 1864.

_____. The Ideas of the Apostle Paul Translated into Their Modern Equivalents. Boston: James R. Osgood, 1884.

_____. "Inspiration of the New Testament," Monthly Journal of the American Unitarian Association, VIII(May, 1867), 154-170.

_____. "Joan of Arc," Christian Examiner, LXV (July, 1848), 1-27.

_____. Letter, Radical, I (December, 1865), 148-152.

_____. Letter, Radical, I (May, 1866), 342-347.

_____. The Letters of James Freeman Clarke to Margaret Fuller. Edited by J. Wesley Thomas. Hamburg, Germany:Cram, de Gruyter and Company, 1957.

_____. "Literary Notices," Western Messenger, II (August, 1836), 71.

_____. "Little Children. A Discourse Delivered Before the Annual Convention of the Sunday-school Society, at Newburyport, Massachusetts, October 8, 1862," Monthly Journal of the American Unitarian Association, III (December, 1862), 529-541.

_____. Memorial and Biographical Sketches. Boston: Houghton, Osgood and Company, 1878.

_____. "Monthly Record," Western Messenger, II (November, 1836), 351-359; III (February, 1837), 500-504.

_____. "The New Theology," Unitarian Review, X (October, 1878), 391-407.

_____. "On a Recent Definition of Christianity," in James Freeman Clarke and Francis Ellingwood Abbot. The Battle of Syracuse: Two Essays. The Index Tracts. No. 15. Boston: The Index Association, 1875.

_____. "On the Positive Doctrines of Christianity," Monthly Journal of the American Unitarian Association, V (February, 1864), 48-64.

_____. "Open Questions in Theology," Christian Examiner, LXXX (January, 1866), 77-90.

_____. "Orestes A. Brownson's Argument for the Roman Church," Christian Examiner, XLVIII (March, 1850), 227-247.

_____. Orthodoxy: Its Truths and Errors. 14th ed. Boston: American Unitarian Association, 1880.

_____. "Parton's Life of Voltaire," Atlantic Monthly, XLVIII (August, 1881), 260-273.

_____. Peter at Antioch; or, the Vatican vs. Bismarck and Gladstone. A Sermon Preached by James Freeman Clarke, To the Church of the Disciples, Boston, December 20, 1874. Boston: Saturday Evening Gazette, 1875.

_____. "Polemics and Irenics. An Address on Theology, Before the Ministerial Conference, at Bedford Street Chapel, Wednesday, May 31, 1854," Christian Examiner, LVII (September, 1854), 163–184.

_____. "The Right Seed. A Paper Read to the National Conference at Saratoga, September 25, 1884," Unitarian Review, XXII (November, 1884), 385–391.

_____. "A Sermon on Scolding," Monthly Journal of the American Unitarian Association, III (August, 1862), 337–352.

_____. A Sketch of the History of the Doctrine of Atonement. Boston: James Munroe and Company, 1845.

_____. Slavery in the United States: A Sermon Delivered in Armory Hall, on Thanksgiving Day, November 24, 1842. Boston: Benjamin H. Greene, 1843.

_____. Steps of Belief; or, Rational Christianity Maintained Against Atheism, Free Religion, and Romanism. Boston: American Unitarian Association, 1880.

_____. Ten Great Religions: An Essay in Comparative Theology. Boston: James R. Osgood and Company, 1871.

_____. "A True Theology the Basis of Human Progress," in Christianity and Modern Thought. Boston: American Unitarian Association, 1880.

_____. "Union of Churches," Monthly Journal of the American Unitarian Association, V (May, 1864), 193–201.

_____. The Unitarian Reform. Boston: James Munroe and Company, 1839.

_____. Vexed Questions in Theology: A Series of Essays. Boston: George H. Ellis, 1886.

_____. "Wanted, a Statesman!" Old and New, II (December, 1870), 644–650.

_____. "Washington City in November," Monthly Journal of the American Unitarian Association, II (December, 1861), 545–565.

_____. The Well-Instructed Scribe, or, Reform and Conservatism. A Sermon Preached at the Installation of Rev. George F. Simmons, and Rev. Samuel Ripley, as Pastor and Associate Pastor Over the Union Congregational Society in Waltham, Massachusetts, October 27, 1841. Boston: Benjamin H. Greene, 1841.

* * *

Bolster, Arthur S. James Freeman Clarke, Disciple to Advancing Truth. Boston: Beacon Press, 1954.

Thomas, John Wesley. James Freeman Clarke: Apostle of German Culture in America. Boston: John W. Luce and Company, 1949.

CHRISTOPHER PEARSE CRANCH

Cranch, Christopher Pearse. *The Bird and the Bell, with Other Poems*. Boston: J. R. Osgood, 1875.

_____. "The Concert and the Church," *Western Messenger*, VI (March, 1839), 339-341.

_____. "Divine Authority," *Unitarian Review*, XII (November, 1879), 465-482.

_____. "Evolution and the Moral Ideal," *Unitarian Review*, XXXVI (August, 1891), 101-113.

_____. "Gnosis," *The Dial*, I (July, 1840), 98.

_____. "Letter on Travelling," *Western Messenger*, V (June, 1838), 183-186.

_____. "The Pelagian Controversy," *Western Messenger*, VI (April, 1839), 395-401.

_____. "A Sign from the West," *The Dial*, I (October, 1840), 161-172.

_____. "Symbolic Conceptions of the Deity," *Unitarian Review*, IX (March, 1878), 241-268.

_____. "The Unconscious Life," *Unitarian Review*, XXXIII (February, 1890), 97-122.

* * *

Scott, Leonora Cranch. *The Life and Letters of Christopher Pearse Cranch*. Boston: Houghton Mifflin Company, 1917.

JOHN SULLIVAN DWIGHT

Dwight, John Sullivan. *An Address Delivered Before the Harvard Musical Association, August 25, 1841*. N.p.: (1843).

_____. "The *American Review's* Account of the Religious Union of Associationists," *Harbinger*, V (June 19, 1847), 28-30.

_____. Book Review of *Italy, Spain and Portugal, with an Excursion to the Monasteries of Alcabaca and Batalha* by William Beckford (New York, 1846), *Harbinger*, III (September 12, 1846), 216-217.

_____. Book Review of *Pictures from Italy* by Charles Dickens (New York, 1846), *Harbinger*, III (June 20, 1846), 27-28.

_____. "Common Sense," *Unitarian Review*, XXXIII (May, 1890), 385-415.

_____. "Letters from Europe," *Dwight's Journal of Music*, XVIII (September 15, 1860, February 9, 1861), 198-199, 364-366; XIX (April 6, 1861), 4-5.

_____. "Music," *Aesthetic Papers*, May, 1849, pp. 25-36.

_____. "Music As a Means of Culture," _Atlantic Monthly_, XXVI (September, 1870), 321-331.

_____. "On the Proper Character of Poetry and Music for Public Worship," _Christian Examiner_, XXI (November, 1836), 254-263.

_____. "Our Dark Age in Music," _Atlantic Monthly_, L (December, 1882), 813-823.

* * *

Cooke, George Willis. _John Sullivan Dwight, Brook-Farmer, Editor, and Critic of Music: A Biography_. Boston: Small, Maynard and Company, 1898.

Mathews, W.S.B. "John S. Dwight, Editor, Critic and Man," _Music_, XV (March, 1899), 525-540.

RALPH WALDO EMERSON

Emerson, Ralph Waldo. Book Review of _Confessions of St. Augustine_ (Boston: n.d.), _The Dial_, III (January, 1843), 414-415.

_____. _The Complete Works of Ralph Waldo Emerson_. 12 vols. in 6. New York: William H. Wise and Company, 1926 [c. 1903].

_____. _The Correspondence of Ralph Waldo Emerson and Hermann Grimm_. Edited by Frederick William Holls. New York: Houghton Mifflin and Company, 1903.

_____. _The Early Lectures of Ralph Waldo Emerson_. 2 vols. Vol. I: 1833-1836. Edited by Stephen E. Whicher and Robert E. Spiller. Cambridge, Massachusetts: Harvard University Press, 1959. Vol. II: 1836-1838. Edited by Whicher, Spiller, and Wallace E. Williams. Cambridge: The Belknap Press of Harvard University Press, 1964.

_____. _Emerson-Clough Letters_. Edited by Howard F. Lowry and Ralph L. Rusk. Cleveland: The Rowfant Club, 1934.

_____. _Indian Superstition_. Edited with a Dissertation on Emerson's Oreintalism at Harvard by Kenneth Walter Cameron. Hanover, New Hampshire: The Friends of Dartmouth Library, 1954.

_____. _Journals of Ralph Waldo Emerson, with Annotations_. Edited by Edward Waldo Emerson and Waldo Emerson Forbes. 10 vols. New York: Houghton Mifflin Company, 1910-1914. Vols. 7-10.

_____. _Journals and Miscellaneous Notebooks of Ralph Waldo Emerson_. Vol. I: 1819-1822. Edited by William H. Gilman, Alfred R. Ferguson, George P. Clark, and Merrell R. Davis, 1960. Vol. II: 1822-1826. Edited by Gilman, Ferguson, and Davis, 1961. Vol. III: 1826-1832. Edited by Gilman and Ferguson, 1963. Vol. IV: 1832-1834. Edited by Ferguson, 1964. Vol. V: 1835-1838. Edited by Merton M. Sealts, Jr., 1965. Vol. VI: 1824-1838. Edited by Ralph H. Orth, 1966. Vol. VII:1838-1842. Edited by A.W. Plumstead and Harrison Hayford, 1869. Vol. VIII: 1841-1843. Edited by Gilman and J.E. Parsons, 1970. Vol. IX:

1843-1847. Edited by Orth and Ferguson, 1972. Vol. X: 1847-1848. Edited by Sealts, 1973. Vol. XI: 1848-1851. Edited by A.W. Plumstead, Gilman, and Ruth H. Bennett, 1975. Vol. XII: 1835-1862. Edited by Linda Allardt, 1976. Vol. XIII: 1852-1855. Edited by Orth and Ferguson, 1977. Vol. XIV: Edited by Susan Sutton Smith and Harrison Hayford, Cambridge, Massachusetts: The Belknap Press of Harvard University Press, 1960-

_____. The Letters of Ralph Waldo Emerson. Edited by Ralph L. Rusk. 6 vols. New York: Columbia University Press, 1939.

_____. "Natural Religion Universal and Sympathetic." Freedom and Fellowship in Religion. A Collection of Essays and Addresses. Edited by a Committee of the Free Religious Association. Boston: Roberts Brothers, 1875.

_____. "Prayers," The Dial, III (July, 1842), 77-81.

_____. Review of A Letter to Rev. William Ellery Channing, D.D. by Orestes A. Brownson (Boston, 1842), The Dial, III (October, 1842), 276-277.

_____. "Thoughts on the Religion of the Middle Ages," Christian Disciple, n.s., IV (November-December, 1822), 401-408. Reprinted in Kenneth W. Cameron. Emerson, Thoreau, and Concord in Early Newspapers. Biographical and Historical Lore for the Scholar and General Reader. Hartford: Transcendental Books, 1958. pp. 273-276.

_____. "War," Aesthetic Papers, May, 1849, pp. 36-50.

_____. Young Emerson Speaks: Unpublished Discourses on Many Subjects. Edited by Arthur Cushman McGiffert, Jr. Boston: Houghton Mifflin Company, 1938.

* * *

Albee, John. "A Tribute to Emerson," The Independent, LV (May 21, 1903), 1178-1181.

Birdsall, Richard D. "Emerson and the Church of Rome," American Literature, XXXI (November, 1959), 273-281.

Brooks, Van Wyck. The Life of Emerson. New York: The Literary Guild, 1932.

Brown, Stuart G. "Emerson's Platonism," New England Quarterly, XVIII (September, 1945), 325-345.

Cabot, James Elliot. A Memoir of Relph Waldo Emerson. 2 vols. New York: Macmillan and Company, 1887.

Cameron, Kenneth W. "Early Background for Emerson's 'The Problem,'" Emerson Society Quarterly, XXVII (1962), 37-46.

_____. Emerson's Workshop: An Analysis of His Reading in Periodicals through 1836 with the Principal Thematic Key to His Essays, Poems, and Lectures. Also Memorabilia of Harvard and Concord. 2 vols. Hartford: Transcendental Books, 1964. Vol. I.

_____. "History and Biography in Emerson's Unpublished Sermons," Proceedings of the American Antiquarian Society, LXVI (October, 1956), 103-118.

_____. Index-Concordance to Emerson's Sermons. With Homiletical Papers. 2 vols. Hartford: Transcendental Books, 1963. Vol. II.

_____. Ralph Waldo Emerson's Reading. A Corrected Edition with Photographs of Literary Concord, Emerson and His Family. Hartford: Transcendental Books, 1962.

Carpenter, Frederic Ives. Emerson and Asia. Cambridge, Massachusetts: Harvard University Press, 1930.

Cooke, George Willis. Ralph Waldo Emerson: His Life, Writings and Philosophy. Boston: James R. Osgood and Company, 1881.

Dillaway, Newton. Prophet of America: Emerson and the Problems of Today. Boston: Little, Brown and Company, 1936.

"The Errancy of Emerson," The Catholic Review, XXII (August 19, 1882), 122.

Gonnaud, Maurice. Individu et Societé dans l'ouvre de Ralph Waldo Emerson. Essai de biographie spirituelle. Etudes Anglaises, No. 20. Paris: Didier, 1964.

Gray, Henry David. Emerson: A Statement of New England Transcendentalism As Expressed in the Philosophy of Its Chief Exponent. New York: Ungar Publishing Company, 1958.

Hopkins, Vivian Constance. Spires of Form: A Study of Emerson's Aesthetic Theory. Cambridge: Harvard University Press, 1951.

Kearns, Francis E. "Emerson and the American Catholic Scholar," Emerson Society Quarterly, XXXIX (1965), 63-68.

Mathews, Joseph Chesley, "Emerson's Knowledge of Dante,"University of Texas Studies in English, XXII (1942), 171-198.

Newman, Franklin B. "Emerson and Buonarroti," New England Quarterly, XXV (December, 1952), 524-535.

Pollack, Robert C. "A Reappraisal of Emerson," Thought, XXXII (Spring, 1957), 86-132.

Roberts, J. Russell. "Emerson's Debt to the Seventeenth Century," American Literature, XXI (November, 1949), 298-310.

Rusk, Ralph L. The Life of Ralph Waldo Emerson. New York: C. Scribner's Sons, 1949.

Shuster, George Nauman. "An Ancient Vision and the Newer Needs," Catholic World, CVI (March, 1918), 733-741.

Welleck, Rene. "Emerson and German Philosophy," New England Quarterly, XVI (March, 1943), 41-62.

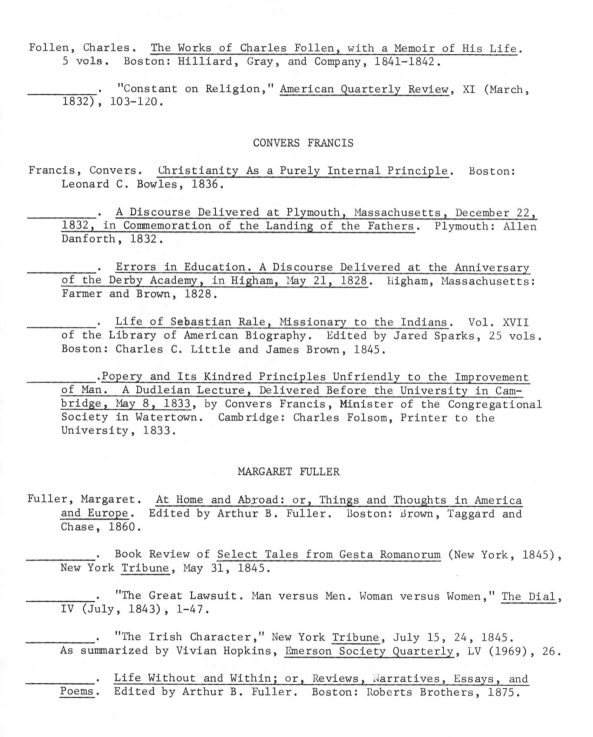

CHARLES FOLLEN

Follen, Charles. The Works of Charles Follen, with a Memoir of His Life. 5 vols. Boston: Hilliard, Gray, and Company, 1841-1842.

_____. "Constant on Religion," American Quarterly Review, XI (March, 1832), 103-120.

CONVERS FRANCIS

Francis, Convers. Christianity As a Purely Internal Principle. Boston: Leonard C. Bowles, 1836.

_____. A Discourse Delivered at Plymouth, Massachusetts, December 22, 1832, in Commemoration of the Landing of the Fathers. Plymouth: Allen Danforth, 1832.

_____. Errors in Education. A Discourse Delivered at the Anniversary of the Derby Academy, in Higham, May 21, 1828. Higham, Massachusetts: Farmer and Brown, 1828.

_____. Life of Sebastian Rale, Missionary to the Indians. Vol. XVII of the Library of American Biography. Edited by Jared Sparks, 25 vols. Boston: Charles C. Little and James Brown, 1845.

_____. Popery and Its Kindred Principles Unfriendly to the Improvement of Man. A Dudleian Lecture, Delivered Before the University in Cambridge, May 8, 1833, by Convers Francis, Minister of the Congregational Society in Watertown. Cambridge: Charles Folsom, Printer to the University, 1833.

MARGARET FULLER

Fuller, Margaret. At Home and Abroad: or, Things and Thoughts in America and Europe. Edited by Arthur B. Fuller. Boston: Brown, Taggard and Chase, 1860.

_____. Book Review of Select Tales from Gesta Romanorum (New York, 1845), New York Tribune, May 31, 1845.

_____. "The Great Lawsuit. Man versus Men. Woman versus Women," The Dial, IV (July, 1843), 1-47.

_____. "The Irish Character," New York Tribune, July 15, 24, 1845. As summarized by Vivian Hopkins, Emerson Society Quarterly, LV (1969), 26.

_____. Life Without and Within; or, Reviews, Narratives, Essays, and Poems. Edited by Arthur B. Fuller. Boston: Roberts Brothers, 1875.

_____. The Love-Letters of Margaret Fuller, 1845-1846. With an Intro-
duction by Julia Ward Howe. To Which Are Added The Reminiscences of
Ralph Waldo Emerson, Horace Greeley, and Charles T. Congdon. London:
T. Fisher Unwin, 1903.

_____. Memoirs of Margaret Fuller Ossoli. Edited by Ralph Waldo Emerson,
William Henry Channing, and James Freeman Clarke. 2 vols. Boston:
Phillips, Sampson and Company, 1851.

_____. "New Year's Letter from a Catholic Priest," New York Tribune,
March 12, 1845.

_____. Papers on Literature and Art. 2 parts. New York: Wiley and
Putnam, 1846. Part II.

_____. "Rev. William Ingraham's Christmas Holidays in Rome," New York
Tribune, December 25, 1845.

_____. "Romaic and Rhine Ballads," The Dial, III (October, 1842), 137-180.

_____. Summer on the Lakes, in 1843. Boston: Charles C. Little and James
Brown, 1844.

_____. Woman in the Nineteenth Century and Kindred Papers Relating to
the Sphere, Conditions, and Duties of Woman, 1855, in Fuller, Writings,
pp. 109-218.

_____. The Writings of Margaret Fuller. Edited by Mason Wade. New York:
The Viking Press, 1941.

* * *

Deiss, Joseph Jay. The Roman Years of Margaret Fuller. New York: Crowell Co.,
1969.

Higginson, Thomas Wentworth. Margaret Fuller Ossoli. Boston: Houghton, Mifflin
and Company, 1884.

Howe, Julia Ward. Margaret Fuller. Boston: Roberts Brothers, 1883.

Rostenberg, Leona. "Margaret Fuller's Roman Diary," Journal of Modern History,
XII (June, 1940), 209-220.

Wade, Mason. Margaret Fuller: Whetstone of Genius. New York: The Viking Press,
1940.

WILLIAM HENRY FURNESS

Furness, William Henry. The Authority of Jesus. A Discourse Delivered Before
a Conference of Liberal Christians Held in Northumberland Pa., April 10,
1867. Philadelphia: King and Baird, 1867.

_____. "The Character of Christ," <u>Christian Examiner</u>, XV (January, 1834), 277-311.

_____(ed.). <u>The Character of Jesus Portrayed. A Biblical Essay, with an Appendix</u> by Daniel Schenkel. Translated from the 3rd German edition, with introduction and notes by William Henry Furness. 2 vols. Boston: Little, Brown and Company, 1866.

_____. <u>A Discourse, Preached in the First Congregational Unitarian Church, on the Morning of the Lord's Day, May 24, 1829. Occasioned by the Recent Emancipation of the Roman Catholics Throughout the British Empire.</u> Philadelphia: R. H. Small, 1829.

_____. <u>Discourses</u>. Philadelphia: G. Collins, 1855.

_____. <u>The Exclusive Principle Considered. Two Sermons on Christian Union and the Truth of the Gospels</u>. Boston: Benjamin H. Green, 1845.

_____. <u>A History of Jesus</u>. Boston: William Crosby and H. P. Nichols, 1850.

_____. <u>Jesus</u>. Philadelphia: J. B. Lippincott and Company, 1870.

_____. <u>Jesus and His Biographers; or the Remarks on the Four Gospels</u>. Revised, with copious additions. Philadelphia: Carey, Lea and Blanchard, 1838.

_____. "Nature and Christianity," <u>Christian Examiner</u>, XLIII (July, 1847), 31-52.

_____. <u>The Power of Spirit Manifest in Jesus of Nazareth</u>. Philadelphia: J. B. Lippincott and Company, 1877.

_____. <u>Remarks on the Four Gospels</u>. Philadelphia: Carey, Lea and Blanchard, 1836.

_____. <u>The Story of the Resurrection Told Once More: with Remarks Upon the Character of Christ and the Historical Claims of the Four Gospels</u>. Philadelphia: J. B. Lippincott and Company, 1885.

_____. <u>Thoughts on the Life and Character of Jesus of Nazareth</u>. Boston: Phillips, Sampson and Company, 1858.

_____. <u>The Veil Partly Lifted and Jesus Becoming Visible</u>. Boston: Ticknor and Fields, 1864.

* * *

Lamson, Alvan. <u>Review of Religion, a Principle, Not a Form. A Discourse, Delivered on the Lord's Day, March 17, 1844, in the First Congregational Church, in Reference to the Question Concerning the Use of the Bible in the Public Schools</u> by William Henry Furness (Philadelphia, 1844), <u>Christian Examiner</u>, XXXVI (May, 1844), 431-432.

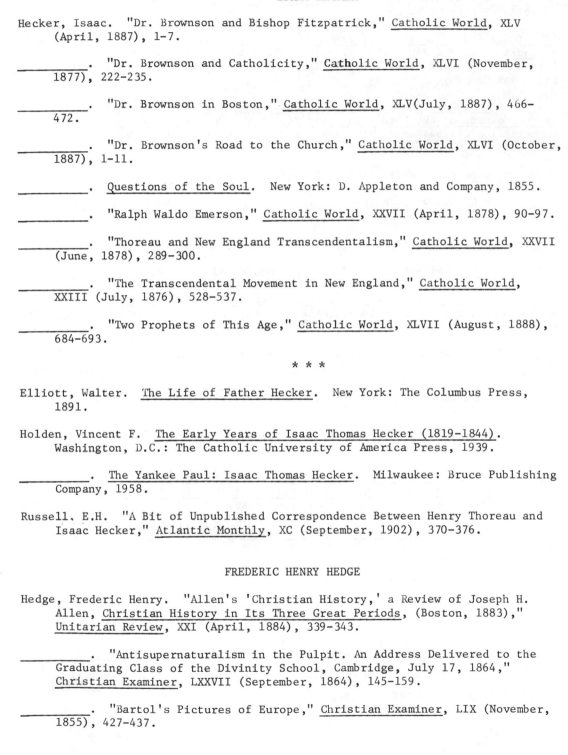

ISAAC HECKER

Hecker, Isaac. "Dr. Brownson and Bishop Fitzpatrick," Catholic World, XLV (April, 1887), 1-7.

_____. "Dr. Brownson and Catholicity," Catholic World, XLVI (November, 1877), 222-235.

_____. "Dr. Brownson in Boston," Catholic World, XLV(July, 1887), 466-472.

_____. "Dr. Brownson's Road to the Church," Catholic World, XLVI (October, 1887), 1-11.

_____. Questions of the Soul. New York: D. Appleton and Company, 1855.

_____. "Ralph Waldo Emerson," Catholic World, XXVII (April, 1878), 90-97.

_____. "Thoreau and New England Transcendentalism," Catholic World, XXVII (June, 1878), 289-300.

_____. "The Transcendental Movement in New England," Catholic World, XXIII (July, 1876), 528-537.

_____. "Two Prophets of This Age," Catholic World, XLVII (August, 1888), 684-693.

* * *

Elliott, Walter. The Life of Father Hecker. New York: The Columbus Press, 1891.

Holden, Vincent F. The Early Years of Isaac Thomas Hecker (1819-1844). Washington, D.C.: The Catholic University of America Press, 1939.

_____. The Yankee Paul: Isaac Thomas Hecker. Milwaukee: Bruce Publishing Company, 1958.

Russell, E.H. "A Bit of Unpublished Correspondence Between Henry Thoreau and Isaac Hecker," Atlantic Monthly, XC (September, 1902), 370-376.

FREDERIC HENRY HEDGE

Hedge, Frederic Henry. "Allen's 'Christian History,' a Review of Joseph H. Allen, Christian History in Its Three Great Periods, (Boston, 1883)," Unitarian Review, XXI (April, 1884), 339-343.

_____. "Antisupernaturalism in the Pulpit. An Address Delivered to the Graduating Class of the Divinity School, Cambridge, July 17, 1864," Christian Examiner, LXXVII (September, 1864), 145-159.

_____. "Bartol's Pictures of Europe," Christian Examiner, LIX (November, 1855), 427-437.

_____. "The Cause of Reason the Cause of Faith," Christian Examiner, LXX (March, 1861), 204-226.

_____. "Characteristics of Genius," Atlantic Monthly, XXI (February, 1868), 150-159.

_____. Christian Liturgy for the Use of the Church. Boston: Crosby, Nichols, and Company, 1853.

_____. "Christian Worship. Extracts from a Sermon Preached at the Dedication of the Union-Street Church in Bangor," Monthly Religious Magazine, X (October, 1853), 462-472.

_____. "Christianity in Conflict with Hellenism," Unitarian Review, XXI (January, 1884), 1-22.

_____. "The Churches and the Church," Christian Examiner, XLI (September, 1846), 193-204.

_____. "Classic and Romantic," Atlantic Monthly, LVII (March, 1886), 309-316.

_____ "Count Zinzendorf and the Moravians," Unitarian Review, XXV (January, 1886), 1-17.

_____. "The Destinies of Ecclesiastical Religion," Christian Examiner, LXXXII (January, 1867), 1-15.

_____. "Dr. Furness's Word to Unitarians," Christian Examiner, LXVII (November, 1859), 431-439.

_____. "The Doctrine of Endless Punishment," Christian Examiner, LXVII (July, 1859), 98-128.

_____. "Ecclesiastical Christendom," Christian Examiner, LI (July, 1851), 112-134.

_____ (ed.). Essays and Reviews by Eminent English Churchmen. 3rd American ed. With an Appendix and a new introduction written expressly for this edition by Frederic Henry Hedge. New York: Henry Holt and Company, 1874.

_____. "European Travel," Christian Examiner, LIII (September, 1852), 239-257.

_____. "Everett's Phi Beta Kappa Address," Christian Examiner, XVI (March, 1834), 1-21.

_____. "Feudal Society," Unitarian Review, XXVIII (July, 1887), 1-19.

_____. "The Historic Atonement. Sermon Preached at the Conference of Unitarian and Other Christian Churches at Syracuse, New York, October 9, 1866," Monthly Journal of the American Unitarian Association, IX (April, 1868), 102-118.

_____. Hours with German Classics. Boston: Roberts Brothers, 1886.

_____, and Frederic D. Huntington (eds.). Hymns for the Church of Christ. Boston: Crosby, Nichols, and Company, 1853.

_____. The Leaven of the Word: A Sermon Preached at the Ordination of Reverend Joshua Young, As Pastor of the New North Church in Boston, Thursday, February 1, 1849. Boston: Dutton and Wentworth, 1849.

_____. "Life and Character of St. Augustine," Putnam's Monthly, VII (March, 1856), 225-240.

_____. "Luther and His Work," Atlantic Monthly, LII (December, 1883), 805-818.

_____. "Madame Ossoli's At Home and Abroad," North American Review, LXXXIII (July, 1856), 261-264.

_____. Martin Luther and Other Essays. Boston: Roberts Brothers, 1888.

_____. "The Method of History," North American Review, CXI (October, 1870), 311-329.

_____. "Mohammedan Mysticism," Unitarian Review, XXIX (May, 1888), 410-416.

_____. "The Mythical Element in the New Testament." Christianity and Modern Thought. Boston: American Unitarian Association, 1880.

_____. "'Natural Religion,'" Christian Examiner, LII (January, 1852), 117-136.

_____. "The Nineteenth Century," Christian Examiner, XLVIII (May, 1850), 373-390.

_____. "The Philosophy of Fetishism," Unitarian Review, XV (March, 1881), 193-203.

_____. Practical Goodness of the True Religion. Boston: James Munroe and Company, 1840.

_____. Presidential Remarks, Thrity-fifth Annual Meeting of the American Unitarian Association, May 29, 1860, Monthly Journal of the American Unitarian Association, I (July, 1860), 302-307.

_____. Presidential Remarks, Thirty-sixth American Unitarian Association Convention, Boston, May 28, 1861, Monthly Journal of the American Unitarian Association, II (July, 1861), 297-305.

_____. Prose Writers of Germany. New York: C. S. Francis and Company, 1847.

_____. _Reason in Religion_. Boston: Walker, Fuller and Company, 1865.

_____. "Romanism in Its Worship," _Christian Examiner_, LVI (March, 1854), 223-243.

_____. _Sermons_. Boston: Roberts Brothers, 1891.

_____. "Shedd's History of Christian Doctrine," _North American Review_, LXXXII (April, 1864), 564-576.

_____. "Synesius," _Unitarian Review_, XXXI (March, 1889), 243-251.

_____. "Thoughts on the Origin and Destination of the Soul," _Unitarian Review_, II (September, 1874), 101-107.

_____. "The Two Religions," _Christian Examiner_, LXVI (January, 1859), 89-112.

_____. "The Unitarian Denomination,--Its Advantages and Mission," _Quarterly Journal of the American Unitarian Association_, III (October 1, 1855), 1-5.

_____. _Ways of the Spirit, and Other Essays_. Boston: Roberts Brothers, 1878.

* * *

Abbot, Francis Ellingwood, "Theism and Christianity," _Christian Examiner_, LXXIX (September, 1865), 157-174.

Long, Orie William. _Frederic Henry Hedge: A Cosmopolitan Scholar_. Portland, Maine: The Southworth-Anthoensen Press, 1940.

Williams, George H. _Rethinking the Unitarian Relationship with Protestantism: An Examination of the Thought of Frederic Henry Hedge (1805-1890)_. Boston: The Beacon Press, 1949.

CALEB SPRAGUE HENRY

Henry, Caleb Sprague. _About Men and Things. Papers from My Study Table Drawer_. New York: Thomas Whittaker, 1873.

_____. _About the Bishop's Declaration on Baptism; with Something About Prayer-Book Revision and Church Progress. A Letter to a Layman_. New York: Pott, Young and Company, 1872.

_____. _A Compendium of Christian Antiquities: Being a Brief View of the Orders, Rites, Customs, and Laws of the Christian Church in the Early Ages_. Philadelphia: Joseph Whetham, 1837.

_____. _Considerations on Some of the Elements and Conditions of Social Welfare and Human Progress. Being Academic and Occasional Discourses and Other Pieces_. New York: D. Appleton and Company, 1861.

_____(ed.). Elements of Psychology: Included in a Critical Examination of Locke's Essay on the Human Understanding, and in Additional Pieces by Victor Cousin. Translated from the French, with an Introduction and Notes by Caleb Sprague Henry, **D.D.** 4th ed. revised. New York: Ivison and Phinney, 1855.

_____. Endless Future of the Human Race. A Letter to a Friend. New York: D. Appleton and Company, 1879.

_____(ed.). General History of Civilization in Europe, from the Fall of the Roman Empire to the French Revolution by Francois Pierre G. Guizot. 3rd American, from the 2nd English ed., with Occasional Notes by Caleb Sprague Henry. New York: D. Appleton and Company, 1842.

_____. The Gospel; a Formal and Sacramental Religion. A Sermon Preached at the Church of the Advent, in Boston, on the Sunday After Christmas, 1845. Boston: Charles Stimpson, 1846.

_____. "Spear's Religion and the State," North American Review, CXXIV (March, 1877), 318-320.

_____. "Tasso and the Alberti Manuscripts," New York Review, IX (October, 1841), 424-444.

SYLVESTER JUDD

Judd, Sylvester. The Birthright Church: A Discourse. Augusta, Maine: William H. Simpson, 1853.

_____. The Church: In a Series of Discourses. Boston: Crosby, Nichols, and Company, 1854.

_____. "The Dramatic Element in the Bible," Atlantic Monthly, IV (August, 1859), 137-153.

_____. Margaret: A Tale of the Real and the Ideal, Blight and Bloom; Including Sketches of a Place Not Before Described, Called Mons Christi. Revised ed. 2 vols. Boston: Phillips, Sampson, and Company, 1851.

_____. Philo: An Evangeliad. Boston: Phillips, Sampson, and Company, 1849.

* * *

Hall, Arethusa. Life and Character of the Reverend Sylvester Judd. Boston: D. C. Colesworthy, 1857.

JAMES MARSH

Marsh, James (ed.). Aids to Reflection, in the Formation of a Manly Character, on the Several Grounds of Prudence, Morality, and Religion: Illustrated by Select Passages from Our Elder Divines, Especially from Archbishop Leighton by Samuel Taylor Coleridge. Preliminary Essay and Additional Notes by James Marsh. Burlington, Vermont: Chauncey Goodrich, 1829.

(_____). Colerdige's American Disciples: The Selected Correspondence of James Marsh. Edited by John J. Duffy. Amherst: University of Massachusetts Press, 1973.

_____. "Evils of Creeds," Christian Palladium, Extra #2, 1841.

* * *

Cheever, George B. Characteristics of the Christian Philosopher: A Discourse Commemorative of the Virtues and Attainments of Reverend James Marsh, Late President, and Professor of Moral and Intellectual Philosophy in the University of Vermont. Delivered Before the Alumni of the University, at Their Annual Meeting, in August, 1843, and Published at Their Request. New York: Wiley and Putnam, 1843.

Feuer, Lewis S. "James Marsh and the Conservative Transcendental Philosophy," New England Quarterly, XXXI (March, 1958), 3-31.

Nicolson, Marjorie H. "James Marsh and the Vermont Transcendentalists," Philosophical Review, XXXIV (January, 1925), 28-50.

CHARLES KING NEWCOMB

Newcomb, Charles King. The Journals of Charles King Newcomb. Editdd by Judith Kennedy Johnson. Providence, Rhode Island: Brown University, 1946.

SAMUEL OSGOOD

Osgood, Samuel. American Leaves: Familiar Notes of Thought and Life. New York: Harper and Brothers, 1867.

_____. "Americansand the Men of the Old World," Christian Examiner, LIX (July, 1855), 1-17.

_____. Book Review of Democracy in America by Alexis De Tocqueville. Part Second (Paris, 1840) Christian Examiner, XXIX (September, 1840), 105-107.

_____. Book Review of Symbolism: or, Exposition of the Doctrinal Differences Between Catholics and Protestants, As Evidenced in Their Symbolic Writings by John Adam Moehler. Translated by James B. Robertson (New York, 1844), Christian Examiner, XXXVII (July, 1844), 119-121.

_____. "The Centenary of Spinoza," North American Review, CXXIV (March, 1877), 265-288.

_____. "Christian Ethics," Christian Examiner, XXIX (November, 1840),153-174; XXX (May, 1841), 145-173.

_____. "The Church of the First Three Centuries," Christian Examiner, LV (November, 1853), 358-374.

_____. The Coming Church, and Its Clergy. Address to the Graduating Class at the Meadville Theological School, June 30, 1858. 2nd ed. New York: Christian Inquirer Office, 1859.

_____. "Debates on the Roman Catholic Religion," Christian Examiner, XXIII (September, 1837), 53-64.

_____. "DeWette's Views of Religion and Theology," Christian Examiner, XXIV (May, 1838), 137-171.

_____. "Doctrine of the Holy Spirit," Christian Examiner, LXXXI (September, 1886), 217-233.

_____. "Education in the West," Christian Examiner, XXIII(November, 1837), 194-207.

_____. "German Hymns," Christian Examiner, LXIX (September, 1860), 234-257.

_____. "The German in America," Christian Examiner, LI (November, 1851), 350-359.

_____. God with Men, or Footprints of Providential Leaders. Boston: Crosby, Nichols, and Company, 1853.

_____. The Hearth-Stone: Thoughts Upon Home-Life in Our Cities. New York: D. Appleton and Company, 1854.

_____. "The Higher Science," Unitarian Review, II (November, 1874), 369-377.

_____. "Hugo Grotius and His Times," Christian Examiner, XLII (January, 1847), 1-30.

_____. Life and Its Record in This Generation. An Anniversary Address Delivered Before the New York Genealogical and Biographical Society, April 11, 1878. New York: The New York Genealogical and Biographical Society, 1878.

_____. Mile Stones in Our Life-Journey. New York: D. Appleton and Company, 1854.

_____. "Modern Ecclesiastical History," Christian Examiner, XLVIII (May, 1850), 411-433.

(_____). "Monthly Record," Western Messenger, II (November, 1836), 283-288.

_____. "The Nemesis of Faith," Christian Examiner, XLVII (July, 1849), 93-96.

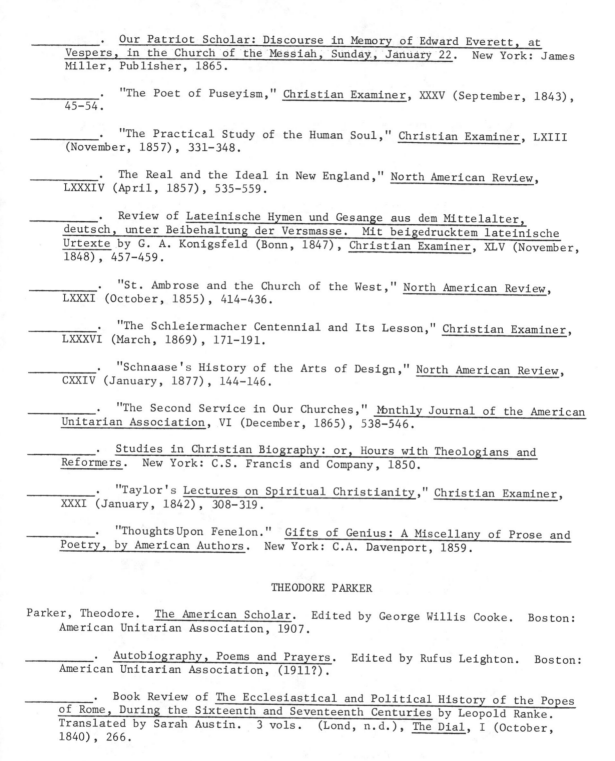

_____. *Our Patriot Scholar: Discourse in Memory of Edward Everett, at Vespers, in the Church of the Messiah, Sunday, January 22.* New York: James Miller, Publisher, 1865.

_____. "The Poet of Puseyism," *Christian Examiner*, XXXV (September, 1843), 45-54.

_____. "The Practical Study of the Human Soul," *Christian Examiner*, LXIII (November, 1857), 331-348.

_____. The Real and the Ideal in New England," *North American Review*, LXXXIV (April, 1857), 535-559.

_____. Review of *Lateinische Hymen und Gesange aus dem Mittelalter, deutsch, unter Beibehaltung der Versmasse. Mit beigedrucktem lateinische Urtexte* by G. A. Konigsfeld (Bonn, 1847), *Christian Examiner*, XLV (November, 1848), 457-459.

_____. "St. Ambrose and the Church of the West," *North American Review*, LXXXI (October, 1855), 414-436.

_____. "The Schleiermacher Centennial and Its Lesson," *Christian Examiner*, LXXXVI (March, 1869), 171-191.

_____. "Schnaase's History of the Arts of Design," *North American Review*, CXXIV (January, 1877), 144-146.

_____. "The Second Service in Our Churches," *Monthly Journal of the American Unitarian Association*, VI (December, 1865), 538-546.

_____. *Studies in Christian Biography: or, Hours with Theologians and Reformers.* New York: C.S. Francis and Company, 1850.

_____. "Taylor's *Lectures on Spiritual Christianity*," *Christian Examiner*, XXXI (January, 1842), 308-319.

_____. "Thoughts Upon Fenelon." *Gifts of Genius: A Miscellany of Prose and Poetry, by American Authors.* New York: C.A. Davenport, 1859.

THEODORE PARKER

Parker, Theodore. *The American Scholar.* Edited by George Willis Cooke. Boston: American Unitarian Association, 1907.

_____. *Autobiography, Poems and Prayers.* Edited by Rufus Leighton. Boston: American Unitarian Association, (1911?).

_____. Book Review of *The Ecclesiastical and Political History of the Popes of Rome, During the Sixteenth and Seventeenth Centuries* by Leopold Ranke. Translated by Sarah Austin. 3 vols. (Lond, n.d.), *The Dial*, I (October, 1840), 266.

_____. Book Review of <u>Rest in Church</u> (by Furlong Elizabeth Shipton Harris), (London, 1848), <u>Massachusetts Quarterly Review</u>, I (June, 1848), 389-393.

_____. <u>A Discourse of Matters Pertaining to Religion</u>. Edited by Thomas Wentworth Higginson. Boston: American Unitarian Association, 1907.

_____. <u>A False and True Revival of Religion. A Sermon Delivered at Music Hall, Boston, on Sunday, April 4, 1858</u>. Boston: William L. Kent and Company, 1858.

_____. "German Literature," <u>The Dial</u>, I (January, 1841), 315-339.

_____. <u>The Great Battle Between Slavery and Freedom. Considered in Two Speeches Delivered Before the American Antislavery Society, at New York, May 7, 1856</u>. Boston: Benjamin H. Greene, 1856.

_____. "Hennell on the Origin of Christianity," <u>The Dial</u>, IV (October, 1843), 137-165.

_____. "Hollis Street Council," <u>The Dial</u>, III (October, 1842), 201-221.

_____. <u>Lessons from the World of Matter and the World of Man</u>. Edited by Rufus Leighton. Boston: American Unitarian Association, n.d.

_____. "The Life of St. Bernard of Clairvaux, a Chapter Out of the Middle Ages," <u>Christian Examiner</u>, XXX (March, 1841), 1-41.

_____. "The Material Condition of the People of Massachusetts," <u>Christian Examiner</u>, LXV (July, 1858), 19-60.

_____. "Matter's History of Gnosticism," <u>Christian Examiner</u>, XXIV (March, 1838), 112-130.

_____. <u>The Nebraska Question. Some Thoughts on the New Assault Upon Freedom in America, and the General State of the Country in Relation Thereunto, Set Forth in a Discourse Preached at the Music Hall, in Boston, on Monday, February 12, 1854</u>. Boston: Benjamin B. Mussey and Company, 1854.

_____. <u>The Philosophical Idea of God and Its Relation to the Scientific and Religious Wants of Mankind Now</u>, 1858. <u>American Philosophic Addresses, 1700-1900</u>. Edited by Joseph Leon Blau. New York: Columbia University Press, 1946.

_____. <u>The Rights of Man in America</u>. Edited by Franklin B. Sanborn. Boston: American Unitarian Association, 1911.

_____. <u>St. Bernard and Other Papers</u>. Edited by Charles W. Wendte. Boston: American Unitarian Association, 1911.

_____. <u>Sins and Safeguards of Society</u>. Edited by Samuel B. Stewart. Boston: American Unitarian Association, 1909.

_____. <u>The Slave Power</u>. Edited by James K. Hosmer. Boston: American Unitarian Association, n.d.

_____. Social Classes in a Republic. Edited by Samuel A. Eliot. Boston: American Unitarian Association, n.d.

_____. Speeches, Addresses, and Occasional Sermons. 3 vols. Boston: Horace B. Fuller, 1855.

_____. Ten Sermons of Religion. Boston: Crosby, Nichols, and Company, 1853.

_____. Theism, Atheism and the Popular Theology. Edited by Charles W. Wendte. Boston: American Unitarian Association, 1907.

_____. The Transient and Permanent in Christianity. Edited by George Willis Cooke. Boston: American Unitarian Association, 1908.

_____. West Roxbury Sermons, 1837-1848. Boston: American Unitarian Association, 1902.

_____. The World of Matter and the Spirit of Man: Latest Discourses of Religion. Edited by George Willis Cooke. Boston: American Unitarian Association, 1907.

* * *

Chadwick, John White. Theodore Parker: Preacher and Reformer. New York: Houghton, Mifflin and Company, 1901.

Commager, Henry Steele. Theodore Parker. 2nd ed. Boston: The Beacon Press, 1947.

Dirks, John Edward. The Critical Theology of Theodore Parker. New York: Columbia University Press, 1948.

Frothingham, Octavius B. Theodore Parker. A Biography. Boston: James R. Osgood and Company, 1874.

Smith, Hilrie Shelton. "Was Theodore Parker a Transcendentalist?" New England Quarterly, XXIII (September, 1950), 351-364.

Weiss, John. Life and Correspondence of Theodore Parker, Minister of the Twenty-Eighth Congregational Society, Boston. 2 vols. New York: D. Appleton and Company, 1864.

ELIZABETH PALMER PEABODY

Peabody, Elizabeth Palmer. (ed.). Crimes of the House of Austria Against Mankind. Proved by Extracts from the Histories of Coxe, Schiller, Robertson, Grattan, and Sismondi, with Mrs. M. L. Putnam's History of the Constitution of Hungary, and Its Relations with Austria, Published in May, 1850. 2nd ed. New York: G. P. Putnam, 1852.

_____. "The Dorian Measure, with a Modern Application," Aesthetic Papers, May, 1849, pp. 64-110.

_____. "A Glimpse of Christ's Idea of Society," The Dial, II (October, 1841), 214-228.

_____. The Identification of the Artisan and Artist, the Proper Object of American Education. Illustrated by a Lecture of Cardinal Wiseman, on the Relation of the Arts of Design with the Arts of Production. Addressed to American Workingmen and Educators, with an Essay on Froebel's Reform of Primary Education. Boston: Adams and Company, 1869.

_____. Record of a School: Exemplifying the General Principles of Spiritual Culture. Boston: James Munroe and Company, 1835.

_____. Reminiscences of Reverend William Ellery Channing. Boston: Roberts Brother, 1877.

_____. "The World's Need of Woman," Christian Examiner, LXIX (November, 1860), 435-445.

GEORGE RIPLEY

Ripley, George. "Arrival of Father Mathew in Boston," Spirit of the Age, I (August 4, 1849), 79.

_____. Book Review of The Early Jesuit Missions in North America. Translated by Rev. William Ingraham Kipp. 2 vols. (New York, n.d.), Harbinger, III (October 24, 1846), 316.

_____. Book Review of Materialism in Religion; or Religious Forms and Theological Formulas by Philip Harwood (London, nd.), The Dial, I (October, 1840), 267-271.

_____. "The Catholics and Associationists," Harbinger, III (September 5, 1846), 193-195.

_____. "Christmas in Philadelphia," Harbinger, VI (January 1, 1848), 69.

_____. Discourses on the Philosophy of Religion. Addressed to Doubters Who Wish To Believe. Boston: James Munroe and Company, 1836.

_____. The Doctrines of the Trinity and the Transubstantiation Compared. Boston: Charles Bowen, 1833.

_____. "European Affairs," Spirit of the Age, I (July 21, August 18, September 1, October 20, November 17, 1849), 46, 108-110, 140-141, 251-252, 317-318.

_____. "Father Mathew," Spirit of the Age, I (August 11, 1849), 93.

_____. "Father Mathew at Work," Spirit of the Age, I (July 21, 1849), 47.

_____. "Festival to Father Mathew," Spirit of the Age, I (August 11, 1849), 93.

_____. Letters on the Latest Form of Infidelity, Including a View of the Opinions of Spinoza, Schleiermacher, and DeWette. Boston: James Munroe and Company, 1840.

_____. Philosophical Miscellanies, Translated from the French of Cousin, Theodore Jouffroy, and Banjamin Constant, with Introductory and Critical Notes by George Ripley. 2 vols. Boston, 1838.

_____ (ed.). Specimens of Foreign Standard Literature. 14 vols. Boston: James Munroe and Company, 1838-1842.

_____. "Town and Country Items," Spirit of the Age, I (July 21, November 24, 1849), 63, 64, 335.

* * *

Burton, Katherine, "Sophia Dana Ripley," The Missionary, LIII (1939), 40-42.

Crowe, Charles. George Ripley: Transcendentalist and Utopian Socialist. Athens: University of Georgia Press, 1967.

Driscoll, Annette S. "Brook Farm Convert," Ave Maria, XXXI (June 7, 1930), 705-711.

Frothingham, Octavius Brooks. George Ripley. Boston: Houghton, Mifflin and Company, 1882.

Schultz, Arthur R., and Henry A. Pochmann. "George Ripley: Unitarian, Transcendentalist, or Infidel?" American Literature, XIV (March, 1942), 1-19.

CALEB STETSON

Stetson, Caleb. A Discourse on the Duty of Sustaining the Laws, Occasioned by the Burning of the Ursuline Convent. Delivered at the First Church in Medford, Sunday, August 24, 1834. Boston: Hilliard, Gray, and Company, 1834.

_____. Two Discourses Preached Before the First Congregational Society in Medford; One Upon Leaving the Old Church; and One at the Dedication of the New. Boston: Isaac R. Butts, 1840.

HENRY DAVID THOREAU

Thoreau, Henry David. Cape Cod and Miscellanies. Vol. IV of The Writings of Henry David Thoreau. 20 vols. New York: Houghton, Mifflin and Company, 1906.

_____. Correspondence. Edited by Walter Harding and Carl Bode. New York: New York University Press, 1958.

_____. Excursions and Poems. Vol. V of The Writings of Henry David Thoreau. 20 vols. New York: Houghton, Mifflin and Company, 1906.

_____. _Journal_. Edited by Bradford Torrey and Francis H. Allen. With a Foreword by Walter Harding. 14 vols. in 2. New York: Dover Publications, 1962.

_____. _The Maine Woods_. Vol. III of _The Writings of Henry David Thoreau_. 20 vols. New York: Houghton, Mifflin and Company, 1906.

_____, and William Cullen Bryant. _Unpublished Poems by Bryant and Thoreau_. Boston: The Bibliophile Society, 1907.

_____. _Walden; or, Life in the Woods_. Vol. II of _The Writings of Henry David Thoreau_. 20 vols. New York: Houghton, Mifflin and Company, 1906.

* * *

Buckley, Frank. "Thoreau and the Irish," _New England Quarterly_, XIII (September, 1940), 389-400.

Cameron, Kenneth Walter. _Companion to Thoreau's Correspondence: With Annotations, New Letters and an Index of Principal Words, Phrases and Topics_. Hartford: Transcendental Books, 1964.

Canby, Henry Seidel. _Thoreau_. Boston: Houghton Mifflin Company, 1939.

Channing, William Ellery, The Younger. _Thoreau the Poet-Naturalist. With Memorial Verses_. Boston: Roberts Brothers, 1873.

Crawford, Bartholow V. _Henry David Thoreau: Representative Selections, with Introduction, Bibliography, and Notes_. New York: American Book Company, 1934.

Harding, Walter Roy. _The Days of Henry David Thoreau_. New York: Alfred A. Knopf, 1965.

_____. _A Thoreau Handbook_. New York: New York University Press, 1959.

_____. _Thoreau's Library_. Charlottesville, Virginia: University of Virginia Press, 1957.

Keiser, Albert. _The Indian in American Literature_. New York: Oxford University Press, 1933.

_____. "Thoreau's Manuscripts on the Indians," _Journal of English and Germanic Philology_, XXVII (April, 1928), 183-199.

Krutch, Joseph Wood. _Henry David Thoreau_. New York: William Sloane Associates, 1948.

Mathews, J. Chesley, "Thoreau's Reading in Dante," _Italica_, XXVII (1950), 77-81.

Miller, Perry. _Consciousness in Concord: The Text of Thoreau's Hitherto 'Lost Journal' (1840-1841)_. Together with Notes and a Commentary by Perry Miller. Boston: Houghton Mifflin Company, 1958.

Moloney, Michael F. "Henry David Thoreau, 1817-1862: Christian Malgre Luī." _American Classics Reconsidered: A Christian Appraisal_. Edited by Harold C. Gardiner, S.J. New York: Charles Scribner's Sons, 1958.

More, Paul Elmer. "Thoreau and German Romanticism," _Nation_, LXXXIII (November 8, 15, 1906), 388-390, 411-412.

_____. "Thoreau's Journal." _Shelburne Essays_. Fifth Series. New York: Houghton Mifflin Company, 1908.

Sanborn, Franklin B. _Henry D. Thoreau_. Boston: Houghton, Mifflin and Company, 1886.

_____. _The Life of Hnery David Thoreau: Including Many Essays Hitherto Unpublished and Some Accounts of His Family and Friends_. Boston: Houghton Mifflin Company, 1917.

Willson, Lawrence. "Thoreau and Roman Catholicism," _Catholic Historical Review_, XLII (July, 1956), 157-172.

_____. "Thoreau's Canadian Notebook," _Huntington Library Quarterly_, XXII (May, 1959), 179-200.

JONES VERY

Very, Jones. _Essays and Poems_. Boston: C. Little and James Brown, 1839.

_____. _Poems and Essays. Complete and Revised Edition. With a Biographical Sketch by James Freeman Clarke and a Preface by Cyrus Augustus Bartol_. New York: Houghton, Mifflin and Company, 1886.

* * *

Bartlett, William Irving. _Jones Very, Emerson's "Brave Saint."_ Durham, North Carolina: Duke University Press, 1942.

Gittleman, Edwin. _Jones Very: The Effective Years, 1833-1840_. New York: Columbia University Press, 1967.

Reeves, Paschal. "Jones Very As Preacher: The Extant Sermons," _Emerson Society Quarterly_, LVII (1969), 16-22.

II ADDITIONAL ARTICLES FROM THE TRANSCENDENTAL PERIODICALS

"An Alarm," _Harbinger_, V (July 3, 1847), 58.

"American Affairs," _Spirit of the Age_, I (December 29, 1849), 408-410.

"Angelus Silesius, the Cherubic Pilgrim," _Massachusetts Quarterly Review_, II (September, 1849), 471-487.

"The Archbishop and the Pope," Harbinger, VIII (December 30, 1848, January 13, 1849), 65, 82.

"Arrival of Father Mathew: Welcome to the City," Spirit of the Age, I (July 14, 1849), 30.

Book Review of Irleand As I Saw It: The Character, Condition, and Prospects of the People by William S. Balch (New York, n.d.), Spirit of the Age, II (February 2, 1850), 77-78.

"The Catholics and Associationists," Harbinger, III (July 25, 1846), 102-104.

"Causes of the Present Condition of Ireland," Massachusetts Quarterly Review, III (June, 1850), 304-337.

Channing, William Ellery, The Younger. "Christian Song of the Middle Ages," The Present, I (November 15, 1843), 136.

Dana, Charles A. Book Review of Father Darcy: An Historical Romance by Mrs. Anne Marsh-Caldwell (New York, 1846), Harbinger, III (September 12, 1846), 218.

_____. Book Review of The Jesuits and The Roman Church and Modern Society by M. M. Michelet and Edgar Quinet (New York, 1845), Harbinger, II (December 20, 1845), 28-29.

_____. "The European Revolution," Spirit of the Age, I (August 18, 1849), 97-98.

"The Disease of the Age and the Cure," The Present, I (December 15, 1843), 173-180.

"The Duties of the Clergy," Western Messenger, VIII (September, 1840), 226-236.

"European Politics," Spirit of the Age, I (July 7, 1849), 12-13.

"The French Clergy," from a Correspondent of the Manchester Examiner, Harbinger, VI (April 29, 1848), 201-202.

Godwin, Parke. "Christian Union," Harbinger, VI (December 18, 1847), 52.

Harris, Thomas L. "The Old Age and the New," Spirit of the Age, II (January 5, 1850), 9-11.

"History of the Early Christian Missions in China," Extract, from Canton Register, Western Messenger, VI (March, 1839), 328-333.

Hudson, H. N. "Religious Union of Associationists," The American Review, V (May, 1847), 492-502.

Ingalls, J. K. "Creed," Spirit of the Age, I (July 7, 1849), 11-12.

Jerrold, Douglass, "The Poor Pope," Harbinger, VIII (January 28, 1849), 91.

"Joan of Arc," Western Messenger, II (November, 1836), 230-231.

Lane, Charles. Book Review of The Life and Times of Girolamo Savonarola: Illustrating the Progress of the Reformation in Italy, During the Fifteenth Century by John A. Heraud (London, 1843), The Dial, III (April, 1843), 536-540.

_____. "Interior or Hidden Life," The Dial, IV (January, 1844), 373-378.

_____. "Popular Music," Spirit of the Age, I (November 17, 1849), 310-311.

Lynch, Anne C. "Day-Dawn in Italy," Harbinger, VI (January 15, 1848), 81.

"La Madonna di San Sisto," The Present, I (December 15, 1843), 165.

Peabody, Ephraim. "History of the Doctrine of Original Sin," Western Messenger, I (January, 1836), 493-499.

Proudhon, P.J. "Confessions of a Revolutionist," (excerpt), Spirit of the Age, II (March 2, 1850), 129-131.

Redfield, James W. "Character of Father Mathew," Spirit of the Age, I (July 21, 1849), 60.

"Reform Movements: Irish Emigrant Protection Societies," Spirit of the Age, II (February 2, 1840), 78.

"Reform Movements: Poor Ireland," Spirit of the Age, II (February 16, 1850), 110.

"The Right to Labor," Spirit of the Age, I (July 21, 1849), 75.

"Social Democracy," Spirit of the Age, II (February 23, 1850), 115-116.

Stone, Thomas T. "Man in the Ages," The Dial, I (January, 1841), 273-289.

T., W. "Religious Persecutions," Western Messenger, VI (November, 1838), 160-165.

Ward, S. G. "Letters from Italy," The Dial, I (January, 1841), 386-400.

Whittier, John Greenleaf. "The Men of Old," Spirit of the Age, I (August 18, 1849), 97.

Wilson, W. D. "The Unitarian Movement in New England," The Dial, I (April, 1841), 409-443.

III GENERAL WORKS

Allen, Joseph Henry. Sequel to "Our Liberal Movement." Boston: Roberts Bros., 1897.

Bean, William G. "An Aspect of Know Nothingism--The Immigrant and Slavery," South Atlantic Quarterly, XXIII (October, 1924), 319-334.

_____. "Puritan Versus Celt," New England Quarterly, VII (March, 1934), 70-89.

Boas, George. "Romantic Philosophy in America." Romanticism in America. Papers Contributed to a Symposium Held at the Baltimore Museum of Art, May 13, 14, 15, 1940. Edited by George Boas. New York: Russell and Russell, 1940.

Brooks, Van Wyck. The Flowering of New England: 1815-1865. Revised edition. New York: E.P. Dutton and Company, 1940.

Cheney, Ednah Dow. Reminiscences of Ednah Dow Cheney. Boston: Lee and Shepard, 1902.

Clemmer, Robert. "Historical Transcendentalism in Pennsylvania," Journal of the History of Ideas, XXX (October-December, 1969), 579-592.

Codman, John Thomas. Brook Farm: Historic and Personal Memoirs. Boston: Arena Publishing Company, 1894.

Cooke, George Willis. An Historical and Biographical Introduction to Accompany The Dial. 2 vols. New York: Russell and Russell, 1961 (c. 1902).

Dwight, Marianne. Letters from Brook Farm, 1844-1847. Edited by Amy L. Reed. With a Note on Anna Q. T. Parsons, by Helen Dwight Orvis. Poughkeepsie, New York: Vassar College, 1928.

Eliot, Samuel A. (ed.). Heralds of a Liberal Faith. 4 vols. Boston: American Unitarian Association, 1910-1952. Vols. II, III.

Fairbanks, Henry G. "Theocracy to Transcendentalism in America," Emerson Society Quarterly, XLIV (1966), 45-59.

Frothingham, Octavius Brooks. Transcendentalism in New England: A History. New York: G. P. Putnam's Sons, 1876.

Gardiner, Harold C., S.J. "The Era of the Half Gods." American Calssics Reconsidered: A Christian Appraisal. Edited by Gardiner. New York: Charles Scribner's Sons, 1958.

Goddard, Harold Clarke. Studies in New England Transcendentalism. New York: Columbia University Press, 1908.

Gohdes, Clarence F. The Periodicals of American Transcendentalism. Durham, North Carolina: Duke University Press, 1931.

Hochfield, George (ed.). Selected Writings of the American Transcendentalists. New York: The New American Library, 1966.

Howe, Daniel Walker. The Unitarian Conscience: Harvard Moral Philosophy, 1805-1861. Cambridge, Massachusetts: Harvard Univeristy Press, 1970.

Hutchison, William R. The Transcendentalist Ministers: Church Reform in the New England Renaissance. New Haven: Yale University Press, 1959.

Jones, Howard Mumford. America and French Culture, 1750-1848. Chapel Hill, North
    Carolina: University of North Carolina Press, 1927.

_____. "The Influence of European Ideas in Nineteenth Century America,"
    American Literature, VII (November, 1935), 241-273.

Kaufman, Paul. "The Romantic Movement." The Reinterpretation of American Liter-
    ature. Edited by Norman Foerster. New York: Harcourt, Brace, and Company,
    1928.

Kenrick, Francis Patrick. The Primacy of the Apostolic See Vindicated. 3rd ed.
    New York: Edward Dunigan and Brother, 1848.

_____. A Vindication of the Catholic Church, in a Series of Letters
    Addressed to the Right Reverend John Henry Hopkins, Protestant Episcopal
    Bishop of Vermont. Baltimore: John Murphy and Company, 1855.

Kern, Alexander. "The Rise of Transcendentalism, 1815-1860." Transitions in
    American Literary History. Edited by Harry Hayden Clark. Durham, North
    Carolina: Duke University Press, 1953.

Kirby, Georgiana Bruce. "Reminiscences of Brook Farm," Old and New, III (February,
    April, 1871), 175-185, 425-438; IV (September, 1871), 347-358; V (May, 1872),
    517-530.

_____. Years of Experience: An Autobiographical Narrative. New York: G. P.
    Putnam's Sons, 1886.

Levin, David. History As Romantic Art. Palo Alto, California: Stanford University
    Press, 1959.

Lewis, R. W. B. The American Adam. Chicago: University of Chicago Press, 1955.

M., S. H. Review of Proceedings of the First Annual Meeting of the Free Religious
    Association, Held in Boston, May 28 and 29, 1868 (Boston, 1868), Radical, IV
    (November, 1868), 391-396.

McAleer, John J. "Transcendentalism and the Improper Bostonian," Emerson Society
    Quarterly, XXXIX (1965), 73-78.

Melville, Annabelle. Jean Lefebvre de Cheverus, 1768-1836. Milwaukeee: Bruce
    Publishing Company, 1958.

"Memoir of Bishop Cheverus," Boston Monthly Magazine, I (June, 1825), 2-21.

Miller, Perry. The American Transcendentalists: Their Prose and Poetry. Garden
    City, New York: Doubleday, 1957.

_____. "Jonathan Edwards to Emerson," New England Quarterly, XIII (December,
    1940), 589-617.

_____. "New England's Transcendentalism: Native or Imported." Literary
    Views: Critical and Historical Essays. Edited by Charles Carroll Camden.
    Chicago: University of Chicago Press, 1964.

_____. The Transcendentalists: An Anthology. Cambridge, Massachusetts: Harvard University Press, 1950.

Mitchell, Anna M. "The Brook Farm Movement Viewed through the Perspective of Half a Century," Catholic World, LXXIII (April, 1901), 17-31.

Myerson, Joel. "Calendar of Transcendental Club Meetings," American Literature, XLIV (May, 1972), 197-207.

Parrington, Vernon Louis. The Romantic Revolution in America, 1800-1860. Vol. II of Main Currents in American Thought: An Interpretaiton of American Literature from the Beginnings to 1920. 3 vols. New York: Harcourt, Brace and Company, 1927.

Persons, Stow. American Minds: A History of Ideas. New York: Henry Holt and Company, 1958.

_____. Free Religion, An American Faith. New Haven: Yale University Press, 1947.

La Piana, Angelina. Dante's American Pilgrimage. A Historical Survey of Dante Studies in the United States, 1800-1944. New Haven: Yale University Press, 1948.

Pochmann, Henry A. German Culture in America: Philosophical and Literary Influences, 1600-1900. With the assistance of Arthur R. Schutz and others. Madison: University of Wisconsin Press, 1957.

Rahv, Philip. "Two Visits." Discovery of Europe: The Story of American Experience in the Old World. Edited with a New Introduction and Commentary by Philip Rahv. Garden City, New York: Doubleday and Company, 1960.

Rice, Madeleine Hooke. American Catholic Opinion in the Slavery Controversy. Gloucester, Massachusetts: Peter Smith, 1964 (c. 1944).

Santayana, George. The Genteel Tradition. Nine Essays. Edited by Douglas L. Wilson. Cambrdige, Massachusetts: Harvard University Press, 1967.

Schneider, Herbert Wallace. A History of American Philosophy. 2nd ed. New York: Columbia University Press, 1963.

Sears, John Van Der Zee. My Friends at Brook Farm. New York: Desmond FitzGerald, 1912.

Sedgwick, Ora Gannett. "A Girl of Sixteen at Brook Farm," Atlantic Monthly, LXXXV (March, 1900), 394-404.

Shuster, Geroge N. The Catholic Spirit in America. New York: The Dial Press, 1927.

Sumner, Arther. "A Boy's Recollections of Brook Farm," New England Magazine, New Series, X (March-August, 1894), 309-313.

Swift, Lindsay. Brook Farm: Its Members, Scholars, and Visitors. New York: Corinth Books, 1961 (c. 1899).

297

"Unitarian Convention," The Independent, XVI (April 6, 1865), 8.

Vogel, Stanley Morton. German Literary Influence on the American Transcendentalists. New Haven: Yale University Press, 1955.

Warren, Austin. New England Saints. Ann Arbor: University of Michigan Press, 1956.

Wasson, David A. Beyond Concord: Selected Writings of David Atwood Wasson. Edited by Charles H. Foster. Bloomington: Indiana University Press, 1965.

Wellek, Rene. "The Minor Transcendentalists and German Philosophy," New England Quarterly, XV (December, 1942), 652-680.

Wells, Ronald Vale. Three Christian Transcendentalists: James Marsh, Caleb Sprague Henry, Frederic Henry Hedge. New York: Columbia University Press, 1943.

White, Joseph Blanco. The Life of the Reverend Joseph Blanco White, Written by Himself; with Portions of His Correspondence. Edited by John Hamilton Thom. 3 vols. London: John Chapman, 1845. Vol. III.

Wilson, John B. "A Transcendental Minority Report," New England Quarterly, XXIX (June, 1956), 147-158.

The Heritage of
American Catholicisim

23. BENITA A. MOORE
   ESCAPE INTO A LABYRINTH:
   F. SCOTT FITZGERALD, CATHOLIC SENSIBILITY, AND THE AMERICAN WAY
   New York 1988

24. MARILYN WENZKE NICKELS
   BLACK CATHOLIC PROTEST
   AND THE FEDERATED COLORED CATHOLICS, 1917-1933:
   THREE PERSPECTIVES ON RACIAL JUSTICE
   New York 1988

25. DAVID L. SALVATERRA
   AMERICAN CATHOLICISM AND THE INTELLECTUAL LIFE, 1880-1920
   New York 1988

26. HELENA SANFILIPPO, R. S. M.
   INNER WEALTH AND OUTWARD SPLENDOR:
   NEW ENGLAND TRANSCENDENTALISTS VIEW THE ROMAN CATHOLIC CHURCH
   New York 1988

27. FAYETTE BREAUX VEVERKA
   "FOR GOD AND COUNTRY:"
   CATHOLIC SCHOOLING IN THE 1920s
   New York 1988

28. TIMOTHY WALCH
   THE DIVERSE ORIGINS OF AMERICAN CATHOLIC EDUCATION:
   CHICAGO, MILWAUKEE, AND THE NATION
   New York 1988